LITERATURE FOR INTERPRETATION

LITERATURE
FOR
INTERPRETATION

By

GLADYS DE SILVA BATES

HELENA KAY

1939

EXPRESSION COMPANY · PUBLISHERS

Boston · · · Massachusetts

COPYRIGHT 1939
By EXPRESSION COMPANY

PRINTED IN UNITED STATES OF AMERICA

FOREWORD

THE literature in this volume found its way there through the experiences of the editors and compilers in teaching the subject over many years. The test of merit is whether the contents have the power to stimulate the reader; whether the events, facts, characters and happenings are significant to him and evoke a response in his thinking and feeling.

The criterion as to whether literature has awakened the self and the degree and quality of response and appreciation is the extent to which it calls forth all the natural languages of tone and body. These are innate, and tend to unite reader and listener in the common experiences of mankind. "No one can give anything to his fellowman but himself." Indeed, unless one has actually shared an experience, he may enter into, understand and appreciate the experiences of others only vicariously through Interpretation.

This requires that the impressions of the author have sufficient appeal and interest to integrate the whole personality and permit the student to breathe his own life into the literary pattern so that it becomes a "living word" possessing definite shape and form. In other words, if the concepts are sufficiently vital they tend to lead the student from subjectivity into the objective forms which characterize Interpretation.

Drill and practice in this speech-form should utilize those literary examples possessing appeal of life and capable of being translated into the consciousness of others through the modulation of body and of tone.

This compilation is strikingly rich in such examples and noteworthy for its balance, wide range of literary exploration, deep insight and cultured taste, and may be safely followed since every reading has been given a class-room test.

Specific forms of literature have been selected because of their special function in interpretation: the Lyric is a deeply subjective and emotional realization giving an intensity of impression, and consists of *personal* concepts; the Narrative or Story-Form is one in which the student learns to understand and appreciate objectively events, persons and happenings from which he secures his sense of sequence—cause and effect—and movement of events; the Ballad may be regarded as a form of "Story-Lyric" or a combination of the Lyric and the Narrative; the Epic may be construed as Narrative Ballad, differentiated by spirit and content and the identification of the individual with the ideals of the race or with the supernatural; the Drama associates the reader through empathy with characters, points of view and situations indispensable in a study of Interpretation. All of these forms of literature and more, are included in this volume.

L. D. FALLIS
Chairman, Department of Speech
Texas Christian University
Forth Worth, Texas

PREFACE

TEACHERS and students of speech are ever in search of compilations of literature which will meet the various needs of the classroom. The aim of this anthology is to stimulate the cause (i.e., the mental or inward activity) and develop the means (i.e., the voice and body, the outward manifestation of physical, mental, and spiritual life).

Prose. Complete stories have been used, with few exceptions. Students should carefully read the story in its entirety. In the longer stories, assignments could be made to several students to relate the story in continuity. Again, the student could make his own arrangement, eliminating some things of lesser value to the audience but important for the background of the story, and concentrating on others necessary for sequence and to give the listener the very essence of the tale. The student, through his personality, vivifies or projects the story to his audience, so if it is to be arranged, he should make his own arrangement. Contrasting stories have been used to develop versatility and to suggest the wide range suitable for oral interpretation.

Stories possessing wit and humor usually find an immediate response from the student. Some of these stories could be put into dialogue form and used for playlets. However, the greater values lie in individual interpretation as a means of establishing a pleasing intimacy with an audience.

Browning's monologues should be made the basis of study in this interesting form of literature. It would be wise to emphasize story-telling before taking up the monologue.

Speeches pertaining to present-day situations will prove

of most interest in the classroom. Editorials and articles in newspapers and magazines furnish a never-ending supply and encourage the student to find material for his assignments.

It should be a matter of choice with the teacher whether the essays are to be interpreted through reading from the printed page, or to have the student assimilate them and give them without the book.

Poetry. There are many excerpts from narrative poems which could be used. A complete arrangement of "Hiawatha" and "Marmion" would prove interesting in the classroom, students preparing the poem. Suitable parts could be read in unison. Many of the ballads can also be used effectively in choral speaking.

The lyrics and problems for oral interpretation have been chosen with the view of giving variation in the student's approach to poetry. Choric speech training is fast proving worthy of consideration. There are obtainable at the present time informative books on this comparatively new form of interpretation.

Drama. It is well to remember in the study of the drama that reading a play is not acting. The distinction cannot be too carefully made. The reader approaches his audience so that the play unfolds through mental vision rather than by the perception of the physical eye. The audience should forget the reader in the thing read.

We read chiefly through our own experiences. We go through and pass out of certain situations, and each leaves its mark—whether it be the responses of the five senses or the aspirations, the apprehensions, the wisdom, the foolishnesses, the joys, the sorrows, the hatreds, the loves, that have been precipitated within us, and result in intellectual and spiritual reactions which we, in turn, share with others.

GLADYS DE SILVA BATES
HELENA KAY

June, 1939

ACKNOWLEDGMENTS

We wish to express our appreciation to the following authors, publishers, and periodicals for the use of literature appearing in this volume, on which all rights are reserved by the holders of the copyright or the authorized publishers:

ADAMS, BILL, for use of a poem.

ADAMS, JAMES TRUSLOW, for use of a formal discourse (from *Our Business Civilization*).

ALFRED A. KNOPF, INC., for a selection by James Oppenheim; for a selection from *The Dream Keeper* by Langston Hughes; for a selection by A. E. Housman from *More Poems*.

ANDERSON, MAXWELL, for scenes from *Mary of Scotland*.

ANDERSON, R. B., translator of works of Bjornson.

ATLANTIC MONTHLY, for material from *The Contributor's Club;* for an essay by Nora Waln; for poems by J. Redwood Anderson and Helene Magaret.

BOBBS MERRILL COMPANY, for a selection from *Complete Works* of James Whitcomb Riley.

CENTAUR PRESS, THE, for use of a poem by Katherine Garrison Chapin.

CHAMBRUN, JACQUES, agent, for prose selections by Finis Farr and Day Edgar.

CHAPIN, KATHERINE GARRISON, for use of a poem.

CHAPMAN AND GRIMES, for use of a poem by Badger Clark.

CHARLES SCRIBNER'S SONS, for selections from *Collected Works* of Francis Thompson; from *Collected Poems* of Edwin Arlington Robinson; for scenes from *And So They Were Married* by Jesse Lynch Williams; from *Victoria Regina* by Laurence Housman.

CHASE, HARRY WOODBURN, for use of a formal discourse.

COFFIN, ROBERT P. TRISTRAM, for use of a selection from *Strange Holiness*.

COLLIER'S MAGAZINE, for stories by John Erskine and Rupert Hughes.

COLLINS, FREDERICK L., for use of a prose selection.

CONNELL, RICHARD, for use of a prose selection.

COUNTRY GENTLEMAN, for a story by Phyllis Duganne.

D. APPLETON-CENTURY COMPANY, for selections from *Narratives in Verse* by Ruth Comfort Mitchell; from *Christmas Night in the Quarters* by Irwin Russell.

DAVIS, MARY OCTAVIA, for use of a poem.

DE LA MARE, WALTER, for use of a poem.

DE LEON, WALTER, for use of a prose selection.

DELINEATOR MAGAZINE, for a story by Karle Wilson Baker.

DODD, MEAD & COMPANY, for a selection from *The Hour Has Struck* by Angela Morgan.

DOUBLEDAY, DORAN & COMPANY, INC., for an article from *Adventures in Solitude* by Ray Stannard Baker; for scenes from *The Circle,* copyright 1921, by W. Somerset Maugham.

DRUMMOND, MAE HARVEY, for a selection from *The Poetical Works* of William Henry Drummond.

DUTTON, E. P. & COMPANY, INC., for scenes from *The Cradle Song* by G. Martinez Sierra, copyright 1921, by John Garrett Underhill.

EMERSON, ELIZABETH H., for use of a poem.

ESQUIRE, for stories by Robert W. Mitchner; by Walter Duranty (arranged for oral reading by permission).

FARJEON, ELEANOR, for use of a poem.

FIELD, SARA BARD, for use of three poems.

FLETCHER, JOHN GOULD, for two selections from *Irradiations.*

FORUM, for a poem by Louise Burton Laidlaw.

GARLAND, HAMLIN, for use of a poem.

GIRLING, KATHERINE PEABODY, for use of a prose selection.

GOLDEN BOOK, for prose selections by T. F. Powys; Frances M. Frost; Charles Battell Loomis; and Ernst Toller (from *Halt the March to War*).

GOULD, ALICE LAWRY, for use of two poems.

HARCOURT, BRACE & COMPANY, INC., for selections from *Smoke and Steel* by Carl Sandburg; from *Roast Leviathan* by Louis Untermeyer; from *Good Morning, America* by Carl Sandburg.

HARPER'S BAZAAR, for a story by Zona Gale.

HARPER & BROTHERS, for a selection from *Color* by Countée Cullen.

HARPER'S MAGAZINE, for prose selections by Leslie Roberts and Harry Hansen.

HARVEY, ALEXANDER, for use of his translation of *The Frogs* by Aristophanes.

HENRY HOLT & COMPANY, INC., for selections from *Peacock Pie* by Walter De La Mare; from *Address to the Living* by John Holmes; from *Slow Smoke* by Lew Sarett; from *North of Boston* by Robert Frost.

HILLYER, ROBERT, for a selection from *Five Books of Youth.*

HOUGHTON MIFFLIN COMPANY, for a selection by Amy Lowell; for selections from *Streets in the Moon, The Happy Marriage and Other Poems* by Archibald MacLeish; for "Song of the Chorus" from *The Frogs* by Aristophanes, translated by John Hook Hamm Frere from *The Chief European Dramatists*.

ICKES, HAROLD L., for use of a formal discourse.

JUDGE, for a story by George Mitchell.

LADIES HOME JOURNAL, for prose selections by Finis Farr and Day Edgar.

LAIDLAW, LOUISE BURTON, for use of a poem.

LEACOCK, STEPHEN, for use of a prose selection.

LE GALLIENNE, RICHARD, for use of a poem.

LITTLE, BROWN & COMPANY, for scenes from *The Barretts of Wimpole Street* by Rudolf Besier.

LIPPMAN, WALTER, for use of a formal discourse.

MACMILLAN COMPANY, THE, for selections from *Collected Poems* by Sara Teasdale; from *Collected Poems* by Vachel Lindsay; from *Wild Earth and Other Poems* by Padraic Colum; from *Strange Holiness* by Robert P. Tristram Coffin; from *Chosen Poems* by Harriet Monroe; for scenes from *John Ferguson* and *Jane Clegg* by St. John G. Ervine.

MARKHAM, EDWIN, for use of a poem.

MARLATT, EARL, for use of two poems.

MASTERS, EDGAR LEE, for use of a poem.

McCARTHY, MRS. DENIS, for use of a poem.

McCREARY, F. R., for use of a poem.

MORGAN, ANGELA, for use of a poem.

MORTON, DAVID, for use of a poem.

NEW REPUBLIC, for a selection by William Rose Benét.

NEW YORKER, for shorter narratives by P. S. Le Poer Trench; Morris Bishop; Frances Warfield; Hannah Lees; Margaret Ford; Wolcott Gibbs; for a poem by Marjorie Allen Seiffert.

NEW YORK HERALD-TRIBUNE, for a formal discourse by Ernst Toller (from *Halt the March to War*).

O'NEILL, EUGENE, for use of a poem.

OUTDOOR LIFE, for monologues by Ray Trullinger.

PHELPS, WILLIAM LYON, for a selection from *Talks About Books and Authors*.

PINKER, ERIC S. & MORRISON, ADRIENNE, INC., for a selection by A. E. Housman from *More Poems*.

POLLOCK, CHANNING, for scenes from *The Fool*.

PORTER, KENNETH, for use of a poem.

PUNCH, for a monologue by Heather White.

RICKETTS, ORVAL, for use of a poem.

ROBERTS, ELIZABETH MADOX, for use of a poem.

SANDBURG, CARL, for selections from *Smoke and Steel* and *Good Morning, America*.

SATURDAY EVENING POST, for shorter narratives by Patricia Collinge, Parke Cummings, Marjorie Henderson, Aleen Wetstein, Doug Welch; for poems by Arthur Stringer and Frances Frost.

SMITH, GORDON ARTHUR, for use of a prose selection (arranged for reading by permission).

SOUTHERN, CLARENCE E., for use of a poem.

STORY MAGAZINE, for prose selections by Martha Foley; I. V. Morris; Manuel Komroff; Richard Sherman.

THEATRE ARTS MONTHLY, for a poem by Phyllis Preston.

THOMPSON, FRANK, for use of a poem.

TILDEN, FREEMAN, for use of a prose selection.

TOWNE, CHARLES HANSON, for use of a poem.

VANGUARD PRESS, THE, for a selection from *The Poet in the Desert* by Charles Erskine Scott Wood.

VIKING PRESS, INC., for a selection from *God's Trombones* by James Weldon Johnson; for a selection by Elizabeth Madox Roberts.

WILDER, ELIZABETH, for an essay from *Umbrian Pilgrimage*.

YALE UNIVERSITY PRESS, for a poem by William Alexander Percy.

YOUNG, OWEN D., for use of a formal discourse.

The compilers are especially appreciative of the helpful suggestions of the poets, Charles Erskine Scott Wood and Sara Bard Field, and also wish to thank Doris Wood and Thelma Lynn, librarians, and Eddie Mae Kay, typist, for their assistance.

CONTENTS

1. PROSE

I. STORIES

II. SHORTER NARRATIVES AND MONOLOGUES

3. CHORIC READING

4. DRAMA
Selected Scenes

1. PROSE

I. Stories

THE BRIDE'S PARABLE

by

Karle Wilson Baker

ONCE upon a time there lived a very great King who had an only son, for whom he was desirous of finding a wife. Nowhere in all the world was there another King so great as he; but there crowded all about him a swarm of petty princedoms, ruled over by little monarchs who paid him tribute. Now, among all these Kings, each one who had a daughter was anxious to wed her to the Prince, the great King's son. And there was a great rivalry among them as to whom should be chosen.

At last upon a day the King set out to journey among his little kingdoms, to choose among the princesses thereof. And when he came to the palace where lived the first princess, after the great feast had been held in his honor, he turned to the Queen Mother,

"Madam," he said, "what is Love like?"

Now she was a tall and stately person, with a weary, faded face, like a rose that has dropped its petals; but she answered, thinking to please the King:

"Love is like a flower, full of beauty and fragrance."

And the blunt old King said, "Flowers fade; keep thy flower, madam."

Then he journeyed on to the next kingdom; and here, as before, when he had feasted and honored, he spake to the Queen Mother:

"Madam, what is Love like?"

Now this was a black-browed matron, quick of speech.

"Ah, your Majesty," she said, while a blush swept up to her forehead, "Love is a flame!"

3

And the old King looked at her under his shaggy brows and said:

"Flame-ashes. My son hath no liking for ashes."

So he fared on to the next kingdom; and once more he put his question to the haughty, imperious mother of the young princess, "What is Love like?"

And she lifted her head a little, that he might see how regally she bore it, and answered:

"Like a star, O King!"

And the King said, "Humph! The stars are far away. Besides, they shine only in fair weather."

And so he passed on from kingdom to kingdom. And at last he came to one where the Queen Mother sat at her tapestry-frame with her daughter beside her; and the two of them had the same broad brow and the same clear eyes, and laughed softly from time to time as they wrought. And the old King looked hard before he spake to the Queen Mother:

"Madam, what is Love like?"

And she considered him with eyes that seemed to look backward on a long pathway, and answered:

"Love, O King, is like a violin, the only thing in all the world that grows finer with age and usage."

And then at last the old King smiled under his grizzled beard, and laid down his great hand on the smooth hair of the maiden.

"Give me thy treasure then," he said, "And come, little maiden. For back at my palace there waits a Prince whose love is like a jeweled bow, straight and strong and faithful, which shall woo her music from her so long as they both shall live."

And so he did.

THE FATHER

by

Bjornson

THE man of whom this story tells was the richest in the
parish. His name was Thord Overaas. He stood one day
in the pastor's study, tall and serious.

"I have gotten a son," he said, "and wish to have him
baptized."

"What is to be his name?"

"Finn, in honor of my father."

"And the sponsors?"

They were named, and proved to be the best men and
women of Thord's kin in the district.

"Is there anything else?" asked the pastor, looking up.

Thord hesitated a moment. "I should like to have my
son baptized alone," he said.

"That is to say on a week-day?"

"On Saturday next, at twelve o'clock, noon."

"Is there anything else?" asked the pastor.

"There is nothing else," answered Thord, taking his
cap to go.

"Just one word," said the pastor, as he arose, stepped
over to Thord, took him by the hand, and looked him in
the eye; "God grant that this child may be a blessing to
you."

Sixteen years later Thord again stood in the pastor's
study.

"You are holding your own well, Thord," said the
pastor, seeing no change in him.

"I have no sorrows," answered Thord.

To this the pastor made no response. But a moment
later he asked: "What is your errand this evening?"

"This evening I come concerning my son, who is to be confirmed to-morrow."

"He is a clever lad."

"I did not care to pay the parson's fee until I heard what rank the boy is to have in the class to-morrow."

"He is to be at the head."

"So I understand, and here are ten dollars for the pastor."

"Is there anything else?" asked the pastor, looking at Thord.

"There is nothing else."

And Thord departed.

Eight years had passed, when one day a bustling was heard at the pastor's study door; a number of men appeared, headed by Thord. The pastor looked up and recognized him.

"You are out in full force this evening, Thord."

"I have come to ask the banns for my son. He is to be married to Karen Storliden, the daughter of Gudmund, who is here with me."

"Why, she is the richest girl in the district."

"So they say," answered Thord, thrusting his hand through his hair.

The pastor sat a moment as in meditation. Without a word he entered the names in his books, and the men signed theirs. Thord laid three dollars upon the table.

"The fee is only one", said the pastor.

"Yes, I know; but he is my only child, and I wish to be generous."

The pastor accepted the money. "This is the third time, Thord, that you have been here in behalf of your son."

"Yes, and now I am done with him," said Thord; he closed his pocketbook, said good-by, and walked slowly out, followed by the others.

Two weeks after that day father and son were rowing across the calm surface of the lake to the Storliden farm to arrange for the wedding.

"This seat does not seem to be right," said the son, and

arose to adjust it. But as he stepped upon the floor-board, it slipped. He threw out his arms, uttered a shriek, and fell into the water.

"Take hold of my oar!" shouted the father as he arose and thrust it out. The son struggled to do so, then suddenly became rigid. "Wait a moment!" called the father as he started to row. But the son rolled backward, cast a dim look at his father—and sank.

Thord could not believe his eyes. He held the boat still, and stared at the spot where the son had sunk, expecting him to rise again. Some bubbles arose, soon a few more, then only one large one that burst—and the lake was again like a mirror.

For three days and nights the father was seen rowing around this spot without stopping to eat and sleep. He was dragging for his son. And on the third day, in the morning, he found him, and carried him up the hills to his home.

It was perhaps a year after that day that the pastor late one autumn evening heard someone moving slowly in the hallway before his door, and fumbling cautiously for the latch. The pastor opened the door, and in stepped a tall man, thin, stooping, and white of hair. The pastor looked long at him before he knew him. It was Thord.

"You are out late," said the pastor, as he stood facing him.

"Yes, I am out late," said Thord, as he sat down.

The pastor, too, sat down, expectant. There was a long silence. Then Thord said: "I have something with me which I should like to give to the poor. I wish to make it a legacy, bearing my son's name." He arose, laid the money upon the table, and then sat down again.

The pastor counted it. "This is a good deal of money," he said.

"It is half the price of my farm; I sold it to-day."

The pastor remained sitting in silence a long time.

Finally he asked in a kindly voice: "What do you intend to do now?"

"Something better."

They sat silent for a while, Thord with his eyes on the floor, and the pastor with his eyes on Thord.

Then the pastor said slowly and gently: "Now I think that your son has at last become a blessing to you."

"Yes, I think so too," said Thord. He looked up, and two tears ran slowly down his face.

THE THICK FOG
by
Freeman Tilden

THE fog, which had been thickening all forenoon, rolled up
the Thames estuary after midday, and blotted London out.
It began by being amber, and ended by being an aerial mud,
impregnated with soft-coal acids which stung in the eyes
like the essence from orange peel. The street lamps became
mere spectral spots of gray, in the darkness. The fog
throttled sound. It was impossible to tell whether the
cursing bus-driver was in the next street, or whether his
front wheels were at your legs.

At two o'clock even the most conservative office mana-
gers permitted the help to venture toward home, and find
home if they could. The taxis went into their holes like so
many rabbits. Pedestrians rammed each other wildly,
muttered a dreary "Sorry!" and stumbled into the nearest
doorway to take account of stock. "Now, then!" cried the
bobbies who were supposed to be directing traffic if they
could see it: but WHAT, then they didn't know. There
was no rain, but there was a layer of thin mud underfoot.
The air was bitter and clammy, like a wet newspaper in
the winter dew.

Mr. Isaac Frawley, respectable metal merchant in
Kensal Rise, shut down his roll-top desk, put on his top-
coat, shut and bolted the safe, and made his way to the
shop door. As he opened it, a billow of gloom enveloped
him. "Bad fog!" he said, aloud. "Very nasty!" He thought
he could get home, for he very often walked the distance
to Wormwood Scrubs, for the sake of his digestion. At any
rate, he knew that it was walk or nothing. A conveyance
was out of the question.

"Let me see," mused Mr. Isaac Frawley, pausing before setting out. "I ought to remember every inch of the road. A few steps to the corner, then across the street, then to the left, and along the High Street—" He therefore went to the corner, as he thought, stepped from the pavement to the street, went across, and ran against a horse. The wet flanks of the animal shivered as his head touched it. He drew back so quickly that he lost his hat. When he looked for his hat, it was nowhere. So he went on without it. He had the unpleasant feeling that the horse had kicked at him, and narrowly missed him.

Mr. Frawley next lurched into someone and begged his pardon, civilly. He then considered that the person he had stumbled against was possessed of a very hard shoulder. He reached out and touched his companion. It was a lamp-post. The fog was that bad, now. "Good Lord, I'm completely lost, already!" muttered Mr. Frawley, "and I haven't gone a hundred steps. Dear me, this is bad!" He heard a child crying lustily for its mother, but from what direction he didn't know.

In the next fifteen minutes Mr. Frawley was conscious of having traveled something less than three hundred yards, and of having got nowhere at all. He had barked his shins against the bottom step of some dwelling, and had been all but crushed under a carter's wagon, driven by a drunkard who had some silly notion that he was on his way home. At last he took to the refuge of a wall, and with his hand running along against the bricks, came to a doorway. Then his hand rested upon a knob. He pushed upon it, and went into some sort of room where a dozen voices were speaking in subdued tones. It smelled like a public house.

"Where am I?" asked Mr. Frawley, now thoroughly frightened; asking of anybody who happened to hear him. He could see that he was in a room, but the room was full of fog.

Somebody replied: "You're in the White Hart."

"Ah!" exclaimed the merchant, in a relieved tone. He

knew where he was, now. "I'd gladly give a pound note," he added, "to any man who could lead me home. My wife isn't well, and will be greatly disturbed."

"I can do it, sir," said a voice.

"Are you sure? I live in Lancaster Road, in Wormwood Scrubs. Do you know the place?"

"Perfectly, sir. I can take you home."

"Where are you? Come up closer. Where is your hand? Ah! Come, then, do you really think you could find the way?"

"Sure of it, sir."

So Mr. Frawley, with his hand in that of the guide, suffered himself to be led forth from the shelter of the pub. He had terrible misgivings. The man might be a ruffian, or a fool, or he might be deceiving himself. But they went along at a decent pace which was, at least, encouraging.

Sometimes the guide said, "Step up, here, sir!" And invariably Mr. Frawley stepped up at the right moment. The man's sense of direction, in the fog, was uncanny! "I wonder if I am losing my sight?" thought the merchant. "Those headaches lately—they might indicate that I need new spectacles."

"Where are we now?" asked Mr. Frawley.

"On the bank of the Grand Junction Canal, sir," was the reply.

"Good God, man!" The perspiration came upon the merchant's forehead. "You shouldn't have come this way! It's—it's dangerous."

"Never fear, sir. Besides, it's the shortest way."

A peevish engine whistle was heard, a little later. "Would this be the bridge over the Great Western Railway?" asked the merchant.

"Right you are, sir."

"Extraordinary!" said Mr. Frawley, a little later. "Really, the fog can't be so bad as I thought. It must be my eyes! Lancaster Road, I said, my man. Number forty-one."

"Yes, sir, and here we are. This is your house, sir."

"Bless my soul, I really believe it is. I can't see it, but I have that feeling. Come up the steps, then. If my key fits—ah! it does, it does! Safely home, by all that's wonderful! Come inside a moment, into the hall. I've got the pound note handy. There you are."

"Thank you, sir. I'd like to see a dozen other gentlemen home at the same price, I would. Good evening, sir!"

"Wait! I'm wondering how you did it. Do you see in the dark, like a cat?" Mr. Frawley chuckled gaily, as he asked the question. Safe at home, he could afford his little joke.

"No, sir, not I. I am blind, sir—blind from birth. Good evening, sir."

WHEN HANNAH VAR EIGHT YAR OLD

by
Katherine Peabody Girling

"WERE you a little girl, Hannah, when you came to America?" I asked.

"No," she replied, letting her sewing fall in her lap as her grave eyes sought mine slowly, "I var a big girl eight yar old."

"Eight years old? How big you must have been! Can you tell me about it? Why you came?"

The recent accounts of people driven to America by tragedy, or drawn by a larger hope of finding a life to live in addition to earning a living, had colored my thoughts for days. Have all immigrants—the will-less, leaden people who pass in droves through our railway stations; the patient, indifferent toilers by the roadside; the maids who cook and mend for us; this girl who sits sewing with me to-day—a memory and a vision? Is each of them in some degree a Mary Antin? So I closed the magazine and asked her—

"A big girl, eight yar old," she said.

"Oh, well," Hannah explained, "in Old Country if you are eight yar old and comes younger child'n in familie, you are old woman; you gotta be, or who shall help de moder?"

"Yes? Did your father and mother bring you?" I continued.

"No—fader and moder var daid. My h'aunt, my fader's broder's wife, se came for us. It cost her twenty-eight dollar, but se do it."

"But surely you can't go to Sweden and return for twenty-eight dollars!"

"Seventeen yar ago, yes, but of course you must to take your own providings. It don't require much." Hannah's

13

shoulders drew together expressively. "Madam knows she is apt to miss her appetite at sea!"

"But too well." I shrugged. Then we both laughed.

"I can tell you how it is I came on Ahmericah, but"—Hannah waited for words to express her warning—"it will make you a sharp sadness."

"Please."

"I don't know if I can tell it to you good, but I tell it so good as I can. My vader he var Swedish fisherman vat h'own his boat and go away by weeks and weeks, and sometimes come strong wedder and he can't make it to get home quick. My moder se var German." Hannah hesitated, and then in lowered tones of soft apology added, "Se var a ver' pretty woman. Var three child'n more as me—Olga var six yar old, and Hilda four, and Jens—well, Jens var just a baby, suppose yar and half. We live in a little house close on by de sea. It is yust a little house, but it can to have a shed with a floor of stone. The door of de shed is broken so it is like a window mitout glass.

"The house is close on by a big dock where in somer time comes big excursion steamer mit—suppose hundert tourist people who climb on de mountain up de road. My moder se sell dem hot coffee, also bread and cheese, but dat is not de reason why we live in de little so lonesome house. It is de big dock is de reason. My fader he can to come home from late fishings mitout needing dat he sall walk on de roads. In Sweden in winter de roads swallow snow till it makes dangersome to you to walk because hides holes to step in. We live dar all somer, but in late autumn my fader he say, 'What about de winter?' My moder se say, 'I don't know, but anyway ve try it vonce'.

"Den my fader he go avay in his boad and my moder se get bad cold and comes sickness on her, and ven se couldn't to keep care on us by reason se is too weak, se lay on de cot in de kitchen-room and vatch on me dat I sall learn to keep care on de child'n."

"What did you live on? How did you keep warm?"

"Oh,—is plenty fuel, and ve make hot stew of dried meat mit rice and raisins.

"One day my moder se say me, 'Hannah,' se say, 'you are a big girl, I must to tell you sometings. You fader is very late, it seems, and winter comes now. I cannot to wait much more. It is soon I got to go. You mustn't take a fear of me if I come all white like de snow and don't talk mit you any more. De little child'n dey will take a fear and cry. I cannot to bring a fear on my little child'n.'

"So se tell me what I sall do—I sall close bot' her eyes up and tie her hands and lock de shed door."

"The shed door!"

"Ya." Hannah resumed her sewing. Her thread snapped as stitch fell by stitch monotonously.

"So one night pretty soon se make dat I sall bring her best nightgown and help her mit to put it on. Den se kiss de little child'n in dair sleppings and se sit on a stool by de fire and say I sall put Jens in her arms. Se try to rock back and fort' and se sing on him a little hymn. But se is too weak, and I must to take him. Den se put on me a shawl and tie it behind under my arms, and se lean heavy on me, and we go out into de shed. My moder se do her bare feet on de stone floor. Se have yust but her nightgown on, but it is her best one with crocheted lace at de neck and wrists. Se tell me I sall put de ironing-board across two chair-seats, but it is too heavy and se sall try to help me, but comes coughing on her and se must to hold on by de shed door. Se look out across de road and de mountain all mit snow white and mit moonlight cold. Well, anyway, we do de ironing-board across de chair-seats and I spread a white sheet and put a head-cushion and my moder lie down and I cover her mit a more other sheet over. 'Oh, moder,' I say, 'let me make some warm coverings on you.'

" 'No,' se say, so soft dat I listen mit my ear, 'I must to come here while I yet have de stren'th, but I want to go quick away, and in de cold I go more quick. Oh, Hannah!' se say, 'my big daughter! You are so comfortable to me!'

"So I hold my moder's hand. Pretty soon it comes cold. I klapp it mit mine, but it comes more cold. I crumple it up and breathe my hot breath in it, but it comes not warm any more. So mit my fader's Sunday handkerchief I bind her eyes like if you play Blindman mit de child'n, and mit an apron-string I tie her hands together. Den I go back and make my hands warm in de kitchen-room and I take de comb down off de string, and I go back to my moder and make her hair in two braids like I did all when se was sick. Den I lock de shed door and crawl in bed mit de child'n to make warm.

"Next day I tell de child'n dat moder is gone away. Dey cry some, but pretty soon dey shut up.

"So I keep care on de child'n and play wid dem, and some days go by. Comes stronger wedder mit storms of sleet and snow, and de wind sob and cry. Comes nobody on. At night when de child'n are sleeping I unlock de shed door and go to see if it makes all right mit my moder. Sometimes it is by the moonlight I see on her, but more often it is by a candle-glimmer."

Hannah broke the subdued tone of her narrative to add in a lower, more confiding note, "It is mit me now dat when I see a candle on light I haf a sharp sadness.

"Pretty soon de wedder is more better, and comes a man trompling troo de snow to tell my moder dat her husband can't come home yust yet—he is drowned in de sea. When he see how it is mit my moder and mit me and de little child'n, de water stands in his eyes—ya. And he go on, troo de snow, tree, four mile nearer on de city to de big castle where live de lady wat h'own all de land and se come in sleigh mit four horsen and big robes of fur and yingling bells. Se see on my moder and se go quick away, but so soon as it can, se come again and se do on my moder a white robe, heavy mit lace, most beautiful! and white stockings of silk and white slippers broidered mit pearlen. Se leaf my moder's hair, as I fix it, in two braids, but se put a wreath of flowers, white and green, yust like real ones.

Is few real flowers in Sweden in winter. Anyway, dese var like de flowers a girl vat gets married should to wear. Den my lady se send her sleigh dat all de people should come and see on de so so brave woman vat couldn't to bring a fear on her little child'n. And de people dey make admiration on my moder. Dey say it is de prettiest dey ever see it, and dey make pity dat se couldn't to see it herself." She paused and breathed deeply. "I wish se could have to seen dose slippers!"

"And did no one tell you that you were a wonderful little girl?"

"Oh, vell—I var eight yar old."

"But what became of you all?"

"My lady took us home in her sleigh mit—I want to stay mit my moder, but se say I sall come to keep care on de child'n dat dey don't cry. And dey don't cry—dey laugh mit se yingling bells. De need was on me strong, but I don't cry before my lady. Se var great dame vat go in de court mit de queen. Se sent men, and dey do my moder in a coffin and carry her to a little chapel house in cemetaire, and in de spring ven de snow is gone dey bury her. My lady se put a white stone mit my moder's name and some poetry—I can't to say it good in English, but it says, 'The stren'th in the heart of her poor is the hope of Sweden.'"

"And then did your aunt come?"

"Ya; my lady se wrote on my fader's broder vat var in Ahmericah. Se say we can to stay mit her, but my onkle he send his wife, and we come back mit her on Ahmericah, und dat is all how I came to be here."

MOTHER SAYS NO

by

Finis Farr

A LOOK passed between Richard and Iris Frazier, the look of young and earnest parents. The woman shook her head to indicate the seriousness of the occasion, then turned to the child playing on the living-room rug.

"But it isn't true," she said, "Mother says it isn't true."

Because they were conscientious parents. Richard and Iris Frazier listened as though to the utterances of an adult to every word that came from the mouth of Richard Frazier III; and now, with unflagging zeal, the mother returned to a familiar duty.

"It was only a big dog, dear," she suggested. "Like Mrs. Beatty's."

This possibility did not even distract the child's attention from the gayly colored picture book that lay between his elbows.

"It was bigger than a dog," he said. "It would eat a dog. It was a tiger."

Young Mrs. Frazier looked reproachfully at her equally young husband.

"Richard," she said, "it's those stories. Dicky wouldn't lie deliberately."

"Don't blame the stories," said the man. "It's his imagination again."

"That's just it," exclaimed Mrs. Frazier. "How can you expect the child to tell right from wrong if his head is stuffed with Jack and the Bean Stalk?"

"Why, any child knows a fairy story couldn't happen," the father protested. "You're making too much of what

18

Dicky said. He was joking—he doesn't really mean he saw a tiger."

"That's what he says."

"He doesn't mean it, though," Mr. Frazier insisted. "Look here, Dick. What was it you really saw out in the yard?"

"A big tiger."

This statement by his son brought to Mr. Frazier's face the hurt expression of a man who has been disappointed by a friend.

"Close that book," he said evenly, "and come over here to me."

The boy approached his father warily, as though realizing that far beyond his control the implacable machinery of circumstance was already set in motion against him.

"We'll settle this once and for all," said Mr. Frazier, grasping his son's arm. "I won't have a—"

"Wait, Richard," his wife interrupted. "Let me talk to him."

She drew the boy to her and spoke with the air of explaining first principles.

"Now, Dicky," she began, "what mother says is true. Isn't it?"

"Yes, mother."

"And mother says you didn't see a tiger."

"Yes, I did," said the boy stubbornly.

"Son, don't you know you must not tell lies?"

"Yes, mother."

"Then why do you tell us you saw a tiger out on the lawn?"

"Because I saw him."

"Mother says no."

"But—"

"You heard your mother," the man interjected. "And we've had about enough of this tiger business. Do you understand?"

"Yes, father."

"That's our truthful little soldier," said Mrs. Frazier. "Now mother wants to hear you admit that you didn't see it."

"He had shiny eyes," the boy said. "He was bigger than a pony."

Laying aside his evening newspaper, Mr. Frazier started to speak but stopped abruptly as his wife again shook her head.

"Dick, mother has said no. Do you mean," she added sorrowfully, "that mother doesn't tell the truth?"

"No," the boy answered, "but I saw his black stripes and long whiskers."

"Dicky!"

"And when he put his feet down," continued the child, "he had long claws."

"Where on earth did he get that description?" Mrs. Frazier asked her husband.

"There's certainly nothing like it in any of his stories," said Mr. Frazier. "So that excuse won't go."

"No, not in his stories, but—oh, of course!" The woman laughed with relief. "It's in his picture book—his animal-picture book!"

"That's it!" cried Mr. Frazier.

"Let mother see the book, Dicky," the young woman directed. "Give it to mother."

After turning several pages, she triumphantly pointed out a crouching yellow tiger in lithograph on a bank of pale green reeds.

"There! That's our old friend, isn't it? The picture's in the book, it couldn't be outside. You understand, don't you, dear?"

"The picture wasn't outside," the child replied uncertainly. "But the tiger was."

Ominously Mr. Frazier rose.

"All right, young man," he said. "We've given you every chance."

He looked inquiringly at his wife.

"There's nothing else to do," she said. "Tell him why you're punishing him, Richard."

Mr. Frazier paused, then delivered a brief lecture explaining that his son's stubbornness had cast a shadow forever on the bright face of truth.

At the end of the sermon he carried his son upstairs and a moment later Dick could be heard screaming in fright and pain.

By the time Mr. Frazier returned downstairs to the living-room the screams had subsided into spasmodic sobbing; and this was dying away when, loud and startling, the doorbell rang.

Mr. Frazier opened the door, his wife peering over his shoulder. On the porch an amiable-looking man in a gray suit was courteously lifting a bowler hat that glistened in the light from the living-room window.

"Good evening, folks," he said cheerily. "Any little ones here?"

The Fraziers stared.

"Any children in this lovely little home?" the stranger repeated.

"Yes—one," admitted Mrs. Frazier. "One boy."

"And the little fellow is safe in bed, no doubt?"

"What is it you want?" demanded Mr. Frazier coldly, with the suspicion accorded drunkards, lunatics and busybodies.

"Why, I've just called," the man replied, "to save the little chap—and your good lady here—from being alarmed."

"What—what do you mean?" Mrs. Frazier asked nervously.

"Madam," said the man, "I represent the Mammoth World's Combined Shows. While passing through your beautiful little city we had the misfortune to upset one of our cars and lose an old tiger. We followed him down this street, and he went through your neighbor's yard. There's no cause for alarm—no cause for alarm."

"A real tiger?"

"Yes, madam, but a gentle old thing," said the showman. "He'd run away from a baby."

"I hope you find him," murmured Mr. Frazier mechanically.

"Three in household," the circus man continued, "and three complimentary admissions to the big show. Bring the little fellow. Let him see the wild animals, the Roman chariots, the funny clowns."

The man's arm moved in an unctuous gesture which had forestalled lawsuits in towns and villages from Virginia to the Dakotas. Into Mr. Frazier's hand he pressed three big red tickets—and was gone through the April dusk.

Beneath the hall light, face to face, the honest couple stood in shame and sorrow.

"We'll both go up," said the man, after a moment of silence.

"Yes," the woman whispered, "and take the tickets with us."

Humbly, reluctantly, they began to mount the stairs.

JUST AS I AM
by
Day Edgar

THE train coasted to a halt and Alan Sheppard, standing in the vestibule of the last car, glanced keenly at his watch. He saw that it was exactly 9:26. Thereupon the engineer, somewhere ahead in the frosty darkness, unconsciously became the recipient of the stern approval which young Alan Sheppard reserved for those who were punctual and efficient. He stepped down to the brick platform. The last car, as he had foreseen, deposited him squarely in front of the waiting room; so, while less farsighted passengers were trudging back the length of many cars, Sheppard walked straight across to the graveled yard. Here he slid into his parked coupe, and as he drove away he was wondering if Edwina would be ready to leave the minute he arrived.

Her most recent offense against punctuality, he recalled, had occurred just two weeks ago. They were going out to dinner and Edwina, after keeping him waiting seven minutes in the car, had objected vigorously because he had repeatedly summoned her by blowing the horn.

"Sometime, when you keep making that racket," she had threatened, "I won't wait to finish dressing. I'll come out just as I am."

The threat had not disturbed Sheppard, and now the memory of it provoked an indulgent smile as he kept the coupe moving at a fast, uniform speed along the winding road. On his right he saw an evergreen tree still spangled with Christmas bulbs of red and green that glittered like false jewels above the snowy lawn. His thoughts traveled across the dark hill on his left to the home of the Ward McCurdys, and this reminded him of the efficiency he had displayed in meeting the difficulties presented by tonight's engagement.

During the past week he had stayed at the office until midnight to handle the rush work that always came with the last days of the old year. Twice this week he had spent the night in town; but tonight, he knew, Edwina was eager to go to the Ward McCurdys' party.

To make this possible, without sacrificing his work, he had once more stayed late at the office and, after a hasty supper at his club, had utilized the minutes before train time by shaving and changing into his Tuxedo. Then he had phoned home. Because Edwina was out he had intrusted his message to the cook. Mrs. Sheppard, he had instructed, was to be ready to start for the McCurdys' as soon as he reached the house. The time of his arrival he had set at 9:34, and a glance at the clock on the dash showed that he was punctual to the minute.

He ran into the house with his brief case. Edwina was not waiting in the hall. Neither was she in the living-room. Annoyed, Sheppard went to the foot of the stairs.

"Edwina?"

"Hello," her voice called. "I'll be down in a minute."

"Aren't you ready?"

"Yes, almost."

Sheppard raised his head toward the upper landing.

"I'll be out in the car."

There was something ominous in his manner as he strode out of the house. In the car he waited exactly one minute and then touched the horn button three times.

In a moment Edwina appeared at her bedroom window, and as she pushed it open Sheppard observed grimly that she was still without her dress.

"Remember what I told you!" she called warningly.

"You're four minutes late," he retorted and blew the horn to drown her reply. He was determined to teach her a lasting lesson. From short toots he graduated into shrill, sustained blasts. Loud and raucous, the horn brayed powerfully through the suburban stillness.

Suddenly, from inside, he heard the sound of swift steps on the stairs. The front door flew open. Edwina, eyes blazing, stood on the threshold, a wrap thrown around her shoulders.

"Alan, stop that racket!"

"I'll stop," he said calmly, "as soon as you're ready."

"Stop it right now!"

"You've already kept me waiting six minutes," he pointed out, "and you're still in your underwear. I intend to keep blowing this horn until you're ready to leave."

Their eyes met, and for a long moment Edwina regarded him inscrutably. Then, visibly, she reached a decision.

"If you blow that horn once more," she said, "I'll get in the car just as I am."

At once his hand came down on the button and another strident blast wailed through the night. Edwina closed the front door and turned. Beneath her scanty wrap the breeze fluttered a garment of delicate green, and her naked legs shone in the light of the rising moon as she came quickly to the car. "We're going to settle this once for all," she said.

Sheppard promptly opened the door. Here, he realized, was the test.

"Get in."

The calmness of his voice was a challenge. Edwina jumped in and the coupe moved slowly out the drive.

"I'm tired of the fuss you make about a few minutes," she said spiritedly. "It's all right in your office. You can be as strict and efficient as you want up there, but our home isn't an office and I won't stand for it any longer."

Sheppard concealed a smile. She was talking, he felt, to keep up her courage. He maintained his dignified silence but watched her out of the side of his eye.

The wrap, held carelessly at her waist, parted high on her lap and exposed bare legs of lovely contours tapering down to pretty knees, legs of streamline symmetry that curved on toward ankles invisible now in the shadows. She was making her legs as conspicuous as she could, Sheppard decided, in an effort to scare him into turning back to the house.

Inexorably he steered the coupe in through a high iron arch and they rolled down the Ward McCurdys' twisting drive. Studying Edwina in the mirror, Sheppard thought he detected nervousness in her attitude as the coupe stopped near the steps of the big Colonial porch. He hopped out.

"Here we are," he said briskly. "Come on!"

Like a queen descending from her coach Edwina stepped gracefully to the ground. While they walked to the porch Sheppard was uneasily assuring himself that she must soon weaken now. Her poise, however, shook his confidence and he had a sudden, horrible vision of a roomful of people who turned from their bridge tables to stare.

Doggedly he escorted her to the wide front door. An amber glow from the fanlight fell on them. He shuddered when he saw Edwina's wrap float back in the night breeze. He saw, too, that there was a mocking gleam in her eyes as she watched him fumbling at his glove.

"Go ahead and ring, Alan," she dared softly. "I'm getting chilly."

He raised his hand to the bell. Beyond the door he heard voices, and suddenly his hand dropped. "Come on home," he said. "Get your dress on."

"I won't move an inch until you promise to stop blowing that horn."

"All right—but hurry!" he whispered and caught her arm. Edwina, withdrawing it, stood her ground. "You promise never to blow the horn at me again?"

"I promise."

"On your honor—whether I'm late or not?"

"Yes, yes!" he said. "I promised once, didn't I? Come on before we—"

A black limousine stopped at the porch steps. People

were climbing out. Sheppard looked around wildly. He wanted to flee, but he saw that he was trapped. The new arrivals were Beth and Harry Lehr.

A queer shiver shook him, and for a frightened moment he wondered if he had gone mad; for as Beth Lehr came running up the steps he saw that she wore, beneath her flapping coat, even less clothes than Edwina.

"Hello!" said Beth breathlessly. "I'm Cleopatria—what are you, Edwina?"

Opening her wrap, Edwina stood revealed in a silken shirt, little boots and short pants of a delicate green.

"I'm a pirate," said Edwina.

"Lovely; you look lovely!" Beth exclaimed. "And what are you, Alan?"

"Alan's not in costume," said Edwina innocently. "He was so busy with the car that he forgot it was a masquerade."

MARRIAGE IN MODERATION
by
John Erskine

THEY were friends of mine, and I tried to improve on their happiness!

He was a writer, a novelist if you must know all, and she painted landscapes.

She came to Eighth Street first, he several weeks after, but fate introduced them promptly. The great days of the Village were already a legend. That was how they had heard of it, he in Altoona, she in Baltimore. They had read of freedom of plain lodgings, two flights up, with a flower box in the window and no running water. She found such a haven at once, he rested cautiously at a small hotel until he got his bearings and found her.

From their reading they both knew you couldn't be free if you were alone. Freedom meant a soul mate, which meant a roommate. But nothing vulgar. No marriage.

Freedom was at its peak when you took your courage in your hand and tacked two calling cards on your door, "Mr. So-and-so," and "Miss This-and-that"—sometimes the girl's name on top and sometimes the man's, but either way you were conscious of independence when you opened the door in the morning to take in the milk, and remembered that the landlady had her thoughts about such things.

I'll call them Wallace and Belle. When I made their acquaintance they had been free for a year, and if they had not outlined their true condition with aggressive frankness I should have taken them for man and wife, signed and sealed, in the sober tradition of Victoria the Queen. Never have I laid eyes on a pair so fitted for domestic propriety, companionship and trust. They had the fiber of constancy

in them, that friendly warp and woof which knits the home
all of a piece, from the first sunshiny spinning of the threads
to the shadowy trimming of the pattern at the end.

I frequented their simple but blessed hearth just to look
on marriage in its essential perfection, and it annoyed me
when they announced again, as they always did before the
evening was over, that they weren't married at all.

"You might as well be!" I protested at last. "It's permanent. Why pretend?"

Belle brushed back her lovely, tousled hair so that her
honest blue eyes could get at me.

"We have the reality. Should we walk up an aisle—
and all that flumdiddle?"

"The city hall would do," I conceded.

Here Wallace got on his long legs, remarked that my
pipe had gone out, and offered fresh tobacco, so I took the
hint and said no more.

But when I called again, off they went on that freedom
theme of theirs, and now I had a better argument ready.

"It's a pity you two don't believe in self-expression.
If you did, you'd be great artists!"

That stirred them, as I knew it would.

"No," I persisted, "if you believed in expression, you'd
marry. You'd do it with the full flumdiddle. An emotion is
stronger, an idea is clearer, for being expressed. In true
art there can't be any hiding. This unadmitted wedlock
of yours—well, it isn't art."

When I left that night, I thought I had merely spoiled
the evening, but the next afternoon Wallace called up to
say that they had been to the city hall, and I was right! You
couldn't realize what marriage was like till you gave it
public expression.

I had them to dinner at the Cafe de Paris, and they talked
of nothing but their new discovery that vows are satisfying,
provided you mean them. They were, if I may say so,
daffy with romance, and the cafe put Europe in their head.

They decided then and there to take an old-fashioned wedding trip.

Where they got the money I don't know. Perhaps the relatives in Altoona and Baltimore made a thank offering. Anyway, they went to England, and I·stood on the dock and waved up at them, conscious of a good job.

A month later I had to go over myself, and I ran into them in Paris. He was halfway through a new book, which she said was inspired, and he didn't argue. She had bought paint and canvas, and was doing an entirely original view of Notre Dame from the river bank.

Also, they had made up their minds to be married in the historic church, and I was to be a witness.

"It's so much more beautiful than the city hall," explained Belle. "It will express our love!"

"You aren't Catholics, are you?" I asked, knowing their indifference to details.

"That can be arranged," said Wallace earnestly, "or if necessary we can join the church."

It took time, but somehow it was indeed arranged, and I looked on with the concierge's wife, and then I gave them a dinner at La Perousse.

We were just uncorking a bottle of Montrachet, when Wallace remarked casually, "I felt it far more deeply this time than at St. Margaret's, in London. The architecture's nobler."

Belle glowed with beatitude. "Or our love has grown!"

My hand shook—I couldn't lift my glass.

"What did you two do at St. Margaret's?" I asked.

"Got married," said Belle. "The charmingest old curate with white hair, and that placid little church, right under the abbey—"

"Did you tell him you were already married?"

"Only a civil ceremony," said Wallace, disposing of me. "Belle, have you tried this spinach? It has cheese on it, and mushrooms."

"Wait a minute!" said I. "Did the French priest know you were married in London?"

"None of his business," said Wallace. "Can't I marry my own wife? If marriage is, as you said, a form of expression, then the more you feel married, the more you ought to express it. Belle and I are happier every day. Aren't we, darling?"

They really were, so I let sleeping dogs lie, and in a week they vanished from Paris, leaving a trail of bliss.

I heard nothing more till I got his telegram.

When they reached Chartres they discovered that the Cathedral was finer than Notre Dame by precisely the proportion that their love meanwhile had matured.

They were moved to express themselves again, and did the necessary registering at the Hotel de Ville, where the clerks are trained to check up on you.

To a marriage in England the French may pay no attention, but to a marriage in France they do.

Wallace's telegram read: "Come down, you misleading idiot, and bail us out. We're arrested for bigamy."

When I got there the charge had been shifted to insanity and Wallace and Belle were quarreling.

I hate to see a man and his wife bandying words, like two dogs with their hind legs tied together!

Wallace and Belle are living in New York now. They're still married.

ONE MAN'S TASTE

by

Richard Connell

MR. AND MRS. WOODLES were proud of their new house. "Simple—but charming" about described it, they thought. They found it in the country, a neglected boarding house for rats, remodeled it, furnished it and transformed it into a thing of beauty. At least, Mrs. Woodles did. About such matters Mr. Woodles admitted he knew little—you might say nothing. He learned that colonial furniture is not bought, but "picked up."

Piece by piece Mrs. Woodles picked up the furniture in sundry barns and attics. With her blood heated by the chase she would shamelessly push into the home of strange rustics and carry off an old four-poster bed right from under Grandpa. Then there would ensue an orgy of scraping, sandpapering, staining and waxing.

There were times when Mr. Woodles felt that he never wanted to smell varnish or hear the word "authentic" again. But he admitted that the result justified the effort and cost. At last the final hooked rug was in precisely the right spot, the framed sampler (by Deborah Wakeman, aged 9) hung over the fireplace, and the chairs, tables and sofas were satisfactorily arranged.

One morning Mrs. Woodles said:

"My cousin Ellery is driving out to see the house. You'll like Ellery, I know. Such exquisite taste! On the subject of what-nots he is an absolute authority."

The authority on what-nots proved to be a long young man, blond and elegant, who inspected Mr. Woodles critically, causing that gentleman to feel like a spurious

32

highboy. As they walked up the path toward the Woodles' house, Ellery stopped and gave a low moan.

"Sick?" queried Mr. Woodles, solicitously.

"That wing, oh, my dear chap, that wing!" moaned Ellery.

"Huh?" said Mr. Woodles. "What's the matter with the wing?"

"Pernicious," murmured Ellery. "One might say fla-grant."

"But we had to put the kitchen some place," said Mr. Woodles.

"Of course, we can easily tear that wing down," said Ellery, thoughtfully. They entered the house.

"And this," said Mrs. Woodles proudly, "is the living-room."

"Not really?" said Ellery. His somewhat piscatorial eye affixed itself to an easy-chair. It was Mr. Woodles' pet chair, placed just right for reading, just near enough to the fire for its occupant to be toasted without being singed.

"That chair," said Ellery, amiably but firmly, "must go. May I?"

He trundled it to a remote corner. It left a gap like a missing front tooth.

"Now I'll just put this Hitchcock chair here," said Ellery. "Not veritable Hitchcock, to be sure, but fairly good."

The moving of the chair necessitated the shifting of a table, and that left an oil painting of a bewhiskered Woodles ancestor dangling in such a way that the sight caused Cousin Ellery acute pain. So the picture had to come down.

"Well, while I'm here I might as well make a good job of it," remarked Ellery, with that happy, almost fanatical gleam that comes only to the eyes of born furniture-rear-rangers. "Just lend me a hand with that desk, will you, Woodles, like a good fellow?"

Looking like anything but a good fellow, Mr. Woodles complied. Mrs. Woodles fluttered about, masking her

distress and saying, "Of course, Ellery, you know best.
I know your taste is exquisite."

Mr. Woodles did emit a feeble protest when his favorite
chair was entirely banished from the room. But his, "Well,
the fact is, I like that chair" only caused the masterful
furniture-rearranger to lift an eyebrow and say, "Really?
How droll!"

Before he had finished, Cousin Ellery had made the
house over. Not even the meat-chopper in the kitchen or
the towels in the towel closet were permitted to remain
where the Woodles wanted them to be.

Ellery was saying, "And now suppose you knock out that
wall and throw the living-room and dining-room together
and move that indecent wing around to the back of the
house, and abolish that uncanny fireplace—" when Mr.
Woodles said, "I'm afraid if you want to get back to the
city for dinner, you'd better start now."

Mr. Woodles escorted Cousin Ellery to his glittering
new car.

"I guess I don't know much about furniture," observed
Mr. Woodles, sadly. Then, with sudden firmness. "But I
do know about haberdashery. And motor cars."

"Ah, really?" murmured Ellery.

"Oh, yes," said Mr. Woodles. "Now, take that hat
you have on. Blatant, my dear fellow, indubitably blatant!"

He removed the bowler from the head of the surprised
Ellery and deftly drop-kicked it over a fence.

"And that collar!" said Mr. Woodles. "Unspeakable!
And that dotted tie! Revolting!"

With a quick movement he tore the collar from its
moorings.

"I'll retie that tie for you as it should be tied," offered
Mr. Woodles; but Ellery, with a treble squeak of dismay,
sprang into his car.

Mr. Woodles eyed the car pensively.

"A bit flamboyant for my taste," he announced. "I
note you have an extra bugle horn on the front. As you

already have a siren, suppose we put the bugle horn on the rear to warn people against bumping into you. Here—I'll move it for you—"

He began to wrench at the bugle horn.

"Hey—now—" the thoroughly disorganized Ellery began to sputter.

"Oh, no trouble at all," said Mr. Woodles. "And while I'm at it, I'll just change the shape of your radiator. I can give it that smart, handmade touch with a few judicious cracks with a heavy hammer. Let me have a hammer from your tool chest, will you, old chap?"

"I will not!" cried Ellery, wildly.

Mr. Woodles stopped twisting at the horn.

"A good-sized stone will serve just as well," he said, "and here is the very stone. What luck!"

But as he stooped to pick up the stone, the frantic Ellery trod heavily on the accelerator and the car whizzed away.

When he returned to the house, Mr. Woodles found his wife in tears.

"I don't like the room this way," she said. "But I suppose Ellery knows best. Such exquisite taste!"

"Let's fix it the way we want it," said Mr. Woodles.

"But Ellery will be furious when he comes again."

"Something tells me he will never come back—if then," said Mr. Woodles. "Where's that chair of mine?"

THE MAN WHO JUST SAT
by
Frederick L. Collins

THAT very evening, "Sitting" Bull—his friends never did
call him Livingston—had looked across the candles at his
beautiful young wife, and thought how much she had contributed to the success of his favorite cult. For, if he had
made his personal freedom his religion, Paula had certainly
made it her profession. It was too bad, he thought, that
all his friends—their guest of the evening, for instance—were
not so helpfully appreciative as his wife. There was no
use denying it. There was something in Jack Weston's
manner which intimated that the Bull was not one of
freedom's heroes, but merely a complacent, indolent rather
fat man; that what he believed to be freedom was really not
freedom at all, but a sort of mental flatulence that would
blow up and burst if you stuck a pin in it. All through
dinner, Weston had been ready with the pin!

"You're free?" he had said, as soon as Paula had gone
upstairs. "You, with your charming and efficient wife, and
your rotten money, and your obsequious servants, and your
house that is a prison in itself? Why, you poor simp!
You're not free at all. There's no such thing as freedom.
And I can prove it. I can prove that you aren't free to do
the simplest thing—here—now—in your own house."

Huh! Not free in his own house to do the simplest thing?
Why, the fellow might just as well have said that he, "Sitting" Bull, could not sit in his own chair, in his own dining
room, in his own home, as long as he liked! And that, as a
matter of fact, is just what he did say.

"For instance, you are sitting quietly in your own chair.
You think you are free to sit there without asking anyone's
permission don't you?"

"I know I am," answered the host.

"You think you can sit there just as long as you wish to, without explaining to anyone what it's all about."

"I know I can."

"Well, I know you can't." Weston looked at his wrist watch. "It is now eight thirty. I'll leave you sitting in that chair. I'll go to the opera and return at twelve. In the meantime, you just sit—sit in the chair and sit tight, understand? And if you are still sitting in that chair when the clock strikes midnight, I'll say you are a free man. But if when I return, you are not in that chair, I'll have proved what I say—that you aren't free at all."

"How ridiculous! As if I didn't know I could sit in my own chair. I'll bet you any amount of money I can sit here all night."

"Never mind the betting. You just attend to the sitting," said Weston, rising, "and never mind all night. You won't last till midnight."

"I'll bet you ten thousand dollars that I will," cried Bull. He was more than annoyed. He was angry. "Ten thousand dollars, see!"

"Are you sure you want to?" said Weston. "It seems a shame—"

"I'm not a child, Weston," Bull interrupted.

"All right, old man, if you insist. Ten thousand bucks if you're in that chair at midnight. You're on." Jack Weston extended a hand which "Sitting" Bull took—without rising.

If Jackson, the butler, had been as familiar with "Historia Religoosa" as he was the matters gastronomic, he might have attached a spiritual significance to his master's extraordinary behavior. He would have recalled that durable old boy, Saint Simeon who sat thirty years on a pillar sixty feet high, and earned world fame as the Sitting Hermit. He would have read into the strained, wan face before him something of the spiritual exaltation which Livingston and Simeon must both have felt. But Jackson had never heard of sitting saints. And so, naturally, he thought his master's trouble was strictly physical, presumably digestive.

"Can't I get you something hot, sir?" queried Jackson anxiously.

"No thank you, Jackson."

For more than an hour "Sitting" Bull had been amusing himself by composing sometimes out loud, heroic stanzas in the meter of "Horatius at the Bridge". In these lyrics he found himself emerging as "Sittingus at the chair."

"A little apple brandy, sir?" pursued the butler.

"No, nothing to drink, thank you."

"Soda and hot water is good, sir. Cook, she says—"

"What are you trying to do to me, Jackson?" he said.

"Well you see, sir," mumbled Jackson, "it's after ten."

"And what of it?"

Jackson was alarmed. His fears for his master's stomach had melted before worry for the condition of his mind. In all events, sudden excitement was to be avoided. Jackson determined on retreat.

"I just thought you might want to know the time, sir." With that he grabbed a tray of dishes and backed discretely toward the screen that hid the pantry door.

"If I want to know the time I'll ask for it," growled his employer.

"Yes sir," agreed Jackson, with a final convulsive backing movement that landed him against the screen instead of behind it. For a second the high tapestried structure rocked on its mahogany foundation, seemed to be tottering pantryward, and then, pitched forward into the room. Before it went Jackson and his loaded tray. Behind it or behind where it had been, were the standers—cook, squat, fat and done to a turn; the second man, a steamy laundress, and scullery maid who looked the part, and Molly, the pretty parlor maid—all drawn by anxious curiosity to witness the extraordinary behavior of the man who just sat.

Oh yes, there was one other interested spectator—O'Brian, the copper on the beat!

Livingston Bull was far too angry to speak, the eavesdroppers far too discomfited. At this critical moment the upstairs bell rang. Never was house bell answered with such alacrity. Cook, butler, second man, and girls. O'Brian's dignity would not permit of such a concourse. Unsupported the representative of the law faced the apostle of freedom—the screen was like a gauntlet flung between them.

"What the devil are you here for?" shouted Bull.

"No offense, Mr. Bull. I just stepped in," stammered O'Brian.

"Well, you'll please step out!"

"Just as you say, Mr. Bull. You seem all right now."

"All right—of course I'm all right!" This was too much. First Jackson thought that he was ill. Now this fellow was inferring he had needed watching. Was he indeed mad? Or wasn't it possible for a gentleman to sit quietly in his own house? He twisted and squirmed in the Jacobean chair, but he did not get up.

"That's what I says to 'em, it's just this 'ere bum hooch, I says. He'll get over it, I says, if he don't go blind."

"Can't a man sit quietly in his own chair, in his own dining room, in his own home, without calling in the police?" he cried, "Without people saying he's sick or drunk or—"

He glared ferociously at the cop, who made a quick jump for the pantry door. Bull heard a slight noise behind him. The folding doors opened. Someone entered the room cautiously and stood at some distance from where he sat. It was his wife. Jackson had done his worst. Paula was pale—and volubly solicitous for his health.

"Me ill? Never felt better in my life. Look!"

"Oh, Livingston, have you been drinking?"

"Has that policeman been talking that stuff to you?"

His wife's eyes filled. This mad raving about the police was the last straw. A policeman—and in her dining room? How absurd!

"No, Livingston, dear," she said soothingly, "you are mistaken. There was no policeman."

There came another of these sudden changes in the man's mood—a most alarming symptom, she had heard; and he straightened up wide-eyed. He seemed to be about to rise.

"That's right, dear," began Paula soothingly. "The best thing for you to do is to get up."

"Get up?" he cried as if she had hit him. For a long time he looked his wife solemnly in the eye. Then he spoke, "Am I, or am I not, a sane human being?"

That question was not to be answered—not then—for Jackson was again standing uncertainly on the threshold. "He's come, ma'am," ignoring Bull completely as if he no longer counted in the world of men.

"Who's sick?"

The family doctor, peering cautiously from behind the protection of the butler, exchanged understanding glances with the madman's wife.

Officer O'Brian had, in his discretion, withdrawn to a telephone booth to consult his captain; and now he was, in his valor, returning to do his duty. His appearance in the pantry door, breaking his way through the row of servants backed this time by two hospital attendants, a white-coated municipal doctor, and a young man in plain clothes, produced a varying effect on the occupants of the room. Dr. Barnard was obviously relieved. Paula just naturally swooned. Livingston Bull alone failed to recognize the gravity of the situation. Peevishness, annoyance, agitation, abuse, even protest dropped from him. There came in their place, laughter, high, convulsive, maniacal laughter, that shook the whole upper part of his frame, that caused the Jacobean chair to rock and teter like a dying top.

Immediately the hospital doctor saw his duty. This was no case for a private house. The patient's condition was clearly institutional.

"For the last time, Mr. Bull"—his tone was increasingly menacing, "I ask you to get out of that chair."

"I won't do it! I won't do it! I tell you to leave me alone. All I want to do is to sit in my own chair. In my own chair, do you understand? In my own chair, ha, ha! Chair, ha, ha, ha! . . .

The hospital doctor had a kindlier side. He too was, in his unprofessional moments, a collector of antiques. He noticed for the first time the quality of the straight, high backed Jacobean chair. He understood how Bull, even in his insanity, might cling to so valuable a possession.

"We'll humor the poor fellow. Strap him to the chair. We'll take 'em both with us."

Two additional uniformed attendants, preceded by a blast of cold air from the front door, swept into the room. Automatically, they thrust the poles of the stretcher under the seat of the precious chair. The two original uniformed attendants seized the poles from the rear. The hospital doctor gave the word of command. They lifted Livingston Bull, chair and all, and bore him from the room.

As Jack Weston and his gay mood and his high hat and his twirling stick swung around the corner into the avenue, he was amazed at the midnight throng around the Livingston Bull front stoop. The place was mobbed. Home-going town cars filled with theater parties had drawn up two and three deep at the curb. Their owners crowded against the steps. The shining black ambulance towered above the motorcycles patrolling the block. From the deep shadows of neighboring windows bald heads and boudoir caps jockeyed for position. Bewildered, even a bit alarmed, Weston approached a man in evening dress, he asked him the cause of the excitement.

"Why, haven't you heard? Old Livingston Bull has gone violently insane."

At this moment, peal on peal of laughter smote the midnight air. All eyes turned toward the open doorway. The first pair of bearers solemnly appeared. Immediately there was a loud and terrifying explosion. The avenue became like midday. The poor wretch in the lifted chair was illumined in all his hideousy. A young man with over developed nasal cavities, jumped out of a drawing-room window, landing on the granite railing at Weston's side.

"Did you get him?" he shouted into the darkness.

"Sure came a voice from a second story window, where Weston could just make out the square build of a newspaperman's cameras.

A distant clock was striking. It was midnight—and "Sitting" Bull, in the cavernous recesses of the police ambulance, still sat, over his face played the sweet smile of a contented mind. He had won ten thousand dollars. More than that he had proved himself a free man.

Some ideas—like freedom—never die!

PORRIDGE ON THE FLOOR

One aristocrat helps another to prove that blue blood will
tell in man or dog, especially dog.

by

Walter Duranty

THE terms of the bet were fantastic as Judge Carter wrote
them in the smoking room of the Berengaria the night
before she reached New York.

"Miles Wynneton, Lord Ashover of Kent, England, bets
Robert Winton of Philadelphia one thousand dollars that:

1. He, Lord Ashover, will order a bowl of porridge to
be served to him on the floor in the middle of the Restaurant
Beauvin at Park Avenue on any day he may select within
two weeks after his arrival in New York.

2. That he can obtain the execution of said order and
consume contents of said bowl without let, hindrance or
interference from anyone.

In token thereof the two gentlemen above-mentioned
have each deposited the sum of one thousand dollars in my
keeping and have agreed to accept my decision as arbiter
should any dispute arise as to the fulfillment of the contract.

Signed, JUDGE ROBERT LEE CARTER

MILES ST.-CLAIR WYNNETON

ROBERT WINTON."

It all began with a discussion about manners and what a
"person of quality" should or should not do, and could or
could not do. The argument which followed was somewhat
sharpened by family pride and a touch of international
rivalry, because Ashover and Winton were distant cousins.

Both branches of the family had prospered—the Philadelphia commoners by frugality and judicious commerce,

the English nobles by no less judicious marriage and their inborn knowledge of the seamy side of Courts.

Robert Winton was a true scion of Harvard and Philadelphia, a tall spare man in the middle forties. He was head of a distinguished law firm, had traveled widely, spoke French and German correctly, and was a connoisseur of food and wines. Good form was his god and the ceremonial rites of eating and drinking his chosen form of worship.

Lord Ashover was twenty-six, tall and blond, with a warm ready smile. He was as clean and polished as Eton and six years in the Coldstream Guards could make him, but behind his gaiety there was a shade of the insolence which comes of youth and unquestioned confidence in one's own position, which exasperated the older man.

Perhaps Judge Carter was really responsible for the bet. It was he who set the ball rolling in the smoking room by raising the vexed question of what constitutes a gentleman. Robert Winton promptly swallowed the bait. "A gentleman," he said, "is one who never puts himself or allows himself to be put in an unsuitable position, unless he cannot possibly help it. Not to do anything unbecoming to one's self or to one's family—that is my idea of *Noblesse oblige*. I—"

"You're entirely wrong," Miles interrupted. "The only true definition of the word is that of a man who is perfectly at ease in any circumstances, however ridiculous. It is precisely, my dear fellow, when a man is placed in an undignified position, whether he chooses it or not, that his breeding shows. I mean it's a question of manners, or rather manner. If you carry yourself right, you can carry off anything right."

Robert Winton was nettled. "To begin with," he said, "it's a contradiction in terms, or rather it's absurd. A gentleman cannot—or should not—behave in an unbecoming way. If he does, he must realize it's unbecoming and feel humiliated and therefore cease to be at ease, or, if you prefer it, to retain the ease of manner about which you are talking. Just imagine, for instance, that instead of your sitting here at this table, the Captain, who is an autocrat while the ship's at sea, ordered you to lap your coffee from a saucer in the middle of the floor under pain of being 'thrown into irons' if you refused. You mean to tell me that you could do a thing like that and retain your ease of manner and not feel that you were making a fool of yourself in front of everybody?"

Miles flushed. "I mean just that. I don't say that if the Captain ordered it . . . that is a different story . . . It would all depend on how far he had the right and power to give such orders . . . but what I mean is, supposing that either by compulsion or choice, I was lapping my coffee from the floor, I would do it without any feeling of humiliation and in such a way that no one would think it especially unnatural. I am convinced that a man can do almost anything if it isn't offensive or indecent or noisy or . . . er . . . as you Americans say, get away with it."

"What you really mean, is that you could make a monkey of yourself in public without feeling any discomfort. Well, that may be true for you personally, or perhaps in England, but you couldn't do it in America. People simply wouldn't tolerate any such exhibition of bad taste as, for instance, taking your meals off the floor in a first-class restaurant. Either they would think you a lunatic and send for a doctor or they would call the head waiter and ask him to have the police remove you as a public nuisance."

That was how the bet was made. With an inward chuckle the Judge realized that the point at issue was both social and international . . . on one side a conflict between the ideas of the Philadelphian bourgeoisie, on the other the almost contemptuous self-assurance of an aristocrat accustomed from birth to the thought that "The King can do no wrong."

The ante-chamber of the restaurant Beauvin opens into a large square room tastefully festooned with flowers. The

patrons and personnel are too well bred and well trained
for any clatter of silver and plates. There is no music.

At eight-thirty one evening a tall young man handed his
dress hat, scarf and silk-lined overcoat to an attendant and
stood a moment under the arch between the ante-room and
restaurant. He was an elegant figure in faultless evening
clothes. All of the tables around the walls were occupied.
In the middle of the room, were a few less favored tables
allotted to late-comers.

Lord Ashover surveyed the scene as if in a search of
friends. He saw his cousin and Judge Carter in a corner
with two young and beautiful companions but made no sign
of recognition. It was understood that they should take
no part save as spectators in the performance to follow.

Past one of the tables on the left came a magnificent
white wolfhound. Indifferent, he neither paused nor wavered
when one of the women guests held out a piece of meat
towards him, but as he thrust his long sharp nose into
Ashover's hand with friendly confidence, the young man
felt that the hound's jaws were dripping.

"Getting on toward your dinner time, old fellow," he
murmured, scratching the narrow head. "Not always easy
to resist temptation, but you did it well."

Legend reports that the *Maitre D' Hotel* at Beauvin's is
a Russian nobleman. Actually he was a head waiter at
the Restaurant Donon, the once peerless resort of Petersburg.

"Monsieur will dine, or does he await friends?"

"What a splendid dog! Was he bred here or imported?"

"His great-grandsire was the pick of the Imperial
kennels. Does Monsieur wait for friends."

"No, I shall dine alone, but the first time in a strange
restaurant I make a rule never to sit at a table. I should
like a bowl of porridge served here on the floor, if it will not
take too long to prepare."

The *Maitre D' Hotel* inclined his head. He had received
far more eccentric orders in St. Petersburg in the long white
nights of summer.

"There will be no delay, and you shall be served immediately, I shall see to it myself."

The young man sauntered forward, took a chair from one of the central tables, lit a cigarette and waited, smiling. He had won the first round.

The *Maitre D' Hotel* himself accompanied the waiter a minute or two later and directed him to lay the cover in the middle of the floor. The man removed the lid from the silver porridge bowl. With perfect composure, Miles sat down cross-legged and began his meal as if it was the most natural thing in the world to be eating off the floor. He did not look around him and his ear detected little change in the tempo of conversation. A girlish giggle or two, and doubtless older eyebrows raised in mild surprise, but nothing more.

Miles glowed with triumph. After all he could teach that starchy cousin of his a thing or two and what it meant to do things in a right manner . . . the bet was as good as won.

But there was something his downcast eyes had missed. The great wolfhound, his hunger still unappeased, had come back from the ante-room and was standing just inside the restaurant with bristling hair and every muscle tense. In the dog's brain a furious conflict raged. Long months of patient training had taught him to weave a graceful course amongst the tables to greet his master's guests, but never to show interest in their food or accept anything they might offer him. Guests' food was served on tables . . . that was the lesson he had learned. It was dogs that took their dinner off the floor.

The wolfhound threw his head back and gave the short savage yelp that has echoed through Russian forests for centuries as he closes with his quarry, then hurled himself at the unsuspecting man.

The hound's shoulder caught Miles squarely in the chest and knocked him flat on the floor with a bang that made his head ring. The wolf-hound planted both feet on his chest and bayed exulting, then without changing position swung his long muzzle swiftly to the silver bowl and devoured what was left of the porridge.

After a moment of frozen silence there was a burst of uproar in the restaurant. The *Maitre D' Hotel* ran forward, shouting orders in crackling Russian. The hound raised his head towards his master as if in inquiry. The order was repeated. The dog's head bent, he licked the hand of the prostrate man, then walked slowly into the ante-room with his usual grace and ease.

Miles sat up rubbing the back of his head and staring stupidly at the crowd of waiters and guests who had left their tables. It seemed to him that they were all talking at once, but he couldn't distinguish what they said.

At that moment Robert Winton did the bravest thing in his life, and justified his notion of *noblesse oblige.* He pushed his way through the throng and taking Ashover by the arm helped him to his feet.

"My dear cousin, I hope you have not been injured by this unfortunate situation. Perhaps a glass of champagne. . . . Allow me." He guided the bewildered youth to the table in the corner.

Fifteen minutes later the incident was closed and nothing save a heightened note to the tone of conversation gave any sign that it had happened. One point, however, remained to be settled: Had Miles won his bet or not?

He declared that he had because its terms said "let, hindrance or interference by anyone," meaning any person; and a dog was not a person. Robert Winton rebuttled that his cousin had failed to finish the porridge; therefore the bet was lost.

They appealed to Judge Carter for a decision.

The Judge paused a moment in thought. "It is not only the terms of the bet—the letter of the law, as one might say—but the spirit in which the bet was made and its underlying purpose that must be considered. That purpose was to determine by a somewhat unusual experiment the meaning of the word gentleman. I believe the Wynneton family claims thirteen generations of nobility, and a conflict has arisen between its senior and junior branches, which I am called upon to arbitrate.

"In this case, however, the matter has been taken from my hands by an aristocrat whose lineage reckons three times thirteen generations of nobility, or more than that. I refer to the Imperial wolf-hound. The bet was to settle whether it is the act of a gentleman to eat porridge on the floor. The wolf-hound made clear his opinion that 'it isn't done'. As I say, he is the ranking aristocrat.

"According to the terms of the bet, Lord Ashover may reasonably claim to have won; according to the wolf-hound he lost. Since the two are incompatible, I declare the bet void."

PARSON SPARROW

by

T. F. Powys

THE Reverend William Sparrow was very much disappointed. He had always believed that a good example worked miracles. He was sure that this would be so when he followed Mr. Loop in the cure.

Mr. Loop was dead, and for the credit of the church he died not a moment too soon. Mr. Loop had been untruthful, he was fond of the drink, he administered the Holy Communion in carpet slippers, and he often walked with Mrs. Betty Wing in Byepath meadow.

Mrs. Wing was a woman, and what more need be said—only that she was too buxom, too young, and too merry to be good, and she liked the meadow stile.

Mr. Loop's garden was so overgrown with great shrubs and brambles that it was hard—and even Mr. Loop had found it so—to discover the path to or from the gate. To remedy this, Mr. Loop had dropped bottles, empty ones, that guided him through the shrubbery when he wished to go to church to preach a sermon, or to meet Mrs. Wing in Byepath meadow.

Mr. Sparrow soon altered all this. He worked harder than any laborer ever does, he cut the bushes, trimmed the hedges, and picked up every one of the bottles with his own hands and buried them. He wished to remove every trace of Mr. Loop.

Mr. Sparrow had a soft, gentle look, he read Keble and Saint Augustine, and hired aged Mrs. Gale as his housekeeper because she was very ugly. Only to look at Mr. Sparrow once, and to notice what he did, was enough for any one, and every word said about him was the same. He was humble, he was kind, there was nothing more to be told.

Mr. Sparrow gave no one any trouble. The baker's account was cast and paid every fortnight, and everything was done so properly at the Rectory that nothing seemed to be done at all.

How different from Mr. Loop, who would be always causing some sensation or another! For when May Green was married to Tom Baker, Mr. Loop went down to the lych-gate to meet them and commenced the burial service, and it was said that he once tried to baptize Betty Wing in Byepath meadow, taking her into his arms as if she were a baby.

Now that everything was so well and Christianly managed in the cure, who would have expected so sad a change to come over Honeyfield, that had been a decent enough village to live in before good Mr. Sparrow was settled there? Mr. Sparrow was all virtue, but the village soon became all sin.

As far as could be remembered in the past only Mr. Loop and Mrs. Wing had walked in Byepath meadow to behave naughtily. Only Mr. Loop had been the one to drop a baby at a christening, only Mr. Loop had told a lie in the pulpit, saying that he owed no man anything. The young girls used to be modest, they were now immodest. They would wait, by the gate into the Byepath meadow, and call to the young men, using unseemly gestures, to follow them to the stile. The old men were as bad as the young. They went to the Inn and met women there who hoped to be treated with port wine. Mr. Tidd, a gentleman who always watched to see what was happening, was heard to say that he wished Mr. Loop was back again, but that if he came he would certainly be extremely shocked by what he saw.

No one took all this new wickedness more to heart than Mr. Sparrow, who feared that he hadn't done his best, and redoubled his efforts for good. He had ever been frugal, but he now hardly ate anything at all. He begged and implored, but to no avail—all the people in Honeyfield

were rushing helter-skelter and tumbling over one another
to perdition.

Mr. Sparrow visited, all the money he saved he spent
upon tracts, he hardly ever went to bed, he prayed night
and day that people should be saved from their sins, but
nothing would do.

Children were born that never should have been born
at all, and were not brought to the font, and not one candi-
date appeared for confirmation when Mr. Sparrow gave
out from the pulpit that the Bishop was coming to lay on
his hands at the next village. Mr. Sparrow found this
neglect hard to bear because when Mr. Loop was Rector a
large number entered their names, for they hoped that Mr.
Loop would instruct them in the catechism with a bottle in
one hand and a pipe in the other—and they were not
disappointed.

At last the naughtiness grew to such a pass that Mr.
Sparrow received a letter from the Bishop informing him
that he had heard sad accounts of the behavior of the people
whose souls were under his care, because since Mr. Loop
had died the people had given themselves up to the Devil
and copied him in everything.

Mr. Sparrow cried over this letter.

"Mrs. Gale," he said to his ugly housekeeper that same
evening, "what can I do?"

"You had better ask Mr. Tidd," replied Mrs. Gale.

Though Mr. Tidd wasn't a holy one, he was always a
watcher. He had once been in trade as a carpenter, but as
the scraping of his jack-plane worried him he gave that up
and became a bankrupt and a looker-on. No one was better
suited as a watcher than Mr. Tidd, and no one was more
religiously inquisitive to see what was happening. He
would stand in the lanes, and if any one came up from
behind him he would look over his left shoulder to see who
it was.

Since he had given up his carpentry and taken to watching, Mr. Tidd had grown very wise, and if any one asked

him a question Mr. Tidd would always give a reply that was much to his credit.

The May sun was shining and the little lambs were leaping innocently, which made Mr. Sparrow sigh the more because the young Honeyfield maidens were so unlike the lambs, when he walked down the lane to find Mr. Tidd. He approached him from behind, but Mr. Tidd looked over his shoulder and saw who was coming.

Mr. Sparrow came to the point at once, as a good man always should.

"Why," he asked, "have the people grown so wicked since I have come amongst them, whereas with Mr. Loop as their Rector they had always been so good? Why, Mr. Tidd, do they never come to church to be christened, confirmed, or married?"

Mr. Tidd nodded at the lambs.

" 'Tis like this," said Mr. Tidd, "there bain't no wickedness in high places for they to watch or talk of, so, in order to have something to say, they must be bad themselves.

"Never a day did pass," continued Mr. Tidd, "when Mr. Loop was here, without there being a fine story to tell. If it wasn't the slippers, 'twas a bottle, and if it wasn't a bottle, 'twas Betty Wing. If a young man and maid did wander too far in the wide fields, thay had so much to tell one another about the dreadful doings of Mr. Loop that they had neither time nor wish to do nothing themselves, but now, alas!" sighed Mr. Tidd, "I fear Hell will have them all."

"Oh, what can I do to save them?" groaned Mr. Sparrow, holding up his hands in horror.

"Why," replied Mr. Tidd coolly, "thee must be a great fool if 'ee don't know how to be wicked."

Mr. Sparrow stepped back a pace.

"You can never mean, Mr. Tidd, that I ought to sin so that the people should have something to talk about and so become good again."

"There bain't no other way," said Mr. Tidd, solemnly.

"And should I," asked Mr. Sparrow, "by sending my soul to perdition, peradventure save all the poor people who now sin so dreadfully?"

" 'Tis most likely thee would," replied Mr. Tidd.

"But how can I?"

"Oh, thee needn't do much," said Mr. Tidd, smiling, "for a little wickedness do make a lot of talk."

"But a little wickedness is as damnable in God's eyes as a great deal."

"Ah," observed Mr. Tidd, nodding at a little leaping lamb, "most like it be."

"But I don't know how to begin," observed Mr. Sparrow, tearfully.

Mr. Tidd regarded the good pastor for a while in silence.

"Thee don't look like a thief," he said.

"I am very sorry," replied Mr. Sparrow.

"Nor a liar, nor yet a drunkard."

"I am most unfortunate," sighed Mr. Sparrow.

"Now don't 'ee be worried," remarked Mr. Tidd, "for, thank the Lord, there be one sin that be easy."

Mr. Sparrow blushed.

"Ah, ha!" said Mr. Tidd, "I believe thee could talk to Betty Wing—"

Never did the manners of a village change so suddenly, and the very next day after Mr. Tidd had given his advice the people of Honeyfield, instead of behaving improperly in divers ways, were all agog to hear what their minister had been doing, who had been noticed by Mr. Tidd to walk in Byepath meadow with Betty Wing, going toward the stile. It is true, as every one said, that they were but talking, but every great matter, Mr. Tidd observed, must have a small beginning.

The following Sunday the Honeyfield Church was well attended, all the village being there, in order to ask one another what the latest news was. Mrs. Wing was in the front pew, and every one listened to Mr. Sparrow's homily against wantonness with the gravest attention.

But that was not all, for when Mr. Sparrow gave out a notice that a confirmation would be held, twenty young persons presented themselves and, during the afternoon service, six children were brought to be baptized.

In a small time Mr. Sparrow was a Rural Dean.

NO FLOWERS

by

Gordon Arthur Smith

ON a Sunday in August of 1918, there were assembled around Steve Dempsey's drafting board an interested and receptive audience of four: Peters, an ensign attached to the "lighter-than-air" section; Madden, a pilot; Erskine, a lieutenant in the Operations Division; and Matthews, a chief yoeman.

"Yes," Dempsey was saying, "I'm beaucoup sorry for these here frawgs. They're just bein' massacred—that's all it is—massacred. And there don't anybody take much notice, either."

"Just how do you display that sorrow?" asked Ensign Madden.

"Well, sir, I displayed it last Sunday."

"What did you do last Sunday?"

"Well, it wasn't very regular, what I done last Sunday, but I'll tell you, if you don't have me up before a court— You remember last Sunday was a swell day. I ain't got a Jane, of course, so I decides to take a little look around, all by myself. Well, I goes down the Chomps-Eleezy feelin' pretty good and sorta peppy and lookin' for trouble. I see all them heroes—the vets and the dentists and the SOS— each with a skirt, and I passes Matthews here, with a skirt clingin' to him, like a cootie."

"Cut it out, you big stiff," interposed Matthews.

"Like a cootie," continued Steve, "and I got sorta depressed. I was just passin' the Loover—that big museum, or whatever it is—when I see a hearse comin' in the opposite direction. It was a pretty sick-lookin' hearse, too. It had a coupla animals hitched to it that was probably called

56

horses when they was young. And there was an old bird sittin' up on the box-seat with a hat like Napoleon One.

"Then I see that there wasn't no flowers. Then I see that there weren't no procession walkin' along behind, except there was one little old woman all in black and lookin' sorta sick and scared. Yes, sir, there she was walkin' all by herself and lookin' lonelier'n hell.

"So I sez to myself: 'It's all wrong, Steve, it's all wrong. Here's a poor dead frawg, the only son of his mother, and her a widow—goin' out to be planted with none of the gang around.' It's tough', I sez. So I sez, 'Laffyette, cheeri-o,' and steps up beside the old lady. That makes two mourners, anyhow.

"Well, the old lady give me the once over and seen Mr. Daniels's uniform and the rooster on my sleeve, and I guess decides that I'm eligible to the club. Anyway, she sorta nodded at me.

"Meanwhile we was crossin' one of them bridges—just crawlin' along like one of the motors had quit and the other was hittin' only on three. If we'd been in the air we'd stalled sure and gone into a tail spin. All the time I was thinkin' how to say 'Cheer up' to the old dame in French, but all I could think of at first was 'Bravo' and 'Vous-ate tray-jolee!' Still it was sorta stupid walkin' along and no conversation, so I guess I musta had an inspiration or something, and I sez, pointing ahead at the coffin, 'Mort avec mon Dieu.' The old lady lost her step at that, because I suppose she was surprised by a Yank speakin' good French. Where was I? Oh yes, we was on the bridge and I'd just told the old lady that the dead soldier was in heaven by now."

"Soldier?" repeated Erskine. "What made you believe he was a soldier?"

"Why, ain't every frawg a soldier now, sir?"

"How did you know, even, that it was a male frog?"

"I'm comin' to that, sir," replied Steve. "That comes next. You see once the old lady knew I could parlez-vous with the best of em, she continued the conversation and sez, 'Mon pover fees.' Get that? 'Mon pover fees.' Well, that means, translated, 'My poor son.' Just then, I seen a marine standin' on the corner tellin' a buncha girls all about Chateau-Teery. Well, I thought that maybe it 'ud be a good thing if he joined the funeral, because, anyway, the girls could hear all about Chateau-Teery from the next marine they saw. So I yell out at him:

" 'Hey, you! Come and join the navy and see the world!'

"Well, he looks around, salutes the corpse and steps in beside me and whispers, 'Say, chief, what's the idea?'

" 'Whadd'ya think, you poor cheese?' I sez, 'D'ya think it's a weddin'? Get in step. We're goin' to bury a French poiloo.'

" 'Is that so?' he sez.

" 'Yes, that's so', I sez. 'Get acrost on the other side of the widowed mother and say somethin' cheerful to her in French—if you know any.'

" 'If I know any!' sez he, 'Wasn't I at Chateau-Teery?'

" 'Well,' I sez, 'don't tell her about that. Tell her somethin' she ain't heard already.'

" 'You go to blazes!' And pretty soon I seen him gettin' all red and I knew he was goin' to shoot some French at the old lady, and sure enough, out he come with, "Madame je swee enchantay.'

"Well, sir, I like to've died trying to keep from laughin' at that because what it means translated is, 'Madam, I'm deelighted.' Trust them marines to say the right thing at the wrong time.

"By the time I got under control we're opposite the French Aviation Headquarters, and I see a doughboy on a motor-cycle with a sergeant sittin' in the side-car. So I step out of the ranks and sez to the sergeant, 'You and your side-car is commandeered for this funeral'. He sez: 'Shure, Oi'll come, and Oi'll be afther gettin' some o' thim other divvles to jine. Me name is Reilly.'

"Well, sir, Reilly was a good scout, and inside of a minute he had six doughboys lined up behind the hearse and him bringin' up the rear in the side-car. The side-car kept back firin', and it sounded like we was firin' salutes to the dead all the way to the park.

"I wanta tell ya, that old lady was tickled. Why, there we was already ten strong, with more to come, because I drafted three gobs at the Bullyvard Raspail. They wasn't quite sober, but I kep' my eye on 'em, and they behaved fine. I sez to them: 'You drunken bums, you! You join this funeral or I'll see you're put in the brig tonight.' But to make sure they'd not disgrace Mr. Daniel's uniform, I put 'em right behind the widow and me.

"Well, it appears that one of 'em talks French good— real good, I mean, sir—like a frawg waiter or a coacher."

"Or a what?" interjected Erskine.

"Or a coacher," repeated Steve with dignity. "The fact is, he talked it so good that—well, never mind that yet. He's a smart fellow, though, Mr. Erskine, by the name of Rathbone. Well, never mind, only, he's a good fellow and 'ud be pretty useful here, with his French, and everything.

"Well, anyway, I begun to wonder after a while where that fellow driving the hearse was takin' us to. We'd gone out the old Bullyvard Raspail a deuce of a way, and the old dame, I could see, was beginnin' to get weak in the knees and was walkin' about as unsteady as the three gobs behind us. So me and the marine each grabbed an arm and she sez, '*Mercy*', and tried to start a smile. I guess it was pretty hard goin', because the smile didn't get far. When we get through the gates I fall back and I sez to the gob, 'Rathbone,' I sez, 'ask the lady where we're headed and if she trusts the driver.'

" 'She says,' sez Rathbone, 'that we're goin' to bury him in a field out here, and that there ain't no priest will bury him and there ain' no cemetery she can bury him in.'

" 'That's funny,' I 'sez—'too poor, I guess. Well, anyway, it's a shame—I'll say it is—it's a shame.'

" 'Yes', sez Rathbone slowly, as if he was thinkin',— 'Yes, it's a shame.'

"And the other two gobs who wasn't as sober as Rathbone, they sez, 'Yes, it's a damn shame.'

" 'That makes the navy unanimous,' I sez.

"Then the old hearse swings to the right through a gate in a stone wall and brings up short in a field.

"There was grass in the field and daisies and things, and a lotta tin crosses stuck on mounds that I guessed was graves.

"We all line up in a sorta circle and Napoleon One climbs down from his box and sez somethin' in French to the old widow and points to two birds who're diggin' a hole half-way acrost the field. Rathbone sez that he sez that that is the grave and that the two birds is the grave-diggers and pall-bearers combined.

" 'They are, are they?' I sez. 'This is a military funeral, ain't it? A military funeral conducted by the navy with the army for pall-bearers.' And I call on Sergeant Reilly to back me up.

" 'Shure,' sez Reilly, 'but who'll be providin' the priest?'

"Well, when he sez that, my old bean give a sort of throb, and I sez: 'Don't bother your nut about the priest. He'll be forthcomin' when and if needed.' So I sez to Rathbone:

" 'Looka here, Rathbone, I'm the priest at this party. See? This dead poiloo ain't gotta priest nor nothin' and there's his poor mother and her a widow. So I'm that missin' priest, and I'm not too proud to perform free and gratis. Get that?'

" 'Hold on, chief,' sez Rathbone. 'You ain't got nothin' to wear.'

" 'Nothin' to wear!' I sez. 'You poor cheese, I'm a navy chaplain.'

" 'You look more like a Charlie Chaplin,' sez Rathbone. I guess that bird wasn't sober yet, after all, because he thought he was funny.

" 'Can the comedy,' I sez, 'an' you go tell the widow that Father Dempsey, the head chaplain of the U. S. Navy, had consented to perform this afternoon. Now, get it straight, and for Gawd's sake don't go and laugh, or I'll put you in the brig.'

"Well, Rathbone looked at me like I was goin' to my death.

" 'Goodby, chief,' he sez. 'Wait till the admiral hears of this.'

" 'Haw,' I sez, 'if he does I'll get decorated.' All forms in a circle with me and the widow facin' each other. And then there's an anxious silence. I'll say right here that I was the most anxious. By luck, I happen to think that I have my old logarithm-book in my pocket—you know, the ones bound in black patent-leather. The widow, bein' a frawg widow, I figgered how'd she'd think may be it was a Yank Bible issued special to the A. E. F., and condensed like malted milk or somethin'.

"So I drew the old logarithm-book outa my coat and eased up gently to the edge of the grave. The doughboys and the gobs begin to nudge each other and snicker. I oughta warned 'em what was comin' but I didn't have no time. So I pretended to read from the book, and sez, in a low voice and very solemn like I was openin' the funeral, 'If any you birds here starts laughin' I'll see him after the show and I'll knock the daylight outa him.'

" 'Amen!' sez Rathbone, very piously.

" 'We've come here today,' I sez, always like I was readin' from the book—'we've come here today to plant a frawg soldier who's the only son of his mother and her a widow. And she's so broke that there ain' no regular priest or no regular cemetery that'll offer their services. So I'm the priest, and it's goin' to make a lotta difference to that poor widow's feelin's when she thinks her son' got a swell U. S. Navy priest administering the rites. Now, get that straight, and don't gum the game.'

"Well, I stop there for breath, and Rathbone, who's

right on the job, comes across with another 'Amen', and Reilly, who's a good Catholic sez, '*Pax Vabiscum.*'

" 'This here poiloo,' I sez, 'I don't know much about him, but he was a regular fellow and a good old bird and treated his mother swell and everything, and I guess if we was wise to everything he'd done we'd be proud to be here and we'd 'a' brung a lotta flowers and things. He most likely was at the battle of the Marne and the Soam and Verdun, and maybe he was at Chateau-Teery. And I wanta tell you that we gotta hand it to these French because they may be little guys, but they carry the longest bayonets I ever see in any man's army.'

" 'Amen,' sez all the doughboys and the gobs, except one that yells, 'Alleluia.' He musta been from the South or somewheres.

"Then I sez, 'Glory be,' and cross myself and signal the doughboys to lower away the coffin, and I flung a handful of dirt on top like I see 'em do always.

"Well, the poor old widow near collapsed and Rathbone and the marine had to hold hard to keep her on her pins, but Reilly created a diversion by startin' up the motorbike, and it back-fired like a buncha rookies tryin' to fire a volley. If we'd hadda bugle we coulda sounded taps, and the musical accompaniment woulda been complete.

"Napoleon One came up and shake hands with me like I'd won the Medeye Militaire, and, before I could side-step, the widow had her arms round my neck and was kissin' me on both cheeks. The cordial entente was pretty cordial on the whole! I'll say it was."

At this point, Lieutenant Erskine ventured a remark.

"This occurred last Sunday?" he inquired, mildly.

"Yes, sir," said Steve, "last Sunday."

"Um," said Erskine, and without further remarks left the office.

On his return he bore a copy of *Le Matin* in his hand.

"I wonder, Steve, if you happened to see this very interesting article?"

"No, sir," said Steve. "I don't read French like I speak it."

"Well," said Erskine, "I'll translate. This paper is dated last Monday, and on page two occurs the following announcement:

" 'American soldiers, sailors, and marines attend funeral of notorious apache. Jean the Rat, convicted murder and suicide, and denied the offices of the Catholic Church, is buried by stalwart Americans. Department of Foreign Affairs reluctant to file protest at present time. Strange demonstration believed to be unofficial and without U. S. Government sanction, although U. S. Navy chaplain delivers oration in English.' "

Steve was very red, even to his ears.

"Gawd!" he spluttered. "Does it really say that, sir? Honest?"

Erskine nodded.

"An apache murderer," Steve groaned. "An' me thinkin' it was a frawg hero. Will I get a court martial for it, sir?"

"I doubt it," said Erskine, "but I don't think you'll get the Congressional Medal or the Legion of Honor, either."

"Well, anyway," said Steve, still violently red about the face and ears. "Anyway, I don't care. Even if it weren't a first-class corpse, it was a first-class funeral."

MARTYR

by

Martha Foley

'AND then I'll see visions.'

Emily rocked back and forth on the sandpaper that was scratching her bottom.

'Visions? You mean like the Virgin Mary and the Angel Gabriel.'

'Yes. Only I won't see an angel. I'll see God himself.'

'But God is invisible.'

'Not when you're a saint and have visions like me.'

Edna stopped flipping the jackstones from the palm of her hand to the back.

'Are you a saint?'

'As soon as I have a vision I'll be.'

'How are you going to get a vision?'

'By suffering.'

'I know—like a toothache.'

'Not exactly. You can't help a toothache but the sufferings a saint does is on purpose. Like my sitting on this sandpaper.'

'But that hurts.'

'Oh course it does. Everything hurts a saint.'

'Well, I don't want to be one then. I don't like being hurt.'

'You'll never see God then.'

'I'll wait until I go to heaven.' Edna returned to her jackstones.

'But you can't be sure of going to heaven unless you are a saint.'

'Twosy, threesy. I'll pray to God to go there. Foursy. Fivesy.'

Emily got up carefully so the sandpaper wouldn't slip out of her drawers. She wished she had enough money to buy a hairshirt. One sheet of sandpaper didn't stay in place. Perhaps when she got her Christmas money her mother would take her to the big store downtown and she could get one in the shirt department where her mother always bought her underwear. But Christmas was a long way off and she would have to do the best she could till then.

She looked disgustedly at Edna and her jackstones. Edna would never get anywhere always playing. As for herself she was going off to her retreat now for fasting and praying. She walked stiffly across the street and into the next yard. She had to hold her hand on her back to keep the sandpaper in place. . . .

Emily looked all around her back-yard carefully. She couldn't be a hermit and have a retreat in the wilderness if anyone saw her now. Heliotrope was picking her way from picket to picket along the fence, but no one else was in sight. She would have to pretend Heliotrope was a lion infesting the wilderness. God would understand that a cat was the best she could do for wild animals here in Boston. Perhaps when the circus came to town a lion or a tiger would escape. The lives of the Martyrs were full of lions.

She looked all around the yard again. She could hear Delia washing dishes in the kitchen. It was all right then. Everything was a wilderness. She got down on all fours and crept into a hole between the back steps and the wall. This made a much better hut for a hermit than under the syringa bush. No one would spray the hose on the back steps as they had on the syringa bush.

Funny the way the light came through the cracks in the steps. There was a funny smell here too. Closed in and dusty. But she must pray.

Oh, God, in your grace and loving kindness look down on this wretched mortal. Oh sacred heart of Jesus I implore you to forgive me all my wickedness. It was right through that crack there she had lost the ring with the green stone that came around the stick of candy. No matter how much she looked she could never find it. The next time she came into this retreat she would bring Johnny's sand shovel and dig up the dirt around the place. Oh, divine solicitude, extend your infinite mercy to this repentant soul. Oh, heavenly father, heavenly father, heavenly, if she couldn't find the ring perhaps she could ask old Mr. Cunningham if he couldn't get some more of those sticks of candy with rings around them then perhaps she could get a blue or purple stoned one instead oh heavenly father who gave your son for thy people's sake bless me, your erring child. Now three Hail Mary's.

Now let's see. What else was it saints did? Oh, yes. Fasting. She wouldn't go in and ask Delia for a piece of bread and butter. And now she thought of it, she was hungry. All the better. She'd fast all the time between breakfast and luncheon. She had been going to buy one of those nice big three-cent ice cream cones when the hokey-pokey wagon came along too. But she'd rather have a halo than an ice cream cone. Only halos must feel awfully warm on your head all the time blazing away like that on Saint Cecilia's head in the piano picture. How could you wear a hat then? And did saints take off their halos when they went to bed? She would have to ask someone about that.

But she'd better be praying again. She'd say three Our Father's this time. She would like to have a vision this morning if possible. She would pray as hard as she could then perhaps a vision would come. For a vision she would like to see the little angels, the cherrybubs on the clouds. She didn't want to see purgatory or hell the way some of the saints did. And she'd just as leave wait awhile before seeing God himself. He might ask her some questions about the catechism and she wasn't sure of the last lesson. The little angels that were always peeking out of the clouds in the holy pictures would be very nice to see.

Each time she said an Our Father she would say very hard at the end and please dear God give me a vision of the cherrybubs.

Emily prayed. The hot summer sun beat down on the steps under which she crouched, bees buzzed in nearby shrubs, sounds of domestic endeavor came from the open kitchen window. It was an ordinary Boston back-yard of a warm June morning. Which is the trouble and why I don't get a vision, she thought. I am not even tormented by fiends like Saint Anthony, I must make a great sacrifice for the Lord. He doesn't like just sandpaper.

She took the square of rough paper out of her drawers and put it away in a corner of the wilderness retreat. I'll try it again some other time, she said. She squeezed herself out from under the stoop just as her brother and two other boys came through the back gate.

'Oh, look at Emily! Watcha doing under there, Emily?'

'Looking for a jackstone I lost.' Dear God forgive me for telling a lie. I can't be a hermit if they know where I'm being one. They'll all want to be hermits too and hermits can't play together. Anyway the Herman boys are Protestants. I can't tell Protestants about such sacred things.

'Walter just found something.'

'What?'

'Look, he found this medal on the sidewalk.'

'Let's see.'

' 'Tisn't yours.'

'Who said it was? I said I wanted to see it.'

'Well, you sounded like you were going to say it was.'

'Please let me see it. I'm not going to say it's mine. I promise. I don't even know anyone who lost a medal.'

'Here then.' Walter held out in his hand a bright yellow disc. On one side was a cross. On the other was a picture of the Virgin with the Christ Child.

'Oh Walter. You shouldn't have that. That's a Catholic medal and you're Protestant.'

'There! I told you. I knew you'd want it.'

'I don't want it. But I know it isn't right for a Protestant to have something that's Catholic.'

'Huh! I found it and it's mine. I can do whatever I

please with it. I can throw it up in the air or burn it or roll it along the ground.'

'Walter! That's sacrilege. You'll go right to hell.'

'Who's said so? If anyone'll go to hell it'll be you for telling me what to do with something I find.'

'I'm going to tell your mamas on both of you. Talking about hell. I'm going right away and tell your mamas—'

'Tattletale! Tattletale! Carry home the cow's tail! We're not doing anything.'

'You are so! You are using the word hell in ordinary conversation. And mama said you can only use it when praying.'

'This is not ordinary conversation. This is religious.'

'But—'

'You shut up right this minute.'

'I won't.'

'All right then. I'll sing a hymn and you know you can't interrupt a hymn. Holy God I praise Thy Name, Lord of all above, I praise Thee—'

The three small boys remained quiet until Emily finished the hymn.

'Walter, let me hold the medal.'

'No. You'll keep it.'

'No, I won't. I promise.'

'Cross your heart and hope to die?'

'Yes. Beat me black and blue.'

Emily examined the medal on both sides. 'This is a holy object.'

'Give it back to me.'

'I'll give you a cent for it.'

'No!'

'Two cents.'

'No, can't you see it's bigger than a quarter?'

'Three cents.'

'I'll give it to you for a nickel.'

'Three cents are all I have. I was saving up for a big cone. Strawberry and chocolate mixed.'

'I like chocolate and nut better. All right. Where's your three cents?'

Emily pulled a small imitation silver mesh bag out of her pocket. In it were a handkerchief, some beads and three coppers. It was a very great sacrifice she was making. She hadn't had an ice cream cone since the little one-cent one last Friday and this was Tuesday.

The Protestant heathen took the three cents eagerly.

'Come on. Let's go out on the front sidewalk and wait for the hokey-pokey man.'

The boys departed. Holding the medal reverently in an out-stretched hand, Emily squeezed her way back under the steps.

'Now, please, dear God, let me have a vision.'

THE HEART BEING PERISHED
by
Frances M. Frost

THE farm lay on the top of the hill, and while the grass meadows were level around the house and the barn, those fields which had to be ploughed, slanted downhill toward hollows that rose immediately into other and lower hills. His father said that if you went up and down the lower hills long enough, you'd get to the big river valley and to Manchester.

Eastward, the higher hills rose in successive ridges above the farm and turned into mountains that loomed deep blue against the sunrise and grew softly and warmly massive in the summer dusks. When he was driving the cows to pasture or crossing the yard to the barn with a pail of garbage to be dumped into the pig-pen, he liked to look at the mountains. When his eyes rested on them, it was as if he had been away and had suddenly come home. It was like having a drink of spring water in the middle of a hot hay field.

He was a good-looking boy, firm-fleshed and brown as an Indian, for he wore no shirt from spring until autumn, liking the feeling of sun and wind and rain on his skin. His mother died when he was ten. His elder brothers, all but Jim, went away and got farms of their own in York State; and when he was eighteen, Jim went, too.

The year he was twenty, his father died of pneumonia, leaving him the farm which was heavily mortgaged. He had had some schooling when the roads were passable, but he had never been beyond the village, which lay in a hollow five miles beyond the farm. His nearest neighbor was Clint Hard, who lived two miles down the road. The day after his father's funeral, Clint drove up and brought him some doughnuts and pies that his wife had made.

"What you goin' to do now, John? Goin' to keep house by yourself?"

"There ain't nothing else to do. I guess I can manage. Dad and I got along all right."

"You ought to get married, a young feller like you."

"I got to pay off the mortgage on this place first."

"Then you'll be married when you're eighty," Clint said.

John said, "Well, I'll think about it. Tell Mrs. Hard thank you for the food, Clint."

"Come on down some Saturday night. We got us a new gramophone for Sally. There's some good cylinders goes with it, too."

"Thanks," John said.

When Clint had gone, and he was doing the milking, he thought about Sally Hard. A year later, they were married.

The first inkling Sally had that she had married a poet as well as a farmer was the forenoon, two weeks after the wedding, when he came to her with some star-flowers he had found in the wood.

"I can't give you a gramophone or nice things," he said, "because we've got the mortgage, but I can bring you wood things, if you like 'em."

She put a hand softly on his cheek. "I like wood things better, John."

"Here's a poem," he said. "It goes like this:

> Thou knowest how poor a trifling thing man is
> And learn'st thus much by our Anatomie,
> The heart being perished, no part can be free.

"It means, we have to keep loving each other and be glad for everything we've got, even if it's not much, because if the heart's dead, we're dead."

She was astonished. "Why, John, that's lovely! Did you make it up?"

He grinned, shamefacedly. "Well—"

"You did! I didn't know you wrote poetry! Do me some more!"

"I'll tell you another one tonight," he said, "after supper."

He left her for the barn and took from a corner of the hay-mow a worm-eaten volume of English poetry. He had found it in the attic while he was cleaning it, before his marriage. It had occurred to him that since he could not offer Sally anything beside himself and a farm with a mortgage, he would give her something else—the most beautiful poetry he could find in the book. He had not expected that she would think he had written it, but he knew now that she loved him the more for it. It was cheating, but she would never know as long as he kept the book hidden. He memorized another lyric, sitting in the hay-mow, and said it over and over to himself all day as he worked in the fields.

In the evening they walked in the yard and looked at the mountains, and he recited in a low voice:

> The earth was green, the sky was blue:
>   I saw and heard one sunny morn
> A skylark hang between the two,
>   A singing speck above the corn.
>
> The corn field stretched a tender green
>   To right and left beside my walks;
> I knew he had a nest unseen
>   Somewhere among the million stalks.
>
> And as I paused to hear his song
>   While swift the sunny moments slid,
> Perhaps his mate sat listening long,
>   And listened longer than I did.

Her delight was better than food and drink to him. After their son was born, he added new poems more slowly, but she liked to hear the old ones over and over, and each time, she said, "That's lovely, John!"

The crops were poor the year Johanna was born. The debts dragged heavily on him: they scrimped and saved frantically to meet the taxes and the interest. On winter nights, when the babies were in bed, and Sally sat sewing by the stove, he would lean back in his chair and watch her, thinking that even the greatest English poetry was none too good for her. And she would look up and smile and say, "Tell me another poem, John."

"I haven't got a new one."

"Tell me the one about 'love, let us be true.'"

And he would say softly:

Ah, love, let us be true
To one another, for the world, which seems
To lie before us like a land of dreams,
So various, so beautiful, so new,
Hath really neither joy, nor love, nor light,
Nor certitude, nor peace, nor help for pain;
And we are here as on a darkling plain
Swept with confused alarms of struggle and flight,
Where ignorant armies clash by night.

The third baby died at birth, and Sally was very ill. A winter of doctor's bills was added to the long procession of debts.

As the years went by, slowly, painfully, they reduced the mortgage.

When Bart finished high school, he said to his father, "I want to go to college, Dad. I want to be an engineer. I'll work my way through."

"You don't want—the farm?"

The boy put his arm around John's shoulders. "I wish I did, Dad. But I don't. I'm sorry."

Johanna, a year later, said, "Dad, I want to teach school. I'll work my way through college, if you'll let me."

"What do you want to teach, baby?"

"English," said Johanna. "Poetry."

John smiled. "I guess your mother will like it."

When the children came home for Christmas, the house was gay with ground-pine wreaths, John had cut a tree and he and Sally had trimmed it.

Sally said, "The children are as sweet as ever, John. Education hasn't spoiled them."

"Of course not. They're your children—why shouldn't they be sweet?"

On Christmas Eve, Johanna said, "Mother, will you come upstairs a minute? I want to tell you something."

They went to Johanna's old room. From her bag she drew a little book.

"What's that?" Sally asked.

"I don't know whether I ought to do this or not," Johanna said slowly. "But I guess I'd better get it off my chest. Mother, you know the poems that Dad has been saying to you all these years?"

"Yes."

"They're all in this book!"

"What do you mean, Johanna?"

"I mean—Dad didn't write them. They were all written a long time ago by English poets. Look here—'O wild West Wind, thou breath of autumn's being . . . ' I remember he said that when I was about ten. And this one—'Go, for they call you, shepherd, from the hill . . .' "

"That one," said Sally, "he said to me the winter the baby died."

"But, Mother, don't you see? He's been cheating! He's been telling you he did them!"

"No," said Sally huskily. "I told *him* he did them. He didn't say anything except the poetry. Johanna, I'll never let him know I know. It would break his heart."

The girl looked hard at her mother. "You two are the grandest people I've ever seen," she said. "I wish I hadn't told you. I wonder where he learned them?"

"I don't know where. I'm glad you did tell me, because

now I know how much he loves me, to have made me so proud of him all these years. It's not easy for your father to deceive me."

The children finished college. Johanna taught for five years and was married. Bart offered to help his father pay off the mortgage, but John only said, "The farm's mine, son, and its debts are mine."

On a spring day, when John and Sally were sixty, John drove to the village and paid the last of the debt. When he returned, he did not go to the house but to the barn; he sat down at the edge of the hay-mow and wept. Sally found him there. They went out into the yard and looked at the mountains.

"They're ours to look at as long as we live," he said.

That week the weather turned raw suddenly, and Sally caught cold. Her cough grew worse, and John drove to the village for the doctor.

"Pneumonia," the doctor said, "I'll stay here tonight, John."

She had a raging fever; John sat beside her, desperate and white, holding her hot fingers.

"John," she said in a choked whisper, "poem. New one."

He swallowed. He had told her over and over all the poems he had memorized.

"All right, darling." Slowly, with terrible effort he put the words together; he made her a poem, his poem, the only one he had ever made in his life.

> These mountains, that are ours
> Forever till we die,
> Fling the drifting flowers
> Of planets up the sky.
>
> With idioms of darkness
> They speak across the night.
> With winged heels of starkness
> The mountain-tops take flight.

My love and I shall follow
Those granite wings in space,
Her head in my arm's hollow,
My lips on her dear face.

"You made it up, John."

"Yes," he said. He never knew that she did not believe him.

He buried her where she could see the mountains, and the book of English poems lay with the wood-flowers on her grave until the seasons had destroyed it.

THE SAMPLER

by

I. V. Morris

IN a certain store where they sell plum puddings, a number of these delicious articles are laid out in a row during the Christmas season. Here you may select the one which is most to your taste, and you are even allowed to sample the various qualities before coming to a decision.

I have often wondered whether this privilege was not occasionally imposed on by people who had no intention of making a purchase, and one day when my curiosity drove me to ask this question of the shop girl, I learned that it was indeed the case.

'Now there's one old gentleman, for instance,' she told me, 'who comes here almost every week and samples each one of the puddings, though he never buys anything and I suppose he never will. I remember him from last year and the year before that, too. Well, let him come if he wants it that bad, say I, and welcome to it. And what's more, I hope there are a lot more stores where he can go and get his share as well. He looks as if he needed it all right, poor fellow, and I guess they can afford it.'

She was still speaking when an elderly gentleman limped up to the counter and began scrutinizing the row of puddings with great interest.

'Why, that there's the very party I've been telling you about,' whispered the shop girl. 'Just you watch him now.' And then turning to him: 'Would you like to sample them, sir?' she asked. 'Here's a spoon for you to use.'

The elderly gentleman who, as the novelists say, was poorly but neatly dressed, accepted the spoon and began eagerly to sample one after another of the puddings, only breaking off occasionally to wipe his red eyes with a large torn handkerchief which he drew from the breast pocket of his shoddy overcoat.

'This is quite good,' he declared in an absurdly rusty voice of one variety, and when he came to the next, 'This is not bad, either, but a trifle too heavy.' All the time it was quite evident that he sincerely believed that he might eventually buy one of these puddings, and I am positive that he did not for a moment feel that he was in any way cheating the shop. Poor old chap! Probably he had come down in the world and this sampling was all that was left him from the time when he could afford to come and select his favorite pudding, which he would later carry home under his arm.

Amidst this throng of happy, prosperous-looking Christmas shoppers the little black figure of the old man seemed incongruous and pathetic, and in a sudden burst of benevolence, one of those bursts which so often bring pain instead of joy, I went up to him and said:

'Pardon me, sir, will you do me a favor? Let me purchase you one of these puddings. It would give me such pleasure.'

He jumped back as if he had been stung, and the blood rushed into his wrinkled face.

'Excuse me,' he said, with more dignity than I would have thought possible considering his shabby appearance, 'I do not believe I have the pleasure of knowing you. Undoubtedly, you have mistaken me for someone else,' and with a quick decision he turned towards the shop girl and said in a loud voice: 'Kindly pack me up this one here. I will take it with me,' and he pointed at one of the largest and most expensive of the puddings.

In surprise, the girl took down the pudding from its stand and proceeded to make a parcel of it, while he extracted a worn little black pocketbook and began counting out shillings and sixpenny pieces onto the counter. To save his 'honour' he had been forced into a purchase which he could not possibly afford and which probably meant many bitter privations in other things. How I longed for the power to unsay my hasty, tactless words. But it was too late, and I felt that the kindest thing I could do now would be to walk away.

'You pay at the desk,' the shop girl was telling him, but he did not seem to understand and kept trying to put the coins into her hand; and that was the last I saw or heard of the old man. Now he can never come there to sample plum puddings again.

NAPOLEON'S HAT UNDER GLASS

by

Manuel Komroff

IN the gorgeous palace of Fontainebleau, just outside of
Paris, on an embroidered silk cushion in a glass case, rests
Napoleon's hat. This is the very hat he wore when, returning from Elba, he saluted his gathering army . . . the
army that he led into the field of Waterloo. But all this was
many years ago, over a hundred years ago, guides say when
they conduct the large parties of visitors through the palace.

And before this glass case with its showpiece of history
now stood a newly-married peasant couple from the country.
She was a rosy-cheeked farmer's daughter and he was the
son of a farmer in southern France. This was their honeymoon.

They stood before the glass case. She fingered her
colored ribbons and he stared at the black felt hat in the
case. Their red faces and big red hands were reflected in
the glass. Their bodies seemed to sway just as they had
swayed that very week when the village priest stood before
them and recited the marriage vows.

"He was the greatest man in the world," she said.

"Yes, he was a great man. He was Emperor of almost
the whole world."

"May his soul rest in peace."

"It must be a hard job to be an Emperor. I don't think
I should like it. Too many papers and documents to read,
and everything is . . . like in the fall of the year when we
have to close ourselves in the house and the leaves become
crisp and brittle. It don't seem natural to be an Emperor,
does it?"

"Sure not, Emil. It must be very hard. But I think

you could do anything you wanted to do. Nobody dreamed you would have the chicken house finished this summer, especially with all the trouble we had with the old wine barrels that leaked and the bugs on the vegetables. But an Emperor don't have to read many papers. They tell him what it says and all he must do is to sign his name. And you can do that, can't you, Emil?"

"Sure."

"But it would be harder for me, Emil. This would be a nice place to live. But the servants would be watching you all day long. I would hate to have strange people watching me; but if you were the Emperor I would just have to do it and say nothing."

"Do what, Marie?"

"Oh, just do everything. Watch the kitchen to see that the rascals did not steal and do the things that ladies do, like making up the beds and sewing up new dresses and taking care of the house."

"It must be a hard job to be an Emperor. I don't think I should like it."

"If you wanted to be, I am sure you could be anything you like. You are so strong—and I love you so much."

At length they moved away from the glass case containing Napoleon's hat, and walked out into the gardens. Here they ate their lunch and looked into each other's eyes.

After a long silence she looked up and said: "You know, Emil, we should go back to the Palace before it closes and see the hat again."

"Poor Napoleon," Emil said.

"Yes. It is so sad. He was once Emperor of the whole world, almost, and now he is dead."

They walked back to have another look at the hat. And in the morning, under the pretext that it was on the way to the station, they went again and had a last gaze at Napoleon's hat under glass.

On the train she sighed: "It was a wonderful honeymoon, wasn't it, Emil?"

"Sure."

Then she whispered in his ear. "I love you, Emil."

He sat up straight and held her red hand. "I—thought maybe you loved Napoleon."

"Oh, yes, but that is different, Emil."

"How different?"

"Well, he is dead and I feel so sorry for him—it is so sad. He was such a great man and it is such a hard job to be an Emperor. You said yourself it was—you know you did."

"Yes, I said so, Marie, but I was thinking of myself and not Napoleon. It was easy for him because he always . . . well, he was all the time doing something big . . . he was a general. It is easy for a general to do all kinds of things."

"He was very brave and that is why. . ."

"That's why you love him."

"I love you too, Emil. I want you to be a great man and have people save your hat and . . . but not to be the Emperor."

Emil was jealous of Napoleon. He kept looking out of the train window watching the green fields and the long rows of tall poplars.

In the evening they were back on the farm. The fragrance of the green shrubbery and the loose damp earth filled their nostrils. In places the grass had grown during their absence. Here was a chance for a second harvest and they lost no time in removing their holiday clothes and getting back into their large comfortable wooden shoes. The shoes that have stamped down the fields of France for centuries. There was only an hour or two before sundown.

At night as they lay in bed breathing heavily, she whispered: "Oh, Emil, it is so good to be home again."

He pressed her hand.

"It must be hard to live in a palace," she added.

Again he pressed her hand.

"And so sad."

"You are thinking of the dead Emperor's hat!" He let go her hand.

"No, Emil, I was thinking, only foolishness. I love you, Emil."

She put her arms about him and he kissed her eyes and fleshy cheeks and her moist red mouth—moist with the dew of the earth.

And Napoleon never came between them again. Only once did he again appear before them. This happened about a year later when Emil became the proud father of a baby boy.

"He is a prize baby," said the father.

And she tickled the child under the chin and added: "We will put him on exhibition . . . under glass."

Then they went through all the names of the ancient kings and Emperors that they could recall, but to their rural ears, each sounded foreign and sad.

The grapes were ripe and there was much work to be done around the place, but at odd moments they deliberated and often thought of Napoleon's hat in the show case. But in the end they named their little son John.

HENRIETTA THE EIGHTH
by
Rupert Hughes

IF the eighteen years that had passed over her pretty fore-head had been eighty, her brows could hardly have been knotted in more torment and alarm or her eyes filled with more anguish. The world was all agog for Haidee Scudder. It usually was. It had begun with her parents. They never appreciated her. They had even named her Ida. And they persisted in calling her "Idie" even after she had changed her name to the far more appropriate Haidee.

Haidee was one who would make tragedy of everything possible. Not the least of her tragedies was the failure of her parents to respond to the terrific importance of her excitements. But they had seen so many of them, and they found a sameness in them that never appeared to Haidee, to whom each was something new and so unbearably hopeless that it was final. Never had there been such a crisis in her affairs as that of this moment and it only partly concerned the book she clenched in her hand and held fast against her breast as she implored her mother:

"Mamma, would you help me? Tonight of all nights I've simply got to have a clear head. I've simply got to get myself ready for the exam tomorrow. It's the last one, thank heavens, and I must not fail. Wouldn't you please make Jimmie quit whistling through his teeth? And tell Nettie to quit practicing those awful scales on that awful piano? And would you ask Papa to please—please! for hem's sakes!—turn off that gastly radio for a while? And if anybody calls me on the telephone or comes to the door I'm out, or sick, or dead or something—unless it's George Ames. I'll speak to him, of course."

Her mother sighed: "Idie—well, Haidee, then—will you please, please calm down a little? You act as if you were going into a conniption fit or something."

"But, Mamma, it's horribly important; my last chance to bone up for the final exam tomorrow. If I pass it I've finished that unbearable high school, and I can begin life. It's the English history exam and I'm so flustered I don't know Henry the Great from Alfred the Eighth or Magna Charta from Maggie Rooney. And, Mamma, won't you please help me? All you have to do is to ask me a few questions and tell me if I give the right answers."

"How could I tell? I never did know much. I've forgotten more than I ever knew."

"The answers are right here in the back of the book. And here are the questions at the end of the chapters. Just ask me the questions and don't give me the answers till I ask for them. But first, for heaven's sake, get the house quiet."

Mrs. Scudder seemed to toss her eyes like marbles into the air, but she rose wearily, went into the living-room and began on the other children:

"Jimmie, I suppose there's no use telling you to quit whistling through your teeth. I declare, I've half a mind to take you to the dentist and have them all pulled out. Go on out on the porch or somewhere. You're glad enough to stay out when I want you in. And, Nettie, come away from that piano. You're driving me mad. Why will you never practice your scales except when they drive everybody mad? And, "Will," this to her husband, "you can turn off the radio for a little while, can't you? Idie has to get her history examination studied up for."

The husband growled, "Oh, Lord, can't you wait till I finish—"

"You can hear the same old jokes tomorrow night—next week—or next year. It's Idie's last chance to study for the final of the finals. And if anybody asks for her at the door—or telephone—tell 'em she's out. And that's no lie, for she is out—of her mind."

Haidee's voice broke through, "If George Ames calls, though, I'm in. I want to talk to George."

"All right," groaned the mother. "Oh, all right," echoed the father. And the house was hushed. Haidee seated herself for cross-examination; her mother sat down and inter-leaved her fingers at various places in the textbook. She began at random.

"How many wives did Henry VIII have?"

Haidee was far away in some reverie and the question had to be repeated. "I say, how many wives did Henry VIII have?"

"Speaking of wives, Mamma, what would you say if I got married when—if—I pass these finals?"

"I'd say you were a bigger fool than I thought you were. Let's get on. How many eights did Henry have?"

"But you were only eighteen when you married Papa."

"The more fool I."

"Oh, Mamma, don't! If you hadn't married Papa then you wouldn't have had me."

"Will you or will you not tell me how many Henrys did eight have?"

"George Ames said that he could take a job in his father's lumber yard and we could get married right away."

"Then he's a bigger fool than I thought he was, and that's saying a lot. You two imbeciles oughtn't to think of getting married for years and years. How many—"

"Oh, Mamma, don't say years! I can't breathe when George is out of my sight for a whole day. I thought I'd die when he took those examinations for Annapolis."

"How'd he come out?"

"He hasn't heard yet. Oh, I hope he didn't pass. He may hear any minute. But he said last night that, even if he did get the appointment, he'd rather give it up and marry me than be all the admirals in the navy."

"Any boy that's as crazy as that—why, it wouldn't be safe to marry him."

"But, Mamma, we love each other."

"Love, pooh! If you love him so much I should think you'd rather have him in the navy than in that lumber yard."

"But if he went to Annapolis it would be four years—four centuries! And after that they don't let them marry for two years. Six years, Mamma! I couldn't stand it! I'd perish! I'd die! I'd kill myself!"

Her mother had heard so many threats of suicide and early death that she was unable to rise to the appropriate alarm. Haidee meant every threat she made at the time. But times changed. Mrs. Scudder's only comment on her daughter's blood-curdling threat was:

"Will you, or will you not, tell me how many wives Henry Clay had?—Henry VIII!!"

"Oh, I know the answer to that one. The thing is, Mamma, that I either marry George or I die."

"All right, but don't die before you pass this examination."

"Very well, Mamma, but after tomorrow it's—"

"The next question is: What relation to Henry VIII was the Virgin Queen? His daughter."

"Mamma! Please, please! don't give me the answer! I could have given that one anyway, but please pay attention to what you're doing."

"Funny that Henry VIII's daughter, the daughter of a man who had six wives, didn't marry at all. Not so funny at that. A wise woman, Elizabeth."

"Mamma! How can you say such things?—with Papa in the next room!"

"Oh, he's heard me say it often enough. And I guess he agrees with me." She laughed bitterly and called out: "Don't you, Will?"

From the next room: "Don't I what?"

"Nothing."

Shocked by youth's earnest shame for the flippancy of the old, Haidee brooded aloud with great originality: "It's terrible the way romance fades—just like the rose—so beautiful, so fragrant! Then it wilts and the petals drop and fall, one by one."

"Is this a botany examination or English history?"

"Still, even if our romance—George's and mine—should fade, it's all we have. It's all we can hope for. I must marry George, and I must marry him soon. I can't wait! I won't! I'd die!"

The telephone bell. The father's voice: "If it's for Idie, did you say I was to say she was out if it was George—or what?"

What a father! He could be relied on only to get everything wrong. Haidee called: "I'll answer it, Papa."

She ran to the telephone and cooed into it:

"Oh, hello, George! Darling!"

The parents heard only one end of the conversation. That was usually enough. Tonight, however, there was drama. They heard Haidee gasp:

"No? You did? Honestly? Why, George!"

She turned away and whispered shrilly: "Mamma, George got the appointment to Annapolis!" She turned back to the telephone. "Oh, George, that's grand! I knew you'd pass. You can do anything. You're the smartest boy that ever lived. What a great satisfaction it will be to you to know that you could have gone to Annapolis if you wanted to. And you're giving it up just for me. It's the most flattering thing that ever happened to me."

Her mother, who had followed to hear the great news, watched her and guessed the truth; saw how she listened with a sort of gluttony for punishment, interjecting little laughs and trying to keep her voice firm though her body swayed till Mrs. Scudder moved close to catch her if she fell.

Haidee was very polite. That was always ominous: "Oh, I see. . . Oh, I understand perfectly. Naturally. Quite. A man's ambition comes first, of course, of course. Oh, no, not at all. . . Ha ha! . . . I agree with you perfectly. . . . You're doing the wise thing. As always. You always do the wise thing, George, no matter what the cost

may be—to others. Goodby, George. Come to see me . . .
sometime . . . before you go."

She laughed for his sake but he could not see the con-
torted face that touched her mother with sincere pity as
Haidee hung up the telephone and toppled into her arms,
her artificial laughter turned to sobs: "He got the appointment, Mamma. And he—he's going to Annapolis without
a—a th—thought of me."

"Poor baby! It's too bad. But it's good riddance of a
selfish brute."

"Oh, Mamma. He—he would rather go to Annapolis
for years than marry me now. I can't bear it. I've got to
die. I'll kill myself."

Her mother could think of no better ruse than to inter-
pose: "But you wouldn't want to die without passing your
last examination, would you?"

"No; I'd hate to flunk in everything. I've been an utter
failure in life. I'm sorry to have been such a disappointment to you, poor Mamma! But I couldn't help it. I
meant well and I loved you. Always remember that—
when—when—"

Her young voice tried to be grim as she set off on her
journey to the grave but it was only more little-girlish than
ever. She shook her head violently in a brave effort to
rally her courage for a little delay:

"What's the next question, Mamma?"

Mrs. Scudder tried one more distraction: "Of course,
if you should want to go on to college yourself, your father
and I—well, we were saying only last night that we'd be
glad to send you to some nice school or college."

"I don't want to go to college. I don't want to live, I
tell you. Please give me the next question."

Mrs. Scudder turned back to the book: "What was
the Spanish Armada and how many ships—"

"Oh, why must you speak of ships? George is going on
a ship! He prefers a ship to me! Why don't you ask me

the questions? Can't you do that much for me before I go mad?"

"Who was the principal poet of Elizabeth's reign and what were his principal plays?"

"George Shakeington—I mean William Ames—and he wrote Hamlet, and Romeo and Juliet. They got married young."

"Yes, and look what happened to them. The cold dark tomb before they knew what it was all about."

"Funny! Romeo and Juliet both died in such misery so young, but Queen Elizabeth—she never married and she lived to be seventy years old. She was a great woman and she never married. Mamma, I'm never going to marry! Not if I live a thousand years. I hate men. They're all alike—especially George Ames. I'm never going to speak to another man as long as I live—except Papa, of course. You say that he and you were talking about sending me to college. College would have been fine if—But no co-ed college with a lot of horrid boys around. I never want to see another boy as long as I live. Annapolis, humph! Well, if he can go to Annapolis I guess I can go to Smith or Wellesley or—Die, Humph! I wouldn't die for all the men in the world. Mamma, you're such a darling. You've helped me. Oh, I can't tell you how you've helped me. What's the next question?"

The telephone bell broke in on it. Haidee shrieked at the next room: "Papa, if that's George Ames, I'm out! If he asks when I am expected back home just say, 'Never forever.' "

"Oh, I just say, 'Never forever.' "

"Yes, Papa, and if—" a brilliant thought dazzled her brain: "If it's any other boy, find out who it is and say you'll see if I'm in or not."

The bell rang again and her father's voice curled through the door: "If it's anybody but George Ames, I'm to say you'll see if I'm in or not. All right. Hello! Oh! Hold the wire. He says his name is Cliff."

"Not Cliff Atterbury?"

"He didn't say what Cliff; just a plain Cliff. Are you in or out or just betwixt and between?"

Haidee brushed him aside and ran to the telephone, sang into it as if she had never known a sorrow and only now knew perfect bliss: "Why, Cliff Atterbury, it can't be you. In hem's name, when did you get back? Only this evening? You di—id? Why, Cliff, how utterly flatt'ring to call me up so right away! I'm all of a twitter. How simply sweet of you! Why, I'm just dying to! But I couldn't, not for half an hour. You see, I'm boning up for the final exam tomorrow. Got to pass somehow so that I can go to college. Mamma and Papa agree with me that I ought to go on to college. You are? How simpully swe—ell! What college are you going to? Yale, Princeton—oh, the State University! But isn't that co-ed? I shouldn't think you'd like tha—at. Oh, how you talk! Well, of course, if you were the other co-ed I might stand it, too—that would be diff'rent. I'll think it over. We'll talk it over. Could you give me half an hour, Cliff? It's only English history and that won't take long. I'm practic'ly through the reign of Queen Liz already. Fine! . . . Grand! . . . Glorious! G'by! Awf'ly glad you're back. G'by, Cliff! G'by—eee—"

She replaced the telephone with the tenderness of a caress, and stood in a trance of beatitude, just being happy through and through. Her mother signed to her father: "Look at her! She looks like a candy doll. And she wonders why I don't get as excited as she does over every tragedy."

Her father studied her stupidly. "What ails her now?"

"Oh, nothing much now. A few minutes ago she was Juliet in the tomb. Then she was Queen Elizabeth, the man-hater. Now I think she's Henrietta the Eighth. I wonder what she'll be tomorrow."

"Can I start the radio again?"

The radio blared. Jimmie came in from the porch and whistled through his teeth. Nettie began to run scales up and down the piano, her fingers stepping on one another and the wrong notes with their usual regularity. Upstairs, Haidee flung out of and into her clothes and powdered her nose, arranged her hair, paying little heed to her mother, who sat on the bed and read:

"What lover of Elizabeth was the hero of what famous novel?"

"Essex and—"

"No."

"Ivanhoe?"

"No!"

"Don't tell me. It was the—the Earl of Leicester."

"Fine! And what famous novel?"

"Uncle Tom's Cab—no . . . Paradise Lost . . . No, don't tell me—er—er—"

"Kenil—"

"Kenilworth! That's it! And that describes George Ames. He's worthy of a kennel. That's good! That's grand! I must tell that to Cliffy. He never did like George Ames any more than I do!"

HAMLET'S DAGGER
by
Manuel Komroff

WHAT a dusty old place! A little, neglected archive of some past forgotten culture. Here in this narrow street, hidden away from the world, was a small shop. In the window stood an odd assortment of old walking-sticks and a few bits of mended English china; but inside—everywhere—on the walls and ledges were engravings of old stage favorites and rows upon rows of little volumes, yellow with age. And through the dust on the books you could read the titles of plays of long ago. Here they had come to rest and their final curtain was a gauze of dust. And the old man in the rear of the shop seemed quite part of his dingy wares.

As I worked my way nearer him I ventured to remark that he had a very good collection of books related to the English stage.

'The stage,' he said, and his deep voice filled the entire room. 'The stage. Ah! Nothing remains of the old glory. Nothing.' He shook back his loose white hair and his fingers trembled as he said those words. Then his ear seemed to catch the echo of his last word and in a whisper he repeated: 'Nothing.'

I walked about and glanced at the odd titles of many of the little books. At length I selected one and brought it back to the old man.

'Ah yes. That is part of the old glory. Do you know what they call these plays today, young fellow? Well, they call them cheap melodrama. They are out of date, out of fashion. And do you know what is in fashion? Talk. Nothing but talk. A few young snips get together before

93

the footlights and for a whole evening they talk away until
they are blue in the face. In the end you are informed that
you have attended a play. And as for acting, like the snakes
in Ireland, there is none. Acting is a lost art. These foot-
light dandies are afraid to act because they know they
can't. And as for melodrama, they fear it because they
think it's unreal. And can you tell me what is real? Do
you think they are real or am I real?'

'I suppose you are real enough. More real than any
ghost I could imagine. But I see you have evidently been
on the stage yourself.'

'Many years.'

'Where did you last appear?'

He was silent. He did not reply to this question either
because he did not want to or because . . . Instead he
said: 'And I could tell you, young fellow, that there is
melodrama in *Hamlet*, and there is melodrama in *Macbeth*,
in *Lear*, in *Othello* . . . and what are *Richard III* and all
the others that lay claim to greatness? It is in melodrama
that the impossible happens, that reality and plausibility
are thrown to the winds and in that . . . (he tapped with
his finger) . . . there lies greatness. There: on just that
impossible and unreal land ride Don Quixote, and Mephisto-
pheles. Here a jealous Moor draws his dagger, a Jew
dangles his scales before a court of justice and here the
conscience of an inn-keeper wrestles with an imaginary rope
around his neck.'

'Inn-keeper?' I inquired.

'Yes. Mathias in *The Bells*. An old melodrama—never
played today. But for twenty-two years . . . And do you
think it is wrong that I should mention it together with
the masterpieces of Shakespeare? Did you ever see the
play?'

I could not admit that I had.

'Well, certainly, one cannot compare it to Shakespeare,
but I mention it only as an example of real theatre. I
mention it because it has something that is lost today.

I still remember every line of that play, every move, every gesture.'

'Then you acted in *The Bells?*'

Again he was silent. He shook his white head sadly and changing the subject said, 'If you would like to have a cup of tea with me upstairs I could tell you more about *The Bells.*'

He locked the shop and we climbed the stair to his room.

Here at the top was a full length portrait of Hamlet. The painting was done in black and gray with a touch of dull yellow in the costume. But the eyes—the eyes stared at you and seemed to follow you as you passed. These were the eyes that had seen the ghost of his father. The legs, in the painting, were thin and spindly, the small waist constricted by a metal belt and the hand rested on the fancy handle of a silver dagger. Below on the frame of the picture was a small brass plate with the words, 'Henry Irving in Hamlet.'

In the room the old man was preparing the hot water for the tea and without delay he began to tell about this old stage melodrama. But my eyes wandered around the walls, there were so many things of interest, and I did not pay very strict attention to all he said.

It was a play, it appears, adapted from a story called *The Polish Jew.* It was first produced in 1871, by Henry Irving, as *The Bells.*

'The first act,' he said, 'takes place in the inn. Outside snow is falling and a sudden gust blows open one of the windows and brings some crockery crashing to the floor. This is an evil omen. From the moment this crash is heard the attention of the audience is held in a grip of iron. For exactly fifteen minutes the company of players carry on preparing the entrance of the star, and at last, quite suddenly, he is before you. This is Mathias the inn-keeper. And from now on you are witness to the struggle of a soul with its conscience. He is poor. He needs money and he plots to kill the Polish Jew who is traveling in a sleigh. He is calm in his reasoning and deliberate in his action. He is impelled by a force greater than the human strength within him and soon the deed is done; the Jew's body is consumed in the flames of a lime-kiln. Now he is free from worry and now he can live. He lives . . .'

As I listen to his words I can see on the wall a dagger that hangs suspended from a metal belt. It is silver, and the handle . . . The very one that the artist painted in the picture of *Hamlet*. How strange.

'Now listen. Mathias lives a blameless life. He is respected in his village. He is loved by his family. He is everything a man should be but—the bells. The bells are ever ringing in his ears. The sleigh-bells of the Polish Jew, that haunting little off-key tinkle, is ever in his ears. And in the last act of the play, fifteen years after he has murdered the Jew, he is still harassed by that insistent melancholy, maddening, snow-in-the-air jingle of the bells.'

My eyes still wandered. A long sword in a black scabbard was on the wall and some framed programs with bold printing: 'Royal Lyceum Theatre.' And on the table before us are some silver spoons and a sugar bowl engraved with the initials, 'H. I.' I could resist no longer. 'All these things belonged to Henry Irving!' I exclaimed.

'Yes,' he said sadly. 'Henry Irving. For twenty-two years I was a member of his company. We traveled everywhere; eight tours to America. Here on the wall is his dagger and there his sword. And all these things he gave me. He gave me all—all except the one little thing I desired most.'

'And what was that?'

Again for a moment he was silent, then his voice took on that deep timbre of the old-school actor. 'Well, as I was saying, for twenty-two years he was haunted . . . He waited. No, no. That's wrong. Excuse me, I do not know what I am saying . . . For fifteen years the bells rang in his ears and in the last act he is weary unto death and he falls asleep. Then he dreams, and you see his dream through a gauze curtain. Through this opening a new scene appears before you. Here a whole court is assembled and three judges sit on a bench of justice. The clerk reads from a paper: "Therefore the prisoner, Mathias, is accused of having, on the night of . . . assassinated the Jew Kovesky . . . to rob him of his gold." The prisoner protests, but the chief justice asks him to answer with calmness. Mathias, rising, replies that nothing can be proved against him; but the chief justice says, "The public voice accuses you. Answer me this. How is it that you hear the sound of bells?" At first the prisoner denies that he hears the bells but then he weakens and admits, "It is nothing. 'Tis but a jangling of mine ears." The court orders the scribe to write down these words. "Yes, but I hear it in a dream." The court again directs the scribe. "Write, that he hears it in a dream." The prisoner cries out furiously, "Is it a crime to dream!" And he appeals to those assembled in the court room, "Listen friends! . . . I am in a dream. If it were not a dream should I be clothed in these rags? . . ." Then he bursts into a loud laugh. "Ha, ha, ha! It is a dream—a dream!" But the chief justice silences the prisoner and explains why the accused is haunted by the sound of the bells. "Because there rankles in his heart the memory of what he would conceal from us." But now the prisoner denies he hears the bells. "No, I hear nothing" . . . but at these words the bells are heard from far far away.'

'And all these things once belonged to the great Henry Irving,' I said. 'The dagger that he wore at his belt in *Hamlet* and . . . And all these he gave to you. But I am curious to know what it was that he refused to give you.'

The kettle was boiling and the old man poured the tea. He continued in a deep bass voice as though he did not hear a word of what I had just said. 'The bells seemed so far away and yet how real they were. The prisoner demands an advocate, but the court only grants him a Mesmerist. Soon this black-haired fellow, master of the art of

sleep, arrives. Mathias sees him and defies him. "I will
not be made the subject of this conjurer's experiments . . .
I have no fear," he cries. But to himself he whispers,
"Courage, Mathias, if you sleep you are lost." But the
Mesmerist throws his spell over the prisoner and Mathias'
eyes become fixed and frozen and his voice speaks from a
distant land. "No—no—I will not sleep—I—will. I will—
not—no—" but he breathes deeply. He is asleep. The
chief justice orders the Mesmerist, "Ask him what he did
on the night of 24th of December, fifteen years ago?" In
a low voice the sleeping man describes, as though it were a
vision before him, how on that very night he murdered the
Polish Jew. He tells all. How the Jew came to the inn,
how he learnt of the money in his belt, how he crossed the
fields to overtake the departing sleigh; and then how he
spoke to himself: "Kill a man!—kill a man! You will not
do that, Mathias—you will not do that. Heaven forbids
it. . ." Then in another voice. "You are a fool! Listen,
you will be rich. . ." Ah! and so the dark deed is described.
And all this time every word he utters has been written
down. Then the prisoner is awakened and his confession
placed in his hands. "It is false!" he cries. "You are a set
of rogues!" But the judges condemn him to be hanged by
the neck until he is dead. And when these words are
spoken . . .'

The old actor knows his lines. His face is alive with
excitement. After twenty-two years with Irving anyone
would know his lines. But what is it he wanted from
Irving? What is he concealing from me? These were the
thoughts that occupied my mind.

'And when these words were spoken the dream scene
behind the gauze curtain grows dim. The lights return to
the stage and Mathias is asleep. But the sleep is a troubled
one. Suddenly his name is called and you hear a loud
knocking upon the door. Many voices call his name and
finally the door is broken down with a crash and many
enter. Mathias staggers out of the alcove, his face is drawn

and deathly pale. His eyes are bulging, his gaze is fixed, and in a voice of strangulation he cries, "The rope! The rope! Cut the rope!" He gasps and he struggles. His last words are, "Take the rope from my neck—take the rope from my neck!" And that is the end. An imaginary rope but a real death. . . There! That is melodrama!'

He poured himself another cup of tea.

'And for how many years did Henry Irving play *The Bells*?'

'From almost the very start of his career, and for over thirty years until the very end. Not *Hamlet*, not *Othello*, nor *Macbeth: The Bells* was his masterpiece.'

'Thirty years is a long time,' I said.

'Yes, a long time. Everything is a long time. Even a moment is capable of being a long time.'

Twilight was creeping in upon us. The dagger on the wall was barely visible. The old man was silent but there was more that he could have said. A good deal more. But he waited. Perhaps he was waiting for the twilight to hide his face before he continued.

At last he said, 'No, I never played in *The Bells*. But I knew every line, every gesture, and every grimace of Mathias' was part of me. Ah, yes. And many other parts grand in manner and noble. . . . But do you know what it is to wait? Ah! That is a lesson I would have no man learn. When I first met Irving I was young. I was playing important parts in a good company. The critics were kind enough to notice my presence and it was said I had a career before me. Irving and I were about the same age, and about the same size. I wore Irving's costumes and his wigs. He made me work hard. I became his understudy. Every line he knew, I knew also. Every movement of his I had learnt . . . And I stood in the wings and waited. Sooner or later I was certain that I would have my chance and then . . . Then I would show the world a piece of acting that would rival the greatest. Sooner or later, if not in *Richard III*, then in *Hamlet* or in *The Lyons Mail* or *The*

Bells. I knew them all and I was ready. First a month
went by and then a season. I wanted to marry but I put
it off until . . . Do you know what it is to be ready, to
step forward and know for certain that the moment you do
so you will be famous? Today your name is of no account
and tomorrow it blazes in glory; and not a glory that is
undeserved. A year went by and I waited patiently in the
wings, dressed in the part, ready for the moment . . . What
is the murder of a Polish Jew? And what his gold? There
are souls more worthy. And can you believe that a man
can be murdered and still may live on? Five years went
by and then ten. When I think back upon those days it
all seems a dream. And is it not possible for a dream to
be true?' His voice grew louder. 'Yes. It is a dream. If
it were not a dream should I be clothed in these rags? Ha,
ha, ha! It is a dream—a dream! Is it a crime to dream!
Courage, if you sleep you are lost. Kill a man! You will
not do that. Heaven forbids it! What am I saying!' He
stopped abruptly . . . His voice grew softer. 'Of course, I
was certain that I would have my chance. In time . . .
Ah, some day. They would not let me die in the wings
without once showing my face to the public. I was always
ready. I could not fall asleep, I dared not grow old. I kept
up the parts and knew my lines . . . And many times after
all had gone, when the stage was empty and the theatre
was dark, when only the old lame watchman was present,
then I would come forward and go through the great moments of the play all alone. I would cry out my lines to
the empty seats and the whole hollow place would tremble
with the terror that was pent up within me . . . You cannot
kill a man! Heaven forbids it . . . Surely sometimes, you
would think . . . But no. My chance never came. Twenty-
two years I waited in the wings, and Irving was never sick!
Not one day in all this time. Not one little hour. For
twenty-two years, dressed in his costumes and wig in hand,
I waited. I was his shadow and when he died that shadow
crept silently into his grave. Then I was an old man. Then

it was over. Wait. Wait, and a life is spent. Wait and some day . . . Ah, that some day is part of a dream that never came.'

He lighted the lamp, and once more one could see the faded playbills on the wall and the long black sword . . . and Hamlet's silver dagger hanging from its metal belt. Ah, you silver-handled little dirk, warmed by the palm of the melancholy black prince of Denmark; that self-centered, ambitious, scheming egotist. Your brooding plots have killed your uncle, your mother, killed your friend and brought madness to your sweetheart, and now, after all these hundreds of years your keen little blade cries for more. Dark prince of ambition, with liquid envy coursing your veins, how many more must you slay! . . . My eyes turned away.

The old gray-headed actor was before me. Now the lamp burned bright and you could see his face. Everything was in that face. The dream, the twenty-two years and everything.

OUR AUNT CONTENT
by
Robert W. Mitchner

AUNT CONTENT has gone, and we are hoping we will
soon be able to mend the threads which had tied us to our
former friends. How warmly will we welcome the brave
soul who must, sooner, we hope, or later, be the first to
cross our doorsill once more.

We were glad to see Aunt Content when she came to
visit us for the first time since, ten years before, we had
left the little village both our families had always lived in
and had moved upstate to the city.

If certain family legends about my dear old aunt had
made us a bit uneasy, Aunt Content dispelled that un-
easiness the first evening as she sat in our living-room,
looking very sweet and placid in her exquisitely old-fashioned
black taffeta dress and her little lace cap.

Mr. and Mrs. Jamison called that evening and they, too,
were charmed by her graciousness. Our conversation, on
topics carefully chosen to suit the delicate tastes of an
elderly maiden, was easy and delightful until the subject
of blindness came up.

"I remember," said Aunt Content, looking down at her
wrinkled hands in her lap, "a school teacher I had when I
was young who lost both eyes in a horrible accident."

The guests clicked their tongues sympathetically, but
Alice and I squirmed a bit and looked at each other un-
happily. Those disturbing legends had included bits about
Aunt Content's childhood memories.

"Yes," Aunt Content went on, "the poor dear lost both
eyes and had to have some glass ones made."

"Did she quit teaching school?" asked Mr. Jamison.

"Oh, no!" our dear old aunt answered. "Through constant practice she soon enabled herself to see with them."

Our friends gasped. Mrs. Jamison was quite pale.

"You—you mean she saw through—that is, she could look at things with her glass eyes?"

"Oh, yes. Her right eye, as I remember, was rather dim, but the left seemed perfectly normal."

Mr. and Mrs. Jamison changed the subject with a jolt, and soon got themselves outside to safety.

After Aunt Content had retired for the night, Alice and I spoke, a bit gingerly, of what we called her infirmity. Alice referred to it as "a tendency to exaggerate" and mentioned her "vivid imagination." I experienced a dull throb of apprehension, something like that felt by a youngster who, having been disobedient, had been told to wait until his father comes home.

Naturally, other friends of ours called, whether through curiosity or because of a real desire to meet our guest, I can't say. At any rate, all of them left as quickly as the Jamisons had, and under similar circumstances.

There was no restraining Aunt Content. After all, it is difficult to request a dainty old lady to watch her conversation.

Alice's buffet supper climaxed Aunt Content's visit.

Thirty acquaintances were invited "to meet John's aunt, Miss Content Darrington." Before the guests arrived, we punished Junior severely in Aunt Content's presence for a lie he was supposed to have told. He wept histronically, and swore that he realized lying was bad and that never again would his lips utter a falsehood. The performance netted him a quarter, as agreed beforehand, but that it had failed to impress Aunt Content became evident soon after the supper had gotten under way.

As our relative was helping herself to the breast of chicken, someone noticed the amethyst ring she wears and asked about it. Aunt Content sighed, attracting all eyes to herself. "I'll tell you its story later this evening," she promised, mysteriously.

The guests clamored for the story as soon as Alice began carrying empty plates to the kitchen. I sat near my aunt, feeling just like an eye-witness to a hanging.

"I got this ring," murmured Aunt Content, "years ago when I was in Egypt."

A crash from near the kitchen door, where Alice had dropped two plates, startled me. The guests, fascinated, ignored the distraction.

"In Egypt? How interesting!" they buzzed.

"Yes, I was twenty and we were traveling around the world. One morning I awoke before the rest of my party and resolved to see the pyramids at dawn. I hired a camel, though its owner was reluctant to see so young a lady venture out alone, and rode toward the desert."

An audible, romantic sigh escaped the ladies in the group as they moved their chairs closer to Aunt Content's.

"I had ridden only a few hours when I noticed a queer shape on the sand ahead of me. As my camel approached it, I could tell that it was a man. Seeing me, he stumbled across my path."

The ladies sighed again. I was in agony. Aunt Content, to my certain knowledge, has never been outside the borders of this state.

"He called to me in a piteous voice, telling me not to be afraid. He was an old Arab, tattered and filthy. 'My good man,' I said, 'what do you want?'

" 'A drink of water, lady, for the love of Allah.'

"Fortunately I had a large thermos jug with me and was able to let him have as much ice-water as he wanted."

"Did they have thermos jugs in those days?" Alice asked, rather belligerently.

Aunt Content smiled at her. "John's Grandfather Darrington invented them, my dear," she said, "and this was the first one ever made."

Alice wilted. From that moment on she simply sat there, opening and closing her mouth.

The guests were impatient at the interruption. "What happened then?" they wanted to know.

"The Arab wiped his mouth with the back of his hand and knelt at my feet. He called down Allah's blessing on me, and then he gave me this ring." Here Aunt Content indulged in a nicely-timed dramatic pause. Then she proceeded.

"Naturally I was greatly pleased—"

Here I broke in. Perhaps she would give up and let the fiction end there. "I should think you would have been pleased," I remarked kindly. Then I turned to my friends. "Would any of you care for another cup of coffee?"

"Naturally I was pleased with the gift for its own sake," Aunt Content resumed, "but the Arab touched the ring mysteriously. 'It has a secret power,' he said."

This I thought too much. "Really," I started to say, "This is—"

A sibilant chorus of hisses for silence halted me completely.

" 'If ever you want to be absolutely alone,' said the Arab, 'you have but to press the amethyst against your chin and every person around you will disappear.' "

Here the guests chuckled at the humorous element which they believed had been introduced. Aunt Content smiled sadly and gazed at the wall above the heads of her audience.

"I was amused, too," she murmured, "and I laughed lightly but kindly at the old man. 'This way?' I asked playfully, and I raised the ring to my chin. To my horror the Arab immediately faded before my eyes."

My aunt's regular, even breathing was the only sound in the room. Every eye was glazed by blank astonishment. I was unable to believe that I had heard this, even from Aunt Content.

"Disappeared?" I croaked.

"Completely!" was my aunt's calm reply. Then she

continued. "Considerably unstrung, I returned to our hotel as quickly as the camel would carry me. When I got there, I ran to my room and threw the ring into my trunk."

Our local banker, a practical fellow, had a solution. "Then did you wake up to find it was all a dream?" he asked. We all breathed again and looked fondly at the banker. *Dear* Mr. Sims!

"Oh, no!" my aunt's thin, high voice went firmly on. "Although, as a matter of fact, the whole occurrence seemed so unreal to me that I forgot about it until one morning, weeks later, when we had returned home, I unpacked my trunk and found the ring wedged in a corner.

"I picked it up and put it on my finger. I reasoned that perhaps some strange tropical disease had caused me to suffer from an hallucination."

We all lavished a hopeless sort of pleading gaze on my aunt's untroubled countenance. Here was another possible egress from this hideous mental maelstrom into which we had been plunged!

"My parents asked me where I got the pretty ring, but I was forced to lie to them. 'I bought it in a Persian bazaar,' I replied, for I dared not tell them the truth. They were satisfied, but my own curiosity was consuming me. I once touched the ring gingerly to my chin before getting into bed at night, but, as I was already alone, any uncanny result was impossible."

"Did—did anything *ever* happen?" I don't know who asked this question, but many heads nodded, indicating that the owners of them were also wondering, yet had not dared ask.

"Yes," replied Aunt Content, and she might as well have dropped a hand-grenade in our midst. "One morning a salesman for kitchen utensils came to our door and forced his way into the parlor. I was alone in the house, and the man seemed determined to sell me a patent egg-beater. Nothing I could think of by way of refusal discouraged him in the least. Finally, becoming desperate, I glanced hastily around to make sure that none of my family had wandered in, closed my eyes, and pressed the amethyst against my chin. The drone of the sales talk ceased. I was afraid to open my eyes. When I did—"

Here my aunt fumbled in the folds of her skirt for her handkerchief.

"When you did—" prompted the widow who is our next-door neighbor, balancing on the extreme edge of her chair.

"When I finally gained the courage to open my eyes, I saw that I was indeed alone. I remember rushing to the window to see if the salesman were in sight and finding the street empty. Then I fainted and my family, returning, found me there on the floor in front of the bay-window."

The widow from next door fell back into her chair. She was pale, and her eyes seemed to have turned back into her head. Like everyone else, I was unable to move, or speak a word, and the widow was left to revive at her leisure and without outside aid.

Aunt Content had started talking again. Like those of snakes swaying before the wails of a Hindu instrument, our eyes followed the ring on her wrinkled hand as she aided her story with small gestures.

"I was confined to my room by illness for nearly a week following that day," mused Aunt Content, "and most of my time was spent in staring at the ring which I had never removed from my finger, hideous though it had become to me.

"After that incident I seemed to be held in the power of the weird ornament. Afraid of what I might be unable to prevent myself from doing, I begged my parents to let me spend a year in New York, ostensibly to study the flute, on which instrument I had become quite proficient. Although such a request was an unusual one for a girl in her twenties to make in those days, my parents, as indulgent as they were wealthy, permitted me to go.

"When in New York, I found myself yielding mentally

to an irresistible desire to press the ring against my chin. The action had been completed so often in my thoughts that at last I actually committed it."

The banker struggled out of the spell my aunt had cast over us to whisper, "And its effect?"

Aunt Content touched her handkerchief gently to her eye with what to me seemed devilish slowness. "Unfortunately," she said, "its effect was as the Arab had said. While attending a rehearsal for a concert a small orchestra to which I belonged was to present within the next month, I suddenly took my flute from my lips and stared at the dull, expressionless faces around me. Before I was aware of what I was doing I had raised the back of my hand to my chin. At once the members of the orchestra disappeared, and their instruments crashed to the floor. I arose and staggered out onto the crowded sidewalks of the city."

"Wh—what happened?" someone gasped.

"The concert was called off," my aunt replied, passing her handkerchief over her mouth.

"After that I was afraid to attend any public gathering, lest I should inadvertently cause the annihilation of hundreds of people. I stayed in my hotel room, not daring to go out or to let anyone enter except the servant who brought my food. Everytime he came in I would sit on my hand.

"Then one day," and again the hand with its fascinating jewel applied handkerchief to eyes, "I received a call from the manager of the hotel, a splendid young man with fair hair and deep blue eyes. He invited me to lunch with him downstairs, and, drawn to him by some pleasant force, I could not refuse.

"Our meal together was most enjoyable, as was our game of cribbage in the lobby that night. And, as I returned to my room later in the evening, the long-absent lightness of my heart convinced me that I was in love with Philip, for that was his name—Philip Ransdale."

Aunt Content smiled, but her smile met no similar response among us.

"Within the week Philip had told me of his love. I confessed that I felt both love and gratitude for him. 'Gratitude?' he asked.

" 'Yes', I answered, 'for you are making me forget things that are not pleasant to remember.' He laughed at me in his hearty way and suggested that we go to the opera that night. Though still afraid, I was unable to give him a reason for refusing, so we went. To my delight I found that I had no desire at all to touch my ring to my chin. As the romantic months of our courtship progressed, Philip unconsciously freed me more and more thoroughly from the ring's power. The day approached when we were to go to my home together to be married. Then—"

Aunt Content now bent her head and rested her face in her palms. Her listeners, pale and taut, were beyond delicacy of feeling.

Their "What thens?" filled the room with sudden, rude sound.

Aunt Content raised her head tragically. "The night before our departure we were in my room, swearing that our love for each other was timeless. 'Are you sure you will never, never tire of me?' Philip asked.

"Flippantly, I pretended to inspect him. In an unconscious attitude of study. I rested my chin on the palm of my hand. After a while I said seriously. 'No, Philip, I can never tire of gazing at your dear features.' Then—then as I moved my hand from my face so that he could take me in his arms some ghastly mischance caused me to touch my chin with the cool amethyst on my finger. So completely had my thoughts of the past left me, I did not realize what I had done, for I had lowered my eyes modestly. Suddenly the icy silence froze my heart. I looked up quickly, and— Philip was gone."

My aunt sighed and smiled a sweet, sad smile. "And that is why I never married," she told us, her limp victims. "Now you know the sad, sad story of my ring."

We still stared, paralyzed by a horrible enchantment,

at the ring. Aunt Content looked down at it, spread her tiny hand out before her own eyes, her arm stiff. Then slowly, very slowly, she brought her hand towards her face. We leaned forward as the ring moved closer, closer to her chin.

Then the widow screamed and, gathering up her skirts sprinted from the room, through the French doors, to her home. The rest of us jumped and stood up, trembling. Within thirty seconds the room was cleared except for Alice and me and Aunt Content.

Slowly the echoes of our guests' hurriedly stammered farewells died away.

"My!" exclaimed Aunt Content as the automobiles plunged into the night. Then she cleared her throat. "It's past my bedtime," she said, and started up the stairs. On the landing she turned and looked down on us fondly.

"It was a lovely party, my dears," she said.

NOW THERE IS PEACE

by

Richard Sherman

THE long, book-lined room was overheated, and the air above the radiators shimmered in upward waves. Outside, in the gray December street whose traffic sounded faintly muffled through the magenta-draped windows, snow had begun to fall; but of the three people seated near the fire, only the boy noticed the flakes, which seemed to be coming not from the sky but from the pavement below. The woman's gaze was on the portrait over the mantel, and the man looked into the coals.

Then the man, shifted, and traced a thin, dry finger over the leather of his chair.

'It was very kind of you to come,' he said. 'I know how precious your holiday time at home must be, and Mrs. Bentham and I appreciate your courtesy.'

'Yes, sir,' the boy answered, and blushed. 'I mean—I mean I was glad to come.'

The woman's eyes left the portrait, to rest on her folded hands.

'Perhaps, Edward, if you would explain to—' she turned: 'Your first name is Martin, isn't it?' The boy nodded, and she again regarded her hands. 'Perhaps if you would explain to Martin why we have asked him here . . .'

Martin spoke quickly. 'I know. You wanted me to tell you about—' And then he stopped, confused.

'About Arthur,' Mr. Bentham said, and at the name his wife's hands unclenched slowly.

'But I can't tell you anything.' The words came even more rapidly now, as if this was all he had to say and as if after he had said it he would leave them there alone. 'You

111

see, this is my first year at the school. Your—Arthur was
my Senior Counselor, but I didn't really know him. He
was older than I am, and—'

'Yes, yes.' Mr. Bentham nodded. 'Dr. Abbott told us
all that. Indeed, it was the fact that you were only slightly
acquainted with him that caused us to send for you.'

'Tell him what you want, Edward.'

'What we want. Yes, my dear.' He rose and began to
pace the room, retreating into a shadowy corner and then
reappearing. 'We are planning,' he said, 'a small memoir
to Arthur, a little book or pamphlet which we hope will be
a tribute to his memory. A tribute to the sort of boy he
was, and an inspiration to others.'

'Oh,' said Martin.

'I have talked with various friends of his, his chums, and
each has volunteered to write a short paragraph or two
about him. Dr. Abbott and several of the instructors have
also signified their willingness, even their desire, to con-
tribute too. We want to have as many different points of
view as possible. Dr. Abbott gave me your name as one
who might picture Arthur as he seemed to a new boy.'

There was a silence in the room, a silence broken only
by the dull murmur of the street outside and the sound of
Mrs. Bentham's nervous breathing. Martin himself said
nothing, had no opportunity to say anything, for almost
at once Mr. Bentham continued.

'I believe that I am not overstating the case,' he announced, 'when I say that Arthur was an unusual boy.
Since his death we have received many letters, some even
from strangers, testifying to his all-round physical and
mental brilliance. Though of slight build, he was a splendid
athlete—'

For the first time, Mrs. Bentham lifted her head and met
her husband's gaze.

'So splendid they killed him,' she said.

'My dear, we have discussed that so often. Simply because one boy is killed in one football game—'

'Killed for sport. Like a bull. . . It wasn't as if he enjoyed playing.' Martin thought that she was going to cry, but she did not. Instead, she returned to her former attitude of lowered eyes and folded hands.

'A splendid athlete,' Mr. Bentham went on, his face serene. 'A distinguished student, a leader in church and social service work—yet not a prig—and extremely popular with his classmates.'

'He was.' The boy's voice was earnest, and it held a note of relief. 'Everybody liked him. He was a big man at the school.'

Mr. Bentham smiled. 'He was indeed. "Always be a leader," I often told him. And he remained a leader to the end.'

'Yes. The end,' Mrs. Bentham said, and then her eyes found Martin's. 'You say they liked him. Did you like him too?'

He replied without hesitation. 'Of course; though I didn't see much of him. You see, he was always so busy.'

At the mantel Mr. Bentham had paused, and was looking upward.

'Here,' he said. 'This is a painting of him, done last summer when he was just eighteen.'

The boy did not move.

'Come over this way,' Mr. Bentham commanded. 'The light is better here.'

Rising slowly from his chair, Martin went toward him.

'It's a very good likeness, isn't it?' he said. 'He was— he was always smiling.'

'It's more than a likeness,' the man answered. 'It is symbolic of Arthur, just as Arthur was symbolic of the best in boyhood, in young manhood. And that is what we want this memoir to be too. We shall call it "Arthur Bentham: The Record of a Happy Boyhood."'

Looking about the room now, Martin saw that everywhere there were relics of the son who had been killed. On the mahogany desk stood two large photographs of him; a catcher's mitt hung incongruously near a family shield; and on a table lay several copies of the school paper of which he had been the editor.

'It is a source of great comfort to us,' Mr. Bentham resumed, not as if he were speaking to Martin but as if he were addressing a larger audience, 'that Arthur's short life was a completely joyous one. Fortunately we were able to surround him with all the material advantages that any boy could wish; and also we tried—and I believe succeeded—to mould his moral and mental character to a point nearing . . .' he fumbled, 'to a point nearing perfection. He lived in the sunlight always. Never did he give us cause for grief or worry.'

There was a pause.

'Edward,' Mrs. Bentham said. 'Perhaps Martin is not interested in all that.'

'Oh, but I am,' Martin put in, embarrassed; 'I—I . . .'

'Of course he is.' Mr. Bentham's tone to his wife was sullen, almost cold. 'And so will other boys be, and their parents. In a way, you see,' he continued, turning to Martin, 'this book will be a guide to adolescence. Not of course that it will be a moral preachment—we want it to be gay and high-spirited, as Arthur was, and vigorous and manly too. But by re-creating his happy life, year by year, and by giving the testimonies of his friends and his teachers as to his character—by doing that we will be helping other parents and their sons.'

'Martin.' Mrs. Bentham stood and waited for him to come to her.

'Martin, why is it that you don't want to write for Arthur's book?'

Involuntarily he caught his breath in a sharp little gasp.

'But I haven't said—'

'Phyllis, my dear,' Mr. Bentham turned from the portrait to face them. 'Of course Martin wants to do it.'

'No, he doesn't.—Do you?'

For a moment the three of them were silent. Then the boy looked at the rug.

'No,' he said.

Mr Bentham started slightly, and a flush began to creep up his cheeks. Then he said, with quiet dignity, 'I am very sorry. I had thought that anyone would welcome the privilege of—'

'Don't, Edward.'

The room had grown darker now, and outside the snow was falling thicker, whiter. Martin looked not at the man but at his wife. Her face, obscure in the gloom, gave no sign of what was in her mind.

'I—I'd better go,' he said, and headed toward the door. Mr. Bentham had already turned away, and was fingering a sheaf of papers. His back was stony, outraged.

'Goodby', said Martin.

Mr. Bentham did not even look up.

Hurrying down the wide, dim hall, he heard light footsteps behind him, and turning, saw Mrs. Bentham.

'Wait', she called.

He stopped, in a sort of alcove. Immediately she was near him, very near.

'Tell me,' she said, in a low, pleading voice; a voice different from that which she had used in her husband's presence.

'It's nothing,' he answered. 'I'd like to do what he asks, but—'

It was as if she had not heard him at all.

'Tell me about Arthur.'

She was almost touching him now—a slight, frail woman, only a little taller than he was, with great eyes. And then she placed a hand on his lapel, lightly.

'Don't think that you will hurt me. Nothing can hurt me now. But I want to know everything about him. You have no right to keep anything from me, bad or good. Don't you understand?'

'It isn't bad. I never knew of him to do or say anything that was bad.'

'What is it then? Why don't you wish to write about him? Is it that you think the idea is sentimental? It *is* sentimental, but—but his father wants it.'

'No. No, it isn't that.'

Her hand fell away from his coat. 'Then you won't tell me. You will go now and leave me knowing that there was something in Arthur's life that was a secret. Something that you, who saw him only a few times, were aware of but won't share with me.'

Their eyes met in a long glance. And then Martin began to speak, uneasily.

'It isn't important. I told you it wasn't important. . . I liked him a lot, even the first time I saw him. He was nice to me, not conceited the way most Senior Counselors are. He talked to me about my studies, and about what activities I should go out for. "If ever you get in trouble," he said, "or if you're homesick, come and see me." He was that way with everybody.'

'Yes.' She knew.

'One afternoon, the day before he was—the day before the game, I went to him. I didn't have anything on my mind, except maybe that I was a little homesick, as he said I might be. I knocked at his door, and no one answered. Then I knocked again, and waited. Somehow I felt that he was there, and I thought maybe he hadn't heard me. So I opened the door. I shouldn't have done it, but I did.'

He stopped, but the pressure of her hand made him go on.

'He was crying. That's all. He was sitting in a chair with his head down and he was crying. You see, it's really nothing at all. But I can't forget it.'

'Why should he cry?' he asked. 'He was always laughing when people were around. Why should he cry up there alone?'

Mrs. Bentham's voice was hardly a whisper.

'I found him that way once, too,' she said. 'A year ago.'

'And don't you know why either?' He was insistent now; demanding. 'Didn't he tell you?'

She had turned away from him, and was looking at the closed door at the end of the hall.

'He didn't have to tell me,' she said. 'I knew.'

'But I can't understand . . .'

Now she was facing him again, and she placed her hands on his shoulders.

'I don't know who your mother and father are,' she said. 'But tell them to let you be what you are, not what they want you to be.'

For a moment he waited for her to continue, and when he saw that she only wanted to be left alone he turned away and began to walk down the hall. At the head of the stairs she called, 'Thank you, Martin.'

He walked down the stairs and out of the house and into a world of white.

THE BOOB
by
Walter De Leon

GOOD old Billy Renton, who can recall nearly everything that happened during the twenty-five years he played piano in vaudeville and musical comedy orchestras, dropped in the other night with a bundle of phonograph records under his arm.

"Anything especially good?" I asked, pointing to the records.

Billy eased his pudgy self into the deep-cushioned chair beside my desk. "Louise Wickhart's newest," he grunted.

"The same Louise Wickhart who has just made the big hit as the star of Moritz's latest Broadway success?"

Billy nodded. "Did you know she started in vaudeville? With her husband, Bob Carol. Wickhart and Carol was the team and a very nice little act it was, too. We used to call Carol the Boob. Louise came on fast—after the Boob split the act and dropped out."

I scented one of Billy's inside stories of stagefolk, the behind-the-curtain stuff that seldom gets into the newspapers. I shoved a box of cigars toward him.

"It doesn't take long for success to go to some people's heads," I said. "I understand Miss Wickhart won't accept any engagement except in Broadway shows."

"She has her reasons," replied Billy, calmly.

"I'd like to hear them."

"Give me a match to go with this cigar and I'll tell 'em to you." When the cigar was drawing to his satisfaction Billy began as usual without preliminary explanations.

When the Boob stepped into the small reception room adjoining the private office of the great Moritz, that summer

118

day, he was still grinning at his success in kidding the girl
at the outside desk into letting him pass. The door to the
private office was slightly ajar. The Boob heard the producer's heavy voice arguing persuasively.

"I want you in my new piece because you've got exactly
the voice, appearance and personality the part calls for. I
can't be franker than that, can I? I've told you I'll give
you as much for yourself as the team got in vaudeville.
What's keeping you from accepting an engagement that'll
mean stardom in a couple of years?"

The Boob shook his head enviously. No manager had
ever begged him to sign a contract.

"I'll be just as frank." A clear, sweet voice broke the
silence. The skin on the back of the Boob's neck prickled
as he recognized his wife's voice. "This is the chance I've
prayed for. But there's Mr. Carol, my—my partner. I
can't very well split the act and—and leave him."

"Why not? He's getting all the benefit out of the part-
nership. He's no good."

"Pardon me, Mr. Moritz, but I sing better when Mr.
Carol plays for me than any other time. Can't you place
him, too, in your new show?"

"I wouldn't have that big tramp in my theater. He ain't
worth a nickel a week to me. Why, the poor boob—"

"The poor boob you speak of is my husband."

Louise's voice was shaky.

"I'm sorry," apologized Moritz, slowly. "But husband
or no husband I can't use him. Now listen, Miss Wickhart—"

The Boob did not linger to hear the producer's new line
of argument. He'd heard plenty to keep his mind busy all
the way back to Oldtown, the village, two hours by train
from New York, where he had grown up, where he and
Louise had gone when the advent of their baby had broken
off their vaudeville route, and where they had lived now
for more than a year.

In Oldtown he walked rapidly up Main Street through

the business section and on into the tree-shaded lanes of
the older residence section. Turning the corner where St.
John's Church stood he hurried past it to the gate in the
white picket fence in front of the parsonage. Old Mrs.
Seamon, the preacher's wife, answered his ring.

"Can I get my child, please?" The Boob grinned, the
lazy, likable grin which, with his drawl and his tall, gangling
figure, had inspired his nickname. As close to him as she
had been, even his wife didn't know the extent to which
the Boob relied on that grin to mask his shyness and almost
childlike sensitiveness.

"She's been as good as pie all afternoon," Mrs. Seamon
said, giving him the baby.

"Thanks for taking care of her," the Boob replied gratefully. Snuggling the sleeping infant in his long arm, he
walked across the street, around the corner to the neat
cottage. As he entered the front door the baby woke up,
smiled and reached out to pull his long nose.

"Nix on the comedy, Little Lou." The Boob carefully
sat his daughter among the pillows of her crib and held out
two fingers for her to grab. "I'm up against a tough proposition. I'm going to explain it to you because I need your
moral support. You and I have been the closest kind of
pals ever since we met each other, and I don't want you
to get me wrong on this proposition. Understand?"

Little Lou squirmed.

"All right. Now listen. For a long time your old man
has had an inward hunch that he don't amount to much.
While he's been silently thinking it, others have been
saying it right out loud. For some reason or other your
mother likes me too much to tell me that I've disappointed
her. But I know I have; in several things—especially
money. She thinks I don't realize the responsibility you
wished on me; that I ought to be tearing around collecting
chunks of money so you can be brought up and educated
the very best possible.

"I realize it, all right, kid. Don't worry about that.

But I haven't got anything that people want to give me large slabs of money for. That's the trouble; see? Now your mother has. Your beautiful mother, Little Lou, is a very wonderful person, and you and me—we ought to feel very proud just to know her. And you and me—see?—we mustn't do anything to keep her from going ahead and becoming still more wonderful.

"A fellow I know who says exactly what he thinks with the door open has offered her a great opportunity. I'd like nothing better than to go on playing piano for your mother the rest of her life. But that wouldn't be fair. No, ma'am; I've got to split the act. Even for you I'm not going to quarrel with your mother—and bust everything that way. I think I can work it another way. But get this, chicken; I want you to thoroughly understand that whatever I say when your mother comes home today I don't mean. At least, not in the way it sounds. Understand?"

Little Lou laughed. She generally did when her daddy scowled at her and talked gruffly.

"It may be comedy for you, Little Lou, but I'll bet it's a long time before I get a laugh out of it."

The baby was undressed, fed and in bed; the dinner table was set—the Boob knew the dinner was safe in the electric cooker—when his wife arrived home.

"Why didn't you meet me this afternoon?" she asked as they sat down to the table.

"Well, I'll tell you, Lou." The Boob's fingers trembled as he started pulling down his house around him. "I've been thinking things over and I decided this afternoon that I've had enough of show business. I'm no actor. You are; you always carried the act. I was just there to play piano for you and—and fill in while you changed costumes. You kept getting better all the time. I didn't."

"That's not true," said Lou, warmly, her eyes flashing. "The act was going better all the time. We'd had two raises in salary—"

"Yeah, but you were the reason. You've got everything

it takes to make a star, honey. You belong on the stage—
not at home taking care of a baby."

"Nonsense. I—"

"Wait a second, Lou." A note of impatient irritation,
foreign to the Boob, caused Lou to glance sharply at him.
"Ever since we've been married you've had your way about
everything. I mean—you've run things."

"Bob! How can you say that! We've always talked
over every plan—"

"Yeah, but always they've been your plans. I'm not
complaining; just explaining why I want you to listen now
to a plan I have. The Booking Office wanted us to go back
into vaudeville six months ago. You said no."

"I did. The thought of dragging around a seven months
baby from town to town, in and out of drafty trains—
having to give her different milk and different water every
week, trusting her to the care of a different nurse every
week, exposing her to all sorts of weather and inconveniences
that even we couldn't enjoy—I couldn't do it, Bob. I still
feel the same way. That's why I've been trying to place us
with a Broadway show, so we could live in one place."

"I know." Again that strangely impatient, fault-finding
tone. "But how do you know I'm not perfectly satisfied to
stay right here in Oldtown, playing piano in the picture
theater and the organ at St. John's on Sundays? I've been
supporting us doing that for the last year and—and I like
it forty times better than stagework." Keeping his eyes
averted from his wife, the Boob gulped a swallow of water
to moisten his dry throat.

"But just because I'm quitting show business is no
reason for you to quit. You're clever and you like it.
That's all right. It just means we split the act."

"Split!" Lou's face went white. "Bob, you—"

"Now don't get excited," the Boob drawled. "If you
land a job with a show, fine and dandy. If you don't there's
nothing to worry about. I can hold my two jobs as long as

I want them. That's bread and butter and coal for the winter. What could be sweeter?"

Lou stared at him, recalling a hundred occasions when she had laughingly given up trying to rouse his ambition.

Though it was not ambition the Boob lacked. His fault was a sweetness of disposition which made him content just to be alive; a rare quality which helped him take the bumps of experience serenely and forget them immediately; a Pollyanna ability to put an amber isinglass in front of the spot-light of reality and appreciate its mellowing effect.

Lou had always held a definite purpose before her. Not content to ride to a fair success on the beauty of her face and figure, she had developed by hard study a naturally pretty voice until her singing had become as great an asset professionally as her appearance. Lou was practical. In their act, while she changed costumes, he had sung little songs of his own composition; hardly songs they were; quaintly humorous bits of verse set to droll, ear-tickling tunes. Audiences loved them.

"Why don't you write some regular songs—for me?" Lou often urged. "You can make a lot of money, Bob. We could help the sales by singing them in the act. Try one, won't you, dear?"

Always the Boob promised. But never had he been able to write a song for Lou that satisfied him. And because he was ashamed to confess his failure, Lou believed he was not trying. It was practical Lou who had suggested applying for the movie theater job, a means of earning money instead of drawing further on their small savings. Again it was Lou who suggested to Bob that he offer his services to Doctor Seamons when the regular church organist was called overnight to California. The Reverend Doctor had baptized the Boob, the son of his life-long friend. It was upon the organ in St. John's that the Boob had studied and played a full year before his legs grew long enough to touch the pedals. When the Doctor gratefully accepted his offer to substitute, so beautifully did the Boob play the service, so full-throated did choir and congregation sing, carried along on his swelling chords and stirring rhythms, that preacher and vestrymen knew they could find none better for the small salary the church could afford to pay.

And that was the easy, futureless living the Boob was insisting he was content with. Lou's lips straightened. She squared her shoulders.

"I saw Moritz this afternoon, Bob. He wants me for his new show."

"No!" exclaimed the Boob, softly. "Say, that's wonderful! You signed right up didn't you?"

"No. He's given me until tomorrow to change my mind—about taking an engagement without you."

"Without me?" The Boob grinned. "I'm through with show business. Ain't it funny how things work out? No sooner do I decide to blow out of the game than you get the big chance you've been wanting. You sign right up, honey. I'm going to stay home and—and take care of the baby." He looked at Lou. She was silently crying. "Gee Whiz, Lou"—he threw his arm across her shoulders—"why the tears? This is an occasion for joy."

"Do"—Lou dabbed her eyes—"do you really *want* me to leave—you?"

The Boob's eyes contracted. "Shucks, honey, it ain't leaving me—exactly. And to think of the money it'll mean for Little Lou!" He glanced at his watch. "Gee, I've got to run right along to the movie house. Good picture they're running today. A lot of laughs in it. See you later, honey." Out in the street, the Boob lit a cigarette with shaking hand, dragged the smoke deep down into his lungs. "If that show isn't a success, I'm going to murder Moritz; that's all," he said, dogging his way toward the smelly picture theater.

A show must be good to stay on Broadway for a solid year. Lou, scoring a personal triumph at every performance, for a year of Saturday nights took a midnight train from New York to Oldtown to spend Sundays and Mondays until three o'clock with Little Lou and the Boob. But because Sunday was his busy day—what with two church services and his picture house grind—and because Monday mornings Lou was always busy overhauling Little Lou's clothes and talking household matters with Mrs. Margot, the house-keeper-nurse, the Boob really did not see an awful lot of his wife. But even after fourteen months of it, when Lou told him that Moritz had offered her a big increase of salary and feature billing to go on the road with the show, because he realized it meant artistic advancement to Big Lou and a whole lot of money for Little Lou, the Boob said simply, "Fine. You'll go, of course."

The three months road tour stretched into four; then five; then plans for its definite termination were discarded. Missing Big Lou more than he let himself think upon, the Boob devoted himself to Little Lou. Every possible minute he could spare he spent with her, answering her questions. Partly because he was naturally whimsical, partly because looking for the humorous helped raise his own spirits, but mostly because he loved to hear Little Lou laugh, to see the dimples deepen in her fat cheeks and the twinkles come and go in her round eyes, in his explanations of creation as it looks to a child the Boob often slighted the truth to make a good story.

He discovered that Little Lou was quickly sensitive to music. Positively against Mrs. Margot's counsel, he used to sing to her every night after she was put to bed. When she tired of the few nursery songs he knew he wrote special songs for her, simple little tunes with simple little words that sent Little Lou into Dreamland with a smile on her lips.

The organ recitals which later caused so much trouble commenced one night in the Spring—when Big Lou had been away eight months—following a gorgeous party in celebration of Little Lou's third birthday. It was a tired, excited youngster whose interior felt none too comfy, who objected strenuously even to think of bed.

"Tell you what we'll do," said the Boob to Mrs. Margot.

"We'll undress her, wrap her up and take her around the corner to the church. That's always a wonderful place to sleep, anyway. Then I'll play something soothing on the organ. Even if it doesn't put her to sleep, I've got a hunch it'll quiet her."

Some minutes later, in the front row of pews, with a few dim lights reflecting softly on the red and purple and green and amber bits of glass in the big memorial window, with the sleepiest music imaginable reaching her as from a long, long way off, Little Lou dropped off to sleep in Mrs. Margot's arms.

The next night at bed-time she insisted the performance be repeated. The Boob laughed and, despite Mrs. Margot's head shaking, bundled her up again. A three cornered compromise was finally reached.

On Tuesdays, Thursdays and Saturdays, subject to good behavior and proper attention to meals, Little Lou knew that at bed-time she would be taken to the pew under the big window where the fuzzy white sheep were eating the grass under the eye of the Shepherd. Then her Daddy would start playing, first a hymn as befitting a church organ. But somehow, in the most surprising way, the hymn would begin sounding farther and farther away, as though it were floating right out of the church; and just when you were straining your ears to see if you could still hear it, it would change to a funny kind of dance, with tiny tinkling bells and the jingle of the silver bangles on the skirts of the fairies who certainly were dancing to that music.

And then you kept very quiet and still because the fairies and the music were coming closer—very close. But always before they flew in through the round hole at the top of the church a dog would bark, or maybe a lion would roar—a loud roar that startled you but didn't make you afraid because you knew it was only a pretend lion that Daddy made roar with his feet. But that would send the fairies scooting away.

Then, each to his own particular kind of a tune, most of

the animals in the menagerie would gather. Birds would sing, and monkeys chatter and pretty soon the big elephant would start doing a clumsy dance. Most times, before he finished, though, a bell would ring slowly—seven times— and everybody knows that animals and chickens and children go to bed when the bell rings seven o'clock.

But Daddy never expected her to go to sleep without a song. Sure enough, all of a sudden the music would change and Daddy would start singing, good little songs that only she and Daddy knew. And pretty soon he'd drift into the song about the Man in the Moon looking out of the moon at all the children on the earth and saying, "Now let me see; who's in bed like a good child tonight? There's little Willie Whiffkins, his foot's sticking out; and naughty Mamie Perkins, gone to sleep in a pout"; but always before he reached her name, something happened. One minute she'd be listening and the next thing she knew it would be morning and the sun would be shining in through the window and her Daddy would be saying, "My Goodness, here it is seven o'clock in the morning and you still in bed. Are you going to sleep all day? Of all the little fat-heads I ever knew—listen, chicken, where did you put your shirt when you went to bed last night?"

"Has Mrs. Carol ever heard you play—like that?" Mrs. Margot asked the Boob as they carried Little Lou home one evening.

"I never played anything like that—before," grinned the Boob. "It's just kid-stuff."

"It's—" But sentimental Mrs. Margot did not say what she thought it was.

Old Doctor Seamon stated his opinion on the matter not only bluntly but militantly when Mr. Grummit, of whom everybody in church always thought when the preacher read that verse in the Bible about the Lord whipping the money-changers out of the temple—anyway, when Mr. Grummit asked the Doctor if he thought it fit that the Boob should play fairy dance music and sacrilegious tunes like that on the church organ, the preacher said:

"There's never a day he plays that my windows aren't open to catch every note. If what Bob plays is sacrilegious, so are my sermons. Because he's expressing the thing I've been pleading with folks for years to express. Love; nothing but love, out of a humble heart."

Then Mrs. Seamon, slipping her hand in that of her husband, smiled gently. "I wish you would come here to-morrow evening and listen with us," she said. "I always get feeling so—so generous toward the world before Little Lou goes to sleep."

Grummit did not go to the parsonage the next evening, but he sent his wife and married daughter, who was visiting them. It was the married daughter, listening to the Boob's songs, who wondered why he didn't publish them. "They're delightful. Can't you persuade him to give me a copy of one or two of them? I'll be glad to pay for them."

The Boob only laughed, embarrassed, when Mrs. Seamon gave him the message.

One day there came a telegram from Lou, playing a return engagement in Boston, the last stand of her season. The wire read: "Cablegram from Moritz states that prima donna of London production won't do. He wants me to take steamer from New York Saturday so I can open in London following week. Have cabled acceptance. Will arrive home tomorrow morning. Love. Lou."

"What do you think!" the Boob said to Little Lou. "Your mother is coming home, tomorrow."

"For real?" asked Little Lou. "To stay wiv you and me?"

"Well, no; not right away, chicken. She's just going to pay us a visit before she goes to London."

"Like de pussy-cat?"

The Boob grinned. "This time the Queen is coming to visit us and our pussy-cat."

Little Lou thought that over. "Daddy, I want to go to Lon'on to visit de Queen wiv Mama."

"And leave me here all alone?"

"No. You come wiv me."

"We'd better wait till your mother invites us, chicken."

When he met Big Lou at the station the next morning she looked more radiantly beautiful than ever as she knelt on the platform and hugged Little Lou to her closely.

"Mama," said her daughter, tearing her eyes from Lou's sparkling ear-drops and the shiny beads around her white throat, "I want to go to Lon'on wiv you."

"Do you, sweetheart?" Lou straightened; looked squarely at the Boob. "I want her, too, Bob."

"That doesn't make it unanimous by a long way," drawled the Boob, remembering Lou hadn't kissed him. "Let's go home and talk it over."

But he knew he was going to lose Little Lou even before her mother stated flatly that she would cancel the London arrangements—break with Moritz—if the alternative meant another six or eight months away from her baby.

"Listen, Bob; why can't you come, too? Pack a trunk and get on the steamer with us—"

She stopped as the Boob shook his head. "I can't leave Doc Seamon and Plunket, at the picture house, in the lurch. I can't do it; that's all. You and Little Lou go. If the play is a hit over there and it looks as though you were going to be there six months or more, I—I'll hop a steamer and—and join you."

The only lie that Bob ever told his daughter was told the morning he took them to the steamer. As he kissed her good-by, for the first time Little Lou realized that her best beloved playmate was being left behind. Tears, large and bitter, a perfect torrent of them, streamed down her plump cheeks. Neither her mother nor Mrs. Margot could quiet her. Convulsively she clung to the Boob.

"Listen, chicken," he picked her up. "You're acting kind of silly for a girl nearly four years old. I'm surprised. I can't go with you today on account of business; understand? As soon as I get through with business, I'll take another big boat and—and"—he gulped—"understand?"

"You mean we go first and you come next?"

"That's it. You first—and me next."

Little Lou, her tears checked, squinted her eyes suspiciously. "How soon—next?"

"Just as soon as I possibly can. Maybe"—the Boob had an inspiration—"maybe I'll get on a boat that goes faster than this boat and maybe I'll get to London before you. Yes, sir; I may get there first. I'll bet you," he dared.

"I bet you," repeated Little Lou, contentedly, long accustomed to win every sporting wager her Daddy proposed.

The Boob stood the empty cottage for a week. Then, at Mrs. Seamon's urging, he moved into a spare room at the parsonage. He and the Doctor were reading in the living room the first Tuesday evening he was there, when Mrs. Seamon entered with her sewing.

"If you don't feel like it, Bob," she said, "don't hesitate to say so; but the Doctor and I do most dreadfully miss the Tuesday, Thursday and Saturday vesper services."

"Vesper services?" inquired the Boob, puzzled.

"The organ recitals you always gave Little Lou. The Doctor claims they're better than his sermons."

"You mean for putting folks to sleep?" asked the Boob, grinning because he felt like crying.

"Why did you ask him to do that?" the Doctor asked his wife as the Boob dragged his unwilling feet across the stretch of lawn between the house and the church.

"He gave up Lou—let her go—a year ago. Now, in his thoughts, he feels that she has taken the baby away from him—permanently. He mustn't give her up in his thoughts. I want him to hold on—tight—to her. Because—"

"Because?" prompted the clergyman as she hesitated.

"Because some day Bob is going to stop groping around in the dark and find the way to show the world his genius. But until that day comes he needs an anchor—ssh!" she cautioned as the first sweet notes of the organ crept through the dusk and in through the open windows.

A few days later came the unexpected cablegram from Lou. "Successful opening. Long run predicted. Critics generous my performance. Send Little Lou songs."

"What does she mean—send Little Lou songs?" the Boob asked Mrs. Seamon.

"The songs you wrote for her," she laughed.

"Oh," said Little Lou's father. "But they're none of them on paper."

"Then you'd better put them on paper as quickly as you can," advised Mrs. Seamon, seizing an opportunity she long had wished.

So the Boob spent many hours writing out all the songs he had done of Little Lou; the words and every note of music he put down neatly and painstakingly. Finally he had them completed, wrapped up for their long voyage, addressed. And, standing in the hallway of the parsonage ready to take them to the post office, suddenly it seemed very clear to the Boob that he was cutting the principal tie that held Little Lou and him together.

He recalled the wording of Lou's cablegram, "*Send* Little Lou songs." If Big Lou had wanted or expected him she would have cabled "*Bring* Little Lou songs."

"Funny I didn't notice that before," he mumbled. "Looks like I was being eased right out of the family." Of a sudden he found himself shaking from head to foot. The hand he raised to his forehead found icy sweat there. "Nerves," said the Boob, through chattering teeth. "Gee, how am I going to play for the pictures this afternoon? I ought to be on my way right now."

As he reached for his hat the bundle of songs rolled unheeded from the stand to the floor.

At the corner drug store he told the clerk—and old friend—to give him some kind of a pick-me-up to carry him through the matinee. With a wink his friend gave him a stout drink of whiskey. And then a second. It was the first drink the Boob had downed since his marriage. The whiskey inside him felt good, steadied him. But he knew its effects would wear off, leave him feeling worse than ever, before his afternoon's work was done. In a poolroom near the theater he bought a flask from another friend. It was in his pocket when he sat down to the piano in the sheltered orchestra pit.

By the time the matinee was over the Boob was hopelessly, miserably drunk. Plunket, the manager, saw him when he staggered out on to Main Street. He placed a steadying hand on the Boob's arm.

"Listen, Bob," he said, not unkindly, "you'd better go home and—"

"Go home? You're crazy." Roughly he shook off Plunket's hand. "I haven't got any home. Understand?" His eyes contracted, narrowed. "I had one—but I couldn't keep it; home and wife and kiddie—but I couldn't hold them. That's the kind of a boob I am."

"That's just the way you're feeling now," said Plunket, placatingly again taking the Boob's arm. With a snarl the Boob shook him off. "Listen," sternly, "you're drunk, Bob—"

"But not nearly drunk enough," the Boob cut in, turned savage. "Not anywhere near drunk enough to forget that nobody gives a damn what happens to me."

The Boob lurched off, down the street toward the railway station, and disappeared, dropped completely out of the sight and ken of every one in Oldtown.

It was not because efforts to locate him were not made that he was not found. Drexell, the music publisher, spent many hours in the parsonage in Oldtown. For Mrs. Seamon, finding the Little Lou songs, had followed her plan to have them copied before the originals were sent across the ocean. These copies she submitted to Drexell. He found in the songs what Mrs. Seamon had found—quaint, irresistible appeal to both old and young—which spelled profits to the publisher. For two months Drexell carried contracts in his pocket, waiting word from the Seamons that the Boob had returned or written to them. Then he made out new contracts containing a larger royalty figure, and inserted advertisements in the trade-papers asking information concerning Bob Carol.

Two months after the Boob had walked into the night, Lou wrote to the Seamons to ask why Bob had not replied to her letter requesting him to join her; and the letter which carried Little Lou's dictated command: "Daddy, you must come—right away quick!" And when another two months passed with no word of the Boob, Lou instructed the Seamons to employ detectives to find him. At the end of six months Mrs. Seamon sensed the mood of desperation in the curt cablegram Lou sent. "Little Lou ill. Returning home. Must find Bob."

The lights in the parsonage burned late the night Little Lou was brought home to toss and fret in the spare room while genial old Doc Runderman shook his head and tried to soothe her mother.

"There's no further danger from the disease," he repeated over and over. "It's a question now of will, whether she wants to fight her way back to health—or not. What is it she keeps mumbling for? What is it she wants?"

"Her father," Big Lou replied, her eyes dark with the shadow of tragedy.

Some sixty miles away, in another small town, at that moment the Boob woke up; woke up on a bench in a deserted park in a steady, drenching downpour of rain; woke up with an urge of purpose fixed uncertainly but tenaciously in his consciousness. There was something, he felt, that he must do; somewhere he must go. It was hard to think straight because of the flashes of heat that shot through his brain and burned the back of his eyes every now and again. All the heat in his body was in his head; legs, arms, chest— they were chilled through. He ought to get a cup of coffee before he started—

Started where? The Boob brushed a hand across his eyes. He had started for many places during the last months; everywhere, nearly, except home. Home? Why,

that was it, of course! He must start home. A gust of
wind shook a tree branch above him, dislodging its accumulated raindrops to shower down on the Boob. Instinctively he rose, pulled his coat tightly over his chest, and
shambled toward the lights of the station.

"How far will this take me toward Oldtown?" he asked
the ticket agent, shoving a collection of coins across the
wicket-shelf. The agent gave him a pasteboard to a village
about two-thirds of the distance to Oldtown, and returned
a five-cent piece. Waiting for his train, the Boob spent the
coin for a cup of coffee.

At seven o'clock the next morning the Boob alighted from
the train and began to walk. It was a day of desolate gray-
ness, of ill-tempered, raw-edged blasts and steady rain,
through which the Boob plugged doggedly, obsessed by one
thought; he must go home. The sight of him, unshaven,
unkempt, his shoes squelching soppily at every step, the
greasy brim of his battered felt hat shedding water on his
white, set face, deterred many a passing motorist from
offering him a lift. So the Boob walked through the day on
into the night.

Doc Runderman went to the parsonage about ten
o'clock that night.

"She's stopped fussing and fretting, but she refuses to
touch any food," the nurse told him.

"That means she's given up," growled the Doc, scowling
and pulling his gray beard lest none guess that he, too, had
given up.

Up the deserted Main Street tramped the Boob; through
the closed-up business section, on into the tree-shaded lanes
of the older residence section. Turning the corner where
stood St. John's, he stumbled up the steps to the vestry-
room. Mechanically he put hand in pocket for a key; unlocked the door. He made his way through the darkness
of the vestry-room to the door which gave in to the choir
benches, between the altar and the raised pulpit. Opening
this door the faint blow of a small light hanging above the

altar reached barely to the front row of pews, in the dark, silent church.

Laboriously the Boob pulled himself up on the organ bench. Automatically he turned the switch that filled the big bellows of the organ with air. His numbed feet felt for the pedals. Trembling fingers, icy cold, hesitated over the stops, indecisively. What was he going to play? He didn't feel like playing at all. He was tired, hungry, sick. His head hurt.

Why was he there? Damn the hunch that had driven him through all those miles, through the mud and rain, slogging along like a poor devil of a soldier—mile after mile—without knowing why or wherefore—marching blindly on orders—tramp, tramp—onward, onward—like a soldier—onward tramping—

The Boob's hand swiftly pulled out a stop. His foot pressed on a pedal. His right hand dropped unerringly on the keys.

"Onward, Christian soldiers,
Marching as to war—"

Softly—so had he often played it for Little Lou—as from a great distance, sounding the melody of the old hymn; momentarily more distinct, ever its majestic rhythm, more accentuated, louder, clearer; closer the host approached until with crashing cymbals and triumphant blare of silver bugles its harmonies filled the church. Filled every arched nook and vaulted space and, overflowing into the night, rolled across the glistening lawn and swept into the parsonage.

Doctor Seamon glanced up from his Bible to look with startled eyes into those of his wife. The same prayer rose silently from both hearts. A long minute; two; then the music gradually diminished; the host was marching on.

Through the door of the spare room slipped Big Lou, her face twitching. "Lou wants to hear it again. She—she thinks it's Bob. Will you—could you ask whoever it is—"

Doctor Seamon sprang to his feet. Swiftly he went to

the outer door and stepped on to the veranda. His wife was beside him.

"I'll go, Mother. It's raining and—"

"I'll go too. If it should be—"

Hatless, coatless, they hurried across the lawn.

"Thank God!" whimpered Mrs. Seamon as she recognized the Boob. The last reverberations of a long-drawn "Amen" chord were rumbling through the church when the clergyman gently laid his hand on the Boob's shoulder.

"Glad to have you home again, Bob," he said quietly. "Mother and I have been waiting for you. No, don't stop playing," he smiled as the Boob dropped his hands from the keys, "at least not until you've played the hymn once more. Will you, Bob? I'll explain as you play."

Weakly obedient, the Boob's fingers sought the keys. Once again the distant throb of marching feet carried out into the night.

"Bob, old chap, you couldn't have come home at a—a better time. You see, we've a little girl visiting us. She's been a very sick little girl and we've all been trying with all our might to keep her interested in living—so that she will live. But she's so tired it has been very hard to make her want to—until just a moment ago. She heard you playing—she's listening now, Bob; listening to every note—and she wants you to keep playing. It's the first thing she's asked for in days."

"Sure, I'll play for the little girl," the Boob muttered. "That's why I came—through the mud."

When Mrs. Seamon quietly entered the church some minutes later with a tray on which was steaming coffee, cream and sugar, the Boob was playing the dance of the fairies that Mr. Grummit had called sacrilegious. Mrs. Seamon's lips quivered as she saw the expression in the Boob's eyes, the beads of sweat on his forehead, the angry red stains on his cheeks.

"There's hot coffee on the bench beside you, Bob," she spoke slowly, clearly.

With his feet, the Boob made the lion roar, the roar that in a moment would send the fairies scampering in all directions.

"How's the li'l girl?" he asked.

"Actually sitting up in bed—and laughing, Bob. Oh, she is so happy! Pretty soon she'll be ready for a fine long sleep and—"

"You—you tell me," the Boob was annoyed to find he had to hunt for the words he wanted. "You tell me—when she's—'sleep. I—I'll play—till—then."

He played; played with his eyes closed because the light hurt them; played to the steady drumming accompaniment of the rain on the roof; played while the nurse arranged a dainty tray of food, and while Little Lou hungrily polished off every dish and drained the pitcher dry of milk.

And then he began singing; first the song about the silly old Chuckle-headed Huckleberry. Little Lou laughed and then laid her drowsy head on the cool, fresh pillow her mother brought.

Mrs. Seamon hurried across the lawn again. She heard the Boob talking while his fingers sent a rippling melody dancing out into the black shadows; swaying back and forth on the organ bench.

"Listen, here's a new one, Li'l Lou; it's 'bout a—a—I tell you what; I'll sing it 'n' you tell me what it's 'bout. Are you listening, chicken? Here goes."

"If you'll play some sleepy music, Bob," Mrs. Seamon said, "I think she'll go to sleep now."

"I don't want her—go to sleep—'less I know she's—going to wake up; see?"

"Oh, she'll wake up," Mrs. Seamon promised, "because we've promised her that tomorrow you'll play games with her."

"Sure; I always play games with Li'l Lou—every morning." He ran his tongue across his parched lips. "Time for her to—go to sleep. How's that song go—Man in Moon—song? That'll do it—if I can remember how it—

sure I know. 'The Man in the Moon looked out of the moon—' "

Doctor Seamon was standing beside the organ bench before the last note of the song floated gently away.

"The little girl is asleep now," he told the Boob. "She's all right—she's going to be all right now."

The Boob's hands slid off the keys. "Then my day's work is done." The next instant he slumped off the bench, a limp, unconscious huddle on the floor.

When he woke up the sun of a brilliant spring morning was flooding the room. Some one was holding his hand. He looked up—into his wife's eyes. Big Lou had to explain that he was not dreaming.

"Little Lou will be in in a few minutes," she finished. Her eyes filled. "Bob, dear, will you please give me the chance to win back the place I once held in your heart?"

The Boob grinned. "Shucks, you don't have to win it back. Just take it, honey."

Billy Renton drew a last puff from his cigar and tossed it in the ash-container.

"You'd be surprised to know what a profitable market there is for kid songs," he said. "And as for those little kid phonograph records,—well, the first batch of his songs Bob sang for the phonograph people has already netted him twenty thousand dollars. That's why I'm in town; to get his new records, just out today.

"Maybe you understand now, with the cosy place they bought thirty-five minutes from Times Square so Lou can get home to Bob and Little Lou every night after the show, maybe you can see why she's sort of lost her taste for show business away from Broadway."

REVENGE IN SPRING
by
Zona Gale

SANTA LIRA is a town, small and sometimes green, lying
in a shallow pocket of the Flor-i-da range of southern New
Mexico. Few tourists ever see the place, for it lies off the
main highways, is reached only by steep and dusty roads,
and has not much to offer to any stranger. But to its own
people, it is a place of romance and all the other ultimate
interests.

Its people are a strange lot, now Mexican, now Spanish,
now French, and with even an Italian name or two. There
is a legend that they all came across the border, less than
sixty miles away, when some slight forgotten Mexican
revolution set a district by the ears and emptied it of all but
the hottest of blood.

But Santa Lira had plenty of hot blood, too. Not a
feast day—and these were many—that some wild color did
not reflect itself—a fight, an old feud blazing, a shooting,
an impudent theft. But no one was greatly disturbed,
unless it was the pure-blood Spanish padre, who admonished
everyone; or the French-Canadian curé from the north,
who drifted often into Santa Lira, especially on feast days,
and quarreled amiably with the padre about the French
culture having done more for the Southwest than had the
Spanish culture. As for the others, they frankly hoped
that something would happen, on every feast day; and old
Nichola, who was Italian and Mexican and God knew what,
and was even called Tante Nichola—old Nichola said that
the way to keep people at their best was to give them something to stir their blood.

"The dead make no progress on the earth," she said, in her outlandish patois. "It is only when they become alive again in glory that they go on. When the blood stirs, a man becomes a man. And," she added, her head wagging, "a woman, too."

Maria Alicia, who had been brought up by Tante Nichola, had been brought up, therefore, on such doctrine, and she took it for granted that it was true. She lived from fiesta to fiesta, and burned candles for a great happening. But all that she had was market days and the fruit picking, and her work at the loom—sent to the border and sometimes sold there, though she herself had never crossed the mountains, where the men went but rarely, the women never.

All that she had was these things until José came— whose father at home on the rancho, obedient to some forgotten blood strain, called him Josef. Josef, too, Maria Alicia called him, from the moment when he had arrived at the market on a day in spring, driving in his Angora goats, and had said that he was on his way to find pasture and would shortly be going on to the south. There was no pasture for miles, and all Santa Lira knew that, but they made him welcome and asked no questions; and Maria Alicia leaned from her fruit stall and offered him a blood orange, new in those parts.

"Are all the girls of the town like you?" Josef had asked, leaning on the stall, peeling his orange slowly, his look slowly moving down her face and resting on her mouth.

"No," she said sadly, "they are more beautiful," and at his shout, she colored and tried to laugh, and corrected herself; "they are beautiful."

He continued to address her mouth.

"But you," he said, "are beautiful enough for me."

"I am not for you at all," she returned, and weighed out vine-berries for a customer. When she had finished, Josef was still there, it seemed, and he had not yet done peeling his orange.

And he said, still to her mouth, "That may be. For

I may find others more to my liking. Yet will you give me the first dance on the square tonight?"

She lifted her head to tell him no, and that smartly; but when she saw his eyes, still fixed so intently on her mouth, her words ran to thin air and she seemed to hear herself answer:

"Yes. If first I do not find someone more to my liking."

He laughed and strolled away without looking at her again.

And so it chanced that when the market day was done, and the musicians were tuning their instruments under the little leaves in the square, Maria Alicia did that which never before had she dared. She cast about her and saw on the edge of the crowd Manuel—a lad with whom she had grown up and who held for her no pang and no breathlessness, but whom she liked well, for he was a good lad.

"Manuel," she said to him softly, "Manuel. Come dance with me—see, this first dance, now, alone on the square."

Into Manuel's round face leaped a swift interest and delight. His cheek blazed scarlet and he said not a word, but he opened his arms to the first wild sound of the piping, and they floated out into the square, under the lighted leaves, the first there of all the couples.

In order that her eyes might sweep the square, and scan the faces of the gathering crowd, Maria Alicia threw back her head and talked into Manuel's face. And because she had no idea what to say to him, save only that she would make herself desirable to one looking on, she talked to him of himself. As,

"Manuel, how you dance! There is no one who can dance like you!" And, "The square is not large enough, I should like to dance with you into the night. . ."

So that when the dance was done, and she stood breathless, and laughing extravagantly beside a piñon tree, and when someone pinioned her arms, and drew her, without a word into the square, and began to sway as she swayed, and

when she looked up into Josef's face, she had no idea at all
what she had said to Manuel—but only that she had succeeded at some blind play.

"Now, I ought to say to you, 'You little devil,' " said
Josef. "But no. I think of you as angel, instead."

This was no talk such as the boys of Santa Lira knew
how to make, and Maria Alicia was dazzled and shaken.
She longed desperately to speak to him as he had spoken,
to be beautiful for him, to fascinate him. But she knew
that she had never fascinated anybody and that assuredly
she was not beautiful. Only, to her amazement, she found
herself able to meet him, a little, in his talk. And this
might have been because no one had ever talked to her in
quite this fashion. Always they had saved their ammunition,
perhaps, for the beauties. In any case, when he said,

"I knew the truth, when I looked at you there, this
morning—that you could dance like this," there came, from
deep caves of her, the power to reply,

"And I knew when I saw you. . ."

She paused and he breathed eagerly, "What?" and
stooped to look at her mouth. So she said, ". . . that you
come from some far place where the real truth isn't known!"

Instead of answering her, he said, "To any other girl I
could give her what she sent. To you I am a fool. That
is what love does."

Now she was shot through by something which in her
life she had never felt, but only dreamed, so that now she
could barely say:

"I shall not be a fool for anyone. I have danced enough.
Let us find the others."

As she spoke, she could have bitten lips and tongue, for
now she must say his name to the beauties, gathering as
the dance ended: Carlotta, Soledad, Rosina. But though
he bowed in the manner of larger town (she was sure), he
gave them no second look but said to Maria Alicia: "I have
the next two dances—you have promised."

Through the evening, she gave him nothing but badinage.

But when she reached her home, where he left her, she was shaking and terrified. Was it like this? Was it like this?

"What is the matter with you?" demanded Tante Nichola, sitting by a window in the moonlight.

"I don't know," said Maria Alicia.

Tante Nichola said, "I need strike no light to look at you. God send he is a decent sort."

"O Tante!" Maria Alicia gasped.

"It is the greatest good and the greatest curse," said Tante, in a businesslike voice, "and nobody but you can say which, for you, it will be."

Maria Alicia was silent. Forgotten stories about Tante Nichola came back to her—about the woman she was even now, with great eyes and soft hands and a way of kissing which left a beholder ill at ease.

Maria Alicia lay down on her bed, and the whole world whirled about her, different in motion, in color, in idea from that which she had supposed her world to be. Her familiar world—where was it? In two weeks they were betrothed as fast as ever they might have been had they known each other for a lifetime. Those beauties of Santa Lira, Josef had hardly looked at them. He had eyes for no one save Maria Alicia. She seemed to herself another girl. She was another girl. She acted as if she had beauty.

"I know your kind," Josef told her seriously. "I know the other kind, too. I have been to the border. I have seen women. But I have lived much with my father on his ranch, and I have had time to think. I know your kind. Will you go far to the south with me, to the pasture land?"

"I will go anywhere with you," said Maria Alicia, "but I should not let you know so," she added, troubled.

"We are past all that—you and I," Josef said brusquely. "We are grown ones. When can the bans be said?"

"When the French curé comes for his service in the church on the hill," she told him. "The padre—he is no man to marry us."

"Better not wait," said Tante Nichola. "You fly in the face of the good God, to wait."

Maria Alicia laughed confidently.

"I waited," said Tante, darkly.

Maria Alicia hardly heard her.

And then, a fortnight before the French curé was due on feast day, came a drover from the north, with his daughter. They put up at the shabby hotel, which seemed so grand to the people of Santa Lira. And from the moment that Josef saw Rena, the drover's daughter, he was a man bereft.

Maria Alicia saw all. She was walking with Josef in the cool of the day, when they passed the little hotel as the drover and his daughter were alighting from a large shabby car. And the low sun shone on the hair of the drover's daughter, and *Dios Mio*, it was like cloudy gold—pale fine gold, such as no woman in that middle of the world wore or hoped for. And her skin was milk white and her eyes blue, and she wore the clothes of the town.

Maria Alicia felt Josef's hand slacken upon her arm. His step slowed and he all but turned and stared at the girl as she walked into the hotel.

"There is your gold hair," said Maria Alicia, like one driving words through her teeth.

"Sweetheart," said Josef, but he said this in some other tongue, not known to her, and he was obliged to translate for her the word.

She knew exactly what happened, as indeed did all of Santa Lira. The truth was that Manuel tried to bring her the tale—not bitterly, but gently, as a brother; but she was not listening to him, because Tante Nichola had told it all to her before he did.

Josef, it seemed, had left her at her door and had gone straight back to the hotel, like an egger-moth to his mate. He walked through to the piazza where the gold woman was sitting, awaiting her father, and he said:

"I am Josef, here with sheep, on my way to the south. I have never even seen a woman with gold hair. DIOS MIO, let me look at you. I am a decent man—anyone will tell you. O—let me look at you!"

He was an amazing person, with his manner of kneeling at a woman's feet with his words and at the same time watching her mouth, as if he would never have done. And Rena was not averse to such adulation. Also, in Santa Lira, she was bored.

"Look at me, then," she said, amused.

"And may God have mercy on my soul," Josef completed that.

The drover was in Santa Lira for three days, waiting for a part of his large and shabby car. In that time, Josef spent every moment of waking by Rena's side. Not only did Maria Alicia see him—but Manuel and Nichola gave her the news.

"He has gone the way of men," said Nichola, "who have women who wait."

"I want no man who will not wait for me," Maria Alicia flung out.

"Oh, yes, you do," Tante Nicholá returned.

"Give me leave to choke his throat?" Manuel said earnestly.

"All to be done, I do myself," Maria Alicia said. And though by this she had meant not a thing in the world when she said it, yet, the words being spoken, teased her with their sound, and she repeated them to herself, and more than once.

Josef was an honest man, and at the end of the third day, and the missing part of the drover's car not yet having arrived, Josef went to Maria Alicia and said, "I love Rena. I must not marry you. I must marry her. And she is willing."

Now this was two days before the fiesta, when the French curé was expected, who was to have read the bans of Maria Alicia and Josef.

Yet Maria Alicia continued to feel tender toward him. She was able to tell him, quite gently, that if he no longer loved her, then he was right not to marry her. But she could not bring herself to say a word about the other woman, and that it was right for him to marry her. When he said, "But you, Maria Alicia, you do not love me any more now? Say so!"

She answered quite gently: "Oh, yes, Josef, I love you. I shall always love you. Have I not given my word?"

At this he looked smitten by death, and he said good-by to her with his shoulders bowed, as if he were a man who has received rather than given, a deadly wound. And he said good-by to her, meeting her eyes in an anguish of self-reproach whose ways seemed greater than those of her own anguish—said good-by to her, looking in her eyes and now not once looking at her mouth.

It was strange, she thought, that for Josef she felt nothing but tenderness and desolation. In vain Tante Nichola, who saw how things had gone, said to her, "Men have been throttled for less. I—I myself had throttled a man for less, in my stronger days."

Maria Alicia said, "No, no, Nichola, I love him. I would see no harm come to him, do you not understand?"

But Nichola said, "If you do not wish harm to come to him now, then you do not love him. I know—I know!" And Nichola regarded the fire and murmured, "Me, I would have seen my false lovers burn!"

And Manuel, who did not come near to her much, yet was about there, brooding over her house at night and from a distance, and occasionally approaching with bright offers to choke Josef's throat. But Maria Alicia looked at him in wonder, saying, "You have not loved, if you can say so."

"I can say so, for I love!" Manuel declared passionately.

But none of them could make her hate Josef whom she loved. Yet Rena. . .

When Rena walked with Josef through the town, Maria Alicia could have fallen upon her and destroyed her. That

lifted baby face, those adoring eyes, that pale frame of
bright hair—she could have fallen upon all. And the
colors that she wore—not honest reds and blacks, no banded
scarfs and fringes of yellow, but instead the blue and pink
of infants, and white thin lace, to distract any man. Oh,
she was shameless. Someone should destroy her, as a benefit
to Santa Lira.

But the drover had interested himself in gaming and
carousing, and his daughter walked the ways about Santa
Lira with Josef, and Maria Alicia began to think openly,
but still with shame, still crossing herself, that this Rena
should be disgraced and humiliated and driven from Santa
Lira.

"If you wished to choke her throat . . ." she muttered
to Manuel.

Manuel hesitated. "I have never choked a lady," he
said, modestly.

Maria Alicia felt troubled about herself, and so she
sought out the Spanish padre, not in confessional, but across
the kitchen fire, when he dropped in for a glass of Tante
Nichola's celery wine. While the old woman puttered about
her jugs, Maria Alicia said, "Padre, I desire the ruin of
a girl. . ."

"That is very easily brought about, one would say,"
said the padre, and shook with his noiseless good-natured
mirth. Because of a wound, one eyebrow seemed very high,
and the lid with it, and he cocked that queer eye and continued to smile.

"I feel hatred—a deadly sin," said Maria Alicia earnestly.

Now the padre talked earnestly, too: The love of God,
his long-suffering, his mercy, his guidance of the children
of Israel, the heavenly home. Maria Alicia listened. But
nothing that he said seemed to be said to her. And when
next she saw Rena, alone, by the door of the hotel, she
flashed upon her such a look of disdain that the small Rena
trembled, though she did not know why.

"You think well of yourself, perhaps," Maria Alicia said

to her, lowering, "to come to a strange town and make much misery."

"I make misery?" the drover's daughter repeated. "Oh, no."

"Oh, yes!" Maria Alicia mocked her. "And then you will go away and leave Josef. . . And require of us that we here take your leavings."

"I shall never leave Josef," said Rena simply. "We are betrothed. He is gone back to his father's ranch with his goats. He comes with my father and me, forever."

Maria Alicia turned without a word. From that moment her hatred began to burn toward Josef, too. This child—she could not help loving him—how could she? But Josef, his was the sin. Nichola was right. Now she must hate him.

So when the French curé appeared in Santa Lira, in good time for the fiesta, Maria Alicia did not seek him out. But she could hardly avoid him, and he cried to her as she crossed the square:

"Haven't you a good word for me this morning?" Then he saw the look in her face. "What then, little daughter?" he asked.

She said, rather proudly, "I am no longer your daughter. My heart is filled with hate. For two people—one more than the other."

He spoke gravely. "Since there are, then, degrees of hating, there is perhaps hope for the hater. Tell me." Grave still, he listened while she poured it out to him and, from her medley of market day, dancing in the square, betrothed, Tante Nichola and drover's daughter, he made out some of the truth. Of a thousand stories in his keeping this story seemed now to be his chief charge. Yet he said little, and gave her only the comfort of listening.

"I hate him. I hate her. I shall make them suffer. I could kill them both. They shall not go unpunished—that would not be right."

"LE PAUVRE DIEU," said the curé. "He then needs your help to punish his children?"

"They are not his children. They are children of the evil one!"

"Also, he needs your help to punish the children of the evil one?"

She cried: "I—I will punish them alone!"

"And yourself as well. That is too small a business. Listen, little daughter. Walk there in the foot-hills this afternoon—you will meet someone who shall help you."

But when, after red sunset, she came in from the foot-hills, in sick disappointment that Josef had not met her there, as she had hoped wildly that the curé had intended; and when the curé explained sternly: "Yourself. It was yourself, daughter, whom I hoped you might come face to face with in the hills, alone," and when she cried out violently that she had seen but yellow sunlight on yellow leaves, the color of the hair of the drover's daughter, and the tree trunks, straight and slim, like the strong body of Josef, then the curé said, "It is green sickness. I can do nothing until you come to yourself."

"I have found a thing to do," said Maria Alicia shortly. And to Tante Nichola she cried, "No woman should stand being flouted to her face!"

And old Nichola cried, her eyes flashing, "Now you speak sense. Yes, yes! It is not holy that she should do so!"

And always Manuel, watching and grieving, insisted in his gentle way, "I—I am the one to take this matter in my hands!"

Santa Lira met its fiesta day with an air, and no matter how many fiesta days were decreed in the year, always it was the same—an air, decoration, events, and shawls or even bed quilts hung from window sills. The little town slept through the year, save only for its fiestas. After midday, the padre and the curé sat on the piazza of the hotel, wrangling gently as was their wont over the sad imposition of French culture, two centuries ago, upon the already well-established Spanish culture of the time, and this, the padre said frankly, had been an outrage.

"As great an outrage," said he, cocking that strange lifted lid of his, "as the imposition of American ideas on the fiesta days. For behold, we now feel that fiesta is not a holiday, but a 'business bringer'—and here in Santa Lira we set up our market on fiesta days!"

"The more business, the less carousing," said the curé. "I find myself in entire sympathy with the picture."

His eye ran across the square to where, at the end of the market row, stood the stall of Maria Alicia, with her fruit, her celery wine and her cordials. There she stood handling her goods, as soberly as another. No time for mischief making, he thought with satisfaction.

In her fruit stall, Maria Alicia smiled at her customers, and rearranged her wares, but her eyes were on the far corner of the square. That way Josef would come, returning without his goats from his father's rancho, returning to claim his love and go away with her and the drover, to the southland, far beyond the range, and never to return. Maria Alicia had seen Rena, walking about the square, or standing on the hotel piazza, watching that same street.

Maria Alicia enacted it all as it would be, Josef would come, so eager, so ready. The dark would fall, the musicians would enter the square, the people would assemble, the fiesta dance would be on. And then she, Maria Alicia, would go to Josef, she would contrive with him a word, she would beg him to give her one dance, one, a last dance for her who had thought to dance with him through her life, but now would be dancing with him no more. He would assent, with a look at Rena, and they would dance away, Maria Alicia and Josef, as they had danced so often. Ah, and what heaven that would be to have his arm about her, his cheek near hers, eyes upon her—ah, but now he would not watch her mouth, would not even meet her eyes. Well! She would have him for a little space for her own.

Then she would tell him. Quite simply and without excitement, she would tell him that he should never be with Rena as he hoped. That she came of a race that did not take such things and suffer them—old Tante Nichola knew—he had but to ask her. No—she would find a way. It might be that she would harm him, it might be that she would harm Rena, but he should know no peace. As they danced, she would tell him, her eyes feeding upon his in a way that she knew, so that he would not expect that blow when it fell: That she might wait a year—two years, but she would never forget. That she would force him to think of her, if only to fear her. Let him ask old Tante Nichola if she, Maria Alicia, did not have it in her blood! She would pursue him, as once he had pursued her. To be sure, never had she practised it in person, but she had been told on good authority, that it was in her blood. He or his yellow-haired love should come to grief—how? Oh, THAT she had not decided. She had many ways. . .

She watched the street and rehearsed this scene. And then she saw Manuel, crossing the square.

Now that she thought of it, she had not seen Manuel all day. Now that she thought of it, she had been wondering where he was, even had been watching for him.

And, as Nichola would say, how he was resplendent! Scarf, sash, and the boots of an elegance, with clanking spurs. He caught off his broad hat, swept her a bow and inquired with an air of casualness, how she did. But she imagined that he did not look at her, that he kept looking about, scanning the square, scanning the piazza of the hotel. . .

Maria Alicia's heart closed. That yellow-haired creature—was she sharpening her claws for Manuel, too. . .

Would Maria Alicia dance? Already the first lazy strains were threading the darkness. Leaving her stall in the care of her small helper, she stepped into the square with Manuel.

He was a dancer divine—every one said so. They were the first couple on the cement. It pleased her to show that she was chosen so early and by one so well dressed, so dashing as Manuel. His spurs clanked pleasantly, he threw back his head and hummed between his teeth. Really, what had come over Manuel! He was acting triumphant. Was it possible that he had choked the throat of Josef? But where was Josef?

Faster, faster he spun her about. Really, Manuel was a great creature. So strong, too! What a night, what a night.

Close by the square, there in Santa Lira, there is a stretch of piñon, stubby and harsh and dusty green. As the others surged into the square, and as they all danced until they were breathless, abruptly Manuel swung Maria Alicia in among the piñons, so that they brushed and scratched her arms and her face, and she cried out.

"Be quiet," said Manuel. "Be quiet! I have pushed you in here to tell you."

"To tell me what?" she gasped.

"That I love you! DIOS MIO, what else? I love you so that I feel insane. I love you so that I think of nothing else! I love you so that I think I am fool before you!"

She saw his face, white in the gloom and close to hers. A new Manuel, indeed! Never, never had he been like this. And never had he once told her that he loved her, no, but only had he acted like a stricken moon-calf. "I love you so that I shall kill you if you do not love me," said this new Manuel.

Maria Alicia sought to straighten and pat her braids, but his hands were closed upon her and his arms were closed about her, so that she could not move.

"Why have you not said this before?" she demanded.

He hardly heard her. "I say it now," he said fiercely. "Love me—you must."

Amazing her herself, there crept and then swept over Maria Alicia something which never had she known before, no, not even with Josef.

"Come then!" she contrived to say. "There is the music. Let us dance!"

She drew him onto the cement and they danced again— but now to dance with Manuel was something else. Now at

last for Maria Alicia, Manuel danced, looked, spoke as one
alive! For as he danced he laughed, caught her again and
kissed her many times and whirled her about, stamping
his grand boots and shouting, very loudly. He was as alive
as Josef. . .

At that thought Maria Alicia stopped dancing, and the
two stood on the edge of the square opposite the hotel, and
just there and at that moment came Josef himself, dragging
his feet, dusty and worn from his long trek from the rancho.
But how bold and glossy was his look toward the hotel,
where Rena was awaiting him! Something stirred in Maria
Alicia that was deeper than anger, something perhaps flowing to her from forgotten sources of pride, and this was a
quick refusal to think long on one who had set love at naught.
That Josef! He who was false, he who went off after another
woman—why should she be any longer shaken by him?

But here was Manuel, so grand in his finery, so loud of
spurs, so seeking of eye, so possessive in the enfolding of
his arms. And now that other strange stirring clamored
in her again. But this new Manuel, besieging, besetting. . .

"I love' you so long," he was murmuring. "You love
me! Say so!"

She could not think very well, for Manuel was kissing
her. As for Josef, he had disappeared within the hotel, the
hotel of Rena. He who was false, he who went off after
another woman, he who could not dance like Manuel nor
had he a voice—and a sash—and a scarf—and such kisses.
Suddenly she was swept by something deeper than pride,
wiser than a wish to spend her life troubling that Josef and
his little yellow-haired beast, when instead she could be
bearing the children of Manuel. . .

"Say so!" his husky voice besought her.

Maria Alicia heard another Maria Alicia, as it were, but
speaking with her own voice, saying slowly, "Manuel! Nice
boy. Have I not known you always—love' you always?
I think so!"

Hurrying from out a side street to watch the fun, came

old Nichola. Very old and furrowed she looked by all her anxieties and all her hates.

"Tante Nichola!" whispered Maria Alicia, "I shall marry Manuel."

Tante Nichola stopped and stared.

"DIOS MIO!" she said. "In my day the blood ran hot. We did not forget so soon, we! We took a revenge with decency, we!"

Laboriously down the steps from the piazza of the little hotel came the padre and the curé. Maria Alicia ran to them.

"Give us your blessings, please," she said, "Manuel and I, we shall wed."

The two priests nodded.

"It is nonsense to bother with revenge, my little daughter," said the curé, patting her arm.

"Si!" said the padre. "All is well—all is well."

Nichola believed one thing, thought Maria Alicia, the curé another; and as for the padre, evidently he thought Josef and Manuel were one and the same fellow.

Maria Alicia looked up at Manuel and laughed, and so he laughed, too. The spring winds blew hot upon Santa Lira, the ranges lay blue under spring moonlight. Assuredly in spring this mating business was far more worthwhile than to choke the throat of anyone!

Music sounded lazily through the square, and Maria Alicia danced away with Manuel under the lighted leaves.

BEHOLD BEHEMOTH!
by
Phyllis Duganne

ONE thing I will say for myself is that I've always had a delicious sense of humor. I mean even when it's me that was funny. There was just one thorn in my armor, though, and Emily Carroll's scavenger-hunt removed that. I don't mean that now I think my driving is funny, because I'm a darn good driver and have been since I was twelve years old, but now I don't get all hot and bothered when people kid me about getting arrested so much.

I mean it really is funny for a good driver to get arrested so often. And now that it doesn't throw me to talk about it, it gives me a lot of good stories to tell—like the time I parked Behemoth in an alley in Boston and then couldn't remember which alley and spent three hours in a pouring rain looking for it and when I finally found it and drove to the station house, how the sergeant laughed and said, "Well, Miss Minot, every time you can think up an alibi that I've never heard before, I'll let you off!" Sam says I ought to write a book called "A Thousand and One Summonses." But it was Emily's scavenger-hunt that cured me of being sensitive.

There were eight of us invited to this house party, and the rest were Emily's regular crowd at Hyannis. I left Marblehead early in the morning, because I knew there'd be a lot of traffic. The roadster was still laid up on account of that hay wagon that crashed into it, so I was driving Behemoth. It's probably a good idea to describe Behemoth right now. It's really Grandfather's car, and Grandfather and Behemoth were young together. Literally, I think they drove it to my christening. It's a touring car, painted a smooth shade of red, and when Behemoth honks, smaller cars climb right out of the way. When Behemoth sideswipes something, it stays sideswiped.

I got through Boston okeh, stopping for all the red lights even when there wasn't a sign of a policeman, or a daisy for one to crouch behind, and all that long straight stretch to Middleboro my arms ached from holding Behemoth back. I wouldn't have known the figure six was on the speedometer. The first few miles after you cross the Canal curve and twist like the road was doing a rhumba, and then there's a fork to the right that is practically a speedway, with no cross traffic and no pedestrians. Well, who am I to disappoint a road like that? Behemoth was eating up the miles like they were peanuts, and I was thinking that for once I'd had an uneventful, 100 per cent legal ride for myself, when I heard a sound that if I heard it at the altar I'd turn and smile the smile I keep for the lads on motorcycles.

I shut my eyes tight and stepped on the brakes and said the first five Presidents of the United States before I looked at the speedometer. It had dropped to forty-five, which seemed a reasonable figure. Then I squinted in the mirror and my hat looked just as good as it had when I mortgaged my next month's allowance to buy it. It's really an awfully cute hat and has paid for itself just about five to one. I mean practically the entire state-police force of Massachusetts has mentioned it in one way or another, from simple, heart-of-gold remarks like, "Some lid, sister!" to the intellectual cop who asked, "Reboux or Maria Guy?"

Well, I reined in Behemoth, and turned my face inquiringly toward the motorcycle. Am I in luck or am I in luck? I asked myself. Tall, dark and handsome; I knew—I mean I thought I knew—that he could be had.

"I'm a stranger here, myself," I said, before he got in a word, "but I'll let you look at my road map, if you're lost."

I could see right away that that didn't make any hit. His face was as responsive as if it had been made of cellophane. "Just how fast do you think you were going?" he asked me coldly.

I raised my hand. "I know that one, teacher! I looked at the speedometer." My voice, which is famous for its range of expression, became confiding and intimate. "Forty-five," I said. My eyes are blue and very appealing when they're anxious. "Was that too fast?" I asked.

Did I say cellophane? His face made Buster Keaton look like Garbo in a Big Moment.

"You girls all think you can get away with murder, don't you?" he asked unpleasantly.

If he hadn't reached in his pocket for his prayer book right then, I might have used the head and seen what was burning him up. If I had tried the womanly-woman line—still, I'd have had to take off that hat to get away with it. Anyway, as I've just said, I was sensitive about getting arrested, and one mistake just naturally followed another.

"Is that your trouble?" I asked pertly. "Are you giving me a ticket because some woman's two-timed you?"

It was a bull's-eye—but it was also a hornet's nest. His face was the color of good red herring as he filled in the blanks. "What's your name?" he barked.

"Leonora Minot," I said. "Please don't shoot, officer!"

"Let's see your license."

"And I thought you were going to be original!" I lamented. "They usually ask me for that first." I gave it to him meekly. "You wouldn't reconsider would you?" I asked, "I mean, you don't think you've been hasty? It's by admitting our errors that we grow in spiritual stature, you know." (That's what Miss Wentworth used to tell us at school.) It's practically impossible to fascinate a man who won't look at you. "Couldn't you just give me a cozy little talk about fast driving?" I pleaded. "Because I realize now that forty-five IS too fast, and—"

He looked at me, unmoved. "You'll appear at the Barnstable courthouse Monday morning at nine," he said, handing me the summons and swinging a really good-looking leg over his motorcycle.

"I don't know how I can wait till Monday," I said weakly.

He might have been the Lady of Shallott; he swung his bike about without a flicker in my direction and zoomed back toward the Canal, the man-hunter in pursuit of his prey.

I felt just like Jimmy Durante. Was I embarrassed! Was my face red! For a minute, I was afraid I must even LOOK like Jimmy Durante, and I peeked in the mirror quickly. My nose was its usual cute shape, though a little shiny from emotion, but except for the glitter, I couldn't see anything wrong with my appearance anywhere. Yet here I was, for the first time in my life arrested by a young and handsome policeman who was letting me stay arrested.

I clucked to Behemoth sadly. It must be pink tooth-brush at last, I thought. But of course it had been too good to last—and one summons to one hundred and fifty miles of highway was still making it in par. Behemoth brightened up before I did—that car has a soul if anything has—and after a few miles I was feeling cheerful again and thinking that, after all, Barnstable was a long way from home and there wasn't any reason why the family should know anything about it. I mean it isn't as though they put a notch on the mudguard every time they give you a summons.

Roads ought to whistle when they throw a curve like the one where I met Sam. I mean a right angle is a right angle, whether you can remember how many degrees are in it or not. PLENTY is the answer, if anyone should ask you. I jammed both feet down so hard that my permanent straightened out—and of course there had to be this shiny yellow roadster with its spare tire lassoing my radiator cap on my side of the road, and this huge red truck coming toward me.

"Behemoth—take your choice!" I murmured, and like a

great big dog going after a rabbit, Behemoth jumped the roadster.

It was wonderful how quickly all three of us were out of our seats and in the road. Sam—only of course I didn't know it was Sam, then—came toward me with the look of a killer in his really swell eyes; his arms swung at his sides in a thrilling way. It flashed through my head what that boy must look like, with any other emotion but blind rage on those features!

I've always believed in getting in the first word, so I started before he got his jaws unclamped, even.

"I MUST apologize for Behemoth," I said. "Of all the cowardly, unsporting attacks I ever saw—I DO hope your little car isn't seriously hurt."

Did I start something? Sam—only, as I say, I didn't know him from Adam, except that it was a hundred to one that he was a million times better looking—slayed me first with a glance, and then began throwing around the English language just as if it was a little invention of his own. I mean, you'd have thought he'd written both the words and music. The truck driver was listening with his mouth wide open, and before I realized how awfully personal all his talk was, I was pretty thrilled myself. The accent, I noticed right away, since I live in Boston, was Harvard, but the appeal was universal. Then—like when you arrive at a Buck dance late and at first it's just a confusion of black coats and evening dresses before you begin to pick out and recognize faces—all of a sudden, I began hearing phrases and simple declarative statements, and there wasn't one of them that I didn't resent bitterly.

I mean he said that drivers like me should have their licenses taken away. He said that cars like Behemoth should be towed out in Boston Harbor and sunk. He said that he could see at a glance that I hadn't the brains of an amoeba. And then he said that I probably wasn't old enough to have a driver's license, anyway!

There was only one thing to do, and I put everything

I had into it. I turned and looked at that truck driver with
a light in my eyes that would double Garbo's salary.

"You saw this accident," I told him, and you could
have whipped cream with the vibrations in my voice.
"You saw me steal quietly around that curve only to find
this—this Harvard student"—Sam blinked—"parked right
in my path. DIDN'T YOU?" I asked passionately, only
the last sounded a little like Wallace Beery in The Champ.

The truck driver reached up and scratched his head,
but Sam, the darling, clinched it for me.

"Why, you low, two-timing little so-and-so!" he addressed me. "You—"

My hero tumbled just like an avalanche. "Say, do
you think that's the way to speak to a lady?" he roared.
"Parkin' on a curve!" He looked at me, and I nodded
soulfully.

"PARKING!" Sam shrieked. "I suppose she called
anything less than fifty miles an hour parking, but—"

"Prob'bly stoppin' for a drink," said my truck driver,
warming to the subject. "Did you see him throw somethin'
that looked like a flask into them bushes, miss?"

I mused. "I wouldn't want to testify to that," I said.
"I mean, after all, it might go hard with him. It probably
isn't his first offense." I'd read about people being purple
with rage, but I'd never seen it before. "I'm willing to just
let the whole thing drop," I said generously. I walked
trippingly across to the yellow roadster. It was so new that
it still had milk behind its fenders, and only one of the mud
guards was bent and the left running board just wrinkled
a little. "Why, it's nothing!" I told the truck driver. "We
don't need to keep this kind gentleman for a witness, do
you think?" I asked Sam.

Sam just looked at me and then he got into his car and
started the engine without a word.

"Prob'ly a beginner," said the truck driver. "Lissen
how he grates his gears."

I shook my head. "These boys certainly make the

highways unsafe," I said. I had a big box of chocolates
in the car. "Here, take a handful," I told him. "It was
swell of you to stop." I smiled, and gave Behemoth his
head; the yellow roadster almost climbed the bank on the
right of the road when I honked to pass it.

By the time I reached Emily's, I was feeling pretty
high. The policeman, of course, had been a complete flop,
but the truck driver had proved that I hadn't lost all my
lure. My only regret was the thought of having a cute
boy like Sam pass right out of my life.

The crowd was on the veranda when I drove up, and
of course Phil Worthington had to come running out and
be funny—looking Behemoth over, he said, for evidences
of the crime.

"What crime?" I asked loftily.

"You needn't try to tell me that you've driven all the
way from Marblehead without ruining something, Leo,"
he said. "Is this an old wound?" he asked, examining a
dent on the left running board.

"Grandfather did that at Gettysburg," I told him.
"And that nick in the bumper is the only genuine relic of
Custer's last stand. It seems that Grandfather had run
out of gas, and the Indians—"

"I surrender, dear," said Phil.

Emily came up then, and we kissed, and Phil got my
bags and trailed us upstairs.

"Run along, little boy," Emily told him. "Us women
have things to discuss." Emily had mainly two things to
discuss; one was that she was practically engaged to Bugs
Carter, only the family wouldn't let them announce it until
Bugs graduated from Princeton—which frankly in my
opinion will be never, but I didn't shatter the girl's illu-
sions—and the other was about this divine boy she had for
me. It seems we were paired for the scavenger-hunt that
night, and—

"What's the matter with him?" I interrupted, knowing
that, engaged or not, Emily wasn't passing up anything

divine without a reason, especially when Bugs was still in Europe.

Well, it seemed that Phil Worthington and Link Miller had gotten sore at her for playing them off against each other while Bugs was away, and they'd been putting her through the jumps, not dancing with her at the club and warning all the new men off. They'd just begun to let up a little, and Emily was on her good behavior—when they could check up on her, anyway.

"Oke," I said, satisfied that there weren't any concealed weapons, because even if Emily is my best friend, really divine boys don't come with every package of wave-setters. "What's his record?"

Name of Sam Vail—and of course I didn't bat an eyelash, never having heard those magic monosyllables before in my life. Sophomore at Harvard; he was driving down from Plymouth, and—

"Wait!" I interrupted, again. "Hold everything! What kind of car? What does he look like?"

When she said a dark blue V-eight sedan and sort of dreamy eyes, I let out my breath. Just for one breath, too, I enjoyed peace, because at that moment there was a terrible rumpus below and we looked out the window and everything went black before my eyes.

"There's Sam, now!" Emily was prattling, delightedly. "Why, he's got a new car!" She beamed at me. "I know you two are going to click," she said. "Come on down."

"Just like a couple of Lewis machine guns," I agreed, following her.

"Leo, darling, this is Sam Vail—Leonora Minot," cooed Emily.

If there was a dream in Sam's eyes, as he looked at me, it was a nightmare.

"Didn't I pass you on the road?" I asked, sweetly.

For a minute, I thought he was going to smite me, but he decided to save it. "Very likely," he answered, politely. "I have a new car and can't drive over thirty."

"How'd you bash your fender, Sam?" Phil, the boy detective, shouted at him.

"Oh—I ran into a hearse," said Sam, and walked across to Jane Hurlburt, leaving me to think that one over.

Of course any other girl would have switched partners for the hunt right then, but I decided that it would be more fun to go through with it. Especially as he took the line of ignoring me; every time he turned those dreamy eyes in my direction, an empty carriage drove up, and I got out. However, not even Emily noticed it, in the general confusion; there were eight of us staying in the house, and ten more piled in for dinner and the hunt.

We danced some during dinner, and though Sam never even leaned in my direction, I noticed that he watched me, more often than not. I had changed to a dark brown dotted Swiss and brown slippers with bronze buckles, having recently discovered that dark colors in sheer materials not only set off my blondeness and made me look deceitfully frail and feminine, but also since ninety-nine out of a hundred girls wear pastel shades in summer, it makes me that much easier to spot.

After we had gorged, Emily brought out the prizes—and anyone who had taken this hunt racket lightly, before, thought better of it. The firsts were the smoothest traveling vanity cases I ever saw, for the girl, pigskin, with a snappy little zippered slip cover and fitted out with enough aids to beauty and general cleanliness to last a lifetime, and for the boy—well, it was the nearest I ever came to wishing I was male! One of those trick new cameras that automatically sets its own stops and gadgets and uses moving-picture film and is 100 per cent foolproof. And the seconds weren't to be sneezed at—female, a portable phonograph, also pigskin; and male, a portable radio.

There was a look of grim determination, do-or-die, on every face in that room, and a sort of cathedral hush. I certainly felt sorry for Emily, because on account of being the hostess, she wouldn't get a prize even if she won. She began reading the boys' names, and each boy went up and got an envelope with his partner's name on it and the list inside. It was so exciting that Sam even forgot to glare when he joined me.

"You know the rules," Emily was saying. "It's ten minutes to nine now. At nine sharp, you look at your lists and you have until twelve to fill them. You have to be back here at the house by midnight. And you can't spend a cent, or get anyone outside to help you—I mean you have to lay hold of all the articles in person."

"How many?" Phil asked.

"Ten."

"Can we get in our cars now?" asked Jane.

Emily shook her head. "We all start at scratch from this room at nine."

I turned to Sam. "Don't you think we'd better take Behemoth? I mean on account of your car being new and—"

"I'll drive," he said, "or we'd probably be disqualified for disabling our opponents."

Then there was a sound of envelopes being torn open, and a breathless silence.

"Oh, this is awf'ly hard!" Pussy Lee's voice rose in a wail. "How can anyone find a bird's nest at night?"

"It's crool!" said Phil. "I ask you—one firefly!"

"Shut up!" I called, my curls pressing against Sam's dark hair as we bent forward, our eyes devouring our own list.

This was it: One live goldfish in good condition; three white hairs; one picture of George Washington; one Boston-to-New York time-table; a four-leaved clover; any one of the Elsie Dinsmore books; one burnt-out electric light bulb; a violin string; one live periwinkle; one—

I lifted my eyes from that final item and looked at Sam Vail. "I'm sure you'll be able to supply the last one," I said coldly, and then I scowled indignantly at Emily, who was watching us like a Cheshire cat. It was not my idea of humor, and my expression told her as much.

Sam was a slower reader than I, but he caught up eventually.

"One police summons, dated today," he read. "Of course you have several of those in your pocketbook, Miss Minot?"

I didn't have the nerve to say that I'd never seen one in my life. I mean, he was sure to find out, eventually, that I'd SEEN one. But I certainly wasn't going to give him the satisfaction of knowing that I did have one—not even for that vanity case!

"Sorry," I answered, stiffly, "but with my car and your driving and three hours to go, that should be the easiest thing on the list." Then my eyes wandered back to those prizes. "Listen," I said, "I don't like you and you don't like me, but those are pretty smooth awards, and for three hours we'd better pull together."

"As you say," he assured me, gallantly, "you're just one big pain-in-the-neck to me, but for three hours—" He held out his hand. "Shake."

We climbed into Behemoth, and even with Casper Milquetoast at the wheel, that car would either get ahead legally or push any obstruction into the ditch. And Sam, for all his faults, was no Timid Soul.

"What's first?" I gasped, clutching the door as we zoomed through the night.

"Railroad station before it closes," he said, and I nodded, approvingly.

"Hey—what's the idea?" I began, as he drew up Behemoth before a fire hydrant, and then I grinned. "Nothing could ever make me like you," I remarked, "but you're not so dumb."

"Thanks," he said.

But the railroad station was closed. We poked around in the rubbish on the tracks, and looked into a couple of trash cans without any success. "So what?" I asked.

"Some of these stores must have time-tables—the news stand, maybe." I started back toward Behemoth, and he grabbed my arm. "Listen, stupid, a watched bus doesn't get a ticket," he cracked. "Leave that car alone to its fate and pray for a fire in the neighborhood. Come on—time's money."

We crossed the street and dashed into a store that had magazines in the window—and what a store! If we'd had time to look around, and any cooperation from the aged citizen who ran it, I bet we could have got everything on the list right there.

"Have you got a Boston-New York time-table, sir?" asked Sam.

"Hey?" said the old boy. "Speak up a little louder, young fella!" Sam shouted it, and Methuselah nodded his head and reckoned that he had. We exchanged a happy smile while he fumbled behind the counter. "You kin look at it," he said, "but you can't take it away."

Well, we argued and we pleaded and we besought—all at the top of our lungs—and we were just wasting our time. Then I had to get an inspiration.

"Will you give me three white hairs?" I screamed at him.

You'd think I'd asked him for his whole head. That old antique just blew up. He said young people had no respect for old age, and it was a pretty pass when—

"Oh, come on, Leo!" said Sam, disgustedly. "We haven't got all night."

"I will NOT come on!" I said. "Sam, you go buy me some chewing gum." Sam started to argue, but there must have been something awe-inspiring in my face, because he shut up and yelled to Santa Claus. I watched them go down to the other end of the store, and then I reached over the counter and grabbed the time-table and stuck it down the neck of my dress, giving me a profile like Mae West.

"Do you realize that it's almost nine-thirty?" Sam asked me coldly, as we went out. "Maybe you'd like to stop and get a shoe shine?"

"Oh, pull in your ears!" I told him. "Here's the time-table."

He brightened at that, but only for an instant. "What the heck?"

Behemoth, positively glowing with righteousness, had moved away from the fire hydrant! We stared wildly at each other, and then the Good Samaritan, in the person of a fatherly individual, came beaming up and said, "I pushed your car down along, folks—you'd get a ticket sure's shooting if a cop saw it by that fire plug."

I was speechless, but Sam managed a hollow thank-you.

We passed every red light on the main street as we went through, and the cops must have thought we were the Lindberghs, or something. Phil Worthington's people had a pool with goldfish, so we went there next. We left Behemoth on the road with no lights and crept across the lawn, Sam with the flash light and me with a child's sand pail I'd quietly lifted from the counter at Old Crosspatch's Shoppe, as we went out.

There were only seven goldfish, but they were all contortionists. And just as Sam's fist was closing over one, there came a growl that made my hair stand on end, and from around the corner of the house came a practically prehistoric looking English bulldog on two wheels. I started to climb into the pool, but Sam held me back. He looked at that raging animal and he waggled a forefinger and he said sternly, "You sit right down there and give me your paw!"

Well, the creature paused and looked at Sam with the most worried expression I've ever seen on an animal. His forehead wrinkled up like an accordion, and he wagged his tail sort of absently and put his head on one side and concentrated. Then he sat down, and with a perfectly froglike gesture, he raised one paw up behind his ear and offered it to Sam.

"Great watchdogs, these," Sam said grinning, and shaking the monster's hands. "Good fellow! Noble animal!"

"Do you know that dog personally?" I asked, in a weak voice.

"I've got one of my own," said Sam. "They're great clowns." He was back again at his fishing, and the bulldog sat there, offering his other paw, and the moon came up behind some trees and Sam caught a fish and looked at his wrist watch and said, "Good grief, it's nearly ten and we've only got two items!"

"It just says hairs," I murmured, thoughtfully. "Not WHOSE hairs. What color would you call that dog?"

Sam looked at me admiringly. "Leo," he said, "if we'd had a different meeting, I think I could almost have learned to like you. C'm here, dog!"

So now we had three items, but when we got out to the road, Behemoth's parking lights were twinkling like a couple of engagement rings.

"It's Hyannis that's paved with good intentions," Sam said, bitterly. "Just a town full of Boy Scouts, that's all. Where do we go from here?"

Violin strings mean music and music means dancing, so, breaking traffic regulations like they were the best phonograph records at a picnic, we dashed to the White Swan where I knew the saxophone player on account of his sister went to the same school where I went last year.

We parked Behemoth where it would be most in the way and went in. The orchestra was playing Night and Day and we were dancing before Sam remembered that he had picked me for a wallflower to press in his memory book. I put my head down on his chest, and somehow felt a lot better.

Then the music stopped and I grabbed Pete, saxaphone and all. "Listen you, find me a violin string somewhere quick!" I hissed. "None of you boys happen to be reading the Elsie books, do you?"

"No, but I know where you can get one," Pete came right back, in the spirit of the thing, he having played scavenger himself in happier days, and when he told me, I threw both my arms around his neck and kissed him.

"Come on, passion flower," Sam's voice said coldly in

my ear. "It's ten-thirty, and you can put the sex in sexa-phones some other time."

We looked hopefully at Behemoth when we came out, but neither of us said anything. It made me a little sick not to be able to get arrested when I was actually trying to. Well, this place where Pete boarded was just beyond a schoolhouse, he said, and there was a complete set of Elsie books in the bookcase in the sitting room. That would mean half our list—and half the time was already gone.

The woman at Pete's boarding house seemed to think it was real sweet of me to want to borrow an Elsie book, but when I asked her if she happened to have any burnt-out electric light bulbs around, she looked at me as if I was really as dumb as I'd have to be to want to read Elsie. Sam was waiting in front of a Private Driveway—Do Not Obstruct sign.

"Little one, we're good!" he greeted me.

"You got a summons!" I cried. "My he-ro!"

He shook his head. "No. But where's there always a picture of George Washington?"

Neither of us had ever expected to break INTO a school-house, but then, the whole evening was like that. Finally we found a window that was unlocked and climbed in. It was pretty spooky and the stairs creaked and just as we got to the top landing, the flashlight went out. Of course I'd used it a long time there on the Worthington's lawn, looking for a four-leafed clover. I yelled and grabbed Sam, and his arm went around me kind of protectingly and he said, "You're a good sport, Leo," and I said "Oke," and we went on into a big silent classroom all white with moon-light, with George on one wall and Abe on the other.

Sam reached up and lifted the father of his country from the hook. It was eleven o'clock.

When we jumped the second traffic light back on the main street, a police whistle rang out and I pressed my hand to my wildly beating heart like I'd heard the voice of my beloved one, if any.

"Say, what's the matter with you?" the officer demanded, sticking his head in the car. "Can't you see a red light?"

"Wasn't looking," snapped Sam, and I said to myself: Five dollars extra for impudence to an officer on duty.

So of course I had to pipe up. "Was that light red?" I asked, in a Gracie Allen voice.

The policeman grinned and stuck his neck out still further like a turtle and took his time about looking me over. "Well, I can't say that I blame you, at that," he told Sam. "Run along and try to look at the road at least once a block."

Sam gulped. "You mean—you aren't going to give me a ticket?"

"You've got trouble enough in the front seat with you already," said the cop, with a wink at me. "Scram!"

Sam just looked at me. "That's right," he said, when he got his voice. "Tha-a-at's right! Pull your stuff—like you did on that truck driver this afternoon!"

"I don't know what you're talking about," I said.

"Not much you don't. You and Dietrich—"

Well, I didn't know whether to be sore or flattered, and before I'd figured it out, we'd reached the shore.

"Do you suppose the guy that made out these lists knew that it would be high tide?" groaned Sam, taking off his shoes and stockings and rolling up his beautifully creased white flannel trow.

"What are you going to do—dive for periwinkles?" I asked, which was a natural Gracie Allen this time, as I really didn't get it.

"Which end do you think I dive with, Brainless?" he retorted. "I'm going to wade out to that dory. There's probably a winkle or two lurking there."

I sat in the car and stared at the list and thought about that vanity case. The fourleafed clover, little emblem of luck, looked to be what was going to throw us. With the flashlight gone dead—I stifled a shriek. Who called who brainless?

Sam was gone such a long time that I began to get nervous. We were so close to success—only two more things to get, now. I picked up the Elsie book, thinking that a really sexy story like that might take my mind off my worries. And was I right? Oh, was I right!

Whatever little hands pressed that clover leaf against the page where Elsie fainted on the piano stool, there's nothing too good for them.

"We Harvard men always get our periwinkle," said Sam, popping into the car and sticking his wrist watch under the dashboard light. "Good grief, kid, was I that long? We're sunk. It's eleven-thirty."

"Sunk, nothing!" I told him. "We're on the top of the wave!" I showed him the clover. "And you called me brainless, big boy! Listen—what makes a flashlight go out?"

"The bulb or the battery," said Sam. "Why?"

I held up the flashlight. "I hadn't thought about it being the battery," I admitted. "But—"

He grabbed it and began taking it apart feverishly. "Gosh, it's the bulb!" he shouted, and kissed me.

I think he was as stunned as I was. I mean, we didn't either of us have a thing to say. He stepped on the starter and off we went and I sat still and thought how there were times to be quiet. His profile, with the moonlight coming sideways into the car, was swell. And his hair wasn't either straight or curly; it looked kind of like birds' feathers.

"We haven't got the summons, though," I said at last.

"We're not home yet," said Sam.

I wasn't using my left hand for anything and it just turned out that he didn't need his right hand to drive, and when he dropped it, it fell over mine and sort of curled.

"You were a fresh little devil this afternoon, Leo," he said, not looking at me.

"I was going to pay for your repairs," I said, "I didn't think you'd drive away like that."

He snorted. "If I'd stuck around any longer, you and

your truck-driving friend would have had me in jail for murdering Costello! How do you do it, Leo?"

"Do what?" I asked. Of course I sort of knew what he meant.

"Make men fall for you," he said.

"Truck drivers, you mean?"

"And dumb gorillas from Harvard. Listen, Leo, you're staying on at Emily's over the week-end, aren't you?"

I nodded. "But I leave at dawn, Monday—I have a heavy date in the morning."

"Oh, you have, have you?" He stopped Behemoth and I saw that we were right outside Emily's gate.

"But we haven't got our summons!" I cried.

He gave me a queer look. "Listen, Fathead," he addressed me tenderly, "I'll take what's coming to me, any day. I mean when I'm at fault, I'll own up to it. And I expect the same of any girl I'm crazy about." His eyes were holding mine in the most thrilling way.

"So what?" I asked, knowing I was lost. But I didn't see how he had found out about the summons.

"So this," he said. "What's your honest, rock-bottom opinion of the cause of our accident today?"

"You mean what do I really think CAUSED it?" I asked. He waited. "It may have been fate," I suggested.

"Come again," said Sam.

"Maybe I took that curve just a wee bit fast," I gulped. I'd never humbled myself like this before a man in my life. "Oh, it was my fault, all right," I said, and reached in my pocketbook for the summons. It was all over with me, anyway.

Sam's face was positively glowing. "Well—here's your vanity case," he said. And he handed me a piece of paper.

"Wh-what's this?" I asked.

"The summons. I crossed a red light at Sandwich— there weren't any cars in sight—and this cop appeared out of nowhere and jumped me." My head was reeling, and there I sat, holding a summons in each hot little hand.

Well, was that a moral issue for a young girl to face? Of course it was easy enough to get out of. But this man trusted me. As I looked into his eyes, my spine got all crawly again, and I just handed him my summons without a word.

"Well, for crying out loud!" said Sam. "And you had this—"

At that minute, a car shot past us and turned up the driveway; then another and another.

"Hey, we better scram!" I said.

The Carrolls' living room looked like a cross between a charity bazaar and the notion counter at the zoo. There was a duck quacking like it had lost its last friend, and a mewing kitten, and a lobster pot with a live lobster in it, and a turtle that kept running around the rug. Phil had caught his firefly, but it had taken him over an hour; it seemed that every list had some time-eater like that on it.

"Who has a complete list?" Emily shouted when the bedlam quieted down enough for a shriek to be heard. "Don't all speak at once."

"Well, we were the only ones. The girls all crowded around my vanity case like it was the only mirror in a dressing room, and Sam kept the lads from taking his camera apart by sheer brute force. Link and Pussy got the seconds, and pretty soon the radio was going in the living room and the phonograph on the porch, and Sam and I were dancing—to the old but appropriate Farewell to Arms.

I put my head down, and I could feel his heart beating, and for a moment we drifted dreamily before I snapped out of it. Don't let it die, Leo! I told myself, because it's always a good rule to say good night about fifteen minutes before a boy starts to think about it. I broke and put out my hand.

"Well—see you in court!" I cooed, and picked up my vanity case and toddled off to bed.

1. PROSE

II. Shorter Narratives
and
Monologues

JOHN TAKES A VACATION

by

George Mitchell

"THERE'S no use talking, Mary, I won't take a vacation. I never take vacations. Don't believe in vacations. Never did. Never will. Can't see anything in 'em for anybody. Waste o'time that should be devoted to business. No, I won't take a vacation."

"John Foster, the way you talk! You need a rest, same's everybody."

"Nobody needs a rest. Never took a rest. Don't believe in rests. Can't see anything to 'em. Never did. Never will. I won't take a rest."

"But, John dear—"

"No use, Mary!"

"—the Doctor said—"

"What's he know about vacations? Doctors don't know anything anyhow. Never did—never will. Besides I gotta go to town. Haven't sold a thing this summer. Rottenest summer I ever had. Don't know what's come over real estate. Nobody buying anything. Never did. Never will. There's that big Shackleton estate I went and bought. Got fifty thousand dollars tied up in it. There's a white elephant on my hands. Can't sell it to anybody and it's costing me three thousand interest to carry it."

"Don't worry—"

"There you go! Who's to worry if I don't? Fifty thousand and nothing stirring and you say: 'Don't worry. Take a vacation.' Women are something I can't understand. Never did. Never will."

"But John, dear, when there's nothing doing—"

"Mary, dear, you talk like a partner. Don't you see I

177

gotta go into town to do it? Can't you see that? Fifty thousand—ask seventy-five—take seventy."

"John, dear, I'm worried about you. You're coming down with something."

"I'm coming down with a crash if I don't sell the Shackleton place. I see that."

"Couldn't you go fishing, John?"

"Fishing! My Godfrey! You mean me, Mary? Only fools fish. You come back with none or the bottom of the boat's alive with the flapping things. I hate 'em. Can't even eat 'em. What are you crying about? Oh, pshaw!"

"The doctor said your nerves—"

"Hang the doctor! Mary—Mary! Oh, well—what are you going to do with a woman? Mary, stop crying, can't you? Well, well, well! There, now. I'll take—I'll take a coupla hours this morning."

"Oh, John dear—you're so funny."

"Sure I'm funny. Ha, ha!"

"Hurry now. Get into an old suit. I'll have a nice warm lunch when you get back."

Half an hour later John shambled his way down the road conscious in the belief that the entire neighborhood was laughing at him behind curtained windows.

Arrived at the country store, he entered and after an altercation with Shlipsky bought a second-hand rod, line and a card of flies, and with the rod clumsily clutched in his hand made his way to the Shackleton estate, his fifty thousand dollar proposition.

"Might as well get something out of it. Costs enough. Three thousand interest on my money. Thirty acres. A big house. Bedrooms and bathrooms all over the place. A trout stream. Fit for a Wall Street prince. Fifty thousand dollars. Asking price seventy-five. Would take sixty—all tied up and me taking a vacation. I'm a fool!"

He would have turned back but Mary'd cry again.

He hooked a fly on the end of his line the way Shlipsky showed him and threw it out over the brook.

For half an hour he fished but took nothing. Then he rose and drew in his line.

"Well, I've seen THAT through. I've fished, and I'm finished with it. But I always knew it. Fish ain't caught. They're bought. Fishing and vacations are for men who have plenty of money and those who think they have it. Me, I'm different. Well, I can still catch the eleven-fifteen and get half a day in at the office."

He disjointed his rod and was about to depart when he was hailed by a jovial, cherry-faced man in khaki who carried a rod and a string of fish.

"Get anything?" he called enthusiastically.

"Fish, you mean?" asked John.

"You don't mean to say you didn't get any? Why, man alive! I never fished a better stream. The brook's full of 'em. Look!" and he held up twelve or thirteen glistening fish.

"Oh, it's a good little brook," said John, remembering his fifty thousand.

"Good? Why I'd give a million for it."

"You would?"

"Well, pretty nearly. You see when a man loves fishing and he finds a real stream—well, I see you wouldn't understand."

"How much WOULD you give for it?"

"Why I've been all over the grounds and through the house and fished the stream and it suits me fine. I understand old Foster wants seventy-five thousand."

"So I hear," said John.

"S'worth it!" said the man. "The brook alone's worth it to a man like me."

"I think I could get it for you for seventy," said John.

"Go ahead and try. Be my agent with the old fool. And I'll split the five thousand with you as a bonus."

"Can you afford it?"

"I guess so. I'm William A. Thatcher—Standard Oil. Guess you've heard my name. What's yours?"

"Mine's John Foster, the old fool that owns this place."

An hour later, with a check to bind the deal, John arrived home.

"Did you catch any fish?" asked Mary.

"Yes, one," said John.

"And did you like your vacation?"

"I'm going to take a coupla months," said John.

WHITE WALLS
by
Patricia Collinge

"YOU see," said Mrs. Smith to the painter, "I want white walls."

"White walls?" asked the painter.

"No, not white walls," said Mrs. Smith. "Not that dead white, but white. That sort of dull oyster white. You know what I mean, don't you?"

The painter looked unhappy.

"You know," she said encouragingly, "white with a little gray in it, only not exactly gray, a sort of brownish gray, oyster white—an off white, that's the color I want."

"You mean you want gray?" said the painter.

"No," said Mrs. Smith, and went over it all again.

The painter shook his head. "We don't generally put nothing but white in kitchens," he said.

"But I don't mean the kitchen," said Mrs. Smith. "I mean the drawing-room—the living room. The big front room," she added as the painter looked confused.

"We don't never put white in living rooms," said the painter. "Yellow is good for living rooms, or green. We paint a lot of living rooms green."

"I'm sure you do," said Mrs. Smith, "but I want mine painted white. Not white, you understand, but white."

The painter sighed heavily and looked at his boots. "Well," he said, "it's your living room."

In a few days Mrs. Smith went over to the new apartment to see how the painter was getting along. He was just finishing up. It was a nice neat job; he had got nearly all the paint on the walls and only a very little on the floors and the windows. He was whistling unhappily in a minor key, and the walls were a nice, cheerful cream.

"I'm sorry, but we'll have to try again," said Mrs. Smith.

The painter looked hurt. "Ain't that the color you wanted?" he said.

"Not quite," said Mrs. Smith, and explained once more.

Two days later the walls were a firm dark gray.

"I'll tell you," said Mrs. Smith. "Let's mix the paint together."

The painter gave her a long look and silently produced his paints, and after some time and the sacrifice of a quite good frock Mrs. Smith got what she wanted.

"Now," she said, "let's put that on."

When it was done, she said, "That's splendid. I'm delighted."

The next day she brought her husband, who had been somewhat doubtful, to be convinced. Her knees shook a little as they gazed together at the walls.

"You had better come over at once," she said to the painter over the telephone. "Something terrible has happened. The walls have turned green—a dirty gray-green. I can't think what it is. Do come at once."

"That might be the glazing," said the painter. "It'll do that if the plaster is damp."

Mrs. Smith counted ten. "Did you glaze the walls?" she asked.

"Sure," said the painter. "Didn't you want them glazed?"

When the walls were once more oyster white, Mrs. Smith moved in. And so did a few carpenters, plumbers, curtain hangers and several unidentified men, none of whom found it possible to get from one end of the living room to the other without placing his hands at intervals on the walls, which rapidly assumed a mottled tone. A fingerprint expert might have enjoyed it, but Mrs. Smith was not a fingerprint expert. When the moving was over she summoned the painter again, who gave the room a fresh coat of paint.

"If you'd glazed them walls you could wash them," he offered, looking happy for the first time.

When the walls were dry Mrs. Smith thought to hang some pictures, thereby discovering that every picture made a mark and, once hung, was irrevocable; and she also discovered that the cleanest fingers left traces, and that even if she locked the living-room doors spirits came in at night and made fingerprints up and down the mantelpiece. But she persevered. She wanted white walls, and she was not a woman easily discouraged. She found a new painter who touched up the places where the men had installed the light fixtures, and where the men had put up the cornices, and where she herself had touched the light button—where anyone, in fact, had touched anything—and when that was all done she issued the strictest orders to the servants and to her husband and admitted her first caller. The caller was enthusiastic. She thought the apartment was lovely, and that the new chintz was lovely, and that the new rug was lovely, and that everything was lovely.

Mrs. Smith relaxed.

"And your walls?" said the caller as she rose to go.

"Yes," said Mrs. Smith. "My walls?"

"What color," said the caller brightly, "are you going to paint them?"

Mrs. Smith took a long, deep breath.

"Green," she said—"I'm going to paint them green."

THE GUSHER

by

Charles Battell Loomis

OF course an afternoon tea is not to be taken seriously, and I hold that any kind of conversation goes, as long as it is properly vacuous and irrelevant.

One meets many kinds of afternoon teas—the bored, the bashful, the intense, and once in a while the interesting, but for pure delight there is nothing quite equals the gusher. She is generally very pretty. Nature insists upon compensations.

When you meet a real gusher—one born to gush—you can just throw all bounds of probability aside and say the first thing that comes into your head, sure that it will meet with an appreciative burst of enthusiasm, for your true gusher is nothing if she is not enthusiastic. There are those who listen to everything you say and punctuate it with "Yes-s-s, yes-s-s, yes-s-s," until the sibilance gets on your nerves; but the attention of the Simon-pure gusher is purely subconscious. She could not repeat a thing of what you have told her a half minute after hearing it. Her real attention is on something else all the while—perhaps on the gowns of her neighbors, perhaps on the reflection of her pretty face—but never on the conversation. And why should it be? Is a tea a place for the exercise of concentration? Perish the thought.

You are presented to her as "Mr. Mmmm," and she is "delighted," and smiles so ravishingly that you wish you were twenty years younger. You do not yet know that she is a gusher. But her first remark labels her. Just to test her, for there is something in the animation of her face and the farawayness of the eye that makes you suspect her sincerity, you say:

"I happen to have six children—"

"Oh, how perfectly dee-ar! How old are they?"

She scans the gown of a woman who has just entered the room and, being quite sure that she is engaged in a mental valuation of it, you say:

"They're all of them six."

"Oh, how lovely!" Her unseeing eyes look you in the face. "Just the right age to be companions."

"Yes, all but one."

The eye has wandered to another gown, but the sympathetic voice says:

"Oh, what a pi-i-ty!"

"Yes, isn't it? But he's quite healthy."

It's a game now—fair game—and you're very glad you came to the tea!

"Healthy, you say? How nice. It's perfectly lovely to be healthy. Do you live in the country?"

"Not exactly the country. We live in Madison Square, under the trees."

"Oh, how perfectly idyllic!"

"Yes; we have all the advantages of the city and the delights of the country. The children bathe in the fountain every morning when the weather is cold enough."

"Oh, how charming! How many children have you?"

"Only seven. The oldest is five and the youngest is six."

"Just the interesting age. Don't you think children fascinating?"

Again the roaming eye and the vivacious smile.

"Yes, indeed. My oldest—he's fourteen and quite original. He says that when he grows up he doesn't know what he'll be."

"Really! How cute!"

"Yes, he says it every morning, a half-hour before breakfast."

"Fancy! How old did you say he was?"

"Just seventeen, but perfectly girl-like and masculine."

She nods her head, and murmurs in musical, sympathetic tones:

"That's an adorable age."

"What, thirteen?"

"Yes. Did you say it was a girl?"

"Yes, his name's Ethel. He's a great help to her mother."

"Little darling."

"Yes; I tell them there may be city advantages, but I think they're much better off where they are."

"Where did you say you were?"

"On the Connecticut shore. You see, having only the one child, Mrs. Smith is very anxious that it should grow up healthy." (Absent-minded nods indicative of full attention.) "He plays with the fisherman's child and gets great drafts of fresh air."

"Oh, how perfectly entrancing! You're quite a poet."

"No; I'm a painter."

Now she is really attentive. She thought you were just an ordinary beast, and she finds that you may be a lion.

"Oh, do you paint? How perfectly adorable! What do you paint—landscapes or portraits?"

Again the eye wanders and she inventories a dress, and you say:

"Oils."

"Do you ever allow visitors to come to your studio?"

"Why, I never prevent them, but I'm so afraid it will bore them that I never ask them."

"Oh, how could anybody be bored at anything?"

"But every one hasn't your enthusiasm. My studio is in the top of the Madison Square tower, and I never see a soul from week's end to week's end."

"Oh, then you're not married."

"Dear, no; a man who is wedded to his art mustn't commit bigamy."

"How clever. So you're a bachelor?"

"Yes, but I have my wife for a chaperone and I'd be

delighted to have you come and take tea with us some Saturday from six until three."

"Perfectly delighted!" Her eye now catches sight of an acquaintance just coming in, and you say:

"Hope you don't mind a little artistic unconventionality. We always have beer at our teas served with sugar and lemons, the Russian fashion."

"Oh, I think it's much better than cream. I adore unconventionality."

"You're glad you met me, I'm sure."

"Awfully good of you to say so."

Anything goes at an afternoon tea. But it's better not to go.

DECEIVED

by

Heather White

I always read the Agony (Personal) Column of my newspaper, and one morning my eye fell upon the following advertisement:

GREEN EYES,—I bumped into you at Hyde Park Corner and did not apologize, as I might have done. May I explain now that the reason was not lack of courtesy but owing to the fact that I was lost in the depths of your lovely green eyes? Am I forgiven?

—BARBARIAN.

Naturally I did not expect that anyone would reply to this fatuous ass. After all, everyone has been bumped into at Hyde Park Corner, and if one person replied a hundred and fifty might equally do so without the real person being included in that number. However, the following morning I saw this:

BARBARIAN,—They're really hazel, but they look green when I'm dressed in green. Which of you was it?

—GREEN EYES.

This, I surmised, would bring forth a spate of answers, but I was wrong again, for there was only one. It ran:

GREEN EYES,—Oh, cruel, cruel! Do all men drown in your translucent depths? Yet after you frowned you smiled on me. Then was the sun upon the waters. Say you remember me.

—BARBARIAN.

Now, I wondered, will the girl play up or will she acknowledge that she has no recollection of the youth by allowing the matter to drop and silence to speak for itself?

188

"GREEN EYES" was more artful than I thought. At breakfast next day I read:

BARBARIAN,—If you're the one that trod on my toe and snapped the handle of my umbrella—yes, I remember you.

—GREEN EYES.

"Minx!" thought I. "She wants a new umbrella and has thought of a way to get one. I hope 'BARBARIAN,' although he's an ass and deserves all he gets, won't rise to this." However, he must have been a simple soul, for he did:

GREEN EYES,—I am prostrate with grief and contrition. I had no idea the damage was so great. Yet the damage to myself was permanent, and even if I replace the umbrella you cannot, I fear, restore to me my heart. Where shall I send it?

—BARBARIAN.

This struck me as over-bold. The girl was unlikely to publish her address. She might, of course, give a club address or a monomark, but that would not be playing fair. The youth had already squandered good money on his advertisements in the hope, obviously, of meeting her again. To take more and give nothing in return would not be just.

In spite of the green eyes the girl was obviously honest, for the following morning she fixed up an appointment. I would have gone to see fair play had not pressure of work prevented me. I regretted that this would obviously conclude the correspondence and that my breakfast Personals would know them no more.

But apparently something went wrong and they missed each other, for "BARBARIAN" was again stricken with grief and still in possession of the umbrella. Couldn't something be done about it?

The next day there was no Personal. Had the girl gone abroad suddenly, or had her parents got wind of the affair? I thought of the umbrella awaiting delivery and wondered what the lad would do with it if "GREEN EYES" passed out of his life forever.

I almost grabbed my paper next day. It was Saturday, and if there was any appointment fixed I knew I should be free. I only wanted to look on from a distance and make sure that the umbrella reached its owner, or alternatively, that the owner-to-be confessed about her own being intact. I saw this:

BARBARIAN,—Was suddenly shy. Silly of me, wasn't it? Were you the tall one in the grey hat? You looked rather a lamb. Meet me at the corner of Surrey Avenue, Hampstead East, at four-forty-five today.

—GREEN EYES.

I took a bus. After a week in the city I wanted a breath of air, I told myself, and I might just as well travel on top of a bus to Hampstead East as anywhere else.

When I reached the corner of Surrey Avenue I thought at first that there must have been an accident. Then we got a little nearer and I saw a huge placard in front of some very tall buildings. This is what I read:

"GREEN EYES" AND "BARBARIAN" WERE MARRIED THIS MORNING. AFTER THEIR HONEYMOON THEY WILL BE OCCUPYING ONE OF THESE ATTRACTIVE AND CONVENIENT FLATS AT A MODERATE RENTAL. BEDROOM, BATH-ROOM, KITCHEN. LARGER FLATS FOR FAMILIES ON VIEW ROUND THE CORNER. DO NOT GO AWAY DISAPPOINTED, BUT VIEW THEM NOW.

PARSONS IS PREPARED

by

P. S. Le Poer Trench

EVEN at college Parsons was always anticipating some kind of minor or major crisis and devising a scheme that would succeed in averting calamity. He knew exactly what to do if his clothing caught fire, and the best way to extinguish blazing oil or gasoline. I remember his telling me once that if the window curtains were ignited by a cigarette, it was of no use to hurl the contents of the goldfish bowl directly at the flames, as I had suggested; the water should be thrown at the top of the curtains.

I happened to stroll into the gymnasium one day with the idea of taking a swing or two at the punching bag. Parsons was perched on the horizontal bar, and as I entered he fell off, landing in a lump on the matress below.

"Are you all right?" I shouted as I ran to him, for he was lying quite still and I was afraid the fool might have broken his collarbone.

"Of course I'm all right," he retorted somewhat testily. "Didn't you see how I fell?"

This didn't seem to make sense, but I let it pass.

"Shall I help you up?"

"Certainly not. I'm studying my position. You see, I'm practicing how to fall. Suppose you fell off a wall or out of a tree or something. What would you do?"

"I'd probably break my neck," I told him.

"No, you wouldn't. Not if you fell the way I do. The whole secret of falling is to be absolutely limp. Now, I could fall off that bar even if the mat wasn't there, and all I should get would be a bruise or two."

191

A few days later I was in the swimming pool with
Parsons.

"What would you do if you saw me in difficulties?" he
asked, suddenly. "I mean, seriously, suppose you saw a
man or a woman struggling in the water somewhere. What
would you do?"

"You mean that old life-saving stuff?" I said. "First,
you have to hit the guy to make him unconscious and dis-
courage him from dragging you under. Then you tow him
to shore by the hair and kneel on his chest until he begins
breathing again."

"Ever tried to knock someone out that way?" Parsons
persisted.

Of course, Parsons was quite right. It would be difficult.
Then he went on to tell me that you should deliberately
submerge the drowning person if necessary. He showed me
how to support an unconscious man so that the mouth and
nose remain above water. Finally, he gave me a demonstration of artificial respiration.

For years after we had both left college—I because I had
graduated, and Parsons because he had sounded a false fire
alarm as an experiment—I used to think about him once in
a while. I knew that, like myself, he was working in New
York, and I wondered if he still acted the same way.

One day I ran into him in the Municipal Building. We
made the usual remarks for such an occasion and got into
an elevator together. The car started upward. I called out
my floor number and turned to ask Parsons where he wanted
to get off. He was studying the sides of the elevator intently.

"What are you looking at?" I asked.

"Yes," said Parsons. "That's the only thing to do."

He stopped talking to himself and addressed me.

"I suppose you know these elevators are the most un-
reliable in the city."

"I know some people think so," I replied.

"Well, haven't you ever considered what you would do if
the car was out of control? Let's see. We're at the seven-

teenth floor. Suppose the car fell from here to the ground floor right now. What would you do?"

The elevators in the Municipal Building are of open design. There are eight cars to each bank of elevators, and you can see through all of the eight shafts. My eyes instinctively turned downward. I could see far down into the pit of an adjoining shaft.

"I'm afraid there's nothing you could do about it," I remarked, feeling slightly sick at the thought.

"Nonsense," said Parsons, and he explained how it would be possible to hang on to the crossbar halfway up the side of the car and draw up your feet so that when the floor of the car hit the bottom of the shaft your legs would not be broken.

"Of course," he admitted, generously, "I realize that your fingers would be crushed if the side of the car buckled, but it would be worth taking a chance on that."

By this time we had both passed our floors. I decided to get out and walk down the stairs. To my annoyance, he accompanied me. As I started down the first flight, he laid a warning hand on my arm.

"Better keep close to the handrail," he urged. "Then you can always save yourself if you miss your footing."

I saw Parsons from time to time afterward. Once we rode in a taxicab together. He sat slouched very low in the seat (to avoid cracking his head against the roof in the event of a collision) and he knew exactly what he would do if the cab turned over. I couldn't follow his explanation.

On another occasion, in the subway, Parsons showed me how to open the door of a train from the outside by means of a gadget which is used by the guards in an emergency and which is never noticed by the average passenger.

The last time I saw Parsons I was walking down Madison Avenue when I suddenly noticed him stepping off the curb on the opposite side of the street. I shouted to him—somewhat unnecessarily, for he was crossing in my direction, keeping a wary eye on the traffic.

Parsons looked around at the sound of his name and spotted me. He waved his hand in recognition and hurried toward me. At the same instant I saw that a taxicab was hurrying toward Parsons. Parsons realized his danger simultaneously, but he stood quite still as the cab bore down on him. There was an alarming squeal of brakes. Parsons bent his knees a little.

I knew what Parsons was planning to do. He was going to imitate the stunt men in Hollywood who are called upon when a street accident is being portrayed. The camera shows an automobile on the point of striking a pedestrian, and the picture is not faked. At the vital moment, however, the stunt man vaults onto the hood of the oncoming car. Parsons had practiced this feat with the help of his friends, so I was not unduly alarmed for his safety.

I watched closely and saw that he sprang into the air with his legs apart when the taxicab was within a few feet of him. To my dismay, however, the cab stopped dead almost immediately.

Instead of landing astride its hood, Parsons fell down in the roadway a few inches in front of the radiator. It was what aviators call a three-point landing and looked extremely painful.

"Damn those hydraulic brakes!" he said, as the taxi-driver and I picked him up.

PROFESSOR'S OFFICE HOUR

by

Morris Bishop

"PROFESSOR, I came to see you about Roswell. . . Oh, I am Mrs. Norton, Roswell's mother. I was so anxious to meet you, because Roswell admires you so much. He was always writing about you in his letters, telling about how interesting you make the work, and how enjoyable your classes are. And so it was such a shock to me to get the mid-term report and to find that he was marked only a D minus."

"Roswell Norton. Let me look a moment. . . I see he was absent eight times this term, and he got a D and an F on his quizzes, and his classwork averages a low D."

"That is what is so dreadful to me. I assure you that report almost stunned me, and I had to go to bed for two days. Roswell always did so well in high school, and they were so proud of him. And as for his absences, Roswell always had a delicate throat, and I have taught him never to take foolish chances in bad weather. For after all, health is really the most important thing, don't you think so?"

"Why, yes, of course—"

"And I want him to be a great surgeon some day, and I know you can't get into the Medical School unless you have good marks. Roswell has very definite leanings toward medicine. He dissected a frog when he was only twelve years old; I remember he had it spread all over the laundry—ugh! And so when I got this terrible report, I decided to sacrifice everything and come down here and help him in every way a boy's mother can. Roswell is my only child, and my own life seems of no importance at all compared to his success."

195

"That's very creditable, I'm sure."

"And so, Professor—or should I say Doctor? I'm afraid you'll think me very ignorant—I shut up my house and came right down here, and I've taken a little furnished apartment near the campus gate. And I've brought down some of Roswell's favorite books and pictures, so that it will seem a little like home to him. And I've bought a little portable radio, so we can listen together to some of the programs we love to listen to together; you know, really good music, Lawrence Tibbett and all that; Roswell loves good music, and evidently at the fraternity they tune in on nothing but jazz, jazz, jazz all the time. I don't think the fraternities are entirely a good influence, do you, Doctor? I mean, they're sort of cheap and coarsening. And Roswell is so young; he's only nineteen, and of course he's very impressionable. He looks up so to the older boys; he seems to think they're a fine lot of boys, but I must say . . .

"Well, anyway, I think it's the bad influence of the fraternity that has pulled down his scholarship. Dances, you know, till all hours of the night. And some of these girls they have to dances seem to me definitely cheap. And Roswell is so naturally friendly, and takes everything at its face value. I suppose these 'crushes,' as we used to call them in my day, are all right, but Roswell is too young to have any real discrimination about people.

"But I think you can be sure that his work will improve now. I get him a nice little dinner every night, the things he likes, in our little apartment, and then I supervise his study. In the fraternities, you know, everything is so noisy, and they're always skylarking around, and it isn't conducive to real study. I often think the trouble with Roswell is he just doesn't know how to study. So now we just sit side by side on the davenport and he studies, unless, of course, there is something *really* good coming over the radio. So I am sure, dear Professor, that you will notice a great improvement in his work from now on. Poor Roswell! I'm afraid he rather regrets his fraternity and all their rowdiness and horseplay sometimes. But of course boys of that age are naturally self-centred, and he doesn't realize the sacrifice I am making, giving up my home and all my friends and everything. But I don't mean to complain, because Roswell's success and happiness is the most important thing in the world to me. Still, I do think it would be a good thing for him just to realize in an indirect sort of way what mothers do for their boys without asking any return but— but love. And I was wondering if—but I'm afraid you will think me very forward—"

"Oh, I am sure, Mrs. Norton—"

"Well, I know how Roswell respects and admires you, and I was wondering if once in a while you couldn't just talk to the class, in a general sort of way, of course, about— well, about how important it is to—to love your—"

"There, there, Mrs. Norton; there, there. Now, don't worry about Roswell; I'm quite certain that his marks are going to be considerably better."

DEAR MARGERY
by
Frances Warfield

MY pretty twenty-year-old cousin from the West was in town for only a few hours before her boat sailed. My lively and lovely young Cousin Margery, to whom I wish all ill fortune.

I drove in from Montclair in the early afternoon and met her train. Though I had not seen her in many years, I expressed no astonishment that she had grown up. She looked very beautiful, but I paid her no compliments, because they would imply that I remembered her as an unpromising little mutt in a middy blouse.

I accepted her at once as an individual in her own right, as a contemporary. I gave no indication of knowing that this was to be her first trip abroad. I let her make her own harebrained arrangements about baggage and laughed spontaneously when she showed me her passport picture. I sat tolerantly smoking while she bought an outlandish, rather nautical, outfit to wear on board ship. When she had finished shopping, I suggested cocktails as a matter of course, not as a treat. I get along awfully well with younger people, you see, and the secret of it is that I never patronize them. I am never guilty of such superiority formulas as "What can *you* know about such things, at your age?" As a matter of fact, I detest formulas of all kinds. If I catch myself in any formularized pattern of behavior or thought, I run like an indignant rabbit to the opposite extreme. That's why I hope Heaven will punish Margery, because now, of course, I'll spend the rest of my life squirming every time I hear a castanet.

Dear Margery. We liked each other immensely. As we

sat comfortably over our Martinis, she said, with a flattering generosity rather rare at her age, that she thought I was
much too attractive to spend all my life cooped up with
a husband and three children. Didn't I ever feel like breaking out with a yell and going travelling, she asked. I said
I had had all I wanted of travelling *per se*, but that there
were plenty of places I'd love to go and live for a while.
Tropical places especially, where life was lax and lavish
and lazy. Where there were bright colors and hot sun and
lots and lots of slow, insidious music. I spoke with animation. Mexico, Rio de Janeiro . . . Margery began to hum
"Carioca."

"Exactly," I said, smiling. In my mind's eye I saw, as
I always see when I hear any kind of Spanish dance music
at all, a vision of myself in swirling skirts, dancing with
exquisite grace, following some faultless, whirling partner
through endless intricate steps. The vision makes me fairly
bite my nails with frustration, because I've always been a
good dancer and I know perfectly well that if I only had a
husband who was the least bit of a gigolo as well as a
thoroughly sound businessman, I could do any of the complicated things you see in night clubs and do them mar-
velously well. I said nothing of this to Margery, but I
leaned back, sipping my cocktail, indulging the vision for
a moment.

Margery put a hand on my arm. "I'll tell you. Why
don't you just leave Cousin Ed and the kids for a few months
and go off high, wide, and handsome? Have yourself a
a time?" Her pretty eyes were warm with interest. She
gave my arm an affectionate squeeze.

Well, would you have bridled like a Jersey matron, even
if you were one, and briskly changed the subject to Tommy's
tonsils? Would you have pulled down your mouth and
replied, "When you are my age, my dear child, you will
know that security is more comfortable than fun"? You
know I have no patience with the idea that one should talk
down to younger people. I laughed and said, "Between

you and me, Margery, I often think of it." I said it lightly, jokingly, and we agreed that we would have time for another cocktail before starting to the pier.

"To the larger life!" Margery said gaily, and we drank a toast.

We were joking, and I can prove it to you, because I went on then to remark, mock sadly, that it was not so much a matter of larger life as of larger opportunities. For example, I had recently run across an old beau, and we had had one of those wistful conversations in which two people exchange stories of the past ten years and find that they have left much to be desired. He had stared at me moodily, his chin in his hand—"I know where I made MY mistake. . . ." My heart had fluttered as I waited for him to say that I was all that had ever mattered, to propose that we abandon our families and fly together. What he had said was, "It may surprise you, but I know darned well that I'd be happier today if I'd only had the patience to learn to play the piano." I told Margery this story with spirited, exaggerated ruefulness. If I'd been in earnest about the whole conversation, I never would have told her a story in which the joke was on myself, would I?

Margery laughed delightedly. "They all do, you know. Haven't you found that out?"

"They all do what?"

"All married men in their thirties think they'd be happy if they could only play the piano really well. At that age, they're just realizing that they're not going to be great men after all. They think that if they could play the piano, they could make enough noise to forget it."

The easy dogmatism of youth. Nevertheless, I looked at Margery appreciatively. With sudden disloyal glee, I recalled that I had heard my own husband say that he wished his parents had stood over him and forced him to practice when he was a kid.

"Now that you mention it," I began, decidedly amused.

"Oh, I've tested it out. I like to get a theory like that

and then experiment to find out if it works. I've been
trying that one on the married men I meet. I lead up to
it by playing something myself, 'Nola' or some other complicated thing. It makes their yearnings crop out like a
rash. The funny part is that each one thinks he's the only
one."

Together we laughed at men—all exactly alike, each
thinking himself unique. We laughed merrily. Right here
I must say that Margery had had two strong cocktails and
that she can hardly be very accustomed to drinking. It's
not the point, but if it hadn't been for the cocktails, I think
she would not have made her next statement.

"Married women are all alike, too," she told me. "In
their thirties, they all dream of having just one adventure
before it's too late."

I watched her finish her drink and silently, grimly,
I addressed God as one adult to another, "If there is an
ounce of justice in the universe, she will swallow—that—
olive—and—*choke to death!*"

Margery set down her glass, and our eyes met. Hers
were so candid that I reproached myself for having mis-
judged her for the moment. Naturally, I realized, she had
accepted the idea of my going off and having a fling for the
joke that it was and had immediately forgotten it. Smiling
gently at her, I decided that for once I had better assert the
superiority of my years and set her right. I opened my
mouth to tell her that that was an amusing generality but
that, like most generalities, it was entirely untrue. My
mouth remained open.

"They all think, in their secret souls," Margery added,
with a giggle, "that if they had a chance, they'd turn out
to be perfectly knockout dancers."

WEDDING BREAKFAST
by
Hannah Lees

THERE was to be a wedding in the afternoon, the wedding of a very close friend, so I came down to breakfast that morning feeling somewhat dewy.

"I told her," I said gently, "that with all the noise of the caterers and florists at their apartment, she must just come here and rest until time for the wedding. I think I'll give her luncheon and then read her to sleep. Wouldn't you?"

Jonas said he should think she would have too much to do to waste her wedding day being read to.

"That's just it," I explained patiently. "She must get away from it all. She must leave all the last-minute fuss for someone else and just relax. She'll probably want to cry. I did, I remember. I cried for about an hour."

"Did you?" asked Jonas.

"Yes," I said, "I did, and she rubbed my head with cologne and told me how nice you were and how much I was going to like you."

"I remember now," said Jonas, his voice getting dreamy. "You were away all that day, weren't you? I remember wishing at lunchtime that you were there. We had the most marvellous lunch; mutton chops grilled on pineapple and topped with bacon, and asparagus with Hollandaise, and I think strawberries."

"I don't remember what I had for lunch that day," I said. "I don't believe I ate any."

"Oh, yes, you did," said Jonas, his memory still holding, "because after the ceremony, Susie was telling me about it. She said the reason you looked so lovely and rested was that you had had a nice lunch and nap. You had creamed sweetbreads and orange Charlotte. I remember because when she told me, I thought how much better ours had been and that you really should have stayed home."

"That was sweet of you," I said. "As a matter of fact, I never looked worse in my life. I looked like an old woman. I remember thinking when I put on my veil that it was a good thing I was wearing one."

"Darling, you looked lovely," said Jonas. I felt he was finally getting the wedding spirit. I reached over and gently patted his hand.

"I remember it all perfectly," he went on. "You looked so calm and sort of gay. I remember thinking how glad I was you weren't one of those languishing brides, and how I wanted to laugh when you started on your second lobster cutlet."

A wife can stand just so much misrepresentation. "Jonas, you're absolutely crazy," I said. "I hardly touched my cutlet. I know because I remember thinking what a shame it was I couldn't eat, because I probably wouldn't have lobster very often in the future."

"But you were wrong, weren't you?" said Jonas smugly. "You've had it any number of times. Think of Cape Cod last summer. You had three that time."

I could see things were rapidly getting out of control.

"You're such a gourmet, dear," I said sweetly. "You'll have to help me. What would be nice to give Susie for lunch? Something light, you know, but tempting."

"Why don't you give her mutton chops grilled on pineapple?" said Jonas. "They're tempting enough. I don't believe I've had one since the wedding." There was a light in his eye I hadn't seen for a long time.

"I'll tell you what," he went on. "You have mutton chops on pineapple, and I'll leave the office early and come home for lunch. Then I can help you amuse Susie till time for her to dress. That will be much better than reading.

Reading would probably give her the jitters. What do you say?"

"I'm afraid mutton chops would be a trifle heavy," I said, gazing out the window over his shoulder. "I think I'll have creamed sweetbreads and orange Charlotte. That won't be quite enough lunch for you, will it, dear?"

LUNCH HOUR

by

Margaret Ford

"WHAT did Herbert say after you and Ed dropped me last night, May?"

"Oh, he said the eats were good and the music was swell and everythin'."

"I mean, did he say anythin' about me?"

"Yeah, I guess he did."

"I was just wondering, see, because I thought he was pretty cute."

"Herbie's all right."

"What I mean is, I was wonderin' what he said, see?"

"Oh, he said he had a swell time. He's crazy about Chinese food, anyway."

"I am, too. I had a swell time. I was tellin' Herbie I was crazy about Chinese food."

"Chinese food is all right, but you get sick of it."

"Is that what he said?"

"Who?"

"Herbie."

"That's what I said. I said you get sick of it. I eat just so much, and then I don't want to see another noodle for six months."

"Herbie and I could never get sick of it. We sort of found out that we liked the same things last night. Did he say anything about the way we both liked the same things, May?"

"Herbie? No . . . Oh yeah, I guess he did say something. I forget."

"Well, try and remember, will you please, May? *Try.*"

205

"What do you want to get so excited about? You'd think you never had Chinese food before."

"No. What I mean is, I just wondered if Herbie mentioned me after you dropped me last night. I mean, I wondered what you were talkin' about and everythin'."

"Oh, he was kiddin'. He wants to take me dancin', see? And he knows as well as you do that I go steady with Ed. I mean, the nerve of him datin' me up right in front of Ed!"

"Take you dancin'?"

"Yeah. He's nuts about it. Kept pesterin' me all the way home. Ed calls him the dancin' fool. . . You used to like to dance, Doris. I should think you'd sort of go for Herbie. I mean, he's cute, and tall, and everythin'."

"He was all right, sure, but to tell you the truth, May, he's just not my type, that's all. I mean, I'm funny about a fellow. If he's not just my type, I don't go for him."

AS USUAL

by

Frances Warfield

IT'S true that I was wearing my most feminine dress and
my most frivolous stockings, and the off-the-face hats just
now are preposterous, but just the same I was feeling perfectly well-poised until eight-year-old Janet came into
the living-room to entertain me while I waited for her
mother. She had on shorts and a flannel shirt with a pocket
in it; her hair was cropped close. She planted her bare,
stocky legs wide apart while she looked at me.

"I never wear a hat or stockings at all," she remarked.
"Not in the worst weather. I don't even own any long
stockings."

"The more fool you, then," I snapped soundlessly, my
back bristling at once. I returned her gaze as critically as
possible. "About the shrewdest move you could make," I
thought, "would be to cover up those legs of yours. They're
far too husky for a girl, in case you don't know it." Aloud,
I said, "Don't you ever catch cold?"

"Of course not," she said. "Of course I don't catch
cold. I'm very, very healthy all the year round."

Unhappily, I coughed just then. "Hunh—never heard
that fragility has charm, have you?" I thought, meeting her
eye with deep antagonism. "Never heard of Camille, eh?
Never even heard of Mimi in 'La Boheme,' I bet. Haven't
got the faintest hunch that the male responds instantly and
satisfactorily to physical weakness in the female?" "That's
awfully nice," I said.

Janet nodded. "And I wear shorts *all* the time now,"
she told me, "instead of just part of the time. Mother

promised me that I don't ever have to wear skirts if I don't want to."

"At your age," I said, in a sour voice, "I used to wear pink and blue dotted-swiss dresses with ruffles over the shoulders and sashes to match the bows in my hair."

"Hair ribbons?" she repeated, looking lofty.

"Yes, hair ribbons," I said. "I used to have very pretty ones." To myself, I said, sulkily, "And I was about one thousand times prettier than you are, my dear. In fact, I was considered a beautiful child. Even now, I'm holding my own remarkably well. Furthermore, if you wanted to see somebody you'll never be able to hold a candle to as long as you live, you should have seen me ten years ago." I took out my compact and powdered my chin out of bravado. "I had a white muff trimmed with ermine tails," I said to Janet, "and a pair of shoes with white kid tops and pearl buttons."

"Goodness!" she said. "Didn't you ever play any games? Didn't you ever play any hockey ball?"

"No," I said, adding silently, "And that's why I haven't any bulging muscles in my arms, like you'll have, see? And that's why my nose has never been broken and I haven't any scars from cuts where stitches had to be taken, like you'll probably have. So there, my fine little Amazon. So there." I was struggling bitterly to keep up my end, but actually I was completely cowed. "I'm afraid I wasn't the least bit athletic, Janet," I apologized.

She corrected me quickly. "Everybody calls me Jiggs."

Squirming, I remembered that I had had an uncle who called me Posy.

Janet was staring at me without admiration. "I guess everything has changed a good deal since you were my age," she said at length, lightly. She stared at me for a long while, and sighed, and was about to give up. Then her mood changed. Her eyes were suddenly bright.

"Want to hear a joke?" she asked, coming closer to my chair. "Why does a chicken cross the road?"

"Let's see," I said, looking baffled. "To meet a friend?"

"No, that's not it." Her eyes snapped with mystery.

"I give up," I said. "Why *does* a chicken cross the road?"

"To get on the other side!" she said, triumphantly. "Did you ever see a banana stand?"

My self-respect poured back over me. "A banana stand?" I repeated, wrinkling my forehead elaborately. "Why, that's impossible. Bananas can't stand."

Janet was dancing up and down with excitement, holding to the arm of my chair. "Yes, they can; yes, they can," she chanted. "A banana stand is where they sell bananas. It's where they sell bananas, see? It's where they sell bananas. Listen, why is a crow?"

"Because!" I said, victoriously.

"No! Be—caw—caw—*caw*—CAW—cause!" she shouted at the top of her lungs. Grinning and exultant, she prodded me heartily in the ribs. I noticed for the first time that she has one very important front tooth missing. I put an arm around her and squeezed her with great affection.

Teeth, too, I reflected, with a lot of sincere satisfaction, are just about the same as they were when I was eight.

LINES FROM BURNS

by

Wolcott Gibbs

FOR some reason, Mr. Ward has never learned how to get up and go away, when he's had enough, without hurting people's feelings. Last Saturday afternoon, for instance, he sat in Mario's for more than three hours while those embattled encyclopedias, Miss Smiley and Mr. Diadem, hounded culture through the ages. They were nicely matched. Miss Smiley had an imposing memory and a voice like a knife; Mr. Diadem used the highly effective technique of making the most improbable statement and then sticking to it, ignoring any proof advanced by the opposition. This was peculiarly maddening to Miss Smiley, who liked to think she preferred logic to force.

"Everybody knows," said Mr. Diadem in one minor skirmish, "that O. Henry died in prison."

"Why, that isn't *so*, Scott!" cried Miss Smiley, who knew a great deal about O. Henry, including his real name. "Sydney Porter died in the Chelsea Hotel, or maybe it was the Chatham. Anyway, he said, 'Please put out the light.' You remember that?"

"O. Henry died in jail," said Mr. Diadem firmly, and because it was also part of his theory that there is no getting around specific data, he added, "He died in Joliet Prison on March 8, 1908."

Arbitrarily then, and over the dead bodies of both Miss Smiley and Mr. Porter, he proceeded to a discussion of poetry. The ballad, he said, is the form from which all poetry derives, and "Good King Wencelaus" is the ballad at its best.

"Edna Millay—" began Miss Smiley.

"Listen," said Mr. Diadem, and began to recite "Good King Wenceslaus" with a great deal of expression. Miss Smiley listened reluctantly until he came to the eighth stanza.

" 'Mark my footsteps, my good page,' " said Mr. Diadem.

"It's 'good my page,' " said Miss Smiley. " 'Mark my footsteps, good my page.' "

"Nonsense," said Mr. Diadem:

> " 'Mark my footsteps, my good page,
>   Tread thou in them boldly,
>   Thou shalt find . . .' "

"I *know* it's 'good my page,' " interrupted Miss Smiley, so loudly and desperately that for once Mr. Diadem stooped to what might very loosely be described as argument.

"I sang that song when I was a mere child," he said severely. "Remember it perfectly. The line is 'Mark my footsteps, my good page.' Isn't that right, Ward?"

Mr. Ward had also sung "Wenceslaus" when he was in school.

"Around Christmas," he said vaguely, "I used to sing the page part because my voice hadn't changed."

This being dismissed as irrelevant, Mr. Ward admitted that he didn't exactly remember the line they were talking about.

"Might have been 'Mark my footsteps *well*, my page,' " he suggested.

At this, the wolves came down on him, yelping.

"Ward," cried Mr. Diadem, "haven't you *any* ear at all?"

"Ear?" said Mr. Ward, yawning.

"Yes," said Miss Smiley. "I mean, goodness, nobody but a barbarian could put a weak, snivelling little word like 'well' into a grand old Anglo-Saxon line like that."

"Oh," said Mr. Ward, and relapsed into a rather moody silence.

Miss Smiley and Mr. Diadem applied themselves fero-

ciously to this new pastime. Miss Smiley very definitely
had an ear. It was indeed so acute that occasionally her
life became almost unbearable.

"Nobody knows," she said, "what I go through with
people who can't get the simplest thing straight. I don't
think I know a single person who can quote eight lines
without making at least one mistake."

"Well, I don't know about that," said Mr. Diadem
irritably. "Of course, I don't pretend to be an authority,
but I imagine that I can quote eight lines without much
trouble. You take—well, let's see—you take 'Cynara'."

They took "Cynara," like Richmond.

" 'I have been faithful to thee, Cynara, after my
fashion,' " said Mr. Diadem when he came to that line.

"Oh, my!" wailed Miss Smiley, addressing Mr. Ward.
"Listen to him! That's all I ask, just listen to that criminal.
Imagine 'after' in that lovely, lovely line!"

Mr. Ward appeared to be asleep, but Mr. Diadem
turned quite lavender with fury.

"Well, what is it then?" he demanded.

" '*In* my fashion', of course," said Miss Smiley. "And
really, Scott, it's a wonder they haven't got your fingerprints at Police Headquarters. 'Scott Diadem, wanted for
the murder of Ernest Dowson.' "

"You're crazy!" shouted Mr. Diadem, but Miss Smiley
only looked at him pityingly, slowly shaking her head.

"Poor Scott!" she murmured.

"Poor hell!" said Mr. Diadem. "You're wrong, and I
can prove it. I can't now, of course, but I will as soon as
I can get my hands on a Bartlett."

"Bet you twenty dollars," said Miss Smiley promptly.

"I don't bet when I'm sure," said Mr. Diadem with
dignity. "I don't want to *steal* your money."

"All right, Santa Claus," said Miss Smiley, "but you
still haven't quoted eight lines."

"Certainly I have. I just did."

"That doesn't count—not till it's proved one way or the

other," said Miss Smiley. "How about 'The Village Black-smith'? They say even little children can usually get that one right."

" 'Under the spreading chestnut tree,' " began Mr. Diadem.

" 'Under *a* spreading chestnut tree,' " Miss Smiley corrected sweetly, "but go on, Scott. I guess we just can't count minor inaccuracies. We'll let it go, if you manage to get the general *sense* of the thing."

For a moment, Mr. Diadem couldn't say anything at all, and Mr. Ward, who apparently hadn't really been asleep, leaned across the table.

"I know one worse than any of those," he said. "Of course you both remember a poem called 'Let's Hae a Wee Drap tae Mither'?"

Miss Smiley and Mr. Diadem nodded.

"Then you must remember that famous line, 'A' my life's a gimble wi' auld Hornie'?"

"Too marvellous!" said Miss Smiley.

"Well," said Mr. Ward slowly, "probably you won't believe me, but the other day I heard a man say 'A' my life's a *gamble* wi' auld Hornie.' "

"Imagine doing a thing like that to Bobbie Burns!" said Mr. Diadem.

Mr. Ward got up. Afterward, Miss Smiley remembered that he was grinning like an idiot.

"As a matter of fact," he said, "Burns didn't write that poem."

They looked at him in bewilderment.

"Not Burns?" said Miss Smiley.

"No," said Mr. Ward. "A man called Goethe. Good-bye," he said.

"SHE'S BOY-CRAZY"

by

Margaret Ford

"THE trouble with most girls," said Jane, who was going on fifteen, "is that they let a man see they're crazy about him. That's what Betty does all the time. She's absolutely balmy, and I told her so."

"What does she do?" I asked. Jane put a very large bonbon in her mouth and chewed it vigorously before she replied.

"Gosh, what *doesn't* she do! She falls all over them. Called Stewy up three times last night, and the last time his mother got furious. She won't let him have the roadster until tomorrow, she's so furious. Betty's nuts. She's always putting her feet all over the place. I don't say anything. I just sort of sit and look as if I was thinking of a lot of things I just didn't care to speak of, and pretty soon all the men leave her flat and come over to me. Last night I had five men talking to me at once."

She offered this bit of information for what it was worth. Probably, she continued, she could have had six talking to her, but Betty grabbed the other man and absolutely forced him to dance. He was only about thirteen anyway, so it really didn't matter, but it just went to show.

"That's a thing I'd never do," she said, through another bonbon. "Absolutely grab a man. I mean, I used to do things like that when I was a kid, but it's too—too—"

"Obvious?" I offered.

"N-no, not that. What I mean is, you can *see* through it. Any dumb-bell can see through it. At Bunny's dance, I couldn't go more than three steps without having someone cut in. Well, you couldn't say I absolutely grabbed anyone and *made* them dance with me, could you?"

No, I agreed, you couldn't very well say that. I wanted to know what the formula was.

"Oh, I mean it's sort of hard to explain, but when you're dancing with a man—well, of course, with some of them you talk and with some of them you don't. It depends. If he says something cute about your hair or your figure or something, you just sort of look like this."

She narrowed her eyes and gazed longingly to the right.

"See?" she pointed out. "The man you're dancing with doesn't know it, but you're looking at some smooth man in the stag line, and when you look at him that way, why he'll be right over in a second, don't worry. Of course you can't look too glad when he cuts in. That's what Betty does. She looks all gaga when anyone cuts in."

"What do you do?"

"Oh, I just sort of act—well, I act as if I just couldn't *bear* to leave the one I was dancing with. Sometimes I give his hand a little squeeze, only not *too* much, and then when I start dancing with the other one, I just act relieved, but I don't *say* anything. That's very important. Betty always says, 'Oh, I'm *so* glad you cut in!' or something, and of course stories like that get back and it's *very* bad. Once I knew an older man," she observed thoughtfully, "who was crazy about me. He smoked a pipe, but he was too short. He's in Harvard now."

She was quiet for a moment.

"I don't think a man respects a girl that pets *all* the time," she said finally. "I think he gets sick of it. I keep telling Betty that, but she's so dumb. Well," she sighed, "here goes my last piece of candy. I'm a nut to eat this when I'm dieting, but you know how it is."

I said I knew how it was, and asked if she and Betty wouldn't like to have tea with me some day soon.

"It would be swell," she said. "The Ritz has the smoothest violinist. But I wish you wouldn't ask Betty. She absolutely makes me nervous, she's so boy-crazy."

CATHERINE'S FIRST PLAY

by
Frances Warfield

YOU know, of course, that hearts break at nine. But can you imagine what luck it would be to discover, at nine, that you can cure heartbreak by writing it out? My niece, Catherine, wrote a play last evening. Partly because in the school play, "The Triumph of the Vitamins," she had the important role of Carrie Carrot, partly because recently she was taken to her first marionette show, and surely because her heart was aching, she wrote a play.

Catherine is just nine, and fierce with dignity. When she came in, pale and slowly, and dropped her crepe-paper favors on the table without a word, I knew that something had gone very wrong at the party.

"Have any fun?" I asked.

"It was all right," she said.

"Who was there?"

"Oh. Everybody."

"Charlie?" Charlie Taylor is her beau.

"Naturally."

She gave a distasteful twitch to her party dress, which she passionately loves, and went to the piano and played "The Jolly Farmer" straight through, frowning. It happens that "The Jolly Farmer" is still the only piece she can play straight through without the music. I said cheerfully that I thought she played it very well indeed, and she swung off the piano stool. "I hate that piece," she said in a low voice. "I can't stand it, it's so silly. It's very childish and silly." She was close to tears. She wandered all around the room dispairingly, giving a furious spin to the telephone dial in passing. She couldn't say what had happened to hurt her feelings at the party, and it was no use to ask her. Finally she picked up the morning newspaper and started toward her room. She is a great newspaper reader.

"Ready for bed?" I asked.

She nodded without turning around, and I let her go. Nine has a right to sorrow.

It was a good while later, on my way to her room, that I found her play. For several months now she has been communicating with us in writing, from time to time, usually leaving these messages conspicuously on the hall table. Her play was like this:

THE DOLLS

Act 1—The dolls were in the living room, talking.

Act 2—The dolls were in the dressing room, chatting.

Act 3—One of the dolls got sick and upset her stomach.

Act 4—A boy doll peeked through the keyhole, and laughed.

As I hurried down the hall to her room, I heard her talking to herself, in a monotone. I found her lying in bed, smiling, repeating "Fiorello, Fiorello, Fiorello," absorbedly, as if she were casting a spell. I tucked in her covers, taking the opportunity to make sure that her forehead was cool. Just to be on the safe side, I got her a pill and a glass of water, which she accepted without comment.

"Fiorello," she said, with a giggle. "That's a funny name."

Calm and restored, she sat in bed drinking the water, and I watched her enviously. She had written it out, do you see? She had written it out and now it didn't matter any more. The harsh blow of Nature to her pride, to her new nine-year maturity, was no longer real. It had simply happened to a doll in a play. I fixed her covers again and said I guessed it was time to put out her light and raise the window.

She waved a hand comfortably. "Okey, Fiorello!" she said.

THE NEW BABY

by

Parke Cummings

"WELL, well, well, so here's the little man. Now isn't he cute? Quite a baby, I'll say! Yes, sir, quite a baby. He's—well, he's certainly quite a baby. . . Only two months old, eh? He's—ah—he's certainly a big baby for that age, isn't he? Look at his nose. That's quite a nose. Yep, that's a cute nose. Say, he's a good-looking baby, all right. A darn good-looking baby, that's what he is. Yes sir. We won't wake him up, will we?

"Yes, his eyes are a lot like yours. They've got the same—well, they certainly look a lot like yours. Hum—ah—say, he's some baby, isn't he? I suppose he walks a little. . . What? . . . Not until they're more than a year? Oh, I didn't know that. Well, then, of course, you couldn't expect him to walk yet a while. O course not.

"Yep, he's really an unusually good-looking baby. He's one of the best-looking babies I ever saw. Because—well, he just is. Don't you think so? . . . No, honest, I'm not just trying to be polite. I really mean it. If I didn't think so I'd come right out and say it. . . Oh, Yes! . . . Of course, he wouldn't be talking yet. They don't talk till they're five, do they? . . . Oh, as soon as that? Well, well. That's something I didn't know.

"Well, well, well. Yes, sir. Some cute baby. You don't often see babies like that. There's something about him that's different. No doubt about it. No, there isn't any doubt about it. Absolutely not. . . What? . . . Yes, he has got a pretty mouth, hasn't he? No doubt about it. A darn cute mouth. It's—well, it's sure cute. As cute as they come. Yep. Well, I never thought I'd be seeing this

218

baby so soon. Yes, I did. I mean—well, I just can't get
used to it. No, I just can't get used to it. I suppose we
ought to leave him; we might wake him up. But he sure is
some baby. I'll tell the world . . . say, Anne, do you think
I could have a drink of water?"

THE BOOK LOVER

by

Marjorie Henderson

OH, hello there, Mr. Smith! I just barged over to return that book you lent me. Thanks ever so much. It was darling of you. Everybody says I'm awfully lucky to have you lend me a book out of your liberry, because it's a very wonderful liberry and you are very particular about who you lend your books to.

And honestly, I thought it was the cutest story! So sort of quaint and everything. The only trouble is you'll have to tell me what happened at the end, because the last hundred pages are all stuck together.

You see, the other night I had it propped up on the edge of the tub while I was taking a bath, which is practically the only time a girl has to read these days, what with one thing and another. And when I reached for the soap, all of a sudden, Ploppo! The book skidded right into the tub. The cover just simply ran all over the place, and there I sat with bright purple legs! It was perfectly harrowing, Mr. Smith; really you have no idea.

But anyways, I'm terribly sorry I got your book so crummy looking, and I would have simply curled up at the edges over the whole episode, if it hadn't been that it was such a sort of old and crummy-looking book to begin with.

Two hundred years old? My goodness, I certainly am relieved! I would of just died if I'd gone and ruined a new one for you!

Well, so long, Mr. Smith, and thanks ever so much. I certainly do appreciate you lending it to me, 'cause I'm just simply cuckoo about good books, I honestly am!

DUCK HUNTER'S HONEYMOON

by

Ray Trullinger

"WAKE up, baby. Open up those big blue eyes and look at the swell breakfast your brand-new husband cooked for you. Hey! you gotta get up. What's the big idea, rolling over like that? It is not the middle of the night! It's four a. m. and high time we got out of this shack and got going, if we're going to get any duck hunting. Come on, hit the deck like a good girl. There now. Take a little nip of this black coffee before you start to dress. Now don't make any wisecracks about that coffee. Certainly it's strong, but I didn't make it with tar as you just hinted. That's good coffee. It'll stiffen up your backbone. Oh, don't be so touchy. Certainly you've got backbone—lots of it. I just meant that the coffee would do you good.

"No dear, put on that woolen underwear I bought you. You'll freeze to death in that silly little silk gadget. Well, suppose it does tickle. Wouldn't you rather be tickled to death than freeze to death? All right then, I'm not going to argue about it with you. Wear whatever you want, but don't tell me that I didn't take the trouble to warn you.

"Come on, baby, let's not fight. Let's get started over to the blind. It'll be daylight before we know it and we've got to be all set for the morning flight when it starts. It's a mile over there. Well, for Heaven's sake, a mile isn't far.

"Well, here's the blind, dear. Wait until I find the flashlight. There now. Watch it! Don't slip! Sit down for a minute and hold on to the dog while the old man slaps out the decoys and pegs Hortense out where she'll do the most good. Yes, I know the seat's frosty and cold, but you won't mind—it'll melt as soon as you sit on it awhile. Water in the bottom of the box? Yes, there usually is. Leaks a little. I'll bale her out as soon as—well, stand on the seat a minute until I go put the decoys out. . .

"Here's Papa back again. Miss me while I was gone? What do you mean, my breath reeks of rum? I haven't had a drink of rum since the dawn of the Noble Experiment. Oh—that. That wasn't rum, baby. Certainly not. That was rye. Well, how did I know you wanted some? Make your wants known after this. Besides, I only brought a quart and it's got to last all day. Honey, please don't poke Papa in the ribs with your gun like that. Yes, dear, I know it isn't loaded but there've been so many people mussed up by unloaded guns that—no, dear, the guns were really loaded but they didn't know it. Well now, let's not go into technical discussion about it. Let's let the matter drop. That's right, stand your shotgun up in the corner of the box until shooting time and—Oop, too bad! Never mind, Hubby will wipe the mud off for you. There now, the gun's all spick and span again. Isn't it a little beauty? Papa paid one hundred and sixty bucks for it.

"What do you mean, you'd rather have an electric washer? What good is an electric washing machine? Well— maybe the old Hubby will buy you one at that. How much do they cost? A hundred dollars! Good Heavens, honey, that's a lot of dough! Wouldn't you rather have a nice Springfield sporter instead? What could you do with it?— now isn't that just like a woman! Tell you what let's do, honey. Let's compromise. I'll get you a nice Springfield and have Griffin and Howe doll it up and in addition to that I'll get you a swell washboard instead of a washing machine. How will that be?

"Darling, why must you wiggle and squirm like that? And do stop scratching yourself! When you move around in a blind all the time you are liable to scare incoming birds. Well, suppose you did pick up a couple of fleas from the dog. The dog couldn't help it, could she? Don't be so fussy!

Anybody would think that you had been assailed by a herd of vampire bats.

"Look!—here comes three blackducks now. Don't move. Don't mo—now what do you suppose made them flare off like that? They were coming right in so nicely, too. Oh, I see—you just pulled your hanky out to blow your nose. Oh, well.

"Don't shoot at that, dear. Don't—oh, hell! Certainly, you killed him. Yes, that was a swell shot, honey. Oh, no, darling, we'll not pick him up. We'll let the tide carry away the evidence of your crime. A duck? No, sweet, that wasn't a duck. That was a seagull. Game wardens get sore when you include a couple of seagulls in your day's bag. Besides, they're not good to eat. No, dear, the seagulls—not the game wardens.

"Here comes another blackduck. Don't move. Keep quiet. There now, how was that for a shot? And maybe you think Gyp wasn't right out there to retrieve him as soon as that duck hit the water. Boy!

"Now don't abuse Gyp just because she shook a little water on you. The dog has to dry herself, doesn't she? Yea, I know there was a teeny little bit of mud with it, too, but after all you needn't act as though it was the Johnstown flood. You can't train an Irish water spaniel to use a Turkish towel every time it gets itself wet. Oh, she did not pick on you. She just happened to shake herself on your side, that's all. Get down, baby, here comes a whole raft of broadbills and they might swing in. Yep, here they come in. Don't move until I give you the word. You shoot the cripples, honey. All set? Wow! Two with the first pipe and there's another with the second. There's still another cripple down. Shoot him before he gets away. Shoot him! Look out for Hortense! Don't shoot poor Hortense! Oh! Look what you've done. You've blasted poor Hortense. Look at her. I would rather have had you shoot your own grandmother than poor Hortense. She was the best call duck in seven states. Now look at her. Oh, sure you're sorry. I know how sorry you are, all right. What do you mean you couldn't tell 'em apart. Does a mallard look like a broadbill? Oh, it does, does it? I suppose broadbills swim around with a collar around their necks. No, I'm going to pick up and go home. This is a hell of a honeymoon. Wish now that I had taken you to Niagara Falls. Certainly, I'm grouchy. Who wouldn't be. It was just plain murder, that's what it was. Where do you see any ducks flying? I don't see anything coming this way. I'm not blind! All right, I won't shoot. You're so good at potting call ducks, let's see you tag one of those babies. No, I won't shoot. They're all yours. Why, that was fine, baby. I'm proud of you. Couldn't have done any better myself! Certainly, you're thrilled. Nothing so cheering as a good shot. I told you all along you'd like duck shooting. You'd really like to stay down for the rest of the week? Come on, now, you're not trying to kid the old man, are you? You really get a kick out of duck shooting? And you want to do more of it? Baby, you're not as dumb as—or rather I meant to say that this marriage is going to be a success. Get down! Here comes a pair of blacks! Ready! Ready! Don't miss them!''

SECRET SOCIETY

by

Aleen Wetstein

OH, I've just been initiated into the duckiest secret society! Like a fraternity, only there aren't any men. Just girls, but you can bring men to the dances. And you ought to see how cute the ritual is.

You can't see it unless you are being initiated though, because it's all a secret; but if only I could tell you about it. I can't, of course, because you have to take a vow not to tell.

Anyhow, you should have seen me in a long white angel robe kneeling before the Aurora—the Aurora is Mabel Cook, only they call her the Aurora in the ritual—making vows right and left. Don't let on you know, but all the girls stand around chanting in white angel robes, all holding sparklers, like the Fourth of July, burning in the dark.

Well, I never was so impressed and—yes, inspired. And just when everyone was bleating about star dust and moon dust and golden chalices, Pauline Mervis—you know how many tons she weighs—comes tripping down the center and falls up the shrine.

Honest! She was supposed to be a glow-worm. I don't know how I ever kept from howling, but I only let out a little chirp or two. I almost strangled but it was worth it.

They have harp music, too; only, personally, I prefer a lute. There's nothing like a lute. In Ernie Jenkin's fraternity's ritual they have a bassoon. I think that's cute, too, but terribly elemental. I wish after this we'd have a lute and a cymbal. I can play a cymbal myself.

Let's see what else. Oh, when I walked in they held a silver broom and a gold blunderbuss over my head. The gold blunderbuss stands for how we fight for our visions, and the silver broom is terribly significant, too—something about sweeping something. Or was it a silver blunderbuss and a gold broom?

That's all I can think of right now. But it'll come to me. . . Oh, and once little Lyndia Peck popped up and said, "I am Womanhood." I nearly split a lung.

I do wish I could talk about it. But it's a secret society, and you know what that means. Ernie Jenkin says the secret of every secret-society ritual is that it is so much like every other ritual that it doesn't matter if you keep it a secret or not. But Ernie Jenkin is so cynical.

As far as I'm concerned I'm simply awed to pieces, and I'm not going to mention it even to myself.

ANCHORS AWAY
by
Doug Welch

WELL, here we are, Joe. Bring on your briny deep. Yo, ho, and a dead man's chest. Pass the grog, shipmates. The glass is a-fallin' fast and she's a-goin' ter blow. Oh, blow the man down—oh, blow the man down. That's the way it makes me feel, Joe. The salt air will do it every time. Well, how do you like our outfits? The admiral and his lady, eh? Not bad, what? . . . No, they didn't cost much. We only spent about a hundred and twenty-five dollars. The way I told Stella, if Joe and Madge are nice enough to invite us to spend our vacation on their yacht— why, the least we can do is to look the part. You wouldn't want me running up the mainmast in a three-button suit, Joe, or have Stella fighting to keep her dresses below her knees. Or maybe you would, you sly old rascal. . . Ha-ha. I'll bet he would, eh, Stella?

Well, bring on the boat. We're dying to see it. . . Where? Down there? That big two-decker with the sporty stack? Say, fella, why didn't you tell us? . . . Yoo, hoo, Stella! Take a look. It's practically the Mauretania! . . . What's that, Joe? . . . Oh, not the big one. Which one? I can't quite make it out from here. You don't mean that little one beside it? The one with the small sort of sail? . . . Oh, I see. . . Well—well, it's a very trim little craft, I must say. . . It's trim, don't you think, Stella? . . . Stella says yes.

I'll bet she cuts through the water like nobody's business, Joe. . . Four knots! Is that a fact! Well, that's faster than walking and a whole lot more restful, eh, Stella? . . . No, don't worry about that, Joe. Stella and I much prefer small boats to large boats, particularly when they look so seaworthy. She looks pretty long when you get up close to her. About fifty feet, I'd guess. . . Only twenty-eight, eh? Well, you'd never know it, Joe. She certainly looks roomy.

A trim little job all around, isn't she, Stella? . . . Stella says yes. Stella's so enthusiastic.

So this is the cabin, eh? . . . Ouch! wow! I just caught my head on the roof. . . There isn't a lot of clearance in here, is there, Joe? . . . Never mind. I'll get used to that. Give me four hours aboard and I'll be ducking in and out of here like a cat. . . All you've got to do is remember to keep your head down, eh, Joe? Down around your knees. Ha-ha. I'm only kidding, Joe. It really is quite roomy, lengthwise.

I suppose this door goes to our cabin? . . . Oh, the engine room. . . You mean, we sleep in here too. You mean, Stella and I have this bunk and you and Madge have that bunk. . . Well, isn't this going to be cozy? It's sort of collegiate. I remember once, going up to the Harvard game, three of us crept into an upper berth. Well, I guess we can manage. It really is a pretty wide bunk. All of three feet, I'd say. . . You'll have to turn when I turn, Stella. Three long blasts and one short blast means turn from your starboard side to your port side. . . Ha-ha! Stella is laughing. She thinks it's funny.

What's this sticking up out of the floor, Joe? . . . It's the keel, eh? . . . Look, Stella, this will keel you. Ha-ha.

Where has she gone? I guess she's gone on deck for a little air. . . No, I didn't think she looked grim. What makes you think she looked grim, Joe?

No, she's going to have a hell of a good time. So am I, Joe. But, listen, Joe. Don't you and Madge feel that you have to keep us out the full two weeks. Any time you want to turn ashore, you do it. You know how Stella and I are. We don't want to monopolize you.

"DON'T SLIP, DARLING"

by
Ray Trullinger

NOW, what's the matter? Hurt you? Well, darling, how many times have I told you not to walk right on my heels when we're going through brush? Of course, you got smacked in the face; branches have a habit of snapping backwards; it's a law of Nature. Keep about ten feet behind me when I'm breaking trail and the naughty limbs won't swat you. I'm not sarcastic. Just sensible. Don't use your rod as a sort of alpenstock either, dear. Rods are made to fish with—not for pole vaulting purposes.

Where you going now? Come here! What funny looking animal? Hey! Come away from that porcupine! Judas Priest, if you pat that critter you'll be picking splinters out of yourself from now until the boys decide what they're going to do about the duck shortage. And that'll be a long time, in case you're interested. You're worse than a kid. Never mind getting chummy with the birds and beasts of the forest. Stick to your tame chipmunk back at camp. Taking you on a fishing trip is like taking the neighbors' kids to the circus. I've got to watch you every minute or you're into something. Next thing, I suppose you'll be trying to play squat tag with an elk. Now don't try to be funny—you know the kind of an elk I mean. The ones I'm talking about don't sing on street corners on Saturday nights.

Well, here we are. How's this for a swell looking trout stream? Take a look at those two pools, will you? If I don't get a creelful by dusk it will be because I've broken my right arm. Wow! Did you see that big walloper jump and grab that bug? No—over there by the edge of that rock. You didn't see him! You must be cockeyed. Funny how you manage to see everything you shouldn't and miss everything else.

We'll just string up our rods right here because I want you to fish those two big pools and that long riffle just beyond the bend. I'm going a little farther up the creek. Meet you here later.

Let's see now, baby, guess I'll tie a No. 10 Caddis on your leader. You'll get fish with that. Of course, you won't get many, darling, because you lack your hubby's skill and finesse, but a few silly ones will probably be deceived by your inexperienced efforts, and I'll make up for what you don't get. Leave it to papa to get the fish. What do you mean I'm conceited? Why, honey, I believe you're getting sarcastic—and you with such a nice disposition, too! *Need* one to get along with me! Well, of all the unjustified accusations. Why, I'm the best husband you ever had. I'll bet you're still sore because I made you get up and build the fire this morning. Wait until you see what the old man has in his basket when he gets back and then you'll regret those unkind words.

No, dear, you can't have that nice big red and white fly. Now don't argue, honey. You fish with a Caddis or a Coachman and you'll catch some trout. Yes, dear, I know it's pretty and all that, but trout flee from it in terror. It's a No. 4 Parmacheene Belle, and they probably mistake it for some new kind of fish-hawk. If you dropped that big red scarecrow in this creek it would probably ruin the fishing for days. It's the last one of a dozen that a slightly misguided salesman put over on me one day last spring at Abercrombie & Fitch's. I gave all the rest of them away to some unsuspecting kids. I must have been pretty well jingled that day—guess I had one too many rounds over at Harry's place on Fortieth Street. Who was I boxing with? Why, I didn't say anything about boxing. You misunderstood me, dear. I simply meant that I'd been putting away a few Tom Collins and was feeling rather—er—shall we say expansive—mellow—when I went over to do some shopping. Anyway, my sales resistance must have been awfully low because the clerk almost talked me into buying a couple of skeet traps. Claimed I could set them up on the roof of the apartment house and shoot a practice string or two every morning. If I'd had another Tom Collins that afternoon, I probably would have fallen for his argument. It wasn't a bad idea at that. Certainly would have been a swell way to get even with that dame on the top floor who kept her electric player piano going on eight hour shifts. Well, if you're so crazy about that Parma Belle, I'll let you wear it in your hat band. It'll add a sort of decorative touch to your chapeau—something like those queer stuffed birds your Aunt Minnie wore on her Sunday hat. For Heaven's sake, don't try to fish with it, though.

There, now, you're all rigged up. Strip off some line and drop your fly right by that big boulder. Right near the edge of the eddy. The big trout that rose a few minutes ago might take a notion to come up again.

Honey, for the love of Pete try to remember what I've told you in the last two days. That's a flyrod—not a communist banner! Don't brandish it like that! Try another cast. Watch your backcast! Look out for those alder branches! Hell's bells! There goes a sixty-cent leader and a two-bit fly. Taking you fishing certainly runs into money fast. Now don't wander off while I'm rigging you up again. Stick around and watch how this is done. Besides, I want to keep my eye on you. I'll bet you were a trial to your mother when you were a little girl. There now. Try it again, but come down about eight clicks on your elevation and keep your line out of the trees. I'm going up the creek a little way and try a few places that I know of. Watch yourself while I'm gone, and don't try to find out how hornets and skunks get that way. 'Bye!

* * *

Yoo Hoo! Where are you? Oh, there you are. My, it's a relief to get back and find you all in one piece. Gosh,

no, I had rotten luck. Tried everything in the flybook and
only got five measly little fish. Guess it must have been
some sort of a trout fast day because they certainly weren't
feeding. Couldn't raise a single decent fish. Do you suppose
that trout observe a Lent of their own?

Why aren't you fishing, honey? You can't catch fish
lying there watching the clouds. You got all you wanted!
Why, there aren't any fish in your basket. It's empty.
You shouldn't begin to lie so early in your fishing career,
baby. That prerogative is reserved for the old, experienced
hand. Still, it's a good sign—an indication that you'll
develop. What do you mean, they wouldn't fit in your
fish-basket? Their tails stuck out! Why darling, you're ill.
Are you sure you didn't stand in the hot sun too long while
I was away? I had a hunch something would happen to
you as soon as you got out of my sight. You're *not* ill and
you *have* some trout? All right, sweet. Have your little
joke. But don't try to take the old man for too much of a
sleigh ride. Papa's been around a little in his time. Heh!
Heh!

Look under what damp ferns? What for? Oh, all right,
but a joke's a joke. I don't see why you want to—great
suffering carfish!! Did you catch . . . where on earth . . .
how . . . why, honey, I'm speechless with surprise! Cut-
throats! Why, they're huge. Marvelous! And you got
'em all out of one pool. Well, what do you know about that!
See, I told you you'd get fish on that little Caddis. You
didn't catch 'em on the Caddis? You did all your fishing
with that big Parmacheene Belle! Do you mean to stand
there and admit that you disobeyed your trusting old hubby
and caught that mess of fish with that red and white mon-
strosity? Where is that fly? What do you mean, you
haven't got it any more? What tree did you lose it in?—
I'll climb it and get that hook down if I break both legs
trying. You gave it away! To whom? *You gave my
beautiful big Parmacheene Belle to the fish warden?* You
mean that big surly oaf who snarled at me up the creek

awhile ago when he asked to see my license? You thought
he was tall and handsome? That guy good looking? Well,
baby, you certainly must have a strange taste in knick-
knacks. He looked like a first class thug to me. He probably
beats his wife and goes around kicking dogs off back porches.
And you gave him my beautiful big Parmacheene Belle
that that highly intelligent young man sold me at Abercrombie's. What in the name of the seven suffering sisters
did you do that for? Oh, I see, you felt sorry for him because he hadn't caught any fish. My, my, what a pity.
Sorry for a fish warden, tsk, tsk! Yes, dear, it surely would
be a shame to see a fish warden go home skunked. The
only fly the big ones were taking—probably the only big
Parma Belle within 500 miles—and you get big hearted
and slip it to a fish warden, of all people. Baby, you certainly are a grand little helpmate. I'll bet that if I ever
fell overboard, you'd toss me a grindstone to save myself
with. No, dear, I'm not mad. Just terribly, terribly ill.

Did the warden have any luck with my fly? Seven big
ones out of the other pool—all of them over fourteen inches.
I see. Did he offer to return the fly to you after he got all
the fish he wanted? He did? But you refused it. That's
right dear, never be an Injun giver—besides, it was probably
worn out by then, anyway. Try to control yourself, though,
if he happens to drop into camp needing a gun. Don't break
down and give him my new Remington. I don't believe I
could stand that. Well, I suppose we might as well start
back to camp. There's no use hanging around here, crying
over things that might have been. No, dear, I'm not angry
with you. Certainly not. Watch out when you climb over
these slippery wet rocks, sweetheart. You're liable to slip
and break your . . . neck.

HOW I SUCCEEDED IN MY BUSINESS

by

Stephen Leacock

I HAD been employed in one business and another quite a good few years, more years than I cared to look back upon; and yet I hadn't made good. I hadn't made good, and I knew I hadn't made good, and sometimes the knowledge that I hadn't made good made me feel bad. Often I said to my wife when I came home nights, "Doll," I said, "I haven't made good." "No, Jim, old boy," she'd say, "I know you haven't made good, but never mind you'll make good yet." And then I'd see a tear fall from her eye onto the dresser. After that I'd go out and sit in the back yard and feel real bad.

Often I used to think it over as to why it was I hadn't made good. I'd had about as much education as most, and more experience than many and better chances than some. I was willing enough and steady enough. I was a non-drinker and a non-smoker; I never touched a card and had never seen a horse race in my life, and never been inside the doors of a poolroom. Yet, I knew as well as anybody just where my shortcomings were: I lacked *pep*, I had no *punch*, I had practically no *magnetism*, and I didn't react quickly on a given environment. And I knew that now-a-days in business it is *magnetism* and pep and reaction that make for success. Then, too, I failed in the little things: I couldn't add up more than one column of figures at a time and my memory was no good: things seemed to slip out of it. Often when I came home of an evening I'd say to my wife, "Doll," I'd say, "my memory is no good." "What is it you can't remember, Jim?" she'd say. "I forget." I'd answer, and I'd groan.

The Diet of a Successful Man

Then, also, though of course I didn't know it, my diet was all wrong. Every morning I filled myself with coffee, and I was a meat eater, and I used to enjoy every meal I ate without any idea of the proper proportion of farraginous and nitrogenous units. I had no notion in those days that for every unit of albuminous farrage that a man eats, he ought to have a definite quantity of hydrogen and a fixed proportion of pollen.

Well, I was thinking it all over one Monday morning in the back yard before going to work, when all of a sudden the reason of my failure came to me like a flash. I had no belief in myself: that was it! I couldn't accomplish anything because I couldn't believe in myself and didn't react upon myself. I got up and I walked right into the house to the kitchen where Doll was getting the breakfast ready. "Doll," I said, "I've found out what was wrong. I've got to believe in myself," and I hit the table with my fist till it jumped up. "Oh, Jim," Doll said, "you frighten me!" "Ha! Ha!" I laughed—that was the first time in six years Doll had ever said that I frightened her—"I frighten you, do I? Well, then, fetch me some farraginous food." "Won't you have your bacon," says Doll, "I was just getting it ready?" "No, Doll," I said, "don't you realize that bacon contains more units of nitrogen than I can absorb in the office. The attempt to absorb nitrogenous food, Doll, depresses the nerve centres and lowers the tone of the system. Get me some sour buttermilk and half a dipper of baked beans so cooked as to emphasize their albuminous properties," "Coffee?" said Doll. "No, Doll," I answered, "not a drop; get me a little popped bran, mixed with warm water."

Well, I got my breakfast and I started down to the office for my new job just feeling fine. I could sense myself reacting against everything. "Jim Dudley" I kept repeating to myself, "You're going to make good." The first person I ran into at the office was the general manager just going in.

"You're ten minutes early, Dudley," he said.

"Mr. Kitson," I answered, "I'd rather be early than not: the employee who values his employer's time more than his own reacts backward to his own emolument."

And with that I opened my desk and got right to work. I guess I never worked in my life as I did that morning. Everything seemed easy. Letters I would have taken half an hour to consider I answered in two minutes. And every letter I answered I tried to put in just a little sunshine. Even if I didn't know who the correspondent was I found time to write in Peek-a-boo! or Keep on Smiling! or some little thing like that. "Jim Dudley", I said to myself, "you're going to make good."

Two or three times in the morning Mr. Kitson walked through the office. "Hard at it, Dudley," he said. "Mr. Kitson," I answered, "the employee who is not hard at it is defrauding both himself and his employer of his proper integument."

Well along about one o'clock Mr. Kitson came over to my desk: "Dudley," he said, "I've something I want to talk to you about, come out to have lunch with me." "All right, Mr. Kitson," I answered, "I've one more postcard to write and then I'll come." "Never mind the postcard, Jim," he said, "that can look after itself." "Mr. Kitson," I said, "Napoleon used to make it a rule never to begin a postcard without finishing it."

Swinging on Spinach

Well, I got the postcard all nicely fixed up and signed and got my hat and went out with Mr. Kitson to a swell club. There was a big bill of fare, but I took no meat at all, only half a bucket of spinach. I noticed that Mr. Kitson ate nothing but boiled watercress.

"Now, Jim," said Mr. Kitson, "I've had my eye on you all the morning, and I believe you're the man we want. The company wants some one to go to Kansas City to line up a man and to swing a big proposition."

"Mr. Kitson," I interrupted, "I can line him up and swing it."

"When can you go?"

"Right now," I said, "as soon as I finish my spinach. Just tell me what it is that I swing when I get there."

"Good!" he said. "The man that you are to see is John Smith of John Street. Can you remember the name? Better write it down."

"I don't need to," I said. "Just say the name over three or four times and my memory will take a grip on it. I'll take a few deep breaths while you say it."

So I went right over to the house and packed my grip.

"Doll," I said, "I'm off to Kansas City."

"What to do?" Doll asked.

"To swing a proposition," I answered. "It's a big thing, Doll, with big people, and if I make good we'll come out big."

I left on the cars that night, and all the way out I ate grass and cultivated my memory and reacted all the time on everything I saw.

Well, when I got to Kansas City, I found I was up against something pretty big, all right. I found John Smith but he wouldn't see me. I went right into his office, and I said, "Mr. Smith, can I see you?" "No," he said, "you can't." However, I hung on. "Let me see you," I said. "No, I won't," he answered. Still I wouldn't give in. I went up to his house that evening and right into his library. "Can I see you now?" I asked. "No," he answered, "you can't see me." "Look here! Mr Smith," I pleaded, "I've come two thousand miles to see you: let me see you!" "No, Dudley," he said, "I won't."

That went on four days and at last he gave in. "All right, Jim," he said. "State your business. What do you want?" "I want to line you up—swing you," I said, "come out with me, Mr. Smith and eat spinach, and I'll tell you about it."

So I took him out to a swell restaurant where they had

the best spinach in Kansas City. "Now," I said, after we had eaten. "You're a big man and this is a pretty big thing; we want to put over something big and you're the man we want in on it. You're big."

"Jim," he said, "you talk well. And what's more, you've got personality and that's the biggest thing in business today. As soon as I see a man who has personality, I do whatever he wants. Personality gets me every time."

So I got what I wanted, and I took the train right back to New York. Doll met me at the depot. I kissed her right there on the platform. "Did you swing it?" she asked. "Yes, Doll, I did," I answered. I saw Doll drop a tear right on the platform. "Good old Jim," she said.

Next morning I found an envelop on my desk with a cheque for five thousand dollars in it.

Well that was how I got my first start. Once the firm found that I could line up a man and swing a thing of that size there was lots more for me to do. So the end of it was they made me the head of the company. "It's no use trying to keep you down, Jim," said Mr. Kitson. "You're the biggest of all of us."

So I went home to Doll and I said, "Doll," I said, "I'm made president of the company." "Oh, Jim!" she said, "you've made good. I'm so proud—and I'm proud of the company, too, now that you're president of it. So you must tell me all about it, what it does and what it makes and sells."

"Doll," I answered, "don't ask me. I've been so busy swinging propositions and lining things up and breathing and eating spinach, that I've never had time to find out what on earth the company does do."

1. PROSE

III. Speeches

NEUTRALITY: THE IMMEDIATE PROBLEM
by
Walter Lippmann

IT is our duty to take every precaution we can take to see to it, if a great war breaks out, that it does not involve the United States.

The practical question now before the country, the question that has to be decided at once, is whether Congress can, before the 29th of February, determine exactly how the United States shall act in the event of a great European and Asiatic war.

This is the fundamental question on which the American people have to make up their minds. It should be clearly grasped. Can Congress in the next four weeks decide how the United States shall act in the event of another great war? This is the real question on which Congress is divided.

The attempt to write a binding, cast-iron law today to fix American neutral policy in another great war is like saying: I may have to play a game of bridge next week and I have decided to lead the eight of diamonds. It is like saying: I may play football next autumn and on the second play I am going to call for a forward pass. It is like saying: I have decided that my grandchild is to be a prize fighter without knowing whether your grandchild is to be a boy or a girl.

In the case of a possible great war in the future nobody knows today, nobody in the Senate, nobody in any country anywhere, when it will break out. Nobody knows where it will break out. Nobody knows who will be fighting. Nobody knows who will be neutral. Nobody knows who will be allied with whom. Nobody knows whether it will be fought on the sea, in the air, or on land. Nobody can look into the future and predict the character of the war which Congress is to make laws about. How, under these circumstances, can any Senator pretend that he knows enough, that he is sufficiently a prophet, to write a law which fixes in advance the correct policy of the United States?

The best proof that this is impossible is to be found in the fact that seventeen years after the end of the World War a Senate Committee has just spent a hundred thousand dollars trying to find out how and why the United States entered it. That war is over. Yet here we are still arguing and quarreling, still writing books, still making speeches, still holding investigations, and still uncertain as to why we entered the war. If we do not know yet why we entered the last war, how on earth can Congress write a law in four weeks telling us exactly how to behave in the next war?

I do not mean to say that we cannot learn much from our mistakes in the last war which will help us to act more wisely the next time. I am sure we can, and that it is our duty to study carefully and dispassionately the history of our attempt to maintain neutrality and the events which caused us to fail. But I am equally certain that we shall not learn much from that experience, if we start with the notion that we already know all about it.

As a matter of fact, if it were possible today to describe the character of the next war, if it were known who is going to fight, and where, and what the military plan of the next war is to be, the next war would almost certainly not take place. If it were known who is going to attack, when he is going to attack, where he is going to attack, who is going to oppose him, there would be no great difficulty in preventing the attack. The very essence of the war danger, however, lies in the inability of the governments and the people to foresee the future. The essence of the danger is that the time, the military strategy, the purposes, cannot be foreseen—that the war, if it comes, will come as a surprise and at a moment when the world is not ready for it.

The moral I draw from this is that for the United States

to tie its hands today is to increase the danger to the United States, not to diminish it. The only way to be prepared for an unpredictable emergency is to be able to move, to have your hands free, to be alert, resourceful, powerful, and unentangled. These proposals to settle American policy in advance are an attempt to say that we know better today what the emergency will require, though we do not know what the emergency will be, than the President and Congress who actually see what the emergency is.

It is a pretty good rule in human affairs that men should solve the problems of their own day and not try to tell their descendants and their successors how to settle their problems.

The policy of the United States Government is to remain unentangled and free. Let us follow that policy. Let us remain unentangled and free. Let us make no alliances. Let us make no commitments. By the same token let us pass no laws which will bind the future, tie the hands of the government, deprive it of its freedom, cause it to be entangled in a statute based on what somebody at this moment thinks the government ought to do in the future.

The simple truth is that we are not wise enough to tell a future Congress and a future President what they must do. We shall be very fortunate if we are wise enough to decide what we must do in the situation that is right before our eyes. We shall need all the wisdom we can find to cross the bridge that we are now trying to cross without deciding also how our successors shall cross the bridges that they will have to cross.

FROM "OUR BUSINESS CIVILIZATION"
by
James Truslow Adams

IN 1719 when an anonymous social critic gave voice to the doctrine that America was young, there was but little more than a fringe of settlement along the Atlantic coast. The wilderness stretched 3000 miles to the Pacific.

Today the doctrine that America is young is as firmly embedded in the popular mind as ever. We still point to the future as the time when we may be expected to begin to devote ourselves to other things than "subduing a continent and accumulating the necessary material resources on which to build a civilization."

I believe that the constant insisting upon this idea of our being a young nation is beginning to do us a deep hurt. I believe that it would be far better for the development of our best selves, individually and nationally, if instead of consistently thinking and speaking of the American people as "young," we should think and say the clear truth, which is that we are an old people.

Every settler who came to America had behind him all the past just as much as did his family or neighbors who remained behind. The 17th century English, Scotch, Germans, Swedes, Dutch, and others who came here in our first century were not barbarians. They were heirs of Greece and Rome, of the Reformation and the Renaissance, as much as those who continued in the old countries; and every man who has come here since has been of the same national age as those he left behind.

Moreover, so rapidly does the loom of history weave that we can now be ranked as among the older nations of western civilization. As an independent and unified nation

244

we long antedate, for example, Italy, which was created in 1860, or Germany, which was first welded into a nation in 1870, to say nothing of many of later growth.

Why should we be content to wait a hundred or two hundred years more before we think we shall be old enough to do something besides provide the material foundation for a civilization which we are told will somehow come of itself when we are grown up? If we believe that no matter what we do we cannot lead a more spiritual life or have the culture of an "old" country in less than so many centuries, are we not giving ourselves an excuse to go on without making an effort to attain to a spiritual instead of a material plane of civilization?

On the other hand, if we think of ourselves as an old race, heirs of all the ages, temporarily set back by having to move into a new house, and that now we have not only got that home in order but have added to it, and that therefore it is high time we turned to something else, I believe it would be far better for our self-respect and for our spiritual growth. To say that we are too young is to put off the time of manhood beyond our power to attain, and to stultify any hopes of our own day and generation.

In many ways we have already added much to the spiritual wealth of the world. In our library systems, in our scientific foundations for research, in a number of other ways, we have led the modern nations. Why, then, still preach this debilitating doctrine that we are young and nothing must be expected of us?

Is it not time to proclaim that we are not children but men who must put away childish things; that we have busied ourselves overmuch with fixing up the new place we moved into 300 years ago, with making money in the new neighborhood; and that we should begin to live a sane, maturely civilized life? To keep on telling our children that they cannot expect this and that of America because she is too young is to make self-indulgent, self-excusing mollycoddles of them and of her.

Everything may be hoped from the child who tries to be a man. Nothing can be hoped from the man who cloaks his shortcomings or spiritual indolence under the pretense of being a child.

FIGHT FOR PEACE!
by
Ernst Toller

THAT state which fires the first shot is not the breaker of the peace. The peace-breaker is the state which teaches its people to glorify war; which teaches its children not the commandment of loving one's neighbor but the art of destroying one's neighbor; which instructs them in the handiwork of the soldier; which lets them play an inhuman game with those hellish productions of our time, poison gases and gas masks.

The word is stronger than weapons. For that reason we need:

The banishment of the spirit of war from schools and universities.

The banishment of the spirit of war from all history books.

The banishment of the spirit of war from all newspapers, films and plays.

The banishment of the spirit of war from word and image and deed.

But this banishment of the spirit of war is only a beginning. Youth does not merely want to know what ought not to be; it wants to know what ought to be.

Teach them that peace is not a state but a risk.

Teach them peace as a dangerous and an adventurous task.

Teach them peace as the revolutionary activity of man.

Teach them that a hero's death is a small thing in comparison with a heroic life for great moral aims, which daily and hourly demand renunciation and manliness, a daring and strong spirit.

Teach them that the senseless adventure of war is nothing beside the adventures of rational life. Peace, as we know it today, is no ideal; it is poisoned by social injustice; it is a mere semblance of that peace which, with the strength of our reason, with the strength of our hearts, we can plan and build.

That peace in which the ideas of human and social justice, the ideas of spiritual freedom, the ideas of the true development of all citizens shall penetrate the work of all nations.

Teach them to love this adventure, and they will turn with contempt from the cannibal customs of degenerate tribes.

OBSOLESCENCE IN THE SOCIAL SCIENCES
Address by
Owen D. Young

I KNOW the failures of my time as well as its most biting
critics, but I am not prepared to admit what is so often
charged, that my generation was bankrupt of accomplish-
ment. What it hands to you is a country so well off in
material things that you can not bankrupt it by any experiment which you may make in your time. You may impair
it but you can not altogether ruin it. I would not say that
it was an impossible task ultimately, but I do say that it
will take more than one generation to destroy what we
have built for you. Indeed, your problem is to deal with a
land which is said to have too much rather than too little.
That, at least, is a new condition in the history of the world.
No people *before* have suffered from too much. Yet that,
we are told, is what has happened. So, however severely
you may indict us for failing wisely to administer, you must
still give us credit for providing the plenty that ruined us.

Our fathers handed us the greatest material potentiali-
ties ever transmitted from sire to son. What were we of
the nineties to do with this wealth of possibilities? What
was the magic key which would unlock them in our hands,
a key which our fathers had not found?

In this quest, as alluring as any that ever excited the
imagination of a nation, it was natural that the most alert
and adventurous brains, both in our colleges and outside,
were attracted to the physical sciences. It was their appli-
cation to these resources that then promised to be and
turned out to be the fairy godmother as we then thought,
or the Pandora, as you now think, who unloosed this
"plenty" which is so cavalierly cursed today.

You ask, and rightly so, if we did so well, how is it we are in the mess we are today? The answer in general terms is not new. The approaching catastrophe had been foreseen by some for many years. The social, political and economic machinery was not being advanced in anything like the degree that forces were being developed and put to work by the physical sciences. The law stood still while business with its new weapons was going over the ramparts into no-man's land.

I hope you in your generation will not confess to your incapacity to keep the sciences of government, of economics, and of the social order in step with the most rapid advances which it is possible for the human mind to make in promoting the material welfare of this world in which we live. Our trouble was not that the physical sciences went too fast but that the social sciences did not go fast enough.

Just as the young men and women of my time were lured to the field of invention and discovery in the physical sciences, so you will have to face the problems of that much more difficult science of human relations. It will not do for you merely to determine what you would like human relations to be. It will be necessary for you to find out what human behavior is, and then fashion the social machinery which will make for human happiness.

You can go no faster and no further than the people as a whole understand and approve. It has ever been the mistake of ardent reformers to go too far and too fast. Just as stand-pat conservatives fail, as history has shown, to move far enough or fast enough. Right now, in this country, I do not fear the extremist because he is likely to carry the American people with him on a rash adventure. They will not go. If I know my America, the torch of the revolutionist is not dangerous because it may start a conflagration. It is disheartening because it will inevitably call out the organized fire departments of reaction which, playing as they must without discrimination, may well dampen our advances for another generation.

The times continue to invite appeals to the emotions. Hot hearts burn in sympathy with suffering. Hot heads raise the sledge hammers of destruction in order to have reconstruction. The fact that they have a following is a stinging indictment of ourselves. They range from the emotional disturbers of the peace to the ambitious masters of great nations, and each is ready as a last resort to precipitate a class war within or a military war without, either to grasp power or to preserve it.

As my generation found its magic key in the physical sciences to unlock a world of plenty from our inheritance, so you will find your major task in the social sciences to control and apportion that world of plenty which is your inheritance. How much organized government must be enlarged, how much the free action of the individual must be curtailed, you will discover. Today we do not know. A social order within a nation must strive not so much for unattainable equality as manageable equilibrium. A world order must seek the same things too. Nothing can be more incongruous or more certain of ultimate failure than the effort to reach social equalization within a nation and at the same time by a policy of reckless nationalism to leave the world outside in consequent turmoil and anarchy, where suspicion and distrust reign supreme and where arms are the only reliance of our faith, even when they blast our fondest hopes for security and peace in a better world.

CAN THERE BE A NEW SOCIAL ORDER?

by

Harry Woodburn Chase

AS most of us read history a generation ago, it was with a deep belief, a rather blind belief, if you please, in the reality of progress. We were progress conscious. . . . We believed in it, and we thought that we found in history ample warrant for believing that the possibility of progress itself depended on an attitude that had regard for the individual. . . . And, because we believed in these things, we believed in the importance of popular education as an instrument both for developing the capacities of the individual and for maintaining the continuity of human progress.

You and I are today citizens of a world in which this whole philosophy has been thrust out of the mind of nation after nation. The movement toward democracy and toward human freedom . . . has not only been definitely checked, it has suffered catastrophic reverses. State after state has come to seek efficiency and security through subordination and regimentation of the individual to centralized and despotic authority. . . .

It is not impossible to regiment the American people. Great sections of them have been regimented more than once in our history. And when regimented, we can be violent and cruel. . . . The problem is one of destiny for us as well as for our neighbors. It is whether we can find a way of life that is both free and workable, whether the intricacies of our modern social and economic order are so beyond the power of free men to deal with that we must sacrifice all the significance of the individual life to maintain a going social order. Must all this striving for human progress end in such dreary futility as Aldous Huxley has portrayed with devastating irony in *This Brave New World?*

Do not misunderstand me. All of us are aware today that we cannot make a twentieth-century society function by following in detail the eighteenth-century formulas of Jefferson and of Adam Smith. The problem is far less simple than it appeared even twenty years ago. But at the heart of it lies the significant choice: Shall we set out arbitrarily to create a social order and then indoctrinate and drive individuals into subordination to it, or shall we center our efforts on the making of men and women who are themselves competent and disposed, as free agents, to do what should be done?

For myself, I confess, there seems but one possible answer. Civilization and human progress must depend in the long run, not on dictatorship, not on social and economic prescriptions, not even on laws, but on the quality of men and women.

THE FUTURE FOR THE BRAIN TRUST

by

Harold L. Ickes

I WONDER if any political party will be willing to write into its next platform a demand that our Government be divorced from brains? The very fact that such an issue as is implicit in the expression "brain trust" should be raised is of itself an eloquent commentary upon the intelligence of those who, seeking to fill the highly important and necessary role of critics of governmental action and policy, have nothing better to offer than an attack upon the Administration for calling experts into counsel upon questions of grave import.

*   *   *

After all, I suspect that what those who decry the use of brains in government fear is not brains as such, but brains that are used for the benefit of the masses of our people instead of for the privileged few. They want brains without heart, brains without soul, brains without conscience, brains without any sense of social responsibility. They want brains that, if they cannot be bought or bullied, are content to lead a quiet existence remote from the practical affairs of life. Those who are using the term "brain trust" as an opprobrious epithet are apprehensive that brains will discover some means of putting an end to that unfair privilege which has resulted in the aggrandizement of the few at the expense of the many. They resent brains that are intent upon forging an improved social order that will mean real equality of opportunity for every man, woman and child in the United States. They are fearful of brains that have undertaken to redress the social and economic abuses which

254

we have too long endured and thus bring about the dawn of a better day, of a happier life for us and for our children.

* * *

Business has always used the best brains available and the bigger the business, the greater its reliance upon brains and the greater the reward it is willing to offer for first-rate brains. . . . Realizing the benefit of brains to their businesses, they outbid the colleges and universities for outstanding men. Brains are employed by banks, by railways, even by Wall Street. . . . A "brain trust" that will jump to the service of business when a button is pressed is a praiseworthy institution. But when the United States Government uses brains to protect the people against special privilege, intelligence all at once becomes a thing that is suspect.

* * *

What nobler ambition can any youth of our land have than that of service to the State? There have been times when men have hurried forth from the colleges to find the easiest way to wealth and an assured future for themselves. This is an understandable ambition and not an unworthy one. But how much finer it would be, as you step out into life, if you would undertake a career which, while it might never give you great wealth or position, would offer you an opportunity to serve your fellow men. The Government needs today, as it never has before, brain power combined with a social sense. We realize now that we must build a new social order. We must set up higher social ideals. Society is no happier or stronger than its most miserable and weakest group. The terrible period through which we have been passing, if it has taught us nothing else, has made us realize our interdependence on each other. If we are to build a happier future for our children and our children's children, we must build it together. We must learn to understand each other. We must cultivate tolerance. We must let live if we would ourselves live, and above all else, we must adopt and adhere to a policy of protecting the weak against the strong; of curbing over-reaching and ruthless power; of assuring to all, both weak and strong, the equality of opportunity under the law which we have boasted to be the cornerstone of our American civilization.

1. PROSE

IV. Essays

FRAGMENTS FROM A FLOWER DIARY

by

Nora Waln

'Habits and customs differ, but all peoples have the love of flowers in common.'

—Chinese Proverb

THE Chinese love of flowers has been rewarded by genius in their cultivation. Certainly this is a transcendent capacity for taking trouble. Aided by their lovers' patient skill, blossoms open for their festivals all over the land despite the diversity of climate which makes the weather below zero in some districts when it is swelteringly hot in others.

Flowers are coddled, nursed, and coaxed. They are fed religiously. There is a vast lore of wisdom passed orally from generation to generation concerning the whims and peculiarities of different plants—also a voluminous detailed gardening literature in which the observations of centuries are garnered. In the House of Exile library there are forty books, considered classics, on the culture of chrysanthemums only, and nearly as many relating to dwarf trees.

In heat, plants are sheltered in the coolest places in the homestead, and shades are erected for blossoming trees, vines, and flowers which are stationary. I have seen people sit all through the breathless tropic noon fanning a drooping flower. In cold, plants are housed in paper shelters, their roots set in loam warmed by subterranean air pipes heated by buried charcoal.

These are constructed to-day exactly as decreed by a ruler of the state of Wei who lived more than two thousand years ago. He ordered that they should be so simply designed that even the poorest and the stupidest of his people

259

might make one. In the most severe weather, florists clothe buds in little paper coats perforated with breathing holes.

Although they perform an infinite amount of toil in bringing their flowers to perfection, florists charge astonishingly low prices. A florist once explained this to me. He told me that a country in which flowers—a necessity for the refinement of the heart—were priced so as to make them a luxury was a country which had yet to learn the first principles of civilization.

*   *   *

According to Chinese legend, a flower presides over each month of the year, celebrating her anniversary on the fifth day after the rise of the new moon. It is usual for a minstrel, when he knocks at a homestead gate on a flower birthday, to ask to come in and sing the flower's ballads. Many tea shops have a story-teller as an attraction to patrons; and, passing on a flower's day, I have often heard the blind-man entertaining the laborers, who gather round him when the day's toil is done, with the flower's fables.

Narcissus is hostess of the first month, violet of the second, peach blossom of the third, which is a favorite month for weddings. In China the peach blossom is the wedding flower as the orange blossom is in America, and in ancient times marriage was celebrated with a festival at the season of the flowering of the peach orchards. Peony gives her name to the fourth month, but rose presides over the month. This is because 'the peony is the millionarie's flower, symbol of riches and power; but the lovely rose belongs to everyone, as she graces cottage and palace impartially with her beauty.'

The gentle jasmine is hostess of the fifth month. The lotus, symbol of purity because she grows out of the mud and is not soiled, reigns over the sixth month; balsam, famous for healing virtues, over the seventh; cassia flower, so small but so fragrant, over the eighth; chrysanthemum, beloved of scholars, over the ninth. Bright cheerful marigold is hostess of the tenth month; camellia of the eleventh; the flowering winter plum, whose petals are like the snowflakes, of the twelfth.

And that no flower shall feel neglected, just because there are not enough months for all, a Birthday of All Flowers is celebrated on the twelfth day of the second month.

On All Flowers' Day it is polite to make 'flower calls,' taking gifts of seeds and slips to one's friends. Every flower birthday is an appropriate occasion for a party. It is not even necessary to possess a garden to give a blossom tea. I know a Chinese lady in Peking, an invalid with neither the means nor the strength to achieve a garden, who has a blossom tea every year. A branch of her neighbor's wisteria extends over her courtyard wall, and each spring, when the wisteria flowers, she asks her friends to come. One year the wisteria did not bloom. She had her party, gay as the previous ones, in memory of the blossoms.

Wealthy families, who can, often give parties which are magnificent flower shows. These usually begin in the morning and last well into the evening. After sunset the homestead is lit with silk lanterns placed to show each plant or flowering tree to the best advantage. Good manners permit one to go as long or as short a time as one chooses.

Chinese people do not like to cut their flowers, and seldom do. The flowers displayed at a party are growing, either in pots or in the ground. Poetry and art through the centuries have endowed each tree, vine, and plant with a symbolic significance, and the cultured are guided by this in their arrangement. In the home of a scholar one is certain to see the 'three friends'—that is, the bamboo, the pine, and the plum—grouped together.

The purpose of a flower party is to view the flowers, and tables for cards or mah jongg are considered in bad taste. Sometimes there is an open-air stage on which actors play the flower classics. At one party I attended, the little children of the house, dressed in flower costumes, danced a flower ballet of their own improvisation. Often someone who reads well is asked to read flower poetry.

Flower picnics are also popular. The Lins give an orchard party when the fruit trees bloom each year. Friends make up travel parties and go from all over China to admire the azaleas near Ningpo. When the lovely lotus opens her tulip-shaped blossoms in the shallow bays of the water highways, families in every province give boat picnics.

When I was preparing to attend the first flower festival to which I was invited, my mother-by-affection spoke to me about my dress. 'One should honor the occasion by care in one's costume,' Shun-ko said. 'But according to an ancient rule of decorum observed by the refined of heart, it is impolite to outdress the flowers. The flower-party gown should be dainty, clean, delicate in color, and fashioned on simple lines. A new fashion, however lovely, is out of place at a flower's party. The courteous hostess and her guests remember that it is to celebrate the flowers that people are gathered, and to wear a gown which distracts attention from the blossoms is rude.'

'MADONNA DEL PARTO'
BY PIERO DELLA FRANCESCA
by
Elizabeth Wilder

IT is not merely difficult, it is impossible to report the effect of a masterpiece. As many photographs as I had seen of this Madonna, as much as I had read in her praise, I had not expected such dignity and such quiet, or such exquisite delicacy of color. How beautifully calm it was! There was a fine appropriateness in coming to such a picture on a serene Sunday morning in June, and finding it alone in the tiny white-washed chapel of a village graveyard. I felt in the setting and in the people around me the same balance of humility and dignity which illuminated the picture. At one minute it seemed to be only a woman great with child—until one saw the angels in their celestial robes holding back the curtains from the Queen of Heaven, until one realized in her face that basic nobility which mysteriously resides in human beings. It was a great picture— a picture of definite presence, which one found it hard to leave and would never forget.

"I THOUGHT I STOOD"
From "Three Dreams in a Desert"
by
Olive Schreiner

I THOUGHT I stood in Heaven before God's throne, and God asked me what I had come for. I said I had come to accuse my brother, Man.

God said, "What has he done?"

I said, "He has taken my sister, Woman, and has stricken her and thrust her out into the streets; she lies there prostrate. His hands are red with blood. I am here to accuse him; that the kingdom be taken from him, because he is not worthy, and given unto me. My hands are pure."

I showed them.

God said, "Thy hands are pure.—Lift up thy robe."

I raised it; my feet were red, blood-red, as if I had trodden in wine.

God said, "How is this?"

I said, "Dear Lord, the streets on earth are full of mire. If I should walk straight on in them my outer robe might be bespotted, you see how white it is! Therefore I pick my way."

God said, "*On what?*"

I was silent, and I let my robe fall. I wrapped my mantle about my head. I went out softly. I was afraid that the angels would see me.

II

ONCE more I stood at the gate of Heaven, I and another. We held fast by one another; we were very tired. We looked up at the great gates; the angels opened them, and we went in. The mud was on our garments. We walked across the marble floor, and up to the great throne. Then the angels divided us. Her, they set upon the top step, but me, upon the bottom; for, they said, "Last time this woman came here she left red foot-marks on the floor; we had to wash them out with our tears. Let her not go up."

Then she, with whom I came, looked back, and stretched out her hand to me; and I went and stood beside her.

God asked me what I had come for; and I drew my sister forward a little that He might see her.

God said, "How is it you are here together today?"

I said, "She was upon the ground in the street, and they passed over her; I lay down by her, and she put her arms around my neck, and so I lifted her, and we two rose together."

God said, "Whom are you now come to accuse before me?"

I said, "We are come to accuse no man."

And God bent, and said, "My children—what is it that ye seek?"

And she beside me drew my hand that I should speak for both.

I said, "We have come to ask that thou shouldst speak to Man, our brother, and give us a message for him that he might understand, and that he might—"

God said, "Go, take the message down to him!"

I said, "But what *is* the message?"

God said, "Upon your hearts it is written; take it down to him."

And we turned to go; the angels went with us to the door. They looked at us.

And one said—"Ai! but their dresses are beautiful!"

And the other said, "I thought it was mire when they came in, but see, it is all golden!"

But another said, "Hush, it is the light from their faces!"

And we went down to him.

A DREAM OF WILD BEES

by

Olive Schreiner

A MOTHER sat alone at an open window. Through it
came the voices of the children as they played under the
acacia-trees, and the breath of the hot afternoon air. In
and out of the room flew the bees, the wild bees, with their
legs yellow with pollen, going to and from the acacia-trees,
droning all the while. She sat on a low chair before the
table and darned. She took her work from the great basket
that stood before her on the table: some lay on her knee and
half covered the book that rested there. She watched the
needle go in and out; and the dreary hum of the bees and
the noise of the children's voices became a confused murmur
in her ears, as she worked slowly and more slowly. Then
the bees, the long-legged wasp-like fellows who make no
honey, flew closer and closer to her head, droning. Then
she grew more and more drowsy, and she laid her hand,
with the stocking over it, on the edge of the table, and
leaned her head upon it. And the voices of the children
outside grew more and more dreamy, came now far, now
near; then she did not hear them, but she felt under her
heart where the ninth child lay. Bent forward and sleeping
there, with the bees flying about her head, she had a weird
brain-picture; she thought the bees lengthened and lengthened themselves out and became human creatures and
moved round and round her. Then one came to her softly,
saying, "Let me lay my hand upon thy side where the child
sleeps. If I shall touch him he shall be as I."

She asked, "Who are you?"

And he said, "I am Health. Whom I touch will have

always the red blood dancing in his veins; he will not know weariness nor pain; life will be a long laugh to him."

"No," said another, "let me touch; for I am Wealth. If I touch him material care shall not feed on him. He shall live on the blood and sinews of his fellow-men, if he will; and what his eye lusts for, his hand will have. He shall not know 'I want.' " And the child lay still like lead.

And another said, "Let me touch him; I am Fame. The man I touch, I lead to a high hill where all men may see him. When he dies he is not forgotten, his name rings down the centuries, each echoes it on to his fellows. Think— not to be forgotten through the ages!"

And the mother lay breathing steadily, but in the brain-picture they pressed closer to her.

"Let me touch the child," said one, "for I am Love. If I touch him he shall not walk through life alone. In the greatest dark, when he puts out his hand he shall find another hand by it. When the world is against him, another shall say, ' *You and I.*' " And the child trembled.

But another pressed close and said, "Let me touch; for I am Talent. I can do all things—that have been done before. I touch the soldier, the statesman, the thinker, and the politician who succeed; and the writer who is never before his time, and never behind it. If I touch the child he shall not weep for failure."

About the mother's head the bees were flying, touching her with their long tapering limbs; and, in her brain-picture, out of the shadow of the room came one with sallow face, deep-lined, the cheeks drawn into hollows, and a mouth smiling quiveringly. He stretched out his hand. And the mother drew back, and cried, "Who are you?" He answered nothing; and she looked up between his eyelids. And she said, "What can you give the child—health?" And he said, "The man I touch, there wakes up in his blood a burning fever, that shall lick his blood as fire. The fever that I will give him shall be cured when his life is cured."

"You give wealth?"

He shook his head. "The man whom I touch, when he bends to pick up gold, he sees suddenly a light over his head in the sky; while he looks up to see it, the gold slips from between his fingers, or sometimes another passing takes it from them."

"Fame?"

He answered, "Likely not. For the man I touch there is a path traced out in the sand by a finger which no man sees. That he must follow. Sometimes it leads almost to the top, and then turns down suddenly into the valley. He must follow it, though none else sees the tracing."

"Love?"

He said, "He shall hunger for it—but he shall not find it. When he stretches out his arms to it, and would lay his heart against a thing he loves, then, far off along the horizon he shall see a light play. He must go towards it. The thing he loves will not journey with him; he must travel alone. When he presses somewhat to his burning heart, crying, 'Mine, mine, my own!' he shall hear a voice—'Renounce! renounce! this is not thine!' "

"He shall succeed?"

He said, "He shall fail. When he runs with others they shall reach the goal before him. For strange voices shall call to him and strange lights shall beckon him, and he must wait and listen. And this shall be the strangest: far off across the burning sands where, to other men, there is only the desert's waste, he shall see a blue sea! On that sea the sun shines always, and the water is blue as burning amethyst, and the foam is white on the shore. A great land rises from it, and he shall see upon the mountain-tops burning gold."

The mother said, "He shall reach it?"

And he smiled curiously.

She said, "It is real?"

And he said, "What *is* real?"

And she looked up between his half-closed eyelids, and said, "Touch."

And he leaned forward and laid his hand upon the

sleeper, and whispered to it, smiling; and this only she heard—"*This shall be thy reward—that the ideal shall be real to thee.*"

And the child trembled; but the mother slept on heavily and her brain-picture vanished. But deep within her the antenatal thing that lay there had a dream. In those eyes that had never seen the day, in that half-shaped brain was a sensation of light! Light—that it never had seen. Light— that perhaps it never should see. Light—that existed somewhere!

And already it had its reward: the Ideal was real to it.

CREDO OF THE FRENCH SOLDIERS

"YOU may be mobilized or you may not be mobilized. If you are not mobilized nothing matters; if you are mobilized one of two things happens. You are sent up to the front or you are not sent up to the front. If you are not sent up to the front nothing matters; if you are sent up to the front one of two things happens. You are sent into the firing line or you are not sent into the firing line. If you are sent into the firing line one of two things happens; you are hit or you are not hit. If you are not hit nothing matters. If you are hit one of two things happens; you are dangerously wounded or you are not dangerously wounded. If you are not dangerously wounded, nothing matters. If you are dangerously wounded one of two things happens; you die or you do not die.

"If you do not die nothing matters.

"If you die nothing matters."

THE WILL OF CHARLES LOUNSBERRY
From "Talks About Books and Authors"
by
William Lyon Phelps

IN the pocket of a ragged coat belonging to one of the inmates of the Chicago poorhouse, I am told, there was found, after his death, a will. The man had been a lawyer. So unusual was it that it was sent to an attorney; and the story goes that he was so impressed with its contents that he read it before the Chicago Bar Association, and that later it was ordered probated. And this is the will of the ragged old inmate of the Chicago poorhouse:

I Charles Lounsberry, being of sound and disposing mind and memory, do hereby make and publish this my last will and testament in order to distribute my interest in the world among succeeding men.

That part of my interest which is known in law as my property, being inconsiderable and of no account, I make no disposition of. My right to live, being but a life estate, is not at my disposal, but, these things excepted, all else in the world I now proceed to devise and bequeath.

Item: I give to good fathers and mothers, in trust for their children, all good little words of praise and encouragement, and all quaint pet names and endearments; and I charge said parents to use them justly, but generously, as the deeds of their children shall require.

Item: I leave to children inclusively, but only for the term of their childhood, all and every flower of the field and the blossoms of the woods, with the right to play among them freely according to the custom of children, warning them at the same time against thistles and thorns. And I devise to children the banks of the brooks and the golden sands beneath the waters thereof, and the odors of the willows that dip therein, and the white clouds that float high over giant trees. And I leave the children the long, long days to be merry in, in a thousand ways, and the night and the train of the Milky Way to wonder at, but subject, nevertheless, to the rights hereinafter given to lovers.

Item: I devise to boys, jointly, all the useful idle fields and commons where ball may be played, all pleasant waters where one may swim, all snow-clad hills where one may coast, and all streams and ponds where one may fish, or where, when grim winter comes, one may skate, to hold the same for the period of their boyhood. And all meadows, with the clover blossoms and butterflies thereof; the woods with their beauty; the squirrels and the birds and the echoes and strange noises, and all distant places, which may be visited together with the adventures there found. And I give to said boys each his own place at the fireside at night, with all pictures that may be seen in the burning wood, to enjoy without let or hindrance or without any encumbrance or care.

Item: To lovers, I devise their imaginary world, with whatever they may need, as the stars of the sky, the red roses by the wall, the bloom of the hawthorn, the sweet strains of music, and aught else they may desire to figure to each other the lastingness and beauty of their love.

Item: To young men jointly I bequeath all the boisterous, inspiring sports of rivalry, and I give to them the disdain of weakness, and undaunted confidence in their own strength, I leave to them the power to make lasting friendships and of possessing companions, and to them, exclusively, I give all merry songs and choruses to sing with lusty voices.

Item: And to those who are no longer children or youths, or lovers, I leave memory; and bequeath to them the volumes of poems of Burns and Shakespeare and other poets, if there be others, to the end that they may live the old days over again, freely and fully without tithe or diminution.

Item: To the loved ones with snowy crowns, I bequeath the happiness of old age, the love and gratitude of their children until they fall asleep.

REFLECTIONS ON THE CHRISTMAS SPIRIT
by
Leslie Roberts

ONE of the surest symptoms of approaching senility is said to be the complaint of the victim that Things As They Are cannot be compared with Things As They Were. There is no more accurate illustration of these circumstances than that to be found in our changed attitude to Christmas. A season which was set apart until recent years for family reunion and rejoicing, with due regard for the spiritual (or, if you insist, the sentimental) significance of the occasion, has been permitted to degenerate into something little better than a salesman's carnival. From the festal season the average householder and his wife emerge worn to the overdraft line of their effort to keep pace with the new social *mores* and they agree, when the battle is over, that they have felt little of the Christmas spirit which they knew as children.

When I was a boy—and my family were city dwellers in moderately comfortable circumstances—preparations for the Yuletide feast were set in motion at the same season which marks the beginning of Christmas organization in today's household, but the activities were vastly different in nature. Mid-November brought the laying in of spices and other ingredients of the mincemeat which would season in stone jars against the day of feasting. Other spices, fruits, and candied peels went into the fashioning of plum puddings and these, in turn, were stowed away to reappear at high noon on the twenty-fifth of December. Last year's decorations were brought out for inspection, and the grocer was asked to reserve a tree. With the arrival of the first tantalizing odors from the kitchen, announcing mother's embarkation on a culinary spree of three weeks' duration, the Christmas season was officially opened. Thereafter usually dilatory children hurried home from school to sample the good things in course of preparation.

Nor was the head of the house excused from the plannings and plottings on foot, for to father fell the duty of invoking the old-fashioned Santa Claus via the living room chimney and of fostering a Yuletide spirit in keeping with the spiritual and mundane estimates of our parents. Every evening there was a Christmas story for the youngsters. Sometimes the tale of the Magi was told, to impress upon our young minds the origin and significance of Christmas-giving. Other fantasies traced the season's lore, weaving a tapestry that was in much closer harmony with the spirit of the Christ-child's holiday than are those produced for today's children by the radio announcers. I submit that father was a happier man before he gave the story-telling hour into the keeping of the program sponsors and fell to brooding on the sorry problem of keeping pace with the Joneses. As for mother's part in the preparations, I am sure that she derived more honest enjoyment from her pre-Christmas activities twenty-five years ago than her daughter can find as she trudges through the shops, trying to make her Christmas shopping list fit the rigors of a 1934 family budget.

In those days our approach to Christmas was made as a family. Early in December we descended on the toy shops to inspect the wares on view and reach conclusions as to our individual requirements. We entered into the Christmas engagements of our church—the carol singing, the preparation of hampers for the poor of the parish, the Sunday School party and, finally, the Christmas morning service—as a family. Another family, less fortunately placed than we happened to be, was sought out and on Christmas Eve we visited their home *en masse*, bearing hampers of food from our own kitchen, articles of warm clothing, and toys for every child. That family was our especial responsibility, even to the point that we youngsters saved our pennies and ransacked our toy chests for presents to bring to the washlady's offspring. Yuletide charity in the old days was distinctly a personal matter which lacked the cold, patronizing quality of the modern Welfare Trust.

On Christmas morning the household was astir almost at the crack of dawn. The great tree had been decorated before children were tucked into their beds, and while we slept Santa Claus had placed presents on and under the green boughs and stuffed with fruits and candies the stockings that were pinned to the mantel. From the ground floor came cries of ecstasy from young throats, while parents donned dressing gowns and carried out hasty morning ablutions above. Almost before the day was fully alight the family had gathered about the tree, where father, in his role of head of the house, set about distributing the beribboned parcels which the rubicund Saint Nick had brought.

After breakfast clockwork trains raced about circular or oval tracks on the living-room rug. New skates were tried on in the storm porch. Meanwhile mother and the hired girl bustled about the house, clearing away the worst of the debris while father joined in the youngsters' fun, testing the power of the baby's new horn, studying the pages of Bob's stamp album, admiring Mary's new doll and Bill's new toboggan. Outdoor sports equipment was given hasty trial in the back yard. Sweaters and mittens were solemnly tested for size. Father examined new ties and socks, with chuckles of amusement as he regarded their assorted color schemes, while mother uttered sounds of pleasure over the array of gifts which had come to her from husband and children.

As ten strokes sounded on the grandfather clock in the hall, children were sent scurrying upstairs to be decked in their finest raiment. Father donned Sunday attire (for the day of the best suit was not yet spent). Soon mother descended the stairs, clad in her church-going finery, and we set off as a family to attend Divine Service and hear the Christmas music.

Church on Christmas morning combined the spiritual and the social in pleasant admixture. Grand hymns boomed out from the organ, to be taken up by the congregation and sung in rousing volume. The brief sermon focussed the attention of parents and children alike on the joy and sanctity of the Christ-child's day. As the Recessional ended the hour of worship, friends and neighbors exchanged smiling Merry Christmases and handshakes in the aisles and on the outer steps, while children whispered to one another of the good things which had been brought to their houses while they slept.

Christmas dinner, served as soon after church as was compatible with mother's kitchen arrangements, was the great feast of the year. The board groaned under its load of good things to eat, beginning with the great bird (which father regarded solemnly from beneath his paper cap, carvers poised points-up), and carrying on through an array of vegetables, stuffings, and sauces to the plum pudding, the mince pies, and the nuts, raisins, and chocolates.

Mid-afternoon brought a lull in the day. Father claimed the privilege of an hour in his den to doze and read, while mother supervised further clearings-away and children scurried about their personal concerns: to skate, to slide, or to compare gifts with those which their friends had acquired. Nightfall brought the family together again for such further repasting as stomachs were able to stand. Thereafter talk and tales before the grate fire in the living room occupied our attention until we were marched off to bed, caring not a whit that a visit to the medicine bottle would mark the beginning of the morning to come.

Such was Christmas when today's gaffers of forty were children. Other families, of course, varied the program outlined, to conform to their own tribal customs, for all that I have attempted here is to recall the Christmas celebrations of the household from which I came. Not all

these good things have been lost. Much of Christmas remains in any home where there are young children. But
something that was good has gone out of the Christmas
spirit since the hand of commercialism (not merely the
commercialism of the shopkeeper, but the comercialism of
his customers as well) seized Santa Claus by the scruff of
the neck and bade him pipe us down the street to the *gifte
shoppe.*

No longer is there peace on earth for the average citizen
as he approaches the season of peace and good will. From
cover to cover the day's newspapers urge the purchase of
This for "Her" and That for "Him." Long rows of Gift
Suggestions indicate innumerable articles suitable as presents
for mother, father, son, daughter, aunt, uncle, wife, husband,
business associate, competitor, friend, enemy, acquaintance,
and all manner of people whom it seems advisable to court,
or at least to recognize. Interlocutors drum their wares on
the radio. Neatly phrased treatises lecture us on the Spirit
of Giving. As one man, we buy—and much of our buying
originates in the fear that we shall be regarded as dead
beats if we fail to march in the gift procession.

Early in November it has become the habit of the lady
of the house to set down on paper the names of numerous
members of what may be termed loosely Our Set, whom it
behooves us to remember with gaily wrapped parcels on
the twenty-fifth. This is the first extra-mural list and it is
accepted at the time as being complete (although we know
that it is nothing of the sort) and an effort is made to work
it into the budget. Some time later, the lord of the manor
(who has been heard to remark time and again that he is
prepared to be damned before he will spend money on
anyone but the children and the immediate family this
Christmas) decides that greeting cards will not suffice in the
cases of certain gentlemen with whom he has enjoyed
profitable business relationships during the year. Furthermore, there is So-and-So, with whom it is hoped to establish
profitable connections during the year to come. These

names must be added. The budget must be expanded again. By the time the final splurge of shopping is upon us and the newspapers are shrieking in bold-face type that only four days remain, the original list has been revised half a dozen times, "because from something Bertha said at bridge yesterday I am sure they are planning to remember us and it would be too humiliating for words if we overlooked them," or else "because Johnson has just been made purchasing agent of his company and I shall be well advised to keep our association on a friendship basis."

As to the great volume of merchandising ballyhoo, I am not suggesting that Christmas gift advertisements, as such, are out of place, nor that the merchant should remain away from print on the assumption that we shall come to his shop for our Yuletide needs in any case. Nevertheless, I grow weary of the constant, insistent drumfire which beats against my eyes, which implies (and occasionally even tells me outright) that something undesirable will happen to my status in the community if I do not join the harassed throng of Christmas shoppers. Then let it happen.

The radio in my living room drives me to the verge of despair during the pre-Christmas weeks. There is a shop in our town which acquires each year the services of its own, personal Santa Claus, and on or about the fifteenth of November it causes that portly saint to begin his southward journey from the Pole, while he regales us each evening with a play-by-play description of his adventures during the previous twenty-four hours. Each day's story, it seems unnecessary to add, is suitably embellished with the announcements of the sponsor who, presumably, has acquired sole rights to the services of Kriss Kringle for our district. The fortnight of journeying down from the great open spaces culminates in a monster parade and broadcast, the former, I am almost ashamed to admit, a highly entertaining spectacle which my children would not miss under any circumstances and which I attend in their company, to our mutual pleasure. Yet there is something in the revel which irritates me as I stand on the side lines and watch Santa ($17.00 per week) doing his stuff atop his float. Perhaps it is because I know that the Old Man will be back in the ranks of the unemployed in another month. Perhaps it is because I know that the young women who will attend to the great volume of business which the Santa broadcasts and the Santa parade brings to the store will not be paid sufficient wages to permit them to enjoy a decent Christmas themselves.

Christmas giving had its origin in a legend. Three wise men, we are told, came from the East bearing gifts. Following a star which shone in the canopy of night, they pressed their pace, pausing at intervals to make inquiry, but always pushing on again, until they reached journey's end at the doorway to the stable in a small Judean village. When they discovered the lowly nature of the birthplace of the royal child on whom they had come to bestow their gifts they did not turn and go away. So far as the legend goes there is not even a suggestion that they put their heads together to question the rightness of their directions and certainly not to ponder the folly of wasting good myrrh on people in such lowly circumstances. On finding the Christ-child couched in a manger, they went to their knees and placed their gifts in the cradle of poverty.

That is the story of the first Christmas giving. For all I know this Magi saga may be nothing but a charming fantasy. I am not even concerned with the question of divinity as it may, or may not, apply to the child on whom the wise men lavished their frankincense. For the legend of this child of Bethlehem who, as a young man, went about doing so much good, I have a deeply rooted respect, however, and am driven to disgust at the manner in which his feast has been degraded.

From the incidents surrounding the story of the birth of Jesus gift legends arose, so that it became the custom of Christians everywhere to commemorate the birth of the Infant by bringing presents to little children. Over the centuries other stories were woven into the warp and woof of Christmas folklore, and soon we had created the rotund figure of jocose Saint Nicholas, patron of the nursery, who typified the jollity of the season with his rosy cheeks, his capacious paunch, and his sack of presents for girls and boys. As time passed, carols were written and waits regaled the householder with these Yuletide songs. People thronged the churches to chant Christmas hymns and to listen to exhortations which told the circumstances of the birth of the Child and pointed out man's rightful celebration of the day. Extra-religious rejoicings were confined to the family circle, where the household and high dining about the family board provided the principal outlet for the season's good will. That was the old-fashioned Christmas.

How we happened to lose sight of the real significance of the season I cannot tell you. Possibly my father felt the first twinges of the desire to promote self-interest by sending gifts to people with whom he hoped to curry favors; but I doubt it. It may not even be important that anything should be done in the direction of rectification, when so many more important elements of our life seem to need repair. On the other hand, it may be extremely important, for so little of our lore and so few of our habits originate in circumstances of unselfishness. Necessity has driven many of us back to the old-fashioned Christmas of late, but more of us would revert to Yule *a la* 1929 if opportunity permitted, if only to show that we are recovering from Hard Times before the rest of the local Joneses. Before doing so we may be well advised to ponder the actual reasons for Christmas celebration, to think back to the Christmas we used to know as children. Those were Christmases worth having. Those were the Good Old Days!

A SHIP OF SOULS
by
Ray Stannard Baker

ANOTHER man I chanced to meet during these days of my own slow recovery had an indescribable fascination for me. *He was going to die and did not know it.* Everyone about seemed aware of it. It was the bandied news of the corridor. A significant look of the eye, a nod of the head as one went by his door—there in that room is a man who is going to die.

It gave me the strangest sense of tense awareness. I had, in the past, seen men die; I had known the sorrow of the death of dear friends; but death—it is curious when I think of it—had never for me, previous to my experience in the hospital, seemed at all a reality. It was something terrible that happened to other people, and though it may appear shocking in the telling, but it is so, I thought of it somehow as their own fault. Here it had come close to me in many forms as a stark reality; something that might even happen to *me*. In this place it was no longer a phenomenon, but a measurable and daily expectancy. It was this new congeries of observation and intense feeling that so stirred my interest in this man who was going to die— and did not know it!

One day I met him. He had read something I had once written and asked if I would come to see him. I went with the greatest hesitation and reluctance, and yet with an overpowering curiosity. How must a man feel who was about to die? What would he think? How would he look? What would he say? As I walked down the corridor with the nurse who brought the message, these questions came upon me with a vividness and power I cannot describe. In my imagination I saw the poor fellow in bed, emaciated, slow of breath, feebly reaching out his hand to touch mine. I could scarcely control the beating of my heart or the trembling of my knees when I stepped around the screen.

"How are you, sir?" said a steady voice. "Come in. I'm glad to see you."

There he sat in his chair, a stout, rather florid man, in a gay-coloured dressing gown. There were flowers on his table—a world of flowers—and pictures of a smiling gray-haired woman and a smiling girl and two little boys. In front of him, on a desk, piles of neatly arranged papers, as though he had just looked up from his daily affairs. It was I who was hesitant and embarrassed: for I could not quickly adjust reality and preconception. It was he who made everything easy and hospitable.

While I sat talking with him a nurse brought in a telegram, which he slit open in the quick, nervous, incidental manner of the business man. He glanced at it and tossed it on the desk, proceeding with his conversation.

It came over me with a kind of shock. What futile urgency—if the man was going to die. Then I remembered, with a wave of pity, that he did not know!

It was not long before I could place him. He was quite a typical American business man—self-confident, positive, vital. He did not tell me in so many words that he was rich; he radiated it. He told me of a "deal" he had just "cleared up" in which he had made a "killing." I found that his secretary came in every morning to take care of "a lot of little matters."

I kept forgetting—but it would come over me suddenly and with a sinking sense of futility, "Why all these deals? What good making any more money? The man is going to die."

The next day when I stopped to see him I found the nurse reading a newspaper aloud, and when he began to talk of the depression in business and the outlook for certain stocks, I kept saying to myself, "Now, what is the use of all that?"

He talked again quite volubly about himself and his affairs: but presently he broke off, and I saw him looking at me with a slow, inscrutable gaze.

"Are you here for long?" he asked.

As I paused I thought his look intensified, and there was something deep down and far back in his narrowing eyes— or did I imagine it?—that was pitiful to see.

"The doctors," said I, "are promising me that I can go home to Christmas."

I shall never forget the pause that followed—my glance drifted away to the picture of the smiling gray-haired woman on his table—nor the peculiar tone of his voice— deep, still—one word:

"Christmas!"

They had all said he did not know, but I knew as well as though he had told me in so many words. He knew! No doubt he had known all along! My whole heart went out to him so that I could scarcely keep the tears from my eyes. I looked at him again. Yes, there was a kind of mediocrity about the man, he had few intellectual resources, but what a fighter! What a fighter! He was playing the game straight through to the end. It seemed to me at the moment as though, of all things in the world, such courage, such steadiness, was most to be admired. He had not thought out a philosophy: he *had* it. He could walk up to death with it.

Telegrams, yes, why not? Deals, yes, why not? A secretary every morning to take his letters, why not? They were not futilities, they were of the essence of the matter. He was refusing to be beaten by the past or crushed by the future. He was living, as a man ought to live, every fibre of him, in the only moment he ever really possesses—this moment! It came to me with intolerable clarity: "Why, we're all going to die and don't know it; and this is what we should do about it."

ORDEAL BY CAMP FIRE

FOR those who need, or think they need, an excuse for going on a camping trip, let me propose such an expedition as a substitute for a trial marriage. Let the prospective bride see how the prospective husband will stand up under the test of actual life as found in a week or so of camping. The experience is bound to be illuminating from the very beginning. Let her make a note of what he says when he discovers that she is taking along two suitcases, a small trunk, and a hatbox. His remarks will indicate his ability to compromise in an emergency. Let her observe the expression on his face when he gets out in the mud to attend to a tire that has gone down for the third time. She will then be able to predict his behavior when the baby demands breakfast at two in the morning. Let her watch his efforts to coax a blaze into a bunch of wet kindling, or as he tries to predict which way the smoke will drift. If he smiles wanly and says, 'Dear me!' let her beware! He is a man of no spirit, or else an accomplished poseur. If, however, when he picks up a hot stone by mistake, or when he drowns out the fire with the pot of coffee, he really rises to a certain eloquence, let her again beware! Self-control and philosophic calm are of the first importance in a husband.

On the other hand, let the young man consider carefully what she may have to say when she discovers what the stew-pan has done to her white skirt. If she takes the incident calmly, let him beware! A repressed desire to throw a fit is as dangerous as the fit itself. Or she may be one of those creatures who take no care of their clothes. But if she lets herself rave over a minor matter like that, what will she do after marriage when a waiter spills the soup into her lap? It's best not to take any risks whatever she

does. Every little incident of camp life throws a brilliant
light on the spiritual life of a man or woman. What he has
to say about mosquitoes, what she has to say about ants—
these are things that should be jotted down for future consideration. Straws, even when you find them floating on
the soup, will show which way the wind blows, and how
hard.

But it is not only in little incidents that the most intimate
glimpses of character are revealed. You swing round a
bend in the highway and suddenly find yourself face to
face with the majestic peak of Mount Shasta towering in a
rosy glow of sunset. If she says, 'Isn't it wonderful! It
looks just like a heaping plate of strawberry ice cream!'
then you know at once that you have not met your true
soul mate, and no wonder she weighs more than you do!
Or again, you are clipping sweetly along, hoping to make
Klamath Falls in time to camp by daylight, when she grabs
your arm. 'Oh, George! Do stop! I saw the cunningest
little Mariposa lily by that rock back there!' And then
you back up a quarter of a mile and she gets out to examine
a tomato can that has been left by some camper a week or
so ago! And even if it had been a lily, this is no time of the
day to stop and pick posies! This is a world where a man
has to hustle, and the question is whether a woman who is
always stopping you to look at tomato cans is going to be
much of a help.

And then, who would have a man that can't take his
mind off the subject of eating? Here we are where we can
see Mount Hood a hundred miles to the north and Mount
Something-or-other a hundred miles to the south, with all
the glittering snow peaks of the Cascades in between, and
all he can think of is, How many cans of apricots did we
bring, and will the bacon hold out till Sunday, and is that
all the canned milk, and what about the bread? Here we
stay in camp all morning mixing and frying pancakes!
What he wants is a cook, not a wife!

On the other hand, what about the man who can't catch

a good mess of trout when that fellow with the Model T in the brown lean-to tent brings in the limit every day? It's humiliating, to say the least. One wonders if he will be any more successful in bringing home the bacon after marriage. And one egg is all he wants for breakfast! And two pancakes! Does one want to spend a lifetime sitting opposite that sort of eater? One would have to resort to solitary eating between meals, and a solitary eater is as bad as a solitary drinker. Better not marry a man who is afraid to look a T-bone in the face!

And what a grand opportunity it is for the prospective parents-in-law to find out whether the young man is a willing performer or not. 'We'll have a good fire this evening. There's a coolish wind off the lake.' You take your axe. You saw a dead cedar on the way in. It was just fallen and the brittle branches will be easy to knock to pieces. You rather pride yourself on your skill with the axe. You give one or two strokes. How good the axe feels as it settles into the wood! 'Here! Let me do it for you!' He does it for you. Thoughtful young fellow!

You begin toasting some bread by the fire. It is a quiet evening and the smoke goes straight up. The fire is fine for toasting. The cedar branches have sunk down into glowing cubes. It is a question whether it is more fun to make toast or to eat it. The question is settled for you. He relieves you of the toasting fork and kindly makes your toast for you. Thoughtful young fellow!

Never mind: you want a drink. You know where the lovely little spring is that bubbles out from under the old laurel. You enjoy going for that cup of water. It is a restful little nook and you want to listen to the stream. You will just slip away and leave those young things sitting on the cedar log in the moonlight talking. Just as you are setting out he grabs the vessel from your hand and hastens to get the water for you. He is so thoughtful! What a wonderful husband he will make for the little girl!

All right—never mind. While he is looking after the

dishes you will have a shave. Surely that is a private and intimate sort of occupation that one might be allowed to do for one's self! But he is an expert at putting an edge on a razor; he can show you how to make a perfect lather in the hardest kind of water; he fixes the mirror in the tree just right for you. . . If the daughter wants to marry a busy bee like that, all right! But you begin laying your plans for a solitary trip into Canada, where they have only mosquitoes.

Oh, camp life is the true test for congenial souls!

SPEAKING ENGAGEMENT
by
Harry Hansen

YOU could have knocked me over with a feather when Mrs. Bonivar called me long distance yesterday and said sweetly, "But you promised to speak to our club, Mr. Doakie, and we're all expecting you. I know your talk will be lovely" . . . and all that sort of thing. Then she gave me details about getting into the heart of New Jersey by way of a ferry, a local accommodation, and a bus, and after she had reminded me again that my lecture would begin promptly at three o'clock—in order not to delay the tea that followed it—she hung up and left me sunk. For the worst storm of the winter was whirling past my office windows, and I kicked myself for having listened to a siren and agreed to an engagement last July, when the sun was shining and the flowers were in bloom.

Just to discover why, I rummaged in my correspondence and there, sure enough, found the original letter from Mrs. Bonivar. She had written:

"As you know the women's clubs have had a hard year, and we can't offer to pay you what you deserve to have, but we hope that you will make an exception in our case and come for less, because the ladies are all so eager to be guided by what you say, and have no other opportunity of hearing you!" . . .

So that was it—she tickled the vanity of the male and he fell. I thought ruefully of my weakness as I braved the winds of the Hudson on the ferry and gazed out over the forlorn sunken meadows of Jersey from the windows of a train that took in all the milk-stops and road crossings. But by the time I reached the town my mind was busy

288

with my subject—Current Trends—which, like Horizons, and Vistas, was one of those blanket assignments that gave a man plenty of space to roam about in.

I didn't have any trouble finding the clubhouse. Women's clubs all look alike, and I've grown so canny in this business that I can spot a clubhouse in the dark. Usually they are built in two parts—the older section was invariably the home of the local banker in 1888, and the newer section, built to house the kitchens and hall, was added in boom days. The old is usually in the tradition of Mansard, complicated by American gingerbread, whereas the new is either colonial Georgian or classic Greek, with a coat of stucco applied over everything to harmonize the whole.

There was no one to receive me at the door, but I am used to that, so I walked boldly in and discovered a woman wrapped in a mink coat hovering about the formal hall. The place was cold as ice, and I attributed this to the lack of money for heating; no doubt the club was economizing. A special room had been reserved for my wardrobe; it smelled of stale tobacco, left over from the last function when males had used the room, and it too was cold and clammy.

The woman who met me was Mrs. Bonivar. It seems that because she had extracted from me the original promise to speak she was now responsible for my comfort. Her relief at my appearance was obvious. "I'm *so* glad you could come, Mr. Doakie," she said. "This is *my* last program of the year and I did want to have it successful. The ladies are all excited to hear what you have to say."

We went in and sat down at the back of the auditorium, but I could discern no excitement. Maybe that was because the ladies were listening to a report of the gardening committee, which dealt with things that would be under-ground for at least another three months. This was followed by a report on finances.

"I'm sorry we are so short of funds this year," whispered Mrs. Bonivar. "But all the clubs have had a hard year.

They tell me that the club in X may lose its clubhouse. We managed to make the interest on our mortgage but we had to pass up the annual payment on the principal. I'll give you your check right now; I think it was wonderful of you to come for this small amount; it should have been much larger, I know."

Her generosity disarmed me. I put the check in my pocket, explaining that I was happy to be of use. I felt that I was amply repaid for my time if the ladies got something out of my talk.

The woman on the platform was explaining about relief. "We have done the best we could," she said, "but there are still a great many families in want. If any of our members have any clothing that they can spare, please give it to the committee. In times like these I am sure we ought all to do what we can. There are also a few ladies who have not paid their special relief assessment. Please don't delay paying me this afternoon."

She adjusted her glasses and consulted a paper. "I am happy to report," she continued, "that we have already collected $11.50. Of course that isn't much, when you consider the cost of things. But it will go a long way to help feed the little folks who really need good food and warm clothing."

Her voice trailed off and I gulped. I found myself suddenly stirred with compassion. Only $11.50 collected for relief, and here they were paying me—well, not what I usually asked, and yet a great deal more than that little $11.50, simply because they had to have a program. It was preposterous to take the money. As against starving children, my talents were worth nothing. I determined then and there to throw the check into the hopper—to turn it over to the club for relief purposes. And as I sat there I began to see reasons for the meager collection. The women were not as prosperous as I had thought them. There were a lot in last year's furs. And there was a big discolored place on the ceiling where the roof had leaked, probably because the club could not afford repairs.

Just then I happened to see that I was not the only male in the room. A lanky, nervous young man, apparently bored, was sitting at one side, shifting his feet and twirling a bowler hat on a cane. His identity was soon disclosed to me. "We have with us today," said the chairman, when the report on relief was finished, "a man whom we have all been eager to hear. I am happy to introduce Mr. Swiffey, who is putting on our annual musical show."

Mr. Swiffey had evidently been waiting for this moment. He rose like a falcon going after its prey. He ascended the platform and faced the women, with his hat in one hand and his cane in the other. He started without the usual urbanities about the privilege of addressing the club. "I'm surprised," said he, "at the little work that has been done by the ladies of this club in selling tickets for the musical comedy. I'm putting on this show at great expense—we've got the finest costumes in New York, professional stuff, direct from the big producers—and we've got a chorus that can kick a hole in the ceiling. It's going to be the biggest production—" and he began pounding the floor with his cane—"that has ever been put on in this town, bar none, a regular Broadway show. But you ladies ain't working. You've got to get out and do your part. You've got to fill the hall."

"Have you any suggestions, Mr. Swiffey?" asked the chairman. I felt sorry for her a moment later.

"Suggestions?" repeated Mr. Swiffey. "I'll say I've got suggestions. You ladies have got husbands. You have got daughters who have men friends. Get them to take ten tickets apiece and sell them to their friends. Everybody likes a good girl show, and we've got a live one. Besides, remember you ladies have put up a lot of money for this show. You've paid out $1,000 already and you've got to get it back. . ."

I leaned over to whisper to Mrs. Bonivar. "Do I under-

stand the club has already paid out $1,000 for this show?"
I asked.

"Yes," she said.

"And collected $11.50 for poor relief?"

"Yes," she said. "Isn't it awful? It costs so much to
put on a show these days."

I pushed the check down in my inside coat-pocket and
started thinking about my lecture. I was suddenly convinced that that would be awful too.

2. POETRY

NOW THE GREAT GOD SUN DESCENDS
by
Robert P. Tristram Coffin

Now the great god Sun descends
As the year draws to its ends.

His feet are golden on the mountains,
Cider runs in amber fountains,
The hornets' wings made out of heat
Swarm on pears burst open sweet,
The sumac bleeds in jubilee,
A hymn stands up where stood a tree,
The maples burn without a sound,
The hounds in wine-vats are unbound.
Pumpkins roll in ponderous mirth,
The wheels of day run low on earth,
Now there smolders in the eyes
The fire of the sacrifice,
And the blood of all the year
Pours out worshipful and clear.

Now the great god Sun descends
As the year draws to its ends.

THE VILLAGE IDIOT
by
Arthur Stringer

Mad Michael streels through glen and moor
　And babbles as he goes
A raft of fool-consated words
　As crazy as his clothes.

He rakes the village midden heap
　And finds with foolish shouts
His treasured rags and rusty cans
　And pots without their spouts.

His brogans have no soles at all,
　His old caubeen no brim,
But night by night, says he, the moon
　Stoops down and talks with him.

When in his liquor, he defies
　God, Saints, and men alike,
And claiming kinship with the stars
　Grows sober 'neath the dike.

For knowledge out of musty books
　He has no foolish wish;
The truth, says he, eats up the truth
　As fishes swallow fish.

Desire is but an old white goat
　That nibbles down a whin,
And works so hard to crop a meal
　He keeps his body thin.

And His Lordship up at Tara Hall,
 Red-faced and scant o' breath,
For all his beef and fifteen stone,
 Is starving, faith, to death.

And the things we hold we never touch,
 And what we lose we gain;
And this solid earth our brogans pound
 Is a shadow in our brain.

That brain, says he, is not your own,
 But a dip net in the sea;
And the green waves washing thro' the threads
 Make thought for you and me.

And tomorrow is still yesterday
 As snow is kin to hail,
For Time, says he, is but a snake
 Devouring its own tail.

We eat the sheep, the sheep the grass
 (The poor fool figures thus),
In turn the grass roots eat the earth,
 And then the earth eats us.

Such moonshine, faith, poor Michael spouts
 You'd know him far from sane—
Yet who of us could squat like him
 Loon-happy in the rain?

O THE FIERCE DELIGHT

by

Hamlin Garland

O the fierce delight, the passion
  That comes from the wild,
Where the rains and the snows go over,
  And man is a child.

Go, set your face to the open,
  And lay your breast to the blast,
When the pines are rocking and groaning,
  And the rent clouds tumble past.

Go swim the streams of the mountains,
  Where the gray-white waters are mad,
Go set your foot on the summit,
  And shout and be glad!

THE FALCON
by
William Rose Benét

Whose eyes have pierced that tragic East
Where a miraculous sun ascends,
Whose flight has hovered above that feast
The lion makes, with lesser friends.

Whose scimitar wings through darkness break,
Through icy cold and gold of dawn
To slant across a lilied lake
And sheathe upon a lilac lawn,—

Proud flier, I can read aright
The bleak, keen brightness in your eyes,
Though cruel wings hunt down the height,
Curved talons track the cruel skies.

Buzzard and vulture linger low
To tear man's heart, but higher, higher
Into a zenith light you go
Unguessed of kite or lammergeier;

And here, upon my shoulder set,
Unhooded, freer than aught that flies,
You bring the heavens' star-spangled net
Trailed from your beak to blind my eyes;

So only since your pride is mine,
Your love of all things wild and fleet,
With golden and with crimson twine
I tie these bells about your feet.

DE FUST BANJO

by

Irwin Russell

Go 'way, fiddle! folks is tired o' hearin' you a-squawkin'.
Keep silence fur yo' betters! don' you heah de banjo talkin'?
About de 'possum's tail she's gwin to lecter—ladies, listen!
About de ha'r whut isn't dar, an' why de ha'r is missin':

"Dar's gwin to be a' oberflow," said Noah, lookin' solemn—
Fur Noah tuk de *Herald*, an' he read de ribber column—
An' so he sot his hands to wuk a-clarin' timber-patches,
An' 'lowed he's gwine to build a boat to beat de steamah
    Natchez.

Ol' Noah kep' a-nailin' an' a-chippin' an' a-sawin';
An' all de wicked neighbors kep' a-laughin' an' a-pshawin';
But Noah didn't min' 'em, knowin' whut wuz gwine to
    happen:
An' forty days an' forty nights de rain it kep' a-drappin'.

Now, Noah had done cotched a lot ob ebry sort o' beas'es—
Ob all de shows a-trabbelin', it beat 'em all to pieces!
He had a Morgan colt an' sebral head o' Jarsey cattle—
An' druv 'em 'board de Ark as soon's he heered de thunder
    rattle.

Den sech anoder fall ob rain! It come so awful hebby,
De ribber riz immejitly, an' busted troo de lebbee;
De people all wuz drownded out—'cep' Noah an' de critters,
An' men he'd hired to wuk de boat—an' one to mix de
    bitters.

De Ark she kep' a-sailin' an' a-sailin' *an'* a-sailin';
De lion got his dander up, an' like to bruk de palin';
De sarpints hissed; de panters yelled; tel', whut wid all de
    fussin',
You c'u'dn't hardly heah de mate a-bossin' 'roun' an'
    cussin'.

Now Ham, de only nigger whut wuz runnin' on de packet,
Got lonesome in de barber-shop, an' c'u'dn't stan' de racket;
An' so, fur to amuse he-se'f, he steamed some wood an' bent
    it,
An' soon he had a banjo made—de fust dat wuz invented.

He wet de ledder, stretched it on; made bridge an' screws
    an' aprin;
An' fitted in a proper neck—'twuz berry long an' taperin';
He tuk some tin, an' twisted him a thimble fur to ring it:
An' den de mighty question riz: how wuz he gwine to string
    it?

De 'possum had as fine a tail as dis dat I's a-singin';
De ha'r's so long an' thick an' strong,—des fit fur banjo-
    stringin';
Dat nigger shaved 'em off as short as washday-dinner graces:
An' sorted ob 'em by de size—f'om little E's to basses.

He strung her, tuned her, struck a jig,—'twuz "*Nebber min'*
    de wedder,"—
She soun' like forty-lebben bands a-playin' all togedder:
Some went to pattin'; some to dancin'; Noah called de
    figgers;
An' Ham he sot an' knocked de tune, de happiest ob niggers!

Now, sence dat time—it's mighty strange—dere's not de
    slightes' showin'
Ob any ha'r at all upon de 'possum's tail a-growin';
An' curyus, too, dat nigger's ways: his people nebber los'
    'em—
Fur whar you finds de nigger—dar's de banjo an' de 'possum!

FOUR LITTLE FOXES
by
Lew Sarett

Speak gently, Spring, and make no sudden sound;
For in my windy valley, yesterday I found
New-born foxes squirming on the ground—
Speak gently.

Walk softly, March, forbear the bitter blow;
Her feet within a trap, her blood upon the snow,
The four little foxes saw their mother go—
Walk softly.

Go lightly, Spring, oh, give them no alarm;
When I covered them with boughs to shelter them from
    harm,
The thin blue foxes suckled at my arm—
Go lightly.

Step softly, March, with your rampant hurricane;
Nuzzling one another, and whimpering with pain,
The new little foxes are shivering in the rain—
Step softly.

A BALLET SONG OF MARY

by

Elizabeth Madox Roberts

Her smock was of the holland fine,
Skinkled with colors three;
Her shawl was of the velvet blue,
The Queen of Galilee.

Her hair was yellow like the wex,
Like the silken floss fine-spun;
The girdle for her golden cloak
Was all in gold bedone.

She sat her down in her own bower place
And dressed herself her hair.
Her gold kemb in her braid she laid,
And a sound fell on the door.

He came within her own bower room
"Hail, Mary, hail!" says he;
"A goodly grace is on your head,
For the Lord is now with thee."

She folded down her little white hands
When Gabriel spoke again.
She set her shawl, the corners right,
For ceremony then.

"And the God will overshadow thee
And bring a holy sweven.
Fear not, fear not," then Gabriel said,
"It's the God of the good high heaven."

"And what must be born it will heal the sick;
It will make a goodly lear;
It will fettle men for christentie
And to keep holy gear."

Then up then rose this little maid
When Gabriel's word was said,
And out of the bower she ran in haste,
And out of the hall she is sped.

She is running far to Zachary's house—
"Is this the way?" says she.
"A little maid in haste," they said,
"Has gone to the hills of Judee."

And what will be born it will ope their eyes;
It will hearten men in their stear;
It will fettle men for christentie
And to have holy gear.

It will scourge with a thong when those make gain
Where a humble man should be;
It will cast the witches from out of his saule
And drown them into the sea.

It will give men drink from the horn of the wind,
And given me meat from the song of a bird;
Their cloak they will get from the sheen of the grass,
And a roof from a singin' word.

And when they come to the Brig o' Dread,
And they cry, "I fall! I'm afear!"
It will close their eyes and give them sleep
To heal them outen their lonesome cheer,
When they come to the Brig o' Dread.

POEM XXXVII
by
A. E. Housman

I did not lose my heart in summer's even
    When roses to the moonrise burst apart:
When plumes were under heel and lead was flying
    In blood and smoke and flame I lost my heart.

I lost it to a soldier and a foeman,
    A chap that did not kill me, but he tried;
That took the sabre straight and took it striking,
    And laughed and kissed his hand to me and died.

TIPPERARY IN THE SPRING
by
Denis A. McCarthy

Ah, sweet is Tipperary in the springtime of the year,
    When the hawthorn's whiter than the snow,
When the feathered folk assemble, and the air is all a-tremble
    With their singing and their winging to and fro;
When queenly Slievenamon puts her verdant vesture on,
    And smiles to hear the news the breezes bring,
And the sun begins to glance on the rivulets that dance—
    Ah, sweet is Tipperary in the Spring.

Ah, sweet is Tipperary in the springtime of the year,
    When mists are rising from the lea,
When the Golden Vale is smiling with a beauty all beguiling,
    And the Suir goes crooning to the sea;

And the shadows and the showers only multiply the flowers
   That the lavish hand of May will fling;
Where in unfrequented ways, fairy music softly plays—
   Ah, sweet is Tipperary in the spring!

Ah, sweet is Tipperary in the springtime of the year,
   When life like the year is young,
When the soul is just awaking like a lily blossom breaking,
   And love words linger on the tongue;
When the blue of Irish skies is the hue of Irish eyes,
   And love dreams cluster and cling
Round the heart and round the brain, half of pleasure, half
      of pain—
   Ah, sweet is Tipperary in the spring.

DESERT DUSK
by
Clarence E. Southern

The dusk comes from the mountain. 'Tis the gray
That lurks in old cathedrals cool and tall;
Behind the purple-silhouetted wall
The sunset's benediction speeds the day.
Dark cactus lifts its arms as if to pray,
While down the wind is heard the wailing coyote's call,
The creeping things that wait for night to fall
Appear, and night upon the desert has her way.

The winds that moan down old arroyos dry
Are strangely like the voice of wand'ring ghosts
Seeking here a sheltered place where they may hide.
They came from distant lands these men, to die
Here in the sand. Their shadows join the hosts
That search for gold along the Great Divide.

MENDING WALL
by
Robert Frost

Something there is that doesn't love a wall,
That sends the frozen-ground-swell under it,
And spills the upper boulders in the sun;
And makes gaps even two can pass abreast.
The work of hunters is another thing:
I have come after them and made repair
Where they have left not one stone on a stone,
But they would have the rabbit out of hiding,
To please the yelping dogs. The gaps I mean,
No one has seen them made or heard them made,
But at spring mending-time we find them there.
I let my neighbor know beyond the hill;
And on a day we meet to walk the line
And set the wall between us once again.
We keep the wall between us as we go.
To each the boulders that have fallen to each.
And some are loaves and some so nearly balls
We have to use a spell to make them balance:
'Stay where you are until our backs are turned!'
We wear our fingers rough with handling them.
Oh, just another kind of out-door game,
One on a side. It comes to little more:
There where it is we do not need the wall:
He is all pine and I am apple orchard.
My apple trees will never get across
And eat the cones under his pines, I tell him.
He only says, 'Good fences make good neighbours.'
Spring is the mischief in me, and I wonder
If I could put a notion in his head:

'WHY do they make good neighbours? Isn't it
Where there are cows? But here there are no cows.
Before I built a wall I'd ask to know
What I was walling in or walling out,
And to whom I was like to give offence.
Something there is that doesn't love a wall,
That wants it down.' I could say 'Elves' to him,
But it's not elves exactly, and I'd rather
He said it for himself. I see him there
Bringing a stone grasped firmly by the top
In each hand, like an old-stone savage armed.
He moves in darkness as it seems to me,
Not of woods only and the shade of trees.
He will not go behind his father's saying,
And he likes having thought of it so well
He says again, 'Good fences make good neighbours.'

THE NEGRO SPEAKS OF RIVERS
by
Langston Hughes

I've known rivers:
I've known rivers ancient as the world and older than the
flow of human blood in human veins.

My soul has grown deep like the rivers.

I bathed in the Euphrates when dawns were young
I built my hut near the Congo and it lulled me to sleep.
I looked upon the Nile and raised the pyramids above it.
I heard the singing of the Mississippi when Abe Lincoln
went down to New Orleans, and I've seen its muddy
bosom turn all golden in the sunset.

I've known rivers:
Ancient, dusky rivers.

My soul has grown deep like rivers.

THE ORIENT, HALF MOROCCO, 8 VO.
by
Ruth Comfort Mitchell

She bought a book, once, with the butter money—
A wild, undreamed of, reckless thing to do!
(So much to manage for the winter schooling;
That split in Hannah Mary's Sunday shoe . . .)

The cover bravely flaunted gold and scarlet,—
Gave hint and promise of the hidden feast,
Fine-grained and limber, sleek beneath the fingers,
Frankly symbolic of the gorgeous east.

She wrapt it up and laid it in the bureau;
She knew she wouldn't get to read it soon,—
Not while she had the harvesters to cook for,
Tho' maybe . . . of a Sunday afternoon. . . .

How often, then, her thought went winging to it,
Thro' all the cumbered days she had to wait,
Till, in a scanty hour of hard-won leisure,
She entered shyly thro' the latticed gate:

Dim har'ms . . . sultans . . . yashmaks . . . cloudy nargillehs,—
Strange sounding words from far-off story lands;
The farm-house fades; the Wishing Carpet bears her
To Kairowan, across the golden sands.

Since then, thro' all the somber woof of living,
For her the mystic Orient weaves its spells;
Faintly, at dawn, down thro' the dairy pasture,
She seems to hear the chime of temple bells.

Now she can see across the piles of mending—
(There is a window in her prison tower!)
Beyond the baking and the baby tending
The Mueddin calls across the sunset hour.

When the fierce August sun in grudging mercy,
Threatening worse torments for the morrow, sets,
The battered barns, the tanks, the gilded hay cocks,
Are distant domes and towers and minarets.

The sullen farmer, summoned in to supper,
Weary and silent as he slouches down,
To her fresh eyes becomes a mighty Caliph
Whose minions tremble at his slightest frown.

Subtlest of all—of course they do not mark it—
She in herself is gently touched with grace—
The swifter carriage of her toil-warped figure,
The ghost of girlhood in her furrowed face.

Sometimes they have to call her twice, and sharply;
(They see her, and they think that she is there!)
Thro' all the homely clamor, she is hearing
Oh, very near and clear, The Call to Prayer!

CHILD OF MY HEART
by
Edwin Markham

Child-heart!
Wild Heart!
What can I bring you,
What can I sing you,
You who have come from a glory afar,
Called into Time from a secret star?

Fleet one!
Sweet one!
Whose was the wild hand
Shaped you in child-land,
Framing the flesh with a flash of desire,
Pouring the soul as a fearful fire?

Strong child!
Song child!
Who can unravel
All your long travel
Out of the Mystery, birth after birth—
Out of the dim worlds deeper than Earth?

Mad thing!
Glad thing!
How will Life time you?
How will God name you?
All that I know is that you are to me
Wind over water, star on the sea.

311

Dear heart!
Near heart!
Long is the journey,
Hard is the tourney:
Would I could be by your side when you fall—
Would that my own heart could suffer it all!

BUT BEAUTY ENDURES
by
Sara Bard Field

The Spring is here. . . . The Spring is flying.
Buds are bursting. No one grieves:
Summer is born when Spring is dying.
Beautiful as buds are leaves.

Summer is here. . . . The Summer is creeping—
Scarlet stain in her emerald bed.
Autumn awakes when Summer is sleeping.
Beautiful as green is red.

Autumn is here. . . . O, the Autumn is banished.
Birds fly over. Leaves let go.
Winter appears when Autumn has vanished.
Beautiful as leaves, the snow.

The Winter is here. . . . Now Winter is sliding
Down the mountain in foamy suds.
Spring will burst in where Winter is hiding.
Beautiful as are snow buds.

WE WHOM THE DEAD HAVE NOT FORGIVEN
by
Sara Bard Field

I cry to the mountains; I cry to the sea.
I cry to the forest to cover me
From the terror of the invisible throng
With marching feet, the whole day long—
The whole night long,
Beating the accent of their wrong.

We whom the Dead have not forgiven
Must hear forever that ominous beat
For the free, light, rippled air of heaven
Is burdened now with dead men's feet:

Feet that make solid the fluid space,
Feet that make weary the tireless wind,
Feet that leave grime on the moon's white face—
Black is the moon for us who have sinned!

And the mountains will not cover us,
Nor yet the forest nor the sea;
No storm of human restlessness
Can wake the tide or bend the tree.

Forever and ever until we die,
Through the once sweet air and the once blue sky
The thud of feet—the invisible throng,
Beating the accent of their wrong.

THE PALE WOMAN
by
Sara Bard Field

Woman, why so pale and thin?
A swan and a raven strive within.

From battling of beak am I wan and worn;
From grappling of white with black wing torn.

Woman, I hear no clash of wing.
In awful silence is done this thing.

They lie on my breast when weary of fight—
Swan on the left; raven on the right.

The left breast burns like a fiery cross;
The right breast blights like frozen moss.

If the white, the black heart slay,
I shall be a nest for day.

But if the swan should vanquished be,
The raven with night will feather me.

Daily I rise and lay me down.
I comb my hair and smooth my gown,
And, basket on arm, go into town.

The neighbors see nothing strange or new—
A woman marketing, as they do:
Butter and eggs and a fish or two. . . .

For who would dream my narrow clay
Could hold the whole of night and day?

Or that the birds of boundless space
Would strive in such a little place?

HOW JACK FOUND THAT BEANS MAY GO BACK
ON A CHAP
by
Guy Wetmore Carryl

Without the slightest basis
For hypochondriasis
A widow had forebodings which a cloud around her flung,
And with expression cynical
For half the day a clinical
Thermometer she held beneath her tongue.

Whene'er she read the papers
She suffered from the vapors,
At every tale of malady or accident she'd groan;
In every new and smart disease,
From housemaid's knee to heart disease,
She recognized the symptons as her own!

She had a yearning chronic
To try each novel tonic,
Elixir, panacea, lotion, opiate, and balm;
And from a homeopathist
Would change to an hydropathist,
And back again, with stupefying calm!

She was nervous, cataleptic,
And anemic, and dyspeptic:
Though not convinced of apoplexy, yet she had her fears.
She dwelt with force fanatical
Upon a twinge rheumatical,
And she said she had a buzzing in her ears!

Now all of this bemoaning
And this grumbling and this groaning
The mind of Jack, her son and heir, unconsciously bored.
His heart completely hardening,
He gave his time to gardening,
For raising beans was something he adored.

Each hour in accents morbid
This limp maternal bore bid
Her callous son affectionate and lachrymose good-bys.
She never granted Jack a day
Without some long "Alackaday!"
Accompanied by rolling of the eyes.

But Jack, no panic showing,
Just watched his beanstalk growing,
And twined with tender fingers the tendrils up the pole.
At all her words funereal
He smiled a smile ethereal,
Or sighed an absent-minded "Bless my soul!"

That hollow-hearted creature
Would never change a feature;
No tear bedimmed his eye, however touching was her talk.
She never fussed or flurried him,
The only thing that worried him
Was when no bean-pods grew upon the stalk!

But then he wabbled loosely
His head, and wept profusely,
And, taking out his handkerchief to mop away his tears,
Exclaimed: "It hasn't got any!"
He found this blow to botony
Was sadder than were all his mother's tears.

The Moral is that gardeners pine
Whene'er no pods adorn the vine.
Of all sad words experience gleans
The saddest are: "It might have beens."
(I did not make this up myself:
'Twas in a book upon my shelf.
It's witty, but I don't deny
It's rather Whittier than I!)

IRRADIATIONS
XXI
by
John Gould Fletcher

Not noisily, but solemnly and pale,
In a meditative ecstasy you entered life:
As performing some strange rite, to which you alone held
    the clue.
Child, life did not give rude strength to you;
From the beginning, you would seem to have thrown away,
As something cold and cumbersone, that armour men use
    against death.
You would perhaps look on him face to face, and so learn
    the secret
Whether that face wears oftenest a smile or no?
Strange, old, and silent being, there is something
Infinitely vast in your intense tininess;
I think you could point out, with a smile, some curious star
Far off in the heavens, which no man has seen before.

IRRADIATIONS
XXX
by
John Gould Fletcher

I have seemed often feeble and useless to myself,
And many times I have wished that the tedium of my life
Lay at last dissolved in the cold acid of death:
Yet I have not forgotten
The sparkling of waters in the sunlight,
The sound of a woman's voice,
Gliding dancers,
Chanting worshippers,
A child crying,
The wind amid the hills.
These I can remember,
And I think they are more of me
Than the wrinkles on my face and the hungry ache at my
      heart.

A BALLADE CATALOGUE OF LOVELY THINGS
by
Richard Le Gallienne

I would make a list against the evil days
  Of lovely things to hold in memory:
First, I set down my lady's lovely face,
    For earth has no such lovely thing as she;
    And next I add, to bear her company,
The great-eyed virgin star that morning brings;
    Then the wild-rose upon its little tree—
So runs my catalogue of lovely things.

The enchanted dog-wood, with its ivory trays,
  The water-lily in its sanctuary
Of reeded pools, and dew-drenched lilac sprays,
    For these, of all fair flowers, the fairest be;
    Next write I down the great name of the sea,
Lonely in greatness as the names of kings;
    Then the young moon that hath us all in fee—
So runs my catalogue of lovely things.

Imperial sunsets that in crimson blaze
  Along the hills, and, fairer still to me,
The fireflies dancing in a netted maze
    Woven of twilight and tranquility;
    Shakespeare and Virgil, their high poesy;
Then a great ship, splendid with snowy wings,
    Voyaging on into eternity—
So runs my catalogue of lovely things.

Envoi

Prince, not the gold bars of thy treasury,
   Not all thy jewelled sceptres, crowns and rings,
Are worth the honeycomb of the wild bee—
   So runs my catalogue of lovely things.

WHO DARES TO LOOK

by

Frances Frost

The glazed tree lifts webbed traceries of thin
   Branches against the blue hoar-frosted air;
And where, a breath ago, small buds were tight
   Along the twigs, clenched buds of ice are clear.

The white hills glitter in the blinding sun,
   Dark pines enameled with silver clamber high
Along the crests, and every summit hardens
   In the cold and brilliant fixative of sky.

Who dares to look on loveliness grown old,
   Still finds that winter's beauty will suffice
To move his heart with a brown weed stiff and gleaming,
   With a single rusty leaf turned into ice.

OURS IS THE SONG
by
Louise Burton Laidlaw

Ours is the song and she the chorister.
   As music pressed from violin and bow,
   Wave upon vibrant wave of love shall flow
From our two souls to form the soul of her.

Undimmed, the radiance of our joy shall be
   Caught in her tiny crescent shimmering
   And from our welded hearts her heart-beats ring
Forged on the anvil of our ecstacy.

Yet, there is magic mystery that lies
   Within the miracle of her small being,
Each year to wax more poignant in her eyes;
   And we shall marvel evermore in seeing
The subtle secret drama that is she
Focused unique against eternity.

KINSHIP
by
Angela Morgan

I am aware,
As I go commonly sweeping the stair,
Doing my part of the every-day care—
Human and simple my lot and my share—
I am aware of a marvelous thing
Voices that murmur and ethers that ring
In the far stellar spaces where cherubim sing.
I am aware of the passion that pours
Down the channels of fire thru infinity's doors;
Forces terrific, with melody shod,
Music that mates with the pulses of God,
I am aware of the glory that runs
From the core of myself to the core of the suns.
Bound to the stars by invisible choir,
Blaze of eternity now in my veins,
Seeing the rush of ethereal rains.
Here in the midst of the every-day air—
I am aware.

COLLEGE COFFEE HOUSE
(as translated by the Man at the Next Table)
by
John Holmes

*Three
sentimental
sophomores are
talking of other
and better days.*

Ah—life is sad. Most exquisitely sad.
Most richly, yearning, sweetly-somber sad,
With husky-throated horns forever blowing
Blended music in a minor key. Slow
Sweeps the pageant by, the wide procession
Of this silly world, muted, once removed,
Softened in velvet to the drowsy mind.
A face in the crowd, a form remembered,
A swift illusion in the color, held
For a moment, and in a moment gone;
A voice; memory; a sweet memory:

*Their words, in
fragments—*

"Once last year—stayed up till morning and sang
To the stars: Deep in My Heart There is a
    Dream—
The old crowd, Larry, Marty, Don and I—
And I remember—freshman year—gone now—
Great boys, great fellows—no one like them
    since."

*They are silent,
remembering.*

The smoke breaks into visible music,
Strata that shift and melt and are blown down.

They wish.

Words, what poor pale muttering sounds are
    words
To tell those golden, lost, once-only nights!
O these four walls should spring cathedral-high,
Open to heaven, there should be a chant—
Words, colors, memory and music mixed,
In praise of what mere words can not bring back.

323

As men of the world they speak, but not so unfeelingly that the Man at the Next Table cannot translate.
But that was long ago, and far away.
Oh, well—and that is life. And life is sad.
So fiercely-tender, aching, throat-full sad
And beautiful that it could break the heart
If it were not that the heart endures this—
God knows why—and finds itself somehow
In love with life, and somehow, therefore, sad.

THEN HE WILL SLEEP
by
John Holmes

Carve these graveyard words for me
On a white board cut from a hardwood tree,
And when these words are worn with weather,
Go get knives and carve another:

"Here lies a man who lies awake,
Having given to death all death can take.
Love still beats in the buried head,
Intent on the days of the great undead."

When the bodies of girls are meaningless,
And no one weeps for music heard,
Nor cares for grace, or the great word;
When down the banners of thankfulness
Are dropped, and flamelight scatters;
When time, time, no longer matters,

Then he will turn on his dark floor,
Glad as he never was before
To be underground and six feet deep;
Then he will sleep.

WOULD I KNEW!
by
William Allingham

Plays a child in a garden fair
  Where the demigods are walking;
Playing unsuspected there
As a bird within the air,
  Listens to their wondrous talking:
  "Would I knew—would I knew
What it is they say and do!"

Stands a youth at city-gate,
  Sees the knights go forth together,
Parleying superb, elate,
Pair by pair in princely state,
  Lance and shield and haughty feather:
  "Would I knew—would I knew
What it is they say and do!"

Bends a man with trembling knees
  By a gulf of cloudy border;
Deaf, he hears no voice from these
Winged shades he dimly sees
  Passing by in solemn order:
  "Would I knew—O would I knew
What it is they say and do!"

THE FAIRIES

by

William Allingham

Up the airy mountain,
  Down the rushy glen,
We daren't go a hunting
  For fear of little men;
Wee folk, good folk,
  Trooping all together;
Green jacket, red cap,
  And white owl's feather!

Down along the rocky shore
  Some make their home,
They live on crispy pancakes
  Of yellow-tide foam;
Some in the reeds
  Of the black mountain-lake,
With frogs for their watch-dogs,
  All night awake.

High on the hill-top
  The old King sits;
He is now so old and gray
  He's nigh lost his wits.
With a bridge of white mist
  Columbkill he crosses,
On his stately journeys
  From Slieveleague to Rosses;
Or going up with music
  On the cold starry night,
To sup with the Queen
  Of the gay Northern Lights.

They stole little Bridget
  For seven years long,
When she came down again
  Her friends were all gone.
They took her lightly back,
  Between the night and morrow,
They thought that she was fast asleep,
  But she was dead with sorrow.
They have kept her ever since
  Deep within the lakes,
On a bed of flag-leaves,
  Watching till she wakes.

By the craggy hill-side,
  Through the mosses bare,
They have planted thorn-trees
  For pleasure here and there.
Is any man so daring
  As dig them up in spite,
He shall find their sharpest thorns
  In his bed at night.

Up the airy mountain,
  Down the rushy glen,
We daren't go a hunting
  For fear of little men;
Wee folk, good folk,
  Trooping all together;
Green jacket, red cap,
  And white owl's feather!

EVENING PRAYER
by
William Allingham

Good Lord, to thee I bow my head;
Protect me helpless in my bed;
May no ill dream disturb the night,
Nor sinful thought my soul affright;
And sacred sleep enfold me round,
As with a guardian-angel's wings,
From every earthly sight and sound;
While tranquil influence, like the dew
Upon thine outer world of things,
Prepares a morning fresh and new.

BEFORE WINTER
by
F. R. McCreary

Long ago
The thunder went talking itself back to the dark hills,
Long ago
The green rows of peas went marching to a tiger lily sunset
While the crickets were sharpening their sickles
For the last of the late August moon.
Now hydrangea breasts hang full and low
To nourish more tenderly
Whatever of sunshine,
And the smell of bruised apples rises from the long rotted
    grass.

Those who come from the fields
Come with their arms overflowing,
And there sounds from the ripe barns
The restless paw of heavy hoofs,
As the smoky wind and the dusk
Go stabling the horses of summer.

Did autumn come with white lips
Sucking at a black beach where no one could listen?
Did she come in a moment neither night time nor day
Whirling red laughter about her,
Long ribbons of ivy leaves, crimson?
Did you see her a gray-shawled woman of the twilight
Seated in a crotch of the hills,
Supping from a half-empty cup?
Or was she a mother, goldenrod tucked in her hair,
Singing to a sunflower poking his head through the corn?
O whoever she is
And however she came
I love her.

I looked hours and hours
Into long golden wells of Indian summer.
I saw my face at the bottom
And staring, remembering,
I suddenly left them
To look at the moon.

For autumn is the sound of a door softly closing at dusk,
Of an old man's voice
Counting over and again
The bushels he stores in the cellar,
The hush of a mother telling herself and her fire,
"Sarah, Thomas and Kate,
These are my children."
Then the curves of a scythe handle tempted my hands.
I grasped them,
And eagerly
I reaped for the last time.

April, June, and August,
I took what was left
And tied it in bundles for the winter.

The dark mistress of fall
Stands in her bare feet by the barn door
Holding a sickle in her hands.
I have helped her gather red apples,
Filling her apron,
And to slit the throats of fat swine;
I have helped her find the hoes and the rakes
And stacked them in a corner with the plow.
So she stands smiling,
Watching the swirl of the smoke mist,
The slow fall of leaves and the night.

I have helped her, but now I must turn from her, whispering,
"Mothers, knit and knit,
As you watch from your windows
The way of your children, their arms full of leaves,
Swaddling the rose bushes.
Barns, hunch your backs to the north,
For your lady is going with her sickle
To beat on the cool door of the snow wind.
Pools, swallow all the stars that you can,
For the ice will come
And cover you over."

September, October, and November,
They are fearless,
So now while the smolder of leaves in the ditches
With tongues of flame and fire
Utter words of autumn prayer,
Let you, my neighbor, and I,
Go through the silence of the tented evening corn.
Let us light a fire at the edge of the fields and the woodside,
And let us stand round it, watching the leap of the shadows,

Saying over and over to ourselves,
"This is our mother, our sky mother autumn,
Who brings shadows and death all about us,
Who fills our hearts with the glory of dying
And soothes us with the promise of snow."
We thrust our hands into the memory of the night
And grasping the hands of our earth fathers, earth mothers,
They who were loyal,
We stand till the last flare and flicker yields to the darkness,
And the darkness is peace.

THE BROOK SONG
by
James Whitcomb Riley

Little brook! Little brook!
You have such a happy look—
Such a very merry manner, as you swerve and curve and
    crook—
      And your ripples, one and one,
      Reach each other's hands and run
      Like laughing little children in the sun.

      Little brook, sing to me:
      Sing about a bumblebee
That tumbled from a lily-bell and grumbled mumblingly,
      Because he wet the film
      Of his wings, and had to swim,
      While the water-bugs raced round and laughed at
        him!

Little brook—sing a song
Of a leaf that sailed along
Down the golden-braided center of your current swift and
strong,
And a dragonfly that lit
On the tilting rim of it,
And rode away and wasn't scared a bit.

And sing—how oft in glee
Came a truant boy like me,
Who loved to lean and listen to your lilting melody,
Till the gurgle and refrain
Of your music in his brain
Wrought a happiness as keen to him as pain.

Little brook—laugh and leap!—
Do not let the dreamer weep:
Sing him all the songs of summer till he sink in softest sleep:
And then sing soft and low
Through his dreams of long ago—
Sing back to him the rest he used to know!

ENCOUNTER

by

J. Redwood Anderson

I met a man upon the public way:
his face was brown as a cut rick of hay;
deep in his blue eyes dwelt that light of pain,
man's ancient heritage that none escape—
the light that dawns on the slow-rousing brain
and makes us Man forever and no more Ape—
though who shall say in those prehuman eyes
What smoulder of eternal anguish lies?

His face was brown and noble as old oak;
and as he passed he smiled and, smiling, spoke
the soft plain greeting of the peasant mind:
"'Tis a fine day!' and so passed on. But I
heard in those words the faith of all mankind
proclaimed, and stared, long after he went by,
as after an angel, cord-clad and leather-shod,
and met at random on the open road.

His wrinkled face, brown as a parchment leaf,
was like a palimpsest where the world's grief
was written: yet he smiled! What secret then
abode with the sad knowledge of his face?
What hope, on this so hopeless way of men,
looked from his eyes to greet life's few fine days?
That look held more of wise and brave and true
than all I have said or thought my lifetime through.

DOMINIQUE

by

William Henry Drummond

You dunno ma leetle boy Dominique?
  Never see heem runnin' about de place?
'Cos I want to get advice how to kip heem lookin' nice,
So he won't be alway dirty on de face—

Now dat leetle boy of mine, Dominique,
  If you wash heem an' you sen' heem off to school,
But instead of goin' dere, he was playin' fox an' hare—
Can you tell me how to stop de leetle fool?

"I'd tak' dat leetle feller Dominique,
  An' I'd put heem on de cellar ev'ry day,
An' for workin' out a cure, bread an' water's very sure,
You can bet he mak' de promise not to play!"

Dat's very well to say, but ma leetle Dominique
  W'en de jacket we put on heem 's only new,
An' he's goin' travel roun' on de medder up an' down,
Wit' de strawberry on hees pocket runnin' t'roo,

An' w'en he climb de fence, see de hole upon hees pant,
No wonder hees poor moder's feelin' mad!
So if you ketch heem den, w'at you want to do, ma frien'?
Tell me quickly an' before he get too bad.

"I'd lick your leetle boy Dominique,
  I'd lick heem till he's cryin' purty hard,
An' for fear he's gettin' spile, I'd geev' heem castor ile,
An' I wouldn't let heem play outside de yard."

334

If you see ma leetle boy Dominique
   Hangin' on to poor ole "Billy" by de tail,
W'en dat horse is feelin' gay, lak I see heem yesterday,
I s'pose you t'ink he's safer on de jail?

W'en I'm lightin' up de pipe on de evenin' affer work,
An' de powder dat young rascal's puttin' in,
It was makin' such a pouf, nearly blow me t'roo de roof—
W'at's de way you got of showin' 't was a sin?

"Wall! I put heem on de jail right away,
   You may bet de wan is got de beeges' wall!
A honder foot or so, w'ere dey never let heem go,
   Non! I wouldn't kip a boy lak dat at all."

Dat's good advice for sure, very good,
   On de cellar, bread an' water—it'll do,
De nice sweet castor ile geev' heem ev'ry leetle w'ile,
An' de jail to finish up wit' w'en he's t'roo!

Ah! ma frien', you never see Dominique,
   W'en he's lyin' dere asleep upon de bed,
If you do, you say to me, "W'at an angel he mus' be,
An' dere can't be not'ing bad upon hees head."

Many t'ank for your advice, an' it may be good for some,
But de reason you was geev' it isn't very hard to seek—
Yass! it's easy seein' now w'en de talk is over, how
You dunno ma leetle boy Dominique.

WINDY NIGHTS
by
Robert Louis Stevenson

Whenever the moon and stars are set,
  Whenever the wind is high,
All night long in the dark and wet,
  A man goes riding by.
Late in the night when the fires are out,
Why does he gallop and gallop about?

Whenever the trees are crying aloud,
  And ships are tossed at sea,
By, on the highway, low and loud,
  By at the gallop goes he.
By at the gallop he goes, and then
By he comes back at the gallop again.

THE FOOL'S PRAYER
by
Edward Rowland Sill

The royal feast was done; the King
    Sought some new sport to banish care,
And to his jester cried: "Sir Fool,
    Kneel now, and make for us a prayer!"

The jester doffed his cap and bells,
    And stood the mocking court before;
They could not see the bitter smile
    Behind the painted grin he wore.

He bowed his head, and bent his knee
    Upon the monarch's silken stool;
His pleading voice arose: "O Lord,
    Be merciful to me, a fool!

"No pity, Lord, could change the heart
    From red with wrong to white as wool;
The rod must heal the sin; but, Lord,
    Be merciful to me, a fool!

" 'Tis not by guilt the onward sweep
    Of truth and right, O Lord, we stay;
'Tis by our follies that so long
    We hold the earth from heaven away.

"These clumsy feet, still in the mire,
    Go crushing blossoms without end;
These hard, well-meaning hands we thrust
    Among the heart-strings of a friend.

"The ill-timed truth we might have kept—
  Who knows how sharp it pierced and stung?
The word we had not sense to say—
  Who knows how grandly it had rung?

"Our faults no tenderness should ask,
  The chastening stripes must cleanse them all;
But for our blunders—oh, in shame
  Before the eyes of heaven we fall.

"Earth bears no balsam for mistakes;
  Men crown the knave, and scourge the tool
That did his will; but Thou, O Lord,
  Be merciful to me, a fool!"

The room was hushed; in silence rose
  The King, and sought his gardens cool,
And walked apart, and murmured low,
  "Be merciful to me, a fool!"

GIVE ME AGAIN

by

Frank E. Thompson

Give me again the trail,
The dripping morning wood,
The whistle now and then of quail,
The scared dash and flirt of cottontail,
Glimpse of far summit draped in cloudy hood,
Keen ache of muscle and the sense of good.
Give me again the trail.

Give me again the pack
Filled with the needed things but none to spare.
Give me the skimpy roll of blanket on the back.
Give me the heart to make a clean attack,
To dash sweat from the eyes without a care.
Give me to wash my mind in God's clean air.
Give me again the pack.

Give me again the thrill of timberline,
The wide, clear world, the sudden lift,
The breeze and light of heaven like a wine,
Bush, shrub and tree defeated here, a sign
Though boundaries to things are set, the gift
Of spirit may o'er pass them. Many may drift
Give me the thrill of timberline.

Give me at last the quiet mountain night,
Hill, slope and jagged peak in soft silhouette,
The moon gone down, the stars alight,

Black shadows in the wood, snow on the height,
The gurgle odd where lake and stream are met,
The eerie mystery, the haunting fret,
   Give me the mountain night.

A BALLAD MAKER
by
Padraic Colum

Once I loved a maiden fair,
   Over the hills and far away,
Lands she had and lovers to spare,
   Over the hills and far away.
And I was stooped and troubled sore,
And my face was pale, and the coat I wore
Was thin as my supper the night before.
   Over the hills and far away.

Once I passed in the autumn late,
   Over the hills and far away,
Her bawn and byre and painted gate,
   Over the hills and far away.
She was leaning there in the twilight space,
Sweet sorrow was on her fair young face,
And her wistful eyes were away from the place—
   Over the hills and far away.

Maybe she thought as she watched me come,
   Over the hills and far away,
With my awkward stride, and my face so glum,
   Over the hills and far away,
"Spite of his stoop, he still is young;
They say he goes the Shee among,
Ballads he makes, I've heard them sung
   Over the hills and far away."

She gave me good-night in gentle wise,
   Over the hills and far away,
Shyly lifting to mine, dark eyes,
    Over the hills and far away.
What could I do but stop and speak,
And she no longer proud but meek?
She plucked me a rose like her wild rose cheek—
   Over the hills and far away.

To-morrow, Mavourneen a sleeveen weds,
   Over the hills and far away,
With corn in haggard and cattle in sheds,
   Over the hills and far away.
And I who have lost her—the dear, the rare—
Well, I got me this ballad to sing at the fair,
'Twill bring enough money to drown my care,
   Over the hills and far away.

THE CREATION
(A Negro Sermon)
by
James Weldon Johnson

And God stepped out on space,
And he looked around and said,
"I'm lonely—
I'll make me a world."

And far as the eye of God could see
Darkness covered everything,
Blacker than a hundred midnights
Down in a cypress swamp.
Then God smiled,
And the light broke,
And the darkness rolled up on one side,
And the light stood shining on the other,
And God said, *"That's good!"*

Then God reached out and took the light in His hands,
And God rolled the light around in His hands
Until He made the sun;
And He set that sun a-blazing in the heavens.
And the light that was left from making the sun
God gathered it up in a shining ball
And flung it against the darkness,
Spangling the night with the moon and stars.
Then down between
The darkness and the light
He hurled the world;
And God said: *"That's good!"*

342

Then God Himself stepped down—
And the sun was on His right hand,
And the moon was on His left;
The stars were clustered about His head,
And the earth was under His feet.
And God walked, and where He trod
His footsteps hollowed the valleys out
And bulged the mountains up.

Then He stopped and looked and saw
That the earth was hot and barren.
So God stepped over to the edge of the world
And He spat out the seven seas—
He batted His eyes, and the lightnings flashed—
He clapped His hands, and the thunders rolled—
And the waters above the earth came down,
The cooling waters came down.

Then the green grass sprouted,
And the little red flowers blossomed,
The pine tree pointed his finger to the sky,
And the oak spread out his arms,
The lakes cuddled down in the hollows of the ground,
And the rivers ran down to the sea;
And God smiled again,
And the rainbow appeared,
And curled itself around His shoulder.

Then God raised His arm and He waved His hand
Over the sea and over the land,
And He said, "*Bring forth! Bring forth!*"
And quicker than God could drop His hand,
Fishes and fowls
And beasts and birds
Swam the rivers and the seas,
Roamed the forests and the woods,
And split the air with their wings.
And God said, "*That's good!*"

Then God walked around,
And God looked around
On all that He had made.
He looked at His sun,
And He looked at His moon,
And He looked at His little stars;
He looked on His world
With all its living things,
And God said, "*I'm lonely still.*"

Then God sat down—
On the side of a hill where He could think;
By a deep, wide river He sat down;
With His head in His hands,
God thought and thought,
Till He thought, "*I'll make me a man!*"

Up from the bed of the river
God scooped the clay;
And by the bank of the river
He kneeled Him down;
And there the great God Almighty
Who lit the sun and fixed it in the sky,
Who flung the stars to the most far corner of the night,
Who rounded the earth in the middle of His hand;
This Great God,
Like a mammy bending over her baby,
Kneeled down in the dust
Toiling over a lump of clay
Till He shaped it in His own image;

Then into it He blew the breath of life,
And man became a living soul.
Amen. Amen.

UNCLE ANANIAS
by
Edwin Arlington Robinson

His words were magic and his heart was true,
  And everywhere he wandered he was blessed.
Out of all ancient men my childhood knew
  I choose him and I mark him for the best.
Of all authoritative liars, too,
  I crown him loveliest.

How fondly I remember the delight
  That always glorified him in the spring;
The joyous courage and the benedight
  Profusion of his faith in everything!
He was a good old man, and it was right
  That he should have his fling.

And often, underneath the apple-trees,
  When we surprised him in the summer time,
With what superb magnificence and ease
  He sinned enough to make the day sublime!
And if he liked us there about his knees,
  Truly it was no crime.

All summer long we loved him for the same
  Perennial inspiration of his lies;
And when the russet wealth of autumn came,
  There flew but fairer visions to our eyes—
Multiple, tropical, winged with a feathery flame,
  Like birds of paradise.

So to the sheltered end of many a year
    He charmed the seasons out with pageantry
Wearing upon his forehead, with no fear,
    The laurel of approved iniquity.
And every child who knew him, far or near,
    Did love him faithfully.

SINE QUA NON
by
Alice Lawry Gould

That each effect must have a cause
Is not a law to flout.
He cannot have a ship come in
Who never sent one out.

HEART'S EYES
by
Alice Lawry Gould

Yes, Camden is a pretty town
They say, exceptionally fair;
I really do not know, myself,
For I was lonely, there.

And Weir is ugly, I suppose,—
Rocky and bleak and bare;
I cannot rightly say, myself,
I was so happy there!

PRECIOUS MOMENTS
by
Carl Sandburg

Bright vocabularies are transient as rainbows.
Speech requires blood and air to make it.
Before the word comes off the end of the tongue,
While the diaphragms of flesh negotiate the word,
In the moment of doom when the word forms
It is born, alive, registering an imprint—
Afterward it is a mummy, a dry fact, done and gone,
The warning holds yet: Speak now or forever hold your
    peace.
Ecce homo had meanings: Behold the man! Look at him!
        Dying he lives and speaks!

JAZZ FANTASIA
by
Carl Sandburg

Drum on your drums, batter on your banjos, sob on the long
cool winding saxophones. Go to it, O jazzmen.
Sling your knuckles on the bottoms of the happy tin pans,
let your trombones ooze, and go husha-husha-hush with
the slippery sandpaper.

Moan like an autumn wind high in the lonesome treetops,
moan soft like you wanted somebody terrible, cry like
a racing car slipping away from a motorcycle-cop,
bang-bang! you jazzmen, bang altogether drums, traps,
banjos, horns, tin cans—make two people fight on the
top of a stairway and scratch each other's eyes in a
clinch tumbling down the stairs.

Can the rough stuff. . . . Now a Mississippi steamboat
pushes up the river with a hoo-hoo-hoo-oo . . . and
the green lanterns calling to the high soft stars . . . a
red moon rides on the humps of the low river hills. . . .
Go to it, O jazzmen.

AUREOLE
by
Helene Magaret

I once praised loneliness, and said:
In this way only shall I grow,
By walking fields no others tread,
By finding lakes no others know.

Deep in my heart I prayed the years
Should grant my spirit be renewed
As Francis' was, in faith and tears,
And self-immuring solitude.

I did not know that those who walk
From year to year, dear Love, alone
Often grow bold-eyed like the hawk,
Or undiscerning like the stone.

Now to my peace I understand
That none may reach the heaven's height
Unless he go there hand in hand
With one who likewise covets light.

MESA

by

Elizabeth H. Emerson

Let the shining light that floods
Your majestic heights at dawn
Turn my leaden world to gold.

Let the boisterous wind that blows
Across your wide expanse
Sweep the turmoil from my soul.

Let the fast mellow glow of the sun
Upon your creviced face
Light the fire of hope in my heart.

Let the silver glow of the moon
Peeping over your measureless rim
Change cold reality to soothing dreams.

VICTORY IN THE CABARETS
by
Louis Untermeyer

The jazz band struck up Dixie. . . . I could see
A boy from Texas slipping down a trench
While some gray phantom with a grinding wrench
Twisted an arm and pulled its bayonet free.
I saw a blur of mud and flies where three
Friends from the South had joked about the stench.
And there, complaining of his lack of French,
A Richmond black felt for his missing knee.

The fife screamed Yankee Doodle . . . and the throng
Danced to a ragtime patriotic air,
The martial fervor grew as several strong
And well-shaped girls not altogether bare
Marched with toy guns and brought the flag along,
While sixteen chorus men sang Over There.

ON SEEING A STATUE OF PAN IN A CLOISTER

by

Earl Marlatt

Pan Speaks

And I, who diced immoderately
For peacocks' tongues
And kisses,
And played upon enchanted reeds
By waters, whose blue sorcery
Seduced Narcissus,
I, who heard the bird-like cry
Of Daphne fleeing from Apollo,
And saw her fragment hair become
The golden, shy
New leaves of laurel,
Must languish in this sterile maze,
Where tonsured eremites,
Self-haloed moral,
Eke out their nymphless nights
And days
With pros and cons and predicates—
Mehercule!
One even writes
An apologia for celibates—
Ye gods, Silenus, Venus,
All the sprites,
Blast them with urchins,
Chilblains, stripes,
And for a gloating moment,
Give me back my pipes.

OVERTONES
by
Earl Marlatt

Are they nowhere,
The songs I did not sing?

In some far, iridescent air
Where silence is a whispering
Of ultra-violet symphonies,
   Are they not there,
Like mysteries,
Or sirens with torrential hair,
Untangled, free,
My vision-songs unjangled,
Pure, unheard,
Unsullied by the harsh despair
Of melody
Or a mouldering word?

Must all the music of infinity
Be sung to be?

THE FLOWER SELLER
by
Eleanor Farjeon

The Flower-seller's fat, and she wears a big shawl;
She sits on the kerb with her basket and all;
The wares that she sells us are not very dear
And are always the loveliest things of the year.
  Daffodils in April,
  Purple flags in May,
  Sweet peas like butterflies
  Upon a summer day,
  Brown leaves in autumn,
  Green leaves in spring,
  And berries in the winter
  When the carol singers sing.
The Flower-seller sits with her hands in her lap,
When she's not crying Roses, she's taking a nap;
Her bonnet is queer, and she calls you My dear,
And sells you the loveliest things of the year.

ANNE RUTLEDGE
by
Edgar Lee Masters

Out of me unworthy and unknown
The vibrations of deathless music:
"With malice toward none, with charity for all."
Out of me the forgiveness of millions toward millions,
And the beneficent face of a nation
Shining with justice and truth.
I am Anne Rutledge who sleep beneath these weeds,
Beloved in life of Abraham Lincoln,
Wedded to him, not through union,
But through separation.
Bloom forever, O Republic,
From the dust of my bosom!

THE POBBLE WHO HAS NO TOES
by
Edward Lear

I

The Pobble who has no toes
　　Had once as many as we;
When they said, "Some day you may lose them all";
　　He replied—"Fish fiddle-de-dee!"
And his Aunt Jobiska made him drink
Lavender water tinged with pink,
For she said, "The World in general knows
There's nothing so good for a Pobble's toes!"

II

The Pobble who has no toes
　　Swam across the Bristol Channel;
But before he set out he wrapped his nose
　　In a piece of scarlet flannel,
For his Aunt Jobiska said, "No harm
Can come to his toes if his nose is warm;
And it's perfectly known that a Pobble's toes
Are safe,—provided he minds his nose."

III

The Pobble swam fast and well,
　　And when boats or ships came near him,
He tinkledy-binkledy-winkled a bell,
　　So that all the world could hear him.
And all the Sailors and Admirals cried,
When they saw him nearing the further side,—
"He has gone to fish, for his Aunt Jobiska's
Runcible Cat with crimson whiskers!"

IV

But before he touched the shore,
   The shore of the Bristol Channel,
A sea-green Porpoise carried away
   His wrapper of scarlet flannel.
And when he came to observe his feet,
Formerly garnished with toes so neat,
His face at once became forlorn
On perceiving that all his toes were gone!

V

And nobody ever knew,
   From that dark day to the present,
Whoso had taken the Pobble's toes,
   In a manner so far from pleasant.
Whether the shrimps or crawfish gray
Or crafty mermaids stole them away—
Nobody knew; and nobody knows
How the Pobble was robbed of his twice five toes!

VI

The Pobble who has no toes
   Was placed in a friendly Bark,
And they rowed him back, and carried him up
   To his Aunt Jobiska's Park.
And she made him a feast at his earnest wish
Of eggs and buttercups fried with fish;—
And she said,—"It's a fact the whole world knows,
That Pobbles are happier without their toes."

ENVOY
by
Francis Thompson

Go, songs, for ended is our brief, sweet play;
Go, children of swift joy and tardy sorrow:
And some are sung, and that was yesterday,
And some unsung, and that may be to-morrow.

Go forth; and if it be o'er stony way,
Old joy can lend what newer grief must borrow:
And it was sweet, and that was yesterday,
And sweet is sweet, though purchased with sorrow.

Go, songs, and come not back from your far way:
And if men ask you why ye smile and sorrow,
Tell them ye grieve, for your hearts know To-day,
Tell them ye smile, for your eyes know To-morrow.

MEMORY
by
Thomas Bailey Aldrich

My mind lets go a thousand things,
Like dates of wars and deaths of kings,
And yet recalls the very hour—
'Twas noon by yonder village tower,
And on the last blue noon in May—
The wind came briskly up this way,
Crisping the brook beside the road;
Then, pausing here, set down its load
Of pine-scents, and shook listlessly
Two petals from that wild-rose tree.

THE GLORY TRAIL
by
Badger Clark

'Way high up the Mogollons,
  Among the mountain tops,
A lion cleaned a yearlin's bones
  And licked his thankful chops,
When on the picture who should ride,
  A-trippin' down a slope,
But High-Chin Bob, with sinful pride
  And mav'rick-hungry rope.

"Oh, glory be to me," says he,
  "And fame's unfadin' flowers!
All meddlin' hands are far away;
I ride my good top-hawse today
And I'm top-rope of the Lazy J—
  Hi! kitty cat, you're ours!"

That lion licked his paw so brown
  And dreamed soft dreams of veal—
And then the circlin' loop sung down
  And roped him 'round his meal.
He yowled quick fury to the world
  Till all the hills yelled back;
The top-hawse gave a snort and whirled
  And Bob caught up the slack.

"Oh, glory be to me," laughs he.
  "We've hit the glory trail.
No human man as I have read
Darst loop a ragin' lion's head,
Nor ever hawse could drag one dead
  Until we've told the tale."

'Way high up the Mogollons,
  That top-hawse done his best,
Through whippin' brush and rattlin' stones,
  From canyon-floor to crest.
But ever when Bob turned and hoped
  A limp remains to find,
A red-eyed lion, belly-roped
  But healthy, loped behind.

"Oh, glory be to me," grunts he.
  "This glory trail is rough,
Yet even till the Judgment Morn
I'll keep this dally 'round the horn,
For never any hero born
  Could stop to holler: 'Nuff!'"

Three suns had rode their circle home
  Beyond the desert's rim,
And turned their star-herds loose to roam
  The ranges high and dim;
Yet up and down and 'round and 'cross
  Bob pounded, weak and wan,
For pride still glued him to his hawse
  And glory drove him on.

  "Oh, glory be to me," sighs he.
    " He kaint be drug to death,
  But now I know beyond a doubt
  Them heroes I have read about
  Was only fools that stuck it out
    To end of mortal breath."

'Way high up the Mogollons
  A prospect man did swear
That moonbeams melted down his bones
  And hoisted up his hair:
A ribby cow-hawse thundered by,
  A lion trailed along,
A rider ga'nt but chin on high,
  Yelled out a crazy song:

  "Oh, glory be to me!" cries he,
    "And to me noble noose!
  Oh, stranger, tell my pards below
  I took a rampin' dream in tow,
  And if I never lay him low,
    I'll never turn him loose!"

SYMBOLS

by

David Morton

Beautiful words, like butterflies, blow by,
  With what swift colors on their fragile wings!—
Some that are less articulate than a sigh,
  Some that were names of ancient, lovely things.
What delicate careenings of escape,
  When they would pass beyond the baffled reach,
To leave a haunting shadow and a shape,
  Eluding still the careful traps of speech.

And I who watch and listen, lie in wait,
  Seeing the cloudy cavalcades blow past,
Happy if some bright vagrant, soon or late,
  May venture near the snares of sound, at last—
Most fortunate captor if, from time to time,
  One may be taken, trembling, in a rhyme.

OVERTONES
by
William Alexander Percy

I heard a bird at break of day
   Sing from the autumn trees
A song so mystical and calm,
   So full of certainties,
No man, I think, could listen long
   Except upon his knees.
Yet this was but a simple bird,
   Alone, among dead trees.

TARTARY
by
Walter de la Mare

If I were Lord of Tartary,
   Myself and me alone,
My bed should be of ivory,
   Of beaten gold my throne;
And in my court would peacocks flaunt,
And in my forest tigers haunt,
And in my pools great fishes slant
   Their fins athwart the sun.

If I were Lord of Tartary,
   Trumpeters every day
To every meal should summon me,
   And in my courtyard bray;

And in the evening lamps would shine,
Yellow as honey, red as wine,
While harp, and flute, and mandoline,
  Made music sweet and gay.

If I were Lord of Tartary,
  I'd wear a robe of beads,
White, and gold, and green they'd be—
  And clustered thick as seeds;
And ere should wane the morning-star,
I'd don my robe and scimitar,
And zebras seven should draw my car
  Through Tartary's dark glades.

Lord of the fruits of Tartary,
  Her rivers silver-pale!
Lord of the hills of Tartary,
  Glen, thicket, wood, and dale!
Her flashing stars, her scented breeze,
Her trembling lakes, like foamless seas,
Her bird-delighting citron-trees
  In every purple vale!

THE SHIP OF RIO
by
Walter de la Mare

There was a ship of Rio
Sailed out into the blue,
And nine and ninety monkeys
Were all her jovial crew.
From bo'sun to the cabin boy,
From quarter to caboose,
There weren't a stitch of calico
To breech 'em—tight or loose;
From spar to deck, from deck to keel,
From barnacle to shroud,
There weren't one pair of reach-me-downs
To all that jabbering crowd.
But wasn't it a gladsome sight,
When roared the deep-sea gales,
To see them reef her fore and aft,
A-swinging by their tails!
Oh, wasn't it a gladsome sight,
When glassy calm did come,
To see them squatting tailor-wise
Around a keg of rum!
Oh, wasn't it a gladsome sight,
When in she sailed to land,
To see them all a-scampering skip
For nuts across the sand!

THERMOPYLAE AND GOLGOTHA
by
Robert Hillyer

Men lied to them and so they went to die.
Some fell, unknowing that they were deceived,
And some escaped, and bitterly bereaved,
Beheld the truth they loved shrink to a lie
And those there were that never had believed,
But from afar had read the gathering sky,
And darkly wrapt in that dread prophecy
Died trusting that their truth might be retrieved.

It matters not. For life deals thus with Man;
To die alone deceived or with the mass,
Or disillusioned to complete his span.
Thermopylae or Golgotha, all one—
The young dead legions in the narrow pass;
The stark black cross against the setting sun.

THE LOST HEART
by
Marjorie Allen Seiffert

The lost heart longs to give itself away,
Like a dog without a master
That lonely runs the fields all day,
Farther and faster,

Its eager eyes half-dazed with loneliness,
Its paws grown sore with thorn and thistle,
A dog that any stranger may possess
By a casual whistle.

Better, lost heart, to chase the crows in the corn,
Or guard a ruined house from danger,
Than follow, follow, hopeful and forlorn,
A whistling stranger!

THE FOUNTAIN SONG
by
Eugene O' Neill

Love is a flower
Forever blooming
Life is a fountain
Forever leaping
Upward to catch the golden sunlight
Upward to reach the azure heaven
Falling,
   falling,
Ever returning,
To kiss the earth that the flower may live.

Life is a field
Forever growing
Beauty a fountain
Forever flowing
Upward beyond the source of sunshine
Upward beyond the azure heaven,
Born of God but
Ever returning
To merge with earth that the field may live.

Death is a mist
Veiling sunrise.

God is a flower
Forever blooming
God is a fountain
Forever flowing

Love is a flower
Forever blooming
Beauty a fountain
Forever flowing
Upward into the source of sunshine,
Upward into the azure heaven;
One with God but
Ever returning
To kiss the earth that the flower may live.

BARTER
by
Sara Teasdale

Life has loveliness to sell
All beautiful and splendid things,
Blue waves whitened on a cliff,
Soaring fire that sways and sings,
And children's faces looking up
Holding wonder like a cup.

Life has loveliness to sell,
Music like a curve of gold,
Scent of pine trees in the rain,
Eyes that love you, arms that hold,
And for your spirit's still delight,
Holy thoughts that star the night.

THE LONG HILL
by
Sara Teasdale

I must have passed the crest a while ago
   And now I am going down—
Strange to have crossed the crest and not to know,
   But the brambles were always catching the hem of my
     gown.

All the morning I thought how proud I should be
   To stand there straight as a queen,
Wrapped in the wind and the sun with the world under me—
   But the air was dull, there was little I could have seen.

It was nearly level along the beaten track
   And the brambles caught in my gown—
But it's no use now to think of turning back,
   The rest of the way will be only going down.

THREE EPITAPHS
by
Countée Cullen

For My Grandmother
> This lovely flower fell to seed.
> Work gently, sun and rain—
> She held it as her dying creed
> That she would grow again.

For a Virgin Lady
> For forty years I shunned the lust
> Inherent in my clay:
> Death only was so amorous
> I let him have his way.

A Lady I Know
> She thinks that even up in heaven
> Her class lies late and snores,
> While poor black cherubs rise at seven
> To do celestial chores.

YEARS AGO

by
Archibald MacLeish

Why should I think of spring in France
When each new April's new mischance
Of gypsy magic and green change
Leaves earth familiarly strange?
Were there not springs before that spring?
Was there not whist and whispering
Of wind in willow until then?
And shall there not be springs again?
I can remember times more near
And longer past than that strange year;
Hip-booted springs, half faun, half boy,
Over the lakes in Illinois,
Following the swollen runnels down
To beaches where the waves broke brown
Shaking the air, and the landward breeze
Smelled of fresh water and far pine trees,
And overnight in the steep ravine
The first hepatica grew green;
And brief, too brief, New Haven Junes,
Green mornings, harbor-smelling noons,
And twilights flat on the shadowy turf
Washed with the footfalls' shallow surf,
With a drifting voice far off and sweet,
And the rumble of wheels on the Chapel Street,
Drowsing and talking whimsily
Of Noah's ark and a life at sea.
I can remember springs more near,
Yet never when the winter's clear
And there's an earthy smoke about

And sluggard black flies blunder out,
Never do I remember these,
But seeing tint the apple trees
I see the orchards north from Meaux
Haggard with dust where the wagons go,
And smelling plow lands under rain
I smell the soft French earth again
Cut deep beneath the clumsy guns,
And hearing how some whistler runs
His broken scale hear then the song
That sunny days and all day long
A dead boy used to sing and sing.
But there were songs before that spring.

ARS POETICA

by
Archibald MacLeish

A poem should be palpable and mute
As a globed fruit

Dumb
As old medallions to the thumb

Silent as the sleeve-worn stone
Of casement ledges where the moss has grown—

A poem should be wordless
As the flight of birds

      *   *   *

A poem should be motionless in time
As the moon climbs

Leaving, as the moon releases
Twig by twig the night-entangled trees,

Leaving, as the moon behind the winter leaves,
Memory by memory the mind—

A poem should be motionless in time
As the moon climbs
           *   *   *

A poem should be equal to:
Not true

For all the history of grief
An empty doorway and a maple leaf

For love
The leaning grasses and two lights above the sea—

A poem should not mean
But be.

THE POET IN THE DESERT
by
Charles Erskine Scott Wood

The desert is a nun withdrawing behind her veil,
Grey, mysterious, meditative, unapproachable.
She is a courtesan, blazing with jewels,
Enticing with a bold smile; adjusting her raiment negli-
    gently,
Showing her brown thighs beautiful and naked.
Her body is tawny with the eagerness of the sun
And her eyes are pools shining in deep canyons.
She is cruel, inviting her victims,
Restlessly moving her wrists bound with rubies,
And her ankles bound with topaz.
Her golden breasts flash with opals.
She slays those who fear her and seek to run away

But runs her hand lovingly over those who dare;
Soothing with a voluptuous caress.
Lying on her floor richly carpeted she displays
The dazzlry of her diadems
And toys with the stars for a coronet,
Smiling inscrutably.

She is a beautiful swart woman who lights the sun
For a torch and sets the high cliffs as sentinels.
She draws morning and evening as curtains before her
    chamber,
And her breasts are the evening and the day stars.
She sits upon her throne of light, proud and silent,
Indifferent to wooers.
The sun is her servitor, the stars her attendants;
Running before her.
She sings a song unto her own ears,
Solitary, but sufficient;
The song of her being.
She is a naked dancer, dancing upon
A pavement of porphyry and pearl,
Dazzling, so that the eyes must be shaded.
She wears the stars upon her bosom
And braids her hair with the constellations.

*   *   *

I will not make a song of balmy Spring
Which lifts so shyly her ecstatic veil,
Jeweled and odorous; showing her buds.
Nor will I sing of Summer, the voluptuous,
Who lies down in the meadows when the birds
Have sunk to silence.

Nor will I celebrate the abundance of bough-bending
    Autumn
When apples lie in golden pools beneath the trees
And the wind whirls painted leaves about,
As a strong youth at play;

Nor of honest Winter, that hopeful mimicry of Death,
White, quiet, cold and fallen to rest, promising the resur-
     rection
When sap shall run in the greening willows.
How can I sing of our playground
While innocent children labor!
Or tell of golden abundance,
While starving children stare into a merciful grave?

                    *   *   *

Who can set a limit to the soul?
Who can explore the infinite?
Light, the swift messenger, which in the winking of
An eye can girdle the earth seven times,
Toils toward us half a million years bringing from
Some outer sentinel the message
Sent before man was "I am here."
And if we reach to the finest stardust of
The Milky-Way—what's beyond?
Infinite is space—but not more infinite than the soul.

I cannot reach to the uttermost bounds
Of the soul of the one I love.
No, not even of the one I love.
Though we are comrades and eagerly try
To approach each other,
There are spaces not to be crossed,
And we wander alone; as much as the moon is alone,
Eager but inexorably forbidden—yearning but inarticulate.
I cannot probe even my own soul.
It eludes me; dissolves and flies like a rainbow
Or the mist in deep canyons, where none can follow.
I am a stranger even to myself.
Mixed, compounded and conditioned by unknown forces
Which have harnessed the stars.
A mystery to myself; to my dear one, a mystery.
He who shall look upon the last sunset
May boast he has known the soul of Man.

*   *   *

Behold silver-kirtled Dawn, the life-renewer,
The comforter, bringer of a new hope.
The skies are listening to Earth's silence.
The Desert is asleep, cool, grey, silent.
A shy little breeze runs across her face
And presently her fretful babies stir upon her bosom.
The comforter casts abroad her gossamer mantle.
A lean coyote, prowler of the night,
Slips to his rocky fastness
And noiselessly, through the grey sage,
Jack-rabbits shuttle.

From castellated cliffs rock ravens launch
On broad black sails.
Wild horses, neighing and tossing their manes,
Having drunk their fill, troop back to pasture;
A sage-brush thrasher warbles a varied ecstasy:
And the waking Desert watches breathlessly
The thin, white skirts of Dawn, Dancer of the sky,
Tripping daintily down the sunrise-molten mountain,
Emptying a golden basin, filled with roses.
Now along the irrigation ditch, from cottonwoods,
Tremulous with caress of unseen fingers,
Orioles begin a rivalry of joy,
And from a pointed poplar top
A red bird, dipped in sunrise,
Cracks an exultant whip above a silver world.

*   *   *

But I have no gladness in the coming day;
For I see an endless procession,
Flowing from life unto death;
Smileless, submissive, starvation-carved, soul-stunted,
Stolidly marching toward the hungry machines,
The clang of hammers and the clank of chains;
The clash and clamour of Industry
And the evil rattle of steel-cranes.

I hear the bellowing of monsters
Which feed on men, belching their black breath against
    the sky.
Naked men sweat in fires of the damned,
Slaves to the demons which they guide:
Grimy alchemists, with faces wan,
Who dully change dull iron to more sordid gold.
The patient sky above waiting;
The patient men below waiting.
The blue sky above forever listening;
Expectant.
The tired men below forever listening;
Expectant.
An iron world without a soul, forever devouring;
Devouring the men who are mates for mothers;
Fathers, steel-muscled, broad-chested, dominant;
The women, mothers of children, weary mothers;
Crypts of the ages; flexible, undulant;
Innocent children, with white bodies, fluent,
Seeds of the unknowable Future.
Devoured for a soulless profit which in the end
Is damnation. Glorious is creation.
But if justice and joy be lacking
Creation is death.

*   *   *

I will sing a song of noisy tumultuous Cities,
Who sit upon the rocks and lure the adventurous youths
With their singing.
The Imperious Ones who bathe their feet in the blood
Of men and women and little children.
They flaunt smoky banners against the morning,
Chanting songs of combat.
For the night-watches, they put on burnished armor
Thick with jewels, marshaling
Their golden phalanxes to the water's edge.
They set watchmen on the hills
With sparkling torches. . . .

*   *   *

Cities, tall Titans, overpowering, majestic;
Challenging with a beautiful defiance.
Domes, spires, minarets, towers, cloud-touching roofs,
Earth's crown in mighty fretwork, set with brilliants
And wrought by miracle-working jinns.
Streaming plumes of steam, and scarfs of smoke restlessly
    coiling
In soft convulations.
Streets, turbulant and murmurous channels
Which the cleansing rain turns to blazing, bewildering
Rivers of light, scintillant, reflecting as mirrors.
Beside these sits a sensuous barbarian,
Crude, childish, inviting, toying with her jewels,
Proud, self-confident, wondering, staring, ominously snarl-
    ing.

*   *   *

The stones of the City are eloquent.
Their laughter is cold; but their tears are hot.
They weep for the little mothers who smile a forced smile,
Selling themselves for bread.
Cripples with leering hypocrisy prey on a greater hypocrisy.
Luxury tramples Misery, and Misery exults secretly
At the day when it shall trample Luxury.
The churches of the city are open and empty;
The jails are barred but full.

*   *   *

I have seen the naked poor enjoying the city-gutters,
In August, and puny children making a brook
Of the filthy waters; refusing to forget Childhood;
Grasping at Childhood, a grey moth
Which flutters by; escaping their thin little fingers.
I thought of all free things: the large sky,
And the rivers which carry the sky
Under the whispering willows;
Rivulets fretting their way

Through the twisted roots of silver-stemmed alders;
Winds dancing with tall grasses;
Striped chipmunks, dragon-flies and wrens;
All quick and shining things, and bees.
But I saw only gaunt ghosts
In the slums of the cities.
I smelled only the stench of Poverty.
Poverty which is made by Man—unnatural, needless.

3. CHORIC READING

TASTING THE EARTH
by
James Oppenheim

In a dark hour, tasting the Earth.

As I lay on my couch in the muffled night, and the rain
    lashed my window,
And my forsaken heart would give me no rest, no pause
    and no peace,
Though I turned my face far from the wailing of my be-
    reavement. . . .
Then I said: I will eat of this sorrow to its last shred,
I will take it unto me utterly,
I will see if I be not strong enough to contain it. . . .
What do I fear? Discomfort?
How can it hurt me, this bitterness?

The miracle, then!
Turning toward it, and giving up to it,
I found it deeper than my own self. . .
O dark great mother-globe so close beneath me. . .
It was she with her inexhaustible grief,
Ages of blood-drenched jungles, and the smoking of craters,
    and the roar of tempests,
And moan of the forsaken seas,
It was she with the hills beginning to walk in the shapes of
    the dark-hearted animals,
It was she risen, dashing away tears and praying to dumb
    skies, in the pomp-crumbling tragedy of man. . .
It was she, container of all griefs, and the buried dust of
    broken hearts,

Cry of the christs and the lovers and the child-stripped
  mothers,
And ambition gone down to defeat, and the battle over-
  borne,
And the dreams that have no waking. . .

My heart became her ancient heart:
On the food of the strong I fed, on dark strange life itself:
Wisdom-giving and somber with the unremitting love of
  ages. . . .
There was dank soil in my mouth,
And bitter sea on my lips,
In a dark hour, tasting the Earth.

A SONG ABOUT MYSELF
OR "NAUGHTY BOY"
by
John Keats

There was a naughty Boy,
  A naughty boy was he,
He would not stop at home,
  He could not quiet be—
    He took
    In his Knapsack
    A Book
    Full of vowels;
    And a shirt
    With some towels—
    A slight cap
    For night cap—
    A hair brush,
    Comb ditto,
    New Stockings,
    For old ones

Would split O!
This Knapsack,
Tight at's back,
He rivetted close
And follow'd his Nose
To the North,
To the North,
And follow'd his nose
To the North.

There was a naughty Boy,
 And a naughty boy was he,
For nothing would he do
 But scribble poetry—
 He took
 An inkstand
 In his hand,
 And a Pen
 Big as ten
 In the other,
 And away
 In a Pother
 He ran
 To the mountains,
 And fountains
 And ghostes,
 And Postes,
 And witches,
 And ditches,
 And wrote
 In his coat,
 When the weather
 Was cool,
 Fear of gout,
 And without
 When the weather
 Was Warm—

Och the charm
When we choose
To follow one's nose
To the North,
To the North,
To follow one's nose
To the North.

There was a naughty Boy,
And a naughty boy was he,
He kept little fishes
In washing tubs three—
In spite
Of the might
Of the Maid,
Nor afraid
Of his Granny—good—
He often would,
Hurly burly,
Get up early,
And go
By hook or crook
To the brook,
And bring home
Miller's thumb,
Tittlebat
Not over fat,
Minnows small
As the stall
Of a glove,
Not above
The size
Of a nice
Little Baby's
Little fingers—
O, he made,
'T was his trade,

Of Fish a pretty Kettle
   A Kettle—
   A Kettle
Of Fish, a pretty Kettle,
   A Kettle!

There was a naughty Boy,
   And a naughty boy was he,
He ran away to Scotland
   The people for to see—
     Then he found
     That the ground
     Was as hard,
     That a yard
     Was as long,
     That a song
     Was as merry,
     That a cherry
     Was as red—
     That lead
     Was as weighty,
     That fourscore
     Was as eighty,
     That a door
     Was as wooden
     As in England—
So he stood in his shoes
   And he wonder'd,
   He wonder'd,
He stood in his shoes
   And he wonder'd.

CICELY AND THE BEARS

by

Lilliput Levee

"Oh, yes! Oh, yes! ding-dong!"
The bellman's voice is loud and strong;
So is his bell: "Oh, yes! ding-dong!"
He wears a coat with golden lace;
See how the people of the place come running to hear what
    the bellman says!
"Oh, yes! Sir Nicholas Hildebrand has just returned from
    the Holy Land,
And freely offers his heart and hand—
Oh, yes! Oh, yes! Oh, yes! ding-dong!"
All the women hurry along,
Maids and widows, a clattering throng.
"Oh, sir, you are hard to understand!
To whom does he offer his heart and hand?
Explain your meaning, we do command!"
"Oh, yes! ding-dong! you shall understand!
Oh, yes! Sir Nicholas Hildebrand,
Invites the ladies of this land
To feast with him, in his castle strong,
This very day at three. Ding-dong!
Oh, yes! Oh, yes! Oh, yes, ding-dong!"
Then all the women went off to dress,
Mary, Margaret! Bridget, Bess, Patty,
And more than I can guess.
They powdered their hair with golden dust,
And bought new ribbons—they said they must—
But none of them painted, we will trust.
Long before the time arrives,
All the women that could be wives

Are dressed within an inch of their lives.
Meanwhile Sir Nicholas Hildebrand
Had brought with him from the Holy Land
A couple of bears—Oh, that was grand!
He tamed the bears, and they loved him true;
Whatever he told them they would do—
Hark! 'tis the town clock striking two!

Among the maidens of low degree
The poorest of all was Cicely—
A shabbier girl could hardly be.
"Oh, I should like to see the feast,
But my frock is old, my shoes are pieced,
My hair is rough!" (It never was greased.)
The clock struck three! she durst not go!
But she heard the band, and, to see the show,
Crept after the people that went in a row.
When Cicely came to the castle gate,
The porter exclaimed, "Miss Shaggypate,
The hall is full, and you come too late!"
Just then the music made a din,
Flute, and cymbal, and culverin,
And Cicely with a squeeze, got in.
Oh, what a sight! Full fifty score of dames that Cicely knew,
And more, filling the hall from dais to door!
The dresses were like a garden bed,
Green and gold, and blue and red—
Poor Cicely thought of her tossy head!
She heard the singing—she heard the clatter—
Clang of flagon and clink of platter—
But, oh, the feast was no such matter!
For she saw Sir Nicholas himself,
Raised on a dais just like a shelf,
And fell in love with him—shabby elf!
Her heart beat quick; aside she stepped:
Under the tapestry she crept,
Tousling her tossy hair, and wept!

Her cheeks were wet, her eyes were red.
"Who makes that noise?" the ladies said;
"Turn out that girl with the shaggy head!"

Just then there was heard a double roar,
That shook the place, both wall and floor:
Everybody looked to the door.
It was a roar, it was a growl;
The ladies set up a little howl,
And flapped and clucked like frightened fowl.
Sir Hildebrand for silence begs—
In walked the bears on their hinder legs,
Wise as owls, and merry as grigs!
The dark girls tore their hair of sable;
The fair girls hid underneath the table;
Some fainted; to move they were not able.
But most of them could scream and screech.
Sir Nicholas Hildebrand made a speech:
"Order, ladies, I do beseech!"
The bears looked hard at Cicely,
Because her hair hung wild and free—
"Related to us, miss, you must be!"
Then Cicely, filling two plates of gold
As full of cherries as they could hold,
Walked up to the bears, and spoke out bold:
"Welcome to you! and to *you*, Mr. Bear!
Will you take a chair? will *you* take a chair?
This is an honor, we do declare!"
Sir Hildebrand strode up to see,
Saying, "Who may this maiden be?
Ladies, this is the wife for me!"
Almost before they could understand,
He took up Cicely by the hand,
And danced with her a saraband.
Her hair was rough as a parlor broom;
It swung, it swirled all round the room—
Those ladies were vexed, we may presume.

Sir Nicholas kissed her on the face,
And set her beside him on the dais,
And made her the lady of the place.
The nuptials soon they did prepare,
With a silver comb for Cicely's hair:
There were bands of music everywhere.
And in that beautiful bridal show
Both the bears were seen to go
Upon their hind legs to and fro!
Now every year on the wedding day
The boys and girls come out to play,
And scramble for cherries as they may.
With a cheer for this and the other bear,
And a cheer for St. Nicholas, free and fair,
And a cheer for Cis, of the tossy hair—
With one cheer more (if you will wait)
For every girl with a curly pate,
Who keeps her hair in a proper state.
Sing bear's grease! curling-irons to sell!
Sing combs and brushes!
Sing tortoise-shell! Oh, yes! ding-dong!
The crier, the bell! Isn't this a pretty tale to tell?

THE ERL KING
by
Goethe

Who rides there so late through the night—dark and drear?
The father it is, with his infant so dear.
He holdeth the boy tightly clasped in his arm.
He holdeth him safely, he keepeth him warm.

"My son, wherefore seek'st thou thy face thus—to hide?"
"Look, father, the Erl king is close to our side:
Dost thou see not the Erl king with crown and with train?"
"My son, 'tis the mist rising over the plain."

"Oh, come, thou dear infant—oh, come thou with me!
Full many a game, I will play there with thee;
On my strand, lovely flowers their blossoms unfold.
My mother shall grace thee with garments of gold."

"My father, my father, and dost thou not hear
The words that the Erl king now breathes in mine ear?"
"Be calm, dearest child, 'tis thy fancy deceives;
'Tis the sad wind that sighs through the withering leaves."

"Wilt go then, dear infant, wilt go with me there?
My daughters shall tend thee with sisterly care,
My daughters by night their glad festival keep,
They'll dance thee, and rock thee and sing thee to sleep."

"My father, my father, and dost thou not see,
How the Erl king his daughters has brought here for me?"
"My darling, my darling, I see it aright,
'Tis the aged gray willows deceiving thy sight."

"I love thee, I'm charmed by thy beauty, dear boy!
And if thou'rt unwilling, then force I'll employ."
"My father, my father, he seizes me fast.
Full sorely the Erl king has hurt me at last."

The father now gallops, with terror, half wild.
He grasps in his arms the poor shuddering child,
He reaches his courtyard with toil and with dread,
The child in his arms finds he motionless, dead.

ALABAMA MOTHER'S LULLABY
by
Kenneth Porter

Haile Selassie's Queen Sheba's son;
His pappy was King Solomon.

He's mules an' automobiles by dozens,
Him an' Jesus Christ is cousins.

Hush, mah baby, doan' yo' weep—
Haile Selassie guards yo' sleep.

His parasol is blood red silk,
His cloak an' cape are white as milk.

His beard is black as a swamp at night,
His eyes are gun barrels, black an' bright.

Baby, hush yo' frettin', do!
Selassie watches over you.

Lions guard his palace grounds,
Fierce as lions, tame as hounds.

Haile Selassie's King of Zion—
At night he can turn *himself* to a lion!

(*Hush, mah baby, doan' yo' weep*—)
Haile Selassie guards yo' sleep.

His folks gather pearls every time it rains;
He has elephants, an' aeroplanes!

There's gold on the butt of his Winchester gun;
He'll never rest till the battle is won.

Baby, hush yo' frettin', do!
Selassie watches over you.

When the war in Africa is done
(*Hush, mah baby, doan' yo' weep*—)
His crown'll shine like the morning sun
(*Haile Selassie guards yo' sleep*).
Over Camp Creek you'll see him comin'
(*Baby, hush yo' frettin', do!*)
You'll hear the silver wings a-drummin'—
The Bosses'll jump an' light a-runnin'!
(*Selassie watches over you!*)

FREE FANTASIA ON JAPANESE THEMES
by
Amy Lowell

All the afternoon there has been a chirping of birds,
And the sun lies warm and still on the western sides of
    swollen branches,
There is no wind;
Even the little twigs at the ends of the branches do not move,
And the needles of the pines are solid
Bands of inarticulated blackness
Against the blue-white sky,
Still, but alert;
And my heart is still and alert,
Passive with sunshine,
Avid of adventure.

I would experience new emotions,
Submit to strange enchantments,
Bend to influences
Bizarre, exotic,
Fresh with burgeoning.
I would climb a sacred mountain
Struggle with other pilgrims up a steep path through pine-
    trees,
Above to the smooth, treeless slopes,
And prostrate myself before a painted shrine,
Beating my hands upon the hot earth,
Quieting my eyes upon the distant sparkle
Of the faint spring sea.

I would recline upon a balcony
In purple curving folds of silk,
And my dress should be silvered with a pattern
Of butterflies and swallows,
And the black band of my *obi*
Should flash with gold circular threads,
And glitter when I moved.
I would lean against the railing
While you sang to me of wars
Past and to come—
Sang, and played the samisen.
Perhaps I would beat a little hand drum
In time to your singing;
Perhaps I would only watch the play of light
Upon the hilt of your two swords.
I would sit in a covered boat,
Rocking slowly to the narrow waves of a river,
While above us, an arc of moving lanterns,
Curved a bridge,
A hiss of gold
Blooming out of darkness,
Rockets exploded,
And died in a soft dripping of colored stars.
We would float between the high trestles,
And drift away from other boats,
Until the rockets flared soundless,
And their falling stars hung silent in the sky,
Like wistaria clusters above the ancient entrance of a temple.

I would anything
Rather than this cold paper;
With outside, the quiet sun on the sides of burgeoning
    branches,
And inside, only my books.

FLOWER OF THE MORNING
by
Bill Adams

Tell them when I'm gone, then
Say, "He was glad to go."
Say, "He heard a ringing voice, a great wind blow."
Say, "He'd always wandered in a sort of maze."
Say, "His life had puzzled him through all his days."
Say, "He knew that this would bring an end to wonder,
Flowers of light, and songs a-wing
And doubting trampled under."
Tell them, "Death is but a birth,
A burst of flowers,
Fairer than the blooms of earth
Its beauty ours."

THEIR GOD
by
Harriet Monroe

I wonder sometimes at their idea of God—these great
    artists who painted for The Catholic Kings.
He is an old man—their God; a senile white-fringed man,
    decaying visibly.
Rafael, showing Elizabeth visiting Mary, both large with
    child,
Has a little flying God Almighty in the sky, carrying the
    two unborn babies in his arms—
A little busy-body white-haired God, powerful as a moth,
    he paints him.
Tintoretto's puny God looks worried, though poised in
    paradise at the top of things, above Jesus and Mary
    and the adoring circles of saints—
How could they adore that God!
And Velasquez, who balked at gods, who made of Mars a
    disreputable hard-boiled brainless bruiser, a bruiser
    with big mustachios,
Even Velasquez had nothing to say about God—he painted
    him bald-headed, decrepit, visibly abdicating as he
    passed on the crown to Mary.

How would you paint God?
    God, eternally young, young as the sun, young as Orion's
    nebula.
God the Creator, stringing worlds like pearls in the sky.
God, molding our little earth after supper of the day he had
    spread the Milky Way like a carpet for his feet;
Fingering forth men in millions with his right hand, and
    beasts, birds, fishes with his left.
God, smiling at life as at a field of nodding flowers,
Finding its good and evil good.

God fecund, magnificent, glorious.

God of the love intolerable, love dark and bright, that
searches, challenges, rewards.

God, moving forever at the centre, with space like a thin
robe around him.

God, facing his universe ever beginning and ending, and
calling it a day.

God of the blazing eyes that see.

God of the secret ears that hear.

"God of God, Light of Light, very God of very God."

How would you paint God?

RED SKY
by
Mary Octavia Davis

God, the Craftsman,
With subtle touch,
Painted a poem
For me to see.
   He scattered the clouds
   And dyed them gold,
   Just to catch my
   Straying fancy.
   Amazed, I watched
   As with bold brush strokes
   He darkened the hills to purple
   And behind them dropped the sun.
Then swiftly,
Lest I learn His secrets,
Dashed His colors
Over the sky—
Leaving
Vermilion, crimson
And scarlet
Dripping among the gold!

LIFE'S DRAMA
by
Louise Burton Laidlaw

Life is Time's great drama,
Earth our sky-lit stage
Whereon mighty peoples
Pass from youth to age.
Yet how strangely different,
This great work of art,
There are no onlookers—
All of us take part!

Our prompter is but common sense
Our mentor sad experience.
No volume holds our varied parts—
No plot is found through craftiest arts.
For woe to him who would but see
The wendings of his destiny.

Some actors in the wings will lurk,
Some strut their foolish parts and shirk,
Ever the center of the stage
For those who love to rant and rage!
At times a savior of his race
Commands all hearts by truth and grace;
Another's greed the world will span
Like some too great Napoleon.

*   *   *   *   *

But those who act their parts the best
Work—fail—strive on—
And early lay self-pride to rest.

OCTOBER MOON
by
Orval Ricketts

There is charm in
Old Santa Fé
In October when light
Of an autumn moon
Floods all the streets
With splintered silver.
I walked along
Cathedral Place
In the deep quiet of the
Moonlight.
There was a hush
Eloquent in silence,
Echoing faint chimes,
A muted melody of
Old bells
That echo thru all the
Forgotten years
On a night like this
In Santa Fé.

BEFORE ARARAT
by
J. Redwood Anderson

Over the leagues of lifeless sea
the white bird passed—repeatedly
the buffets of the savage wind assailed her flight;
while in the West, under the frown
of purple thunders southward rolled
along the marches of the night,
mantled in light and, like some old
rich-frescoed saint, gold-aureoled,
the sun went down.

The white bird passed: no sign was there
of living thing in all the dark
vast waters spread, and over head
no sign in all the empty world of air;
no sign of land—no mountain peak
pointed above the seas its naked reef,
no top of tallest tree from which her beak
might pluck one token-leaf:
nothing save, far below her flying,
in the gray troughs of ocean lying,
the tempest-battered ark.

And Noah looked forth:
east and west and south and north
stretched fierce and wide
the sombre waters desolate,
while in the West the last dun light
of the sun died,

and night
came down upon the world—menace and fear and hate—
through which not one star burned,
not one small lamp of hope through all the skies of fate.

And as the white bird, wearily
and heavily flying at her journey's end,
returned
and at the feet of Noah fell dead,
Noah, sighing, to his children said:
'To-morrow I will send
over the lifeless leagues of sea,
over the world deep-drowned in misery,
another dove:
for God is not perpetual wrath, but everlasting love.'

AN ACTOR TO APOLLO
by
Phyllis Preston

Will you breathe on me, O God?
If I can discipline this mind
Into the groove you carve, and I so ardently choose,
And the more difficult thing, if I can give this body all that
     it needs, and never a bite nor a drink nor a breath nor
     an hour of sleep over,
And make it a tight-strung unbreakable lyre for the fingers
     of perception to play on,
Every nerve responsive and quiet, every muscle relaxed
     and tensing immediately,
As a wild animal's do, to every demand put upon it—

And if I can show you a mind controlled, that it may go
    freer,
Toward nothing that is not alive—
My thoughts hinged like a book, one side of the leaf sweet
    and one bitter, and the two sides making the whole—

If I can keep out all that is weak, and all that is cruel,
(No, it is not possible.) If I can keep out all that is weak,
And all that I can that is cruel—
If I can show you an unleashed spirit with a lean mind like
    a peeled stick in a sentient body,
Will you breathe on me, O God?
Will you breathe on me, O God?
As the wind sweeps the harp, as the sun quickens the seed,
    so the fingers of your inspiration
Can wake some chords harmonious and strong.

Must I play my lyre myself? Guide then my heart's hands,
Which are too stiff with clenching, and too soft with ease,
Point its blunt spreading fingers, to pluck
The slimmest note of feeling without tearing;
Quicken the slow-moving knuckles,
That will not flex, and loose its wrists
To noble rhythm.

Will you breathe on me, O God?

A THANKSGIVING
by
Charles Hanson Towne

Lord, I am glad for the great gift of living—
  Glad for Thy days of sun and of rain;
Grateful for joy, with an endless thanksgiving,
  Grateful for laughter—and grateful for pain.

Lord, I am glad for the young April's wonder,
  Glad for the fullness of long summer days;
And now when the spring and my heart are asunder,
  Lord, I give thanks for the dark autumn ways.

Sun, bloom, and blossom, O Lord, I remember,
  The dream of the spring and its joy I recall;
But now in the silence and pain of November,
  Lord, I give thanks to Thee, Giver of all!

THE LORD'S PRAYER

The following beautiful composition was found in Charleston during the Civil War in the United States.
(*Unknown source*)

Thou to the mercy seat our souls
  dost gather   Our Father
To do our duty unto Thee.

To Whom all praise, all hounor,
  should be given,   Who art in heaven,
For Thou art the great God

Thou by Thy wisdom rulest the
  world's whole frame,   Hallowed be Thy name;
For ever therefore

Let nevermore delay divide us
  from   Thy will be done
Thy good pleasure,

And let our promptness to obey
  be seen   In earth as it is in heaven;
The very same

Therefore our souls, O Lord, we
  also pray   Give us this day
Thou would'st be pleased to

The food of life wherewith our
  souls are fed,   Our daily bread,
Sufficient raiment, and

With every needful thing do
    Thou relieve us,
And of Thy mercy pity

And forgive us

All our misdeeds, for Him whom
    Thou did'st please
To make an offering for

Our trespasses,

And forasmuch, O Lord, as we
    believe
That Thou wilt pardon us

As we forgive

Let that love wherewith Thou
    doth acquit us
To pardon all

Those who trespass
    against us;

And though sometimes Thou
    findest we have forgot
This love for Thee, yet help

And lead us not

Through soul's or body's want
    to desperation,
Or let earth's gain drive us

Into temptation,

Let not the soul of any true be-
    liever
Fall in the time of trial,

But deliver

Yea, save them from the malice
    of the devil,
And both in life and death keep

Us from evil,

Thus pray we, Lord, for that of
    Thee from Whom
This may be had,

For Thine is the kingdom,

This world is of Thy work, it's
    wondrous story;   The power, and the glory
To Thee belong

And all Thy wondrous works
    have ended never,   For ever.
But will remain for ever and

Thus we poor creatures would
    confess again,   Amen.
And thus say eternally,

THE VOICES

Isaiah 40

Comfort ye, comfort ye my people, saith your God.
Speak ye home to the heart of Jerusalem and call unto her,
That her affliction is ended, that her debt is paid;
That she hath received from the hand of Jehovah double
    for all her sins.
Hark, one calling:
"In the wilderness prepare ye a way for Jehovah!
Make straight in the desert a highway for our God!
Let every valley be exalted,
And every mountain and hill be made low;
And let the rugged be made a plain,
And the ledges of rocks a valley,
And the glory of Jehovah be revealed,
And all flesh shall see it together;
For the mouth of Jehovah hath spoken it."

Hark! one saying, "Cry!"
And I said:
        "What can I cry?

All flesh is grass,
And all its beauty as a wild-flower,
Grass is withered, flower faded:
For the breath of Jehovah hath blown upon it.
Surely grass is the people."
"Grass withereth, flower fadeth:
Yet the word of our God will stand forever."

Up on a high mountain, get thee up,
O Evangelistess Zion!
Lift up thy voice with strength,
Evangelistess Jerusalem!
Lift up, be not afraid, say to the cities of Judah:
Behold your God.
Behold the God, Jehovah: as a mighty one will He come,
His arm ruling for Him;
Behold, His reward is with Him,
And His recompence before Him.
He will feed His flock like a shepherd,
Gather the lambs with His right arm
And carry them in His bosom,
And tenderly lead the ewe-mothers.

LAMENT FOR THE STOLEN
by
Katherine Garrison Chapin

This is a terrible thing to be done in our time
    This is a terrible thing!
Woman to woman, shoulder to shoulder,
    The wide world over,
    Stand and look at this thing.
Evil, out of the night betraying,
Evil, the hand that stole, the slaying
Hand reaching out of the night,
Into the sheltered circle of light,
Into the harmless innocent circle of light,
    This is a terrible thing!

Ah, the heart stands still for the empty room,
    The empty bed,
There is fear in the open window, fear unspoken, unsaid,
    Ah, the cold fear unsaid.

Ah pity, ah anguish, ah pain, ah despair!
The search goes out over the waves of the air,
On the electrical waves of the air, as night closes down,
And the long cold winds of the terrible spring blow on!
Woman to woman, our hands reach out to her side,
Dumb with compassion, dumb with pity, strong only in
    pride.
Pride for the silent courage, the tears unwept
And the long endless vigilance kept,
    The vigilance kept.

410

Shoulder to shoulder the wide world over,
    We suffer this thing.
The breathless suspense, the torment, the waiting,
Hope in the heart abating, abating,
But grief and horror time cannot mend
Wait at the vigil's end,
    The vigil's end.

      Now it is ended,
      Hope is suspended,
        Nothing comes after.
      So frail to suffer death.
      In innocent breath
      The innocent light laughter
        Is stilled.
      Quick gentle heart broken,
      The tender words unspoken,
      Tender hopes unfulfilled.

      Let the earth cover
      In silence deep
      The wounds and the wounded
      In a long sleep
    Let the earth cover . . . in a long sleep
But woman to woman the watch shall keep!

Woman to woman, where there is love, is pity
Will cry these wrongs to an answering height.
From hillside to farm, from village to city
Break the heart in anger, shatter the night!
Reach for the evil with merciless hand,
Wipe the long blood stains from a trampled land!
    Not vengeance, but justice,
    Not destruction, but peace,
Wipe the long blood stains, wipe the long blood stains,
That childhood shall sleep . . . in peace . . . in peace.

THE SANTA FÉ TRAIL

(*A Humoresque*)
by
Vachel Lindsay

(I asked the old negro: "What is that bird that sings so well?" He answered: "That is the Rachel-Jane." "Hasn't it another name—lark, or thrush, or the like?" "No, Jus' Rachel-Jane.")

I. IN WHICH A RACING AUTO COMES FROM THE EAST

This is the order of the music of the morning:—
First, from the far East comes but a crooning.
The crooning turns to a sunrise singing.
Hark to the *calm*-horn, *balm*-horn, *psalm*-horn   *To be sung delicately, to an improvised tune.*
Hark to the *faint*-horn, *quaint*-horn, *saint*-horn. . . .

Hark to the *pace*-horn, *chase*-horn, *race*-horn.   *To be sung or read with great speed.*
And the holy veil of the dawn has gone.
Swiftly the brazen car comes on.
It burns in the East as the sunrise burns.
I see great flashes where the far trail turns.
Its eyes are lamps like the eyes of dragons.
It drinks gasoline from big red flagons.
Butting through the delicate mists of the morning,
It comes like lightning, goes past roaring.
It will hail all the windmills, taunting, ringing,
Dodge the cyclones,
Count the milestones,
On through the ranges the prairie-dog tills—
Scooting past the cattle on the thousand hills. . .

412

Ho for the tear-horn, scare-horn, dare-horn,
Ho for the *gay*-horn, *bark*-horn, *bay*-horn.
Ho for Kansas, land that restores us
When houses choke us, and great books bore us!
Sunrise Kansas, harvesters' Kansas,
A million men have found you before us.
A million men have found you before us.

To be read or sung in a rolling bass, with some deliberation.

II. IN WHICH MANY AUTOS PASS WESTWARD

I want live things in their pride to remain.
I will not kill one grasshopper vain
Though he eats a hole in my shirt like a door.
I let him out, give him one chance more.
Perhaps, when he gnaws my hat in his whim,
Grasshopper lyrics occur to him.

In an even, deliberate, narrative manner.

I am a tramp by the long trail's border,
Given to squalor, rags and disorder.
I nap and amble and yawn and look,
Write fool-thoughts in my grubby book,
Recite to the children, explore at my ease,
Work when I work, beg when I please,
Give crank-drawings, that make folks stare
To the half-grown boys in the sunset glare,
And get me a place to sleep in the hay
At the end of a live-and-let-live day.
I find in the stubble of the new-cut weeds
A whisper and a feasting, all one needs:
The whisper of the strawberries, white and red
Here where the new-cut weeds lie dead.

But I would not walk all alone till I die
Without some life-drunk horns going by.
And up round this apple-earth they come
Blasting the whispers of the morning dumb:—
Cars in a plain realistic row.
And fair dreams fade
When the raw horns blow.

On each snapping pennant
A big black name:—
The careering city
Whence each car came.
They tour from Memphis, Atlanta, Savannah,
Tallahassee and Texarkana.
They tour from St. Louis, Columbus, Manistee,
They tour from Peoria, Davenport, Kankakee. *Like a train-caller in a Union Depot.*
Cars from Concord, Niagara, Boston,
Cars from Topeka, Emporia, and Austin.
Cars from Chicago, Hannibal, Cairo.
Cars from Alton, Oswego, Toledo.
Cars from Buffalo, Kokomo, Delphi,
Cars from Lodi, Carmi, Loami.
Ho for Kansas, land that restores us
When houses choke us, and great books bore us!

While I watch the highroad
And look at the sky,
While I watch the clouds in amazing grandeur
Roll their legions without rain
Over the blistering Kansas plain—
While I sit by the milestone
And watch the sky,
The United States
Goes by.

Listen to the iron-horns, ripping, racking.
Listen to the quack-horns, slack and clacking.
Way down the road, trilling like a toad,
Here comes the *dice*-horn, here comes the *vice*-horn *To be given very harshly,*
Here comes the *snarl*-horn, *brawl*-horn, *lewd*-horn, *with a snapping explosiveness.*
Followed by the *prude*-horn, bleak and squeaking:—
(Some of them from Kansas, some of them from Kansas.)
Here comes the *hod*-horn, *plod*-horn, *sod*-horn,
Nevermore-to-*roam*-horn, *loam*-horn, *home*-horn.
(Some of them from Kansas, some of them from Kansas.)

Far away the Rachel-Jane

Not defeated by the horns

To be read or sung, well-nigh in a whisper.

Sings amid a hedge of thorns:—

"Love and life,

Eternal youth—

Sweet, sweet, sweet, sweet,

Dew and glory,

Love and truth,

Sweet, sweet, sweet, sweet."

WHILE SMOKE-BLACK FREIGHTS ON THE DOUBLE-
TRACKED RAILROAD

Louder and louder, faster and faster.

DRIVEN AS THOUGH BY THE FOUL FIEND'S OXGOAD,

SCREAMING TO THE WEST COAST, SCREAMING TO THE EAST,

CARRY OFF A HARVEST, BRING BACK A FEAST,

AND HARVESTING MACHINERY AND HARNESS FOR THE BEAST,

THE HAND-CARS WHIZ, AND RATTLE ON THE RAILS,

THE SUNLIGHT FLASHES ON THE TIN DINNER-PAILS.

And then, in an instant, ye modern men,

Behold the procession once again,

In a rolling bass, with increasing deliberation.

The United States goes by!

Listen to the iron-horns, ripping, racking,

Listen to the *wise*-horn, desperate-to-*advise* horn,

Listen to the *fast*-horn, *kill*-horn, *blast*-horn. . .

With a snapping explosiveness.

Far away the Rachel-Jane

Not defeated by the horns

To be sung or read well-nigh in a whisper.

Sings amid a hedge of thorns:—

Love and life,

Eternal youth,

Sweet, sweet, sweet, sweet,

Dew and glory,

Love and truth.

Sweet, sweet, sweet, sweet.

The mufflers open on a score of cars

With wonderful thunder,

To be brawled in the beginning with a snapping explosiveness, ending in a languorous chant.

CRACK, CRACK, CRACK,

CRACK-CRACK, CRACK-CRACK,

CRACK, CRACK, CRACK,
Listen to the gold-horn. . .
Old-horn. . .
Cold-horn. . .
And all of the tunes, till the night comes down
On hay-stack, and ant-hill, and wind-bitten town.
Then far in the west, as in the beginning,
Dim in the distance, sweet in retreating,
Hark to the faint-horn, quaint-horn, saint-horn,
Hark to the calm-horn, balm-horn, psalm-horn. . .

To be sung to exactly the same whispered tune as the first five lines.

They are hunting the goals that they understand:—
San Francisco and the brown sea-sand.
My goal is the mystery the beggars win.
I am caught in the web the night-winds spin.
The edge of the wheat-ridge speaks to me.
I talk with the leaves of the mulberry tree.
And now I hear, as I sit all alone
In the dusk. By another big Santa Fé stone,
The souls of the tall corn gathering round
And the gay little souls of the grass in the ground.
Listen to the tale the cottonwood tells.
Listen to the windmills, singing o'er the wells.
Listen to the whistling flutes without price
Of myriad prophets out of paradise.
    Harken to the wonder
    That the night-air carries. . . .

This section beginning sonorously, ending in a languorous whisper.

    Listen . . . to . . . the . . . whisper . . .
    Of . . . the . . . prairie . . . fairies
    Singing o'er the fairy plain:—
    "Sweet, sweet, sweet, sweet.
    Love and glory,
    Stars and rain,
    Sweet, sweet, sweet, sweet. . . ."

To the same whispered tune as the Rachel-Jane song—but very slowly.

THE LEPRACAUN OR FAIRY SHOEMAKER
(A Rhyme for the Children)
by
William Allingham

Little Cowboy, what have you heard
　　Up on the lonely rath's green mound?
Only the plaintive yellow bird
　　Sighing in sultry fields around,
Chary, chary, chary, chee-ee!—
Only the grasshopper and the bee?—
　　　　"Tip-tap, rip-rap,
　　　　Tick-a-tack-too!
　　Scarlet leather, sewn together,
　　　　This will make a shoe.
　　Left, right, pull it tight;
　　　　Summer days are warm;
　　Underground in winter,
　　　　Laughing at the storm!"
Lay your ear close to the hill.
Do you not catch the tiny clamour,
Busy click of an elfin hammer,
Voice of the Lepracaun singing shrill
　　As he merrily plies his trade?
　　　　He's a span
　　　　And a quarter in height.
Get him in sight, hold him tight,
　　And you're a made
　　　　Man!

You watch your cattle the summer day,
Sup on potatoes, sleep in the hay;
　　How would you like to roll in your carriage,
　　Look for a duchess's daughter in marriage?

Seize the Shoemaker—then you may!
  "Big boots a-hunting,
    Sandals in the hall,
  White for a wedding-feast,
    Pink for a ball.
  This way, that way,
    So we make a shoe;
  Getting rich every stitch,
    Tick-tack-too!"
Nine-and-ninety treasure-crocks
This keen miser-fairy hath,
Hid in mountains, woods, and rocks,
Ruin and round-tow'r, cave and rath,
  And where the cormorants build;
    From times of old
    Guarded by him;
    Each of them fill'd
    Full to the brim
      With gold!

I caught him at work one day, myself
  In the castle-ditch where foxglove grows,—
A wrinkled, wizen'd, and bearded Elf,
  Spectacles stuck on his pointed nose,
  Silver buckles to his hose,
  Leather apron—shoe in his lap—
    "Rip-rap, tip-tap,
    Tack-tack-too!
  (A grig skipp'd upon my cap,
    Away the moth flew!)
  Buskins for a fairy prince,
    Brogues for his son,—
  Pay me well, pay me well,
    When the job is done!"
The rogue was mine, beyond a doubt.
I stared at him; he stared at me;
"Servant, Sir!" "Humph!" says he,
  And pull'd a snuff-box out.

He took a long pinch, look'd better pleased,
  The queer little Lepracaun;
Offer'd the box with a whimsical grace,—
Pouf! He flung the dust in my face,
    And, while I sneezed,
      Was gone!

4. DRAMA

LOVE FOR LOVE
by
William Congreve

Note: First printed in the year 1730

As the play opens we find Valentine Legard, the philosophical son of Sir Sampson Legard, in love with Angelica, an heiress who treats him with equanimity bordering upon indifference. In the course of his life as a student and man of fashion, Valentine has accumulated some large bills, and his creditors have become embarrassing. His father has previously spent large sums for his profligacy and now lays down severe conditions for the payment of these debts. He stipulates that if Valentine will sign a deed of conveyance of all his rights to his father's estate in favor of his brother Ben, who is about to return after roaming the seas for three years, he will immediately give him four thousand pounds with which to meet his obligations and make his fortune.

The ladies in the comedy are all related to one Foresight, a doting old pedant. Angelica is his niece, and Miss Prue, a hoydenish minx, is his daughter by his first wife. The Mrs. Foresight of the play is his second wife, and considerably younger than he. Her sister, Mrs. Frail, is none too discreet in her pursuit of men. Scandal, a friend of Valentine and general man wit is introduced together with Tattle, who makes the usual pretenses of wit, fashion and amours.

Angelica calls upon Valentine in his lodgings (at the beginning of Act 4) having heard that he is suffering from a mental aberration—because she believes his madness may have been caused by his unrequited love for her; but she suspects a trick and leaves without seeing him. Later Valentine confesses to Angelica that he has feigned madness in order to secure his inheritance that he may better provide for her.

Angelica decides in the last act to make final proof of Valentine's love and constancy by leading his father to propose marriage to her and letting it be known that she intends to accept him. When at last Valentine is about to sign away his inheritance, Angelica tears up the bond and rewards his constancy and generosity with her love and fortune.

The two-fold moral sentiment is voiced in the final speeches of Scandal and Angelica, that parents should not deal tyrannically with their children, and that a constant lover is more rare than a kind woman.

*   *   *

ACT 2. SCENE 9

A room in the Foresight Home

Mrs. Foresight and *Mrs. Frail*

Mrs. Frail. What have you to do to watch me? Slife, I'll do what I please.

Mrs. Foresight. You will?

Mrs. Frail. Yes, marry will I—a great piece of business to go to Covent Garden-Square in a hackney coach and take a turn with one's friend.

Mrs. Foresight. Nay, two or three turns, I'll take my oath.

Mrs. Frail. Well, what if I took twenty—I warrant if you had been there, it had been only innocent recreation—Heavens, where's the comfort of this life, if we can't have the happiness of conversing where we like?

Mrs. Foresight. But can't you converse at home? I own it, I think there's no happiness like conversing with an agreeable man; I don't quarrel at that, nor I don't think but your conversation was very innocent: but the place is public, and to be seen with a man in a hackney coach is scandalous:—How can anybody be happy, while they're in perpetual fear of being seen and censur'd. . . . Besides it would not only reflect upon Sister, but me.

Mrs. Frail. Pooh, here's a clutter . . . why should it reflect upon you? I don't doubt but you have thought yourself happy in a hackney coach before now. . . . If I had gone to Knights Bridge or to Chelsea with a man alone, something might have been said.

Mrs. Foresight. Why was I ever in any of those places? What do you mean Sister?

Mrs. Frail. Was I? What do you mean?

Mrs. Foresight. You have been at a worse place.

Mrs. Frail. I at a worse place, and with a man!

Mrs. Foresight. I suppose you would not go alone to the World's End?

Mrs. Frail. The World's End! What, do you mean to banter me?

Mrs. Foresight. Poor Innocent! You don't know there's a place called the World's End? I'll swear you can keep your countenance purely, you'd make an admirable player.

Mrs. Frail. I'll swear you have a great deal of confidence, and in my mind too much for the stage.

Mrs. Foresight. Very well, that will appear who has most; you never were at the World's End?

Mrs. Frail. No.

Mrs. Foresight. You deny it positively to my face?

Mrs. Frail. Your face! What's your face?

Mrs. Foresight. No matter for that; it's as good a face as yours.

Mrs. Frail. Not by a dozen years wearing—But I do deny it positively to your face then.

Mrs. Foresight. I'll allow you now to find fault with my face for I'll swear your imprudence has put me out of countenance: But look you here now,—where did you lose this gold bodkin? (*Brings the bodkin in view.*) Oh, sister, sister!

Mrs. Frail. My bodkin!

Mrs. Foresight. Nay, 'tis yours, look at it.

Mrs. Frail. Well, if you go to that, where did you find this bodkin? Oh, sister, sister!

Mrs. Foresight. Oh devil on't that, I could not discover her without betraying myself.

Mrs. Frail. I have heard gentlemen say, sister, that

one should take great care when one makes a thrust in fenc-ing, not to lay open ones self.

Mrs. Foresight. It's very true, sister. Well, since all's out, and as you say, since we are both wounded, let us do what is often done in duels, take care of one another, and grow better friends than before.

Mrs. Frail. With all my heart, ours are but slight flesh wounds and if we keep 'em from air, not at all dangerous: Well, give me your hand in token of sisterly affection.

Mrs. Foresight. Here 'tis with all my heart.

Mrs. Frail. Well, as an earnest of friendship and con-fidence I'll acquaint you with a design I have. To tell truth and speak openly one to another; I'm afraid the world has observed us more than we have observed one another. You have a rich husband, and are provided for; I am at a loss and have no great stock either of Fortune or Reputation; and therefore must look sharply about me. Sir Sampson has a son, a sailor, Ben, that is expected to-night, and by the ac-count I have heard of his education, can be no conjuror. The estate you know is to be made over to him: Now if I could wheedle him . . . sister, ha? You understand me?

Mrs. Foresight. I do, and will help you to the utmost of my power. And I can tell you one thing that falls out luck-ily enough, my awkward daughter-in-law, Prue, who you know is designed to be his wife, is grown fond of Mr. Tattle; now if we can improve that, and make her have an aversion for the booby, Ben, it may go a great way towards his liking you. Here they come together and let us contrive some way or other to leave them together.

*   *   *

ACT 2.   SCENE 11

Miss Prue and *Mr. Tattle*

Miss Prue. What makes them go away, Mr. Tattle? What do they mean, do you know?

Tattle. Yes, my dear—I think I can guess—But hang me if I know the reason for it.

Miss Prue. Come, must not we go too?

Tattle. No, no, they don't mean that.

Miss Prue. No! what then? what shall you and I do together?

Tattle. I must make love to you, pretty miss; will you let me make love to you?

Miss Prue. Yes, if you please.

Tattle. Frank, Igad, at least. (*Aside.*)

Miss Prue. Well and now will you make love to me. . . . Come, I long to have you begin—must I make love too? You must tell me how.

Tattle. You must let me speak, miss; you must not speak first; I must ask you questions, and you must answer.

Miss Prue. Why, is it like the catechism? Come then ask me.

Tattle. Do you think you can love me?

Miss Prue. Yes.

Tattle. Pooh, you must not say yes already. I shan't care a farthing for you then in a twinkling.

Miss Prue. What must I say then?

Tattle. Why, you must say no, or you believe not, or you can't tell—

Miss Prue. Why, must I tell a lie then?

Tattle. Yes, if you'd be well-bred. All well-bred persons lie—besides, you are a woman, you must never speak what you think: Your words must contradict your thoughts; but your actions may contradict your words. So, when I ask you, if you can love me, you must say no, but you must love me too—If I tell you you are handsome, you must deny it, and say I flatter you. But you must think yourself more charming that I speak you;—and like me for the beauty which I say you have. . . . If I ask you to kiss me, you must be angry, but you must not refuse me. If I ask you for more, you must be more angry—but more confusing; and as soon as ever I make you say you'll cry out, you must be sure to hold your tongue.

Miss Prue. Oh, heavens, I like it better than our old-fashioned country way of speaking one's mind—and must you not lie too?

Tattle. Hum—yes—but you must believe I speak Truth.

Miss Prue. O Gemini! Well, I always had a great mind to tell lies—but they frighted me, and said it was a sin.

Tattle. Well, my pretty creature, will you make me happy by giving me a kiss?

Miss Prue. No, indeed; I'm angry at you. (*Runs and kisses him.*)

Tattle. Hold, hold, that's pretty well—but you should not have given me, but have suffered me to have taken it.

Miss Prue. Well, we'll do it again.

Tattle. With all my heart—now there my little angel.
(*Kisses her.*)

Miss Prue. Pish!

Tattle. That's right, again my charmer. (*Kisses her.*)

Miss Prue. O fie, now. I can't abide you.

Tattle. Admirable! That was as well as if you have been born and bred in Convent Garden—and won't you show me, pretty miss, where your lodging is?

Miss Prue. No, indeed won't I: but I'll run there—

Tattle. Oh my dear apt Scholar.

Miss Prue. Well, now I'll run and make more haste than you.

Tattle. You shall not fly so fast, as I'll pursue.

*   *   *   *   *

Act 3.   Scene 7

Ben, and *Miss Prue*

Ben. Come mistress, will you please to sit down? For and you stand a stern a that'n, we shall never grapple together—Come, I'll haul a chair; there, and if you please to sit, I'll sit by you.

Miss Prue. You need not sit so near one. If you have any thing to say, I can hear you farther off, I am not deaf.

Ben. Why that's true, as you say, nor I am not dumb; I can be heard as far as another—I'll heave off, to please you. (*Sits further off.*) And if we were a League asunder, I'd undertake to hold discourse with you, and if it were not a main high wind indeed, and full in my teeth. Look you, forsooth, I am as it were bound for the Land of Matrimony; 'tis a voyage, do you see, that was none of my seeking. I was commanded by Father, and if you like it, maybe I may steer into your Harbour. How say you, mistress? The short of the thing is, that if you like me, and I like you, we may chance to swing in a hammock together.

Miss Prue. I don't know what to say to you, nor I don't care to speak with you at all.

Ben. No, I'm sorry for that—But pray why are you so scornful?

Miss Prue. As long as one must not speak one's mind, one had better not speak at all. I think, and truly I won't tell a lie for the matter.

Ben. Nay, you say true in that, it's but a folly to lie. For to speak one thing, and to think just the contrary way, is as it were, to look one way, and to row another. Now, for my part, do you see, I'm for carrying things above Board, I'm not for keeping anything under Hatches, . . . so that if you were as willing as I, say for a God's name, there's no harm done. Perhaps you may be shamed-faced, some maidens, though they love a man well enough, yet they don't care to tell him to his Face. If that's the case, why Silence gives Consent.

Miss Prue. But I'm sure it is not so, for I'll speak sooner than you should believe that; and I'll speak Truth, though one should always tell a Lie to a Man; and I don't care, let my Father do what he will, I'm too big to be whipped; so I'll tell you plainly, I don't like you, nor love you at all, nor never will, that's more; so there's your answer for you; and don't trouble me no more, you ugly thing.

Ben. Look, you, young woman, you may learn to give good Words however. I spoke you fair, you see and civil. . . . I like you as little as you do me. . . . What I said was in Obedience to Father; Gad, I fear a whipping no more

than you do. But I tell you one thing, if you should give
such Language at Sea, you'd have a cat o' Nine Tails laid
across your shoulders. Flesh! who are you? You heard of
another handsome young Woman speak civilly to me, of her
own Accord: whatever you think of yourself, gad I don't
think you are any more to compare to her, than a can of
small-beer to a Bowl of Punch.

Miss Prue. Well, and there's a handsome Gentleman
and a fine gentleman, and a sweet gentleman, that was
here, that loves me, and I love him, and if he sees you speak
to me any more, he'll thrash your jacket for you, he will,
you great Sea-Calf.

Ben. What, do you mean that fair-Weather Spark, that
was here just now? Will he thrash my jacket?—Let him,
let him—But he comes near me, perhaps I may give him
a salt El for his supper, for all that. What does Father
mean, to leave me alone as soon as I come home, with such
a dirty Dowdy—Sea-Calf? I'm not Calf enough to lick your
chalked Face, you cheese-curd, you—Marry thee? Ons,
I'll marry a Lapland Witch as soon, and live upon selling
Contrary Winds, and wrecked Vessels.

Miss Prue. I won't be called names, nor I won't be
abused thus, so I won't—If I were a man—(*Cries.*) You
dare not talk at this rate—no you dare not, you stinking
Tar-Barrel.

*   *   *

ACT 5.   SCENE 2
A room in Foresight Home

Enter Sir Sampson. Discovers Angelica.

Sir S. I have not been honoured with the commands of
a fair lady a great while—Odd, madam, you have revived
me—not since I was five and thirty.

Angelica. Why, you have no great reason to complain,
Sir Sampson—that's not long ago.

Sir Sampson. Zooks, but it is madam, a very great
while to a man that admires a fine woman as much as I do.

Angelica. You are an absolute courtier, Sir Sampson.

Sir Sampson. Not at all, madam. Odsbud, you wrong me—I am not so old, neither, to be a bare courtier—only a man of words. Come, come, let me tell you, you women that a man old too soon,—faith and troth! you do—Come, don't despise fifty; odd, fifty, in a hale constitution is no such contemptible age!

Angelica. Fifty contemptible! Not at all! A very fashionable age, I think. I assure you, I know very considerable beaux that set a good face upon fifty—Fifty! I have seen fifty in a side-box, by candlelight, out blossom five and twenty.

Sir Sampson. Outsides, outsides! a prize take them, mere outsides! Hang your side-box beaux; no, I'm none of those. . . . I am of a long-lived race, a branch of one of the antidiluvian families; fellows that the flood could not wash away. Well, madam, what are your commands? Has any young rogue affronted you, and shall I cut his throat or—

Angelica. No, Sir Sampson, I have no quarrel upon my hands. I have more occasion for your conduct that your courage at this time. To tell you the truth, I am weary of living single and want a husband.

Sir Sampson. Madam, you deserve a good husband and were a pity you should be thrown away upon any of these young idle rogues about the town. Odd, there's never a young fellow worth hanging—that is a very young fellow.

Angelica. Therefore I ask your advice, Sir Sampson. I have fortune enough to make any man easy that I can like; if there were such a thing as a young agreeable man, with a reasonable stock of good nature and sense—for I would neither have an absolute wit nor a fool.

Sir Sampson. Add, you are hard to please, madam: to find a young fellow that is neither a wit in his own eye, nor a fool in the eye of the world, is a very hard task. But faith and troth! You speak very discreetly. I hate a wit. I had a son that was spoiled among them, a good hopeful lad, till he learned to be a wit, and might have risen in the state.

But, a plague on it, his wit ran him out of his money, and now his poverty has run him out of his wits.

Angelica. Sir Sampson, as your friend, I must tell you, you are very much abused in that matter—he is no more mad than you are.

Sir Sampson. How madam! Would I could prove it!

Angelica. I can tell you how that may be done—but it is a thing that would make me appear to be too much concerned in your affairs.

Sir Sampson. Odsbud, I believe she likes me. (*Aside.*) If I had Peru in one hand, and Mexico in the other, and the eastern empire under my feet, it would make me only a more glorious victim to be offered at the shrine of your beauty.

Angelica. Bless me, Sir Sampson, what's the matter?

Sir Sampson. Add, madam, I love you—and if you would only take my advice in a husband—

Angelica. Hold, hold, Sir Sampson, I asked your advice for a husband, and you are giving me your consent. I was indeed thinking to propose something like it in jest, merely to satisfy you about Valentine; for, if a match were seemingly carried on between you and me, it would oblige him to throw off his disguise of madness, in apprehension of losing me, for, you know, he has long pretended a passion for me.

Sir Sampson. Gadsooks, a most ingenious contrivance— if we were to go through with it! But why must the match only be seemingly carried on? Odd, let it be a real contract.

Angelica. O fie, Sir Sampson, what would the world say?

Sir Sampson. Say! They would say you were a wise woman, and I a happy man. Odd, madam, I'll love you as long as I live, and leave you a good fortune when I die.

Angelica. Ay, but that is not in your power, Sir Sampson, for when Valentine confesses himself in his senses, he must make over his inheritance to his younger brother.

Sir Sampson. Odd, you're cunning, a wary baggage. Faith and troth! I like you the better. But I warrant you,

I have a promise in favour of myself. Odsbud—I'll find an estate.

Angelica. Will you? Well, do you find the estate, and—

Sir Sampson. Oh, rogue! but I'll trust you. And with your consent. It is a match then?

Angelica. Let me consult my lawyer concerning this obligation; and, if I find what you propose practicable, I'll give you my answer.

Sir Sampson. With all my heart. Come in with me, and I'll lend you the bond—Odso, here's somebody coming.

THE FROGS
by
Aristophanes

Translated by Alexander Harvey

From SCENE V

(*Pluto enters followed by Aeschylus, a hobbling old man of ninety-two, very bald, with long beard, dressed in a dirty gown from which his slippered feet protrude gigantically. Behind Aeschylus walks Euripides, a distinguished figure, well groomed, bearded, most deferential in gesture and clad in a tunic over which a beautiful cloak is thrown. Bacchus is just behind him.*)

Euripides. I won't get off the throne. Don't suggest it. I say that I'm better artist than he is.

Bacchus. Aeschylus, why your reticence? You hear his remark.

Euripides. He will play the lofty creature to begin with. It's the grand manner he invariably struts with in his tragedies.

Bacchus. Oh, dear man, don't talk so big!

Euripides. I know this fellow and have long seen through him. He's a savage mortal in achievement, brazen in vocabulary, having an unharnessed, unbitted, unrestrained, unshut oral cavity, unspeakable in dissertation, indomitably loquacious, vociferating a vain syllabification.

Aeschylus. Is that so, you son of a kitchen garden goddess? (His mother peddled vegetables.) You hurl those words at me, do you? Compiler of inconsequentialities, purveyor of paucities, dramatiser of indigence, exploiter of histrionic beggary and ranting ragamuffin that you are! You won't say such things and laugh.

434

Bacchus. Whoa, Aeschylus! Don't, in your fury, make a brewery of your intestines.

Aeschylus. Not until I have fully exposed this creator of crippled caricatures for the braggart that he is!

Bacchus (pretending to speak to people in the chorus). Boy! Boy! Bring out a black lamb. A tempest is ready to break forth over our heads.

Aeschylus (to Euripides). Oh, you collector of Cretan solos, you innovator of incestuous inclinations in the field of dramatic art! (Euripides did not keep one half of a chorus dancing while the other sang. He took to such themes as the passion of Phaedra for her stepson and the love of Pasiphae for the bull.)

Bacchus. Stop this, oh, highly esteemed Aeschylus! After this hail storm, oh naughty Euripides, get yourself out of the way if you know what's what, so that he does not beat your brow with some word that would break a head and let the supreme creation of your brain escape. And you, Aeschylus, don't argue furiously but question and be questioned meekly. It is not becoming in men of poetical genius to rail at one another like women selling bread in the streets. You start roaring like a tree afire.

Euripides. Ready—that's what I am, to bite or to be bitten first just as this fellow pleases. The words, the music, the choruses, the very nerves of tragedy—I'm ready. And by Jove, for the Peleus too, and the Aeolus, and the Meleager (his tragedies) and for the Telephus, I'm ready! (The Telephus was said to have been the supreme Euripidean tragedy—now lost.)

Bacchus. Now, say, Aesychylus, what are you going to do?

Aeschylus. I didn't think of fighting here. A fight between the pair of us would not be on equal terms.

Bacchus. How's that?

Aeschylus. Because my poetical gift did not perish with me, but his did with him so that he will have it to recite here. (He means that his plays are still alive on earth and are hence not in Hades, like those of Euripides, which are dead on earth and have therefore descended to Hades.) However, since it seems proper to you, I needs must do what you say.

Bacchus. Let someone bring me incense and flame so that I may pray before the masterpieces and act as well as judge of this most literary of compositions. (*To the chorus.*) Will you be good enough to sing some song to the Muses?

Chorus. Oh, you nine holy virgins of Jove who gaze below upon the lightly worded conceits of men who make popular phrases each time they strive together like sophisticated wrestlers, come down now to contemplate the dire power of mouths apt in their equipment of syllables and saw dust. Now the gigantic intellectual fray is getting down to business!

Bacchus. Now pray, the two of you, before you say a word.

Aeschylus. Ceres, you who nursed my intellect, may I be worthy of your mysteries!

Bacchus (*to Euripides*). Now it's your turn to distribute a little incense.

Euripides. That's all right—but the gods to whom I pray are other ones.

Bacchus. Some that are peculiar to yourself or of a new crowd? (A charge against Socrates.)

Euripides. Why, certainly!

Bacchus. Then go and pray to your private and personal gods.

Euripides. Ether, my nurse, and pendulum of my tongue, and conscience, and scented orifices of my nasal organ, teach me well what words I am to choose! (*Goes inside followed by the others.*)

Chorus (*amid blowing of reeds and dancing*). And we too want to hear from these two wise men some words of sweetness. (*Spoken by a giant.*)

Let the two tongues be savage! (*Spoken by an elderly hag.*)

The mood of the pair is not without its touch of defiance. (*The speaker flourishes a club.*)

Nor are their minds unmoved. (*All now put in a word to egg on the pair.*)

It's obvious that one will say something he picked up in the city that will sound sophisticated.

The other fellow will tear his words up by the roots and rush at his foe while he scatters verses explosively. (Aeschylus will advance with an artillery of fine language which Euripides will meet after a raking fire of sarcasms.)

Scene VI

(*Euripides emerges from the shadowy palace in a military costume with shield, escorted by ghosts of admirers. Bacchus with his retinue comes next. At last Aeschylus limps forth majestically unattended but in a gorgeous robe with a garland on his bald head.*)

Bacchus. We must all begin to speak as soon as possible. Speak what is urban in its amenity and don't use figures of rhetoric or say what anyone might think of.

Euripides. As regards myself and the kind of poetry I make, I will speak last of all. I'll say first of this fellow that he is a humbug and a fizzler in the things he fools audiences with. They come to him already accustomed to the imbecilities of Phrynicus. (A famed playwright prone to lyric effects who relied upon one brilliant actor and a finely trained chorus for his great scenes.) To begin with he made it a practice to begin with a seated figure—Achilles or Niobe— all muffled up so that the face did not show, a mere hint of tragedy without one spoken word.

Bacchus. No, not one.

Euripides. And his chorus would bombard us with four volleys of lyrics, one right after another, and the actors remained dumb.

Bacchus. I rejoiced at the silence. This thing pleased me no less than do those who do so much talking now.

Euripides. You were incompetent to pass judgment—rest assured of that.

Bacchus. I seem so even to myself. Why did he do such things—this, this—what do you call him? (*He indicates Aeschylus.*)

Euripides. It was his impudence, for the sake of keeping the man in the audience sitting in suspense until Niobe said something. Meanwhile the play would be nearly over.

Bacchus. The rascal—how I was fooled by him! (*To Aeschylus.*) Why do you gape and seem ill at ease?

Euripides. Because I'm testing him. Now when he had fooled away time like that and the play was half done he roared some dozen words like a bull having brows and plumes grim and terrible in their goblin-faced aspects and all unfamiliar to the audience.

Aeschylus. Well, I declare!

Bacchus. Hold your tongue!

Euripides. Yet not one plain word did he speak. Not one.

Bacchus (*to Aeschylus*). No clenching of teeth.

Euripides. It was with him either "Scamander" (a river famed in war) or "ditches" or "shields" or eagles like griffins on shields of brass, to say nothing of jaw breakers in the form of words that it was not possible to make sense of.

Bacchus. By the gods, I have myself already in the course of one long night gone without my sleep meditating upon his golden cock. What bird is that?

Aeschylus. A device on the ships, you unteachable lout. Painted!

Bacchus. Eryxis, son of Philozenus—that's who I thought it was (A deformed reprobate who devoured prodigiously.)

Euripides. Was it becoming to drag a cock into a tragedy?

Aeschylus. And you, enemy of the gods that you are, what were the things that you dragged into it?

Euripides. Not cocks, by Jove, nor goat billies in your

style, which is that of the hanging curtains of the Medes
with pictures on them. When I took over the art from you,
the first thing I did was to reduce the bloated phraseology
and the weight of words. I strained away the fatted ver-
biage with little lines that told what the plot was. I administered chatter in small doses taken from books. I
brought tragedy up by means of monodies helped out with
an infusion of Cephisophon (a slave who is said to have
helped Euripides write his plays but this slave was later
involved in a love affair with the wife of Euripides. The
latter was noted for his domestic troubles.) Nor did I
jabber away on any trifling theme nor by rushing at once
into the heart of the plot did I bewilder the spectator of
my pieces. The actor who came first on the stage told the
audience what kind of a play it was, giving indeed the
pedigree of the character he enacted.

Bacchus. That was better than giving your own. (Although of low birth, Euripides was suspected of trying to
ape aristocracy.)

Euripides. Then from the very first words, I did not
suffer the action to lag. Either a woman spoke up in my
piece or a slave did no less or the master of the house or a
maid or an old hag.

Aeschylus. And ought you not have perished for daring
such things?

Euripides. By Apollo—I did these things to be demo-
cratic.

Bacchus. Let this go, nevertheless. You're not going
your best in turning around and about this.

Euripides. Well, I taught the characters to talk like
that.

Aeschylus. Even I admit that. Before you taught
anything of the kind you should have broken apart in the
middle.

Euripides. And you taught the lugging in of queer
quips and the lipping of lilting lingoes and other things to

contrive, to see, to wink at, to drivel, to improvise, to ape, to clown, to invent knowingly all sorts of things.

Aeschylus. That I, too, acknowledge.

Euripides. You dragged in people's domestic troubles, things that we all had learned of or were mixed up with, so that I might be put to the proof or even annoyed (his own domestic troubles were notorious). These people (the audience) knowing all about the matter, would thus be able to criticise my devices (as if they were borrowed from his own personal troubles rather than taken from actual historical tradition). But I did not use lofty language so as to be above their heads and I did not stagger them with the introduction of swans and statues or horses hung with bells. You can easily tell his followers from mine. This fellow's followers are Phormisius (a ranking orator politician) as well as Magaenetus (a servile character) from Magnesia, bewhiskered buglers or lancers and grimacing bandits of the pine trees who sneer through the piece they play where as my followers include Cleitophon (a dilettante but a genius) and Theramenes of polished manners. (The pine tree torture refers to a bandit who tied his victims to trees bent back which later flew apart and tore the helplessly bound in two.)

Bacchus. Theramenes? Wise was that man and dire in all things—so that even if he fell into difficulties or was involved in them he knew how to fall out of them too.

Euripides. I really did teach my pupils in the playwright's art to be plausible by making the drama seem real (to the audience) so that now people know more about real life than they did and can manage their domestic affairs more wisely and see how complications may be smoothed away. Hence they may ask "how did this happen?" and "who took this?" and "how has this gone?" (A political hit. The theory of the Athenian law was that the jury ran the trial, not the judge and that the jury decided domestic difficulties, by passing a sentence instead of the judge.)

Bacchus. By the gods! Now every man among the Athenians when he comes home asks the members of the household all sorts of questions. "What's the jug?" "Who's been nibbling at this fish?" "Last year's bowl has disappeared." "Where's yesterday's garlic?" "Who ate the rest of the olives?" Until now they were intellectually incurious, milk sops, worldless, brainless dunces.

Chorus (*its members mimicking the famous scene in the "Myrmidons" of Aeschylus*). You behold these things, faithful Achilles? (*Spoken by a girl or by an actor dressed as a girl.*)

Come now, you, what will you say to this? (*Spoken by one dressed as a juryman asking it of one attired as a defendant.*)

Don't let your anger run away with you and drive you out of the relevant. (*This member of the chorus continues the burlesque of a juryman who is also a judge.*)

He has accused you of grave things! (*Pointing to a defendant.*)

(*The chorus is now burlesquing a trial in which neither litigant can be represented by counsel, for the profession of lawyers was abolished.*)

Now, my noble man, see that you do not in your reply be transported with rage.

Shorten sail, make use of the tops of your halyards and masts and work your way slowly and gradually so that you'll get every advantage from the wind. (*A sailor on the jury speaks to the litigant represented in this vaudeville effect.*)

You, who first among the Greeks (*to Aeschylus*) built holy towers of sacred words, and adorned tragedy with emptiness, discharge your verbal stream with boldness.

(*Din of kettledrums in the chorus. All dance.*)

Aeschylus (when the chorus has worn itself out). I'm enraged at this collision and my bowels are all wrought up seeing that I am forced to reply to this fellow. However, so that he may not say I'm not equal to him, I ask him and how to tell me why a man who is a poet ought to be regarded with wonder.

Euripides. For his brilliance and intellect and because he has made city dwellers brighter and more beautiful (intellectually).

Aeschylus. But if you haven't done this but instead have represented good and worthy beings as monsters of iniquity what will you confess yourself fit to suffer?

Bacchus. Oh, Death! But don't ask him. (The burlesque of an Athenian jury trial is proceeding.)

Aeschylus. Consider, now, what sort of characters he got from me to begin with (the heroes and heroines of mythology and legend, Jove, Hercules, Hecuba and so on.) See if they were not noble and strapping figures, and not slackers and loafers and loungers as they are now, nor malefactors. They were men who breathed defiantly, bore the lance, and white plumed helmets and battle axes and armor and had moods of roaring seven yells! (A challenge to the foe. Or, had seven-hided souls.)

Euripides. This nuisance is spreading. With his making of many helmets, he will bowl me over.

Bacchus. And what did you do that rendered them such noble beings? (*Aeschylus remains mute.*) Aeschylus, speak, don't be insolently majestic of mien and make trouble in that style.

Aeschylus. I made a theatre changed with war.

Bacchus. How so?

Aeschylus. I dramatized the seven against Thebes. (The seven commanders who led seven hosts to the seven gates of Thebes comprised one of the renowned expeditions of antiquity and the play of Aeschylus on the subject was always highly esteemed.) Every man who witnessed it burned to be a torch bearer.

Bacchus. This was a vile deed of yours. The Thebans have been rendered all the more courageous for the war. And for this you must be penalised.

Aeschylus. Yet it was in your power to exercise the same courage. You did not practice it. Then having afterwards performed the "Persians" (dealing with the battle of Salamis

and the flight of Xerzes) I put in them enough courage to
make them burn to triumph over their foes, a most magnificent masterpiece (of tragedy) being thus embellished.

Bacchus. I was glad then—because I heard Darius was
dead and the chorus instantly clapped its hands and yelled
"Hurrah!" (The chorus really lamented in that tragedy.)

Aeschylus. The very things that poetical men should
do. Consider how from the beginning how helpful the poets
have proved. Orpheus it was who showed us the mysteries
and taught us to keep from killing. Musaios taught us
cures for disease and oracles (some suspect that Moses is
somehow traceable in this obscure allusion). Hesiod told
us about works, the fruit seasons and the plowings. The
divine Homer himself—from what did he derive honor and
glory if not from teaching what is good, what is virtuous,
the drill and the discipline of troops?

Bacchus. He did not teach Pantacles though, that most
unenlightened of mankind! Only lately when he was
parading he tied his helmet on backward and then tried to
put the plume on it. (This individual was an office holder
who thus revealed his ignorance of military matters in war
time.)

Aeschylus. Many another good man I had for one of my
characters—among them Lamachus was a hero. (A stupid
and incompetent commander in the Sicilian expedition.
The idea of making him a hero was absurd.) It was from
him that I got my ideas of heroic Patroclus (in the Ilaid)
and his indomitable soul, and for Teucer of the lion heart
(a legendary hero of epics). Thus I sought to excite the
voters to rise to the level of such beings each time the
trumpet sounded (in the theatre). Not, by Jove, did I
drag unchaste Phaedras upon the scene (heroine of the
"Hippolytus" of Euripides) or Sthenoboea (she played the
part of Patiphar's wife in an episode like that of Joseph).
Nobody ever saw either an infatuated woman in any play
I made.

Euripides. By Jove, neither was there any comprehension of the goddess of love in your work!

Aeschylus. Never may I do that sort of thing! But in you and in your work she was potent and yet in the end she got the best of you and worsted you (his wife proved faithless).

Bacchus. By Jove, that fits you well! The very thing you invented for others was the thing that tortured you.

Euripides. And what harm, you wretched man, does my Sthenoboea do the town?

Aeschylus. You led well-born dames and the wives of well-born men to suicide from shame brought upon through the example of your Sthenoboea (the scandalous private lives of some Athenians was said to have been encouraged by the plays of Euripides) and your Bellerophon.

Euripides. Is it that I invented a fanciful tale about Phaedra?

Aeschylus. By Jove, it was true! But the evil is what a poet should hide and not lead it forth as a model for imitation. To the childish he is their teacher who makes phrases to them and only to the mature is he the poet. Hence it is essential in us all to speak only of what is good.

Euripides. If then you drag in Lycabettus (a mountain) and Parnes (another mountain) is this teaching what is good by one who ought to use human language? (In one of the lost plays of Aeschylus the dialogue of the divinities on the mountain peaks was too sublime to be intelligible.)

Aeschylus. But, you wicked devil, the reason of great ideas and intellectual superiorities is for the begetting of big words. Moreover it is fitting that people who are half gods should use words more tremendous than our own. In fact they have clothes far holier than those we wear. When I had these things well established (in the theatre) you degraded them all.

Euripides. How?

Aeschylus. In the first place you put kings before us

in rags so that they might seem objects of pity to ordinary men.

Euripides. Whom did I injure in doing so?

Aeschylus. These things have made the wealthy citizens intensely reluctant to hold the office of trierarch (admiral or captain in the fleet) and so he puts on rags and weeps and says he is a pauper (to escape the assessment).

Bacchus. With a fine under garment on, by Ceres! And while he is lying like that he goes where the fish are sold (for a fine meal).

Aeschylus. Moreover, you taught the people to be wordy and chattering so that they do not go upon the drill ground but wear out their skins on seats too comfortable when they are young. Then you taught the crew of the state galley to argue with their captains (because that was enacted in his plays). Now when I was alive they did not even know how to dare such things but only called for their porridge and yelled for the anchor to be heaved.

Bacchus. By Apollo, he did that—and they learned to discharge their bowels in the countenances of the men who plied the oars below on rows under their own (in the galleys) and if they got shore leave they only learned how to steal and now they have got so bad that they argue with their commanders and can no longer row forward or backward or this way or any other. (Or, nowadays the oarsman gainsays his orders and refusing to row any longer, he sails about hither and thither.)

Aeschylus. What evils has he not originated? Has he not brought procuresses upon the stage and illegitimate births in the holy places and sisters in incest with their brothers. Has he not said that to live is not to be alive? It is because of this our town is filled with scribblers and creatures who ape men (pretending to be actors) and thus befooling the people. As for carrying a torch, no one is able to do that any more for want of practice. (Hence the signals necessary in war could no longer be relied upon.)

Bacchus. By Jove, No—I was nearly dead from laughing at the Athenian revels when a slow man, all white and obese, pasty faced and puffing, seemed bent in two with his strainings and blowings, outrun as he seemed to be by all the other races and himself in a terrible stew about it all, acting terribly. The men of Cerameicus, at the gates, where he was running the gauntlet of the line of sight seers there dealt him slap after slap as he passed, some on the paunch, the sides, the thighs. Pummeled yet again and that by so many hands, he blew out the torch and fled. (The prize went to him who first raced with the torch lighted to the goal.)

Chorus (its members still burlesquing a jury):
The case is a celebrated one.
The feuds are many. (*Each remark by a separate speaker.*)
The war is getting hot.
It will be hard to decide.
When one pulls powerfully this way the other seems capable of straining with no less force the other way.
Now don't sit perpetually in one place.
There are ever and ever so many other arguments to come.
Whatever you have to fight about, speak it out, spit it forth, rake up what is new and what is old.
Do try hard to say something clever as well as wise.
If you are afraid to do that, because we spectators are so stupid and your brilliance will thus be above our heads, remember that you have ceased to be such fine wits as you were (or, we have been so sharpened that we are as bright as yourselves).
They are fighters themselves for they have each a book and from it they picked up the art of quarreling. (Or, they learned the right lessons.)
Their natures are powerful.
Their wits have been whetted.
Don't be afraid.

Spit it all out, for the benefit of the audience, just as if it were made up of intelligent people.

(*Din of kettledrums. Dancing around. Bacchus leads the rout behind the palace, Euripides dancing along while Aeschylus hobbles painfully after.*)

THE CIRCLE
by
W. Somerset Maugham

ACT II

The drawing-room of Aston-Adey.

Characters: *Lord Porteous, Lady Kitty, Anna, Teddie, Elizabeth,* and *Champion-Cheney*

(*Porteous and Lady Kitty, Anna and Teddie, are playing bridge. Elizabeth and Champion-Cheney are watching. Porteous and Lady Kitty are partners.*)

C.C. When will Arnold be back, Elizabeth?

Eliza. Soon, I think.

C.C. Is he addressing a meeting?

Eliza. No, it's only a conference with his agent and one or two constituents.

Port. (*Irritably.*) How anyone can be expected to play bridge when people are shouting at the top of their voices all round them, I for one cannot understand.

Eliza. (*Smiling.*) I'm so sorry.

Anna. I can see your hand, Lord Porteous.

Port. It may help you.

Lady K. I've told you over and over again to hold your cards up. It ruins one's game when one can't help seeing one's opponent's hand.

Port. One isn't obliged to look.

Lady K. What was Arnold's majority at the last election?

Eliz. Seven hundred and something.

C.C. He'll have to fight for it if he wants to keep his seat next time.

Port. Are we playing bridge, or talking politics?

Lady K. I never find that conversation interferes with my game.

448

Port. You certainly play no worse when you talk than when you hold your tongue.

Lady K. I think that's a very offensive thing to say, Hughie. Just because I don't play the same game as you do, you think I can't play.

Port. I'm glad you acknowledge it's not the same game as I play. But why in God's name do you call it bridge?

C.C. I agree with Kitty. I hate people who play bridge as though they were at a funeral and knew their feet were getting wet.

Port. Of course you take Kitty's part.

Lady K. That's the least he can do.

C.C. I have a naturally cheerful disposition.

Port. You've never had anything to sour it.

Lady K. I don't know what you mean by that, Hughie.

Port. (*trying to contain himself.*) Must you trump my ace?

Lady K. (*innocently.*) Oh, was that your ace, darling?

Port. (*furiously.*) Yes, it was my ace.

Lady K. Oh, well, it was the only trump I had. I shouldn't have made it, anyway.

Port. You needn't have told them that. Now she knows exactly what I've got.

Lady K. She knew before.

Port. How could she know?

Lady K. She said she'd seen your hand.

Anna. Oh, I didn't. I said I could see it.

Lady K. Well, I naturally supposed that if she could see it, she did.

Port. Really, Kitty, you have the most extraordinary ideas.

C.C. Not at all. If anyone is such a fool as to show me his hand, of course I look at it.

Port. (*fuming.*) If you study the etiquette of bridge, you'll discover that onlookers are expected not to interfere with the game.

C.C. My dear Hughie, this is a matter of ethics, not of bridge.

Anna. Anyhow, I get the game. And rubber.

Teddie. I claim a revoke.

Port. Who revoked?

Teddie. You did.

Port. Nonsense. I've never revoked in my life.

Teddie. I'll show you. (*He turns over the tricks to show the faces of the cards.*) You threw away a club on the third heart trick, and you had another heart.

Port. I never had more than two hearts.

Teddie. Oh, yes, you had. Look here. That's the card you played on the last trick but one.

Lady K. (*delighted to catch him out.*) There's no doubt about it, Hughie. You revoked.

Port. I tell you I did not revoke. I never revoke.

C.C. You did, Hughie. I wondered what on earth you were doing.

Port. I don't know how anyone can be expected not to revoke when there's this confounded chatter going on all the time.

Teddie. Well, that's another hundred to us.

Port. (*To Champion-Cheney.*) I wish you wouldn't breathe down my neck. I never can play bridge when there's somebody breathing down my neck.

(*The party have risen from the bridge-table, and they scatter about the room.*)

Anna. Well, I'm going to take a book and lie down in the hammock till it's time to dress.

Teddie. (*Who has been adding up.*) I'll put it down in the book, shall I?

Port. (*Who has not moved, setting out the cards for a patience.*) Yes, yes, put it down. I never revoke.

(*Anna goes out.*)

Lady K. Would you like to come for a little stroll, Hughie?

Port. What for?

Lady K. Exercise.

Port. I hate exercise.

C.C. (*looking at the patience.*) The seven goes on the eight.

(*Porteous takes no notice.*)

Lady K. The seven goes on the eight, Hughie.

Port. I don't choose to put the seven on the eight.

C.C. That knave goes on the queen.

Port. I'm not blind, thank you.

Lady K. The three goes on the four.

C.C. All these go over.

Port. (*furiously.*) Am I playing this patience, or are you playing it?

Lady K. But you're missing everything.

Port. That's my business.

C.C. It's no good losing your temper over it, Hughie.

Port. Go away, both of you. You irritate me.

Lady K. We were only trying to help you, Hughie.

Port. I don't want to be helped. I want to do it by myself.

Lady K. I think your manners are perfectly deplorable, Hughie.

Port. It's simply maddening when you're playing patience, and people won't leave you alone.

C.C. We won't say another word.

Port. That three goes. I believe it's coming out. If I'd been such a fool as to put that seven up, I shouldn't have been able to bring these down. (*He puts down several cards while they watch him silently.*)

Lady K. and C.C. (*together*) The four goes on the five.

Port. (*throwing down the cards violently.*) Damn you! why don't you leave me alone? It's intolerable.

C.C. It was coming out, my dear fellow.

Port. I know it was coming out. Confound you!

Lady K. How petty you are, Hughie!

Port. Petty, be damned! I've told you over and over again that I will not be interfered with when I'm playing patience.

Lady K. Don't talk to me like that, Hughie.

Port. I shall talk to you as I please.

Lady K. (*beginning to cry.*) Oh, you brute! You brute! (*She flings out of the room.*)

Port. Oh, damn! now she's going to cry.

*   *   *

ACT II

Drawing-room.

Characters: *Arnold* and *Elizabeth*

Arn. Hulloa! (*He comes in.*) Oh, Elizabeth, I've found an illustration here of a chair which is almost identical with mine. It's dated 1750. Look!

Eliz. That's very interesting.

Arn. I want to show it to Porteous. (*Moving a chair which has been misplaced.*) You know, it does exasperate me the way people will not leave things alone. I no sooner put a thing in its place than somebody moves it.

Eliz. It must be maddening for you.

Arn. It is. You are the worst offender. I can't think why you don't take the pride that I do in the house. After all, it's one of the show places in the county.

Eliz. I'm afraid you find me very unsatisfactory.

Arn. (*good-humoredly.*) I don't know about that. But my two subjects are politics and decoration. I should be a perfect fool if I didn't see that you don't care two straws about either.

Eliz. We haven't very much in common, Arnold, have we?

Arn. I don't think you can blame me for that.

Eliz. I don't. I blame you for nothing. I have no fault to find with you.

Arn. (*surprised at her significant tone.*) Good gracious me! what's the meaning of all this?

Eliz. Well, I don't think there's any object in beating about the bush. I want you to let me go.

Arn. Go where?

Eliz. Away. For always.

Arn. My dear child, what *are* you talking about?

Eliz. I want to be free.

Arn. (*amused rather than disconcerted.*) Don't be ridicu-ous, darling. I daresay you're run down and want a change. 'll take you over to Paris for a fortnight if you like.

Eliz. I shouldn't have spoken to you if I hadn't quite made up my mind. We've been married for three years, and I don't think it's been a great success. I'm frankly bored by the life you want me to lead.

Arn. Well, if you'll allow me to say so, the fault is yours. We lead a very distinguished, useful life. We know a lot of extremely nice people.

Eliz. I'm quite willing to allow that the fault is mine. But how does that make it any better? I'm only twenty-five. If I've made a mistake, I have time to correct it.

Arn. I can't bring myself to take you very seriously.

Eliz. You see, I don't love you.

Arn. Well, I'm awfully sorry. But you weren't obliged to marry me. You've made your bed and I'm afraid you must lie on it.

Eliz. That's one of the falsest proverbs in the English language. Why should you lie on the bed you've made if you don't want to? There's always the floor.

Arn. For goodness' sake, don't be funny, Elizabeth.

Eliz. I've quite made up my mind to leave you, Arnold.

Arn. Come, come, Elizabeth, you must be sensible. You haven't any reason to leave me.

Eliz. Why should you wish to keep a woman tied to you who wants to be free?

Arn. I happen to be in love with you.

Eliz. You might have said that before.

Arn. I thought you'd take it for granted. You can't expect a man to go on making love to his wife after three years. I'm very busy. I'm awfully keen on politics, and I've worked like a dog to make this house a thing of beauty. After all, a man marries to have a home, but also because he doesn't want to be bothered with sex and all that sort of

thing. I fell in love with you the first time I saw you, and
I've been in love ever since.

Eliz. I'm sorry, but if you're not in love with a man, his
love doesn't mean very much to you.

Arn. It's so ungrateful. I've done everything in the
world for you.

Eliz. You've been very kind to me. But you've asked
me to lead a life I don't like and that I'm not suited for. I'm
awfully sorry to cause you pain, but now you must let me go.

Arn. Nonsense! I'm a good deal older than you are,
and I think I have a little more sense. In your interests as
well as in mine I'm not going to do anything of the sort.

Eliz. (*with a smile.*) How can you prevent me? You
can't keep me under lock and key.

Arn. Please don't talk to me as if I were a foolish child.
You're my wife, and you're going to remain my wife.

Eliz. What sort of a life do you think we should lead?
Do you think there'd be any more happiness for you than
for me?

Arn. But what is it precisely that you suggest?

Eliz. Well, I want you to let me divorce you.

Arn. (*astounded.*) Me? Thank you very much. Are
you under the impression I'm going to sacrifice my career
for a whim of yours?

Eliz. How will it do that?

Arn. My seat's wobbly enough as it is. Do you think
I'd be able to hold it if I were in a divorce case? Even if it
were a put-up job, as most divorces are nowadays, it would
damn me.

Eliz. It's rather hard on a woman to be divorced.

Arn. (*with sudden suspicion.*) What do you mean by
that? Are you in love with some one?

Eliz. Yes.

Arn. Who?

Eliz. Teddie Luton.

(*Arnold is astonished for a moment, then bursts into a
laugh.*)

Arn. My poor child, how can you be so ridiculous? Why, he hasn't a bob. He's a perfectly commonplace young man. It's so absurd I can't even be angry with you.

Eliz. I've fallen desperately in love with him, Arnold.

Arn. Well, you'd better fall desperately out.

Eliz. He wants to marry me.

Arn. I daresay he does. He can go to hell.

Eliz. It's no good talking like that.

Arn. Is he your lover?

Eliz. No, certainly not.

Arn. It shows that he's a mean skunk to take advantage of my hospitality to make love to you.

Eliz. He's never even kissed me.

Arn. I'd try telling that to the horse marines if I were you.

Eliz. It's because I wanted to do nothing shabby that I told you straight out how things were.

Arn. How long have you been thinking of this?

Eliz. I've been in love with Teddie ever since I knew him.

Arn. And you never thought of me at all, I suppose.

Eliz. Oh, yes, I did. I was miserable. But I can't help myself. I wish I loved you, but I don't.

Arn. I recommend you to think very carefully before you do anything foolish.

Eliz. I have thought very carefully.

Arn. By God! I don't know why I don't give you a sound hiding. I'm not sure if that wouldn't be the best thing to bring you to your senses.

Eliz. Oh, Arnold, don't take it like that.

Arn. How do you expect me to take it? You come to me quite calmly and say: "I've had enough of you. We've been married three years, and I think I'd like to marry somebody else now. Shall I break up your home? What a bore for you! Do you mind my divorcing you? It'll smash up your career, will it? What a pity!" Oh, no, my girl, I may be a fool, but I'm not a damned fool.

Eliz. Teddie is leaving here by the first train to-morrow.
I warn you that I mean to join him as soon as he can make
the necessary arrangements.

Arn. Where is he?

Eliz. I don't know. I suppose he's in his room.

(*Arnold goes to the door and calls.*)

Arn. George!

(*For a moment Arnold walks up and down the room im-
patiently. Elizabeth watches him. The Footman comes in.*)

Footman. Yes, sir.

Arn. Tell Mr. Luton to come here at once.

Eliz. Ask Mr. Luton if he wouldn't mind coming here
for a moment.

Footman. Very good, madam. (*He goes out.*)

Eliz. What are you going to say to him?

Arn. That's my business.

Eliz. I wouldn't make a scene if I were you.

Arn. I'm not going to make a scene. (*They wait in
silence.*) Why did you insist on my mother coming here?

Eliz. It seemed to me rather absurd to take up the attitude that I should be contaminated by her when—

Arn. (*interrupting.*) When you were proposing to do
exactly the same thing. Well, now you've seen her, what
do you think of her? Do you think it's been a success? Is
that the sort of woman a man would like his mother to be?

Eliz. I've been ashamed. I've been so sorry. It all
seemed dreadful and horrible. This morning I happened to
notice a rose in the garden. It was all over-blown and be-
draggled. It looked like a painted old woman. And I remembered that I'd looked at it a day or two ago. It was
lovely then, fresh and blooming and fragrant. It may be
hideous now, but that doesn't take away from the beauty
it had once. That was real.

Arn. Poetry, by God! As if this were the moment for
poetry!

*   *   *

Act III

Drawing-room.

Characters: *Elizabeth* and *Lady Kitty*

Eliz. They've told you?

Lady K. Yes, and now they have, I think I knew it all along.

Eliz. I don't expect you to have much sympathy for me. Arnold is your son.

Lady K. So pitifully little.

Eliz. I'm not suited for this sort of existence. Arnold wants me to take what he calls my place in Society. Oh, I get so bored with those parties in London. All those middle-aged painted women, in beautiful clothes, lolloping round ball-rooms with rather old young men. And the endless luncheons where they gossip about so-and-so's love affairs.

Lady K. Are you very much in love with Mr. Luton?

Eliz. I love him with all my heart.

Lady K. And he?

Eliz. He's never cared for anyone but me. He never will.

Lady K. Will Arnold let you divorce him?

Eliz. No, he won't hear of it. He refuses even to divorce me.

Lady K. Why?

Eliz. He thinks a scandal will revive all the old gossip.

Lady K. Oh, my poor child!

Eliz. It can't be helped. I'm quite willing to accept the consequences.

Lady K. You don't know what it is to have a man tied to you only by his honour. When married people don't get on, they can separate, but if they're not married, it's impossible. It's a tie that only death can sever.

Eliz. If Teddie stopped caring for me, I shouldn't want him to stay with me for five minutes.

Lady K. One says that when one's sure of a man's love, but when one isn't any more—oh, it's so different. In those circumstances one's got to keep a man's love. It's the only thing one has.

Eliz. I'm a human being. I can stand on my own feet

Lady K. Have you any money of your own?

Eliz. None.

Lady K. Then how can you stand on your own feet
You think I'm a silly frivolous woman, but I've learned
something in a bitter school. They can make what laws
they like, they can give us the suffrage, but when you come
down to bedrock, it's the man who pays the piper who calls
the tune. Woman will only be the equal of man when she
earns her living in the same way that he does.

Eliz. (*smiling.*) It sounds rather funny to hear you talk
like that.

Lady K. A cook who marries a butler can snap her
fingers in his face because she can earn just as much as he
can. But a woman in your position and a woman in mine
will always be dependent on the men who keep them.

Eliz. I don't want luxury. You don't know how sick
I am of all this beautiful furniture. These over-decorated
houses are like a prison in which I can't breathe. When I
drive about in a Callot frock and a Rolls-Royce I envy the
shop-girl in a coat and skirt whom I see jumping on the tail-
board of a bus.

Lady K. You mean that if need be you could earn your
own living?

Eliz. Yes.

Lady K. What could you be? A nurse or a typist. It's
nonsense. Luxury saps a woman's nerve. And when she's
known it once, it becomes a necessity.

Eliz. That depends on the woman.

Lady K. When we're young, we think we're different
from everyone else, but when we grow a little older, we discover we're all very much of a muchness.

Eliz. You're very kind to take so much trouble about
me.

Lady K. It breaks my heart to think that you're going
to make the same pitiful mistake that I made.

Eliz. Oh, don't say it was that, don't, don't.

Lady K. Look at me, Elizabeth, and look at Hughie. Do you think it's been a success? If I had my time over again, do you think I'd do it again? Do you think he would?

Eliz. You see, you don't know how much I love Teddie.

Lady K. And do you think I didn't love Hughie? Do you think he didn't love me?

Eliz. I'm sure he did.

Lady K. Oh, of course in the beginning it was heavenly. We felt so brave and adventurous and we were so much in love. The first two years were wonderful. People cut me, you know, but I didn't mind. I thought love was everything. It *is* a little uncomfortable when you come upon an old friend and go towards her eagerly, so glad to see her, and are met with an icy stare.

Eliz. Do you think friends like that are worth having?

Lady K. Perhaps they're not very sure of themselves. Perhaps they're honestly shocked. It's a test one had better not put one's friends to if one can help it. It's rather bitter to find how few one has.

Eliz. But one has some.

Lady K. Yes, they ask you to come and see them when they're quite certain no one will be there who might object to meeting you. Or else they say to you: "My dear, you know I'm devoted to you, and I wouldn't mind at all, but my girl's growing up—I'm sure you understand; you won't think it unkind of me if I don't ask you to the house?"

Eliz. (*smiling.*) That doesn't seem to me very serious.

Lady K. At first I thought it rather a relief, because it threw Hughie and me together more. But you know, men are very funny. Even when they are in love, they're not in love all day long. They want change and recreation.

Eliz. I'm not inclined to blame them for that, poor dears.

Lady K. Then we settled in Florence. And because we couldn't get the society we'd been used to, we became used to the society we could get—Loose women and vicious men. Snobs who liked to patronise people with a handle to their names. Vague Italian princes who were glad to borrow a few francs from Hughie and seedy countesses who liked to drive with me in the Cascine. And then Hughie began to hanker after his old life. He wanted to go big game shooting, but I dared not let him go. I was afraid he'd never come back.

Eliz. But you knew he loved you.

Lady K. Oh, my dear, what a blessed institution marriage is— for women, and what fools they are to meddle with it! The Church is so wise to take its stand on the indi— indi—

Eliz. —solu—

Lady K. —bility of marriage. Believe me, it's no joke when you have to rely only on yourself to keep a man. I could never afford to grow old. My dear, I'll tell you a secret that I've never told a living soul.

Eliz. What is that?

Lady K. My hair is not naturally this colour.

Eliz. Really?

Lady K. I touch it up. You would never have guessed, would you?

Eliz. Never.

Lady K. Nobody does. My dear, it's white, prematurely of course, but white. I always think it's a symbol of my life. Are you interested in symbolism? I think it's too wonderful.

Eliz. I don't think I know very much about it.

Lady K. However tired I've been, I've had to be brilliant and gay. I've never let Hughie see the aching heart behind my smiling eyes.

Eliz. (*amused and touched.*) You poor dear.

Lady K. And when I saw he was attracted by some one else, the fear and the jealousy that seized me! You see, I didn't dare make a scene as I should have done if I'd been married—I had to pretend not to notice.

Eliz. (*taken aback.*) But do you mean to say he fell in love with anyone else?

Lady K. Of course he did eventually.

Eliz. (*Hardly knowing what to say.*) You must have been very unhappy.

Lady K. Oh, I was, dreadfully. Night after night I sobbed my heart out when Hughie told me he was going to play cards at the club, and I knew he was with that odious woman. Of course, it wasn't as if there weren't plenty of men who were only too anxious to console me. Men have always been attracted by me, you know.

Eliz. Oh, of course, I can quite understand it.

Lady K. But I had my self-respect to think of. I felt that whatever Hughie did, I would do nothing that I should regret.

Eliz. You must be very glad now.

Lady K. Oh, yes. Notwithstanding all my temptations I've been absolutely faithful to Hughie in spirit.

Eliz. I don't think I quite understand what you mean.

Lady K. Well, there was a poor Italian boy, young Count Castel Giovanni, who was so desperately in love with me that his mother begged me not to be too cruel. She was afraid he'd go into a consumption. What could I do? And then, oh, years later, there was Antonio Melita. He said he'd shoot himself unless I—well, you understand I couldn't let the poor boy shoot himself.

Eliz. D'you think he really would have shot himself?

Lady K. Oh, one never knows, you know. Those Italians are so passionate. He was really rather a lamb. He had such beautiful eyes. (*Elizabeth looks at her for a long time and a certain horror seizes her of this dissolute, painted old woman.*)

Eliz. (*Hoarsely.*) Oh, but I think that's dreadful.

Lady K. Are you shocked? One sacrifices one's life for love, and then one finds that love doesn't last. The tragedy of love isn't death or separation. One gets over them. The tragedy of love is indifference.

THE CRADLE SONG

by

G. Martinez Sierra

English Version by John Garrett Underhill

Act I.

A room opening upon the cloister of a convent of Enclosed
Dominican Nuns.

Characters: *Sister Sagrario, Sister Joanna of the Cross, Sister
Maria Jesus, Sister Marcella, Prioress, Vicaress, Mistress of Novices,* and *Sister Inez*

(*The bell rings by the grille.*)

Sagrario. The bell! I wonder who it is?

Joanna. Better ask. That's why they left us here.

Maria. Who'll do it? I won't. I'm afraid.

Sagrario. So am I.

Marcella. You're not usually so bashful, I must say. I'll
ask, though I was the last to enter the house. (*Going up to
the grille, she says in a timid voice:*) Ave Maria purissima:
(*A moment's silence.*) No one answers.

Joanna. Try again. Say it louder.

Marcella. (*Raising her voice.*) Ave Maria purissima:

Sagrario. Nothing this time, either.

Maria. (*Summoning her courage, in a high-pitched voice.*)
Ave Maria purissima! (*Another silence. The Novices look
at each other in surprise.*)

Marcella. It is very strange.

Maria. It must be spirits.

Sagrario. Oh, I'm afraid!

Joanna. Nonsense! It's some little boy who has rung
the bell on his way home from school, so as to be funny.

Maria. Peep through the hole and see if anybody is
there.

Marcella. (*Stooping down to look.*) No, nobody. But it looks as if there was something on the wheel. Yes . . .

Joanna. Let me see! Yes . . . Can't you turn it? (*She turns the wheel, and a second basket appears, carefully covered with a white cloth like the first.*) A basket!

Sagrario. Another present for our Mother.

Maria. Of course it is! And here's a paper tied fast to it.

Joanna. (*Reading, but without unfolding the paper.*) "For the Mother Prioress."

Sagrario. Didn't I tell you?

Marcella. Somebody wants to give her a surprise.

Joanna. I wonder if it's Don Calixtus, the chaplain?

Marcella. Of course it is, child!

Maria. Or maybe it's the Doctor.

Joanna. No. He was just here and he didn't say anything about it.

Sagrario. All the same it might be from him. Maybe he wants to keep it a secret.

Maria. Let's take it off the wheel.

Marcella. (*Lifting and carrying it to the table.*) We'd better put it here by the canary. My! But it's heavy!

Sagrario. I wonder what it is?

Marcella. Let's lift the corner and see.

Maria. No, for curiosity is a sin.

Marcella. What of it? Come on! Let's do it. Who will ever know? (*She lifts the corner of the cloth a little and starts back quickly with a sharp cry.*) Ay!!

Joanna. (*Hurrying to look.*) *Jesus!*

Maria. Ave Maria! (*Looking too.*)

Sagrario. (*Following.*) God bless us!

(*The Convent is aroused at the cry of Sister Marcella. Presently The Prioress, The Vicaress, The Mistress of Novices and the other Nuns enter from different directions.*)

Prioress. What is the matter? Who called out?

Vicaress. Who gave that shout?

Novices. Is anything wrong? (*The four Novices, trembling, stand with their backs to the basket, their bodies hiding it completely.*)

Vicaress. It is easy to see it was Sister Marcella.

Prioress. What has happened? Speak! Why are you all standing in a row like statues?

Novices. Has anything happened to you?

Joanna. No, reverend Mother, not to us; but—

Maria. No reverend Mother; it's . . .

Marcella. Someone rang the bell by the wheel . . . and we looked . . . and there was nobody there . . . and they left a basket . . . this basket . . . and . . . and your sister had the curiosity to undo it. . . .

Vicaress. Naturally, you couldn't do otherwise.

Marcella. And it's . . .

Prioress. Well? What is it?

Marcella. It's . . . I . . . I think it would be better for your Reverence to look yourself.

Prioress. By all means! Let me see. (*She goes up to the basket and uncovers it*) *Ave Maria!* (*In a hoarse whisper.*) A baby!

All. (*Variously affected.*) A baby? (*The Vicaress, horrified, crosses herself.*)

Prioress. (*Falling back.*) Your Reverences may see for yourselves. (*The Nuns hurry up to the basket and surround it.*)

Vicaress. Ave Maria! How can such an insignificant object be so pink?

Novices. It's asleep.

Joanna. See it open its little hands!

Maria. Why! It has hair under the edge of its cap!

Sagrario. It is like an angel!

Vicaress. A pretty angel for the Lord to send us.

Joanna. Ay, Mother Vicaress! You mustn't say that.

Prioress. (*Tenderly*) Where do you come from, little one?

Vicaress. From some nice place, you may be sure.

Prioress. Who can tell, Mother? There is so much poverty in the world, so much distress.

Vicaress. There is so much vice, reverend Mother.

Novices. You say that there was nobody at the grille?

Marcella. Nobody; no, Mother. The bell rang; we answered . . . but there was nobody there.

Sagrario. (*Picking up the paper which has fallen on the floor.*) Here is a paper which came with it.

Prioress. (*Taking the paper*) "For the Mother Prioress."

Vicaress. An appropriate present for your Reverence.

Prioress. Yes, it is a letter. (*She unfolds the paper and begins to read.*)

"Reverend Mother:

Forgive the liberty which a poor woman takes, trusting in your Grace's charity, of leaving at the grille this newborn babe. I, my lady, am one of those they call women of the street, and I assure you I am sorry for it; but this is the world, and you can't turn your back on it, and it costs as much to go down as it does to go up, and that is what I am writing to tell you, my lady. The truth is this little girl hasn't any father, that is to say it is the same as if she didn't have any, and I—who am her mother—I leave her here, although it costs me something to leave her; for although one is what one is, one isn't all bad, and I love her as much as any mother loves her baby, though she is the best lady in the land. But all the same, though she came into this world without being wanted by anyone, she doesn't deserve to be the daughter of the woman she is, above all, my lady, of her father, and I don't want her to have to blush for having been born the way she was, nor for having the mother she has, and to tell it to me to my face, and I pray you by everything you hold dear, my lady, that you will protect her and keep her with you in this holy house, and you won't send her to some orphanage or asylum, for I was brought up there myself, and I know what happens in them, although the sisters are kind—yes, they are—and have pity. And some day, when she grows up and she asks for her mother, you must tell her that the devil has carried her away, and I ask your pardon, for I must never show myself to her, nor see her again, nor give you any care nor trouble, so you can do this good work in peace, if you will do it, for I implore you again, my lady, that you will do it for the memory of your own dear mother, and God will reward you, and she will live in peace, and grow up as God wills, for what the eyes have not seen, the heart cannot understand, my lady."

Vicaress. Bless us! *Ave Maria!*

Novices. Poor woman!

Joanna. Baby dear! Darling baby!

Vicaress. What pretty mothers the Lord selects for His children!

Prioress. God moves in His own ways, Sister. God moves in His own ways.

Inez. Is that all the letter says?

Prioress. What more could it say?

* * *

Act II
Parlor of a Convent.

Characters: *Teresa, Sister Joanna of the Cross.*

(*Teresa and Sister Joanna of the Cross remain behind picking up and arranging the papers, patterns and scraps that have been left on the seats or about the floor. They say nothing but presently Teresa throws herself on her knees before the Nun.*)

Teresa. Sister Joanna of the Cross!

Joanna. What do you want, my child?

Teresa. Now that we are alone, bless me while there is no one here to see—no, not one—for you are my mother, more than all the rest!

Joanna. Get up. (*Teresa gets up.*) Don't talk like that! We are all equal in God's house.

Teresa. But in my heart you are the first. You mustn't be angry at what I say. How can I help it? Is it my fault, though I have struggled against it all my life, that I have come to love you so?

Joanna. Yes, you have struggled. You have been wilful . . . (*Then seeking at once to excuse her.*) But it was because you were strong and well. When a child is silent and keeps to herself in a corner, it is a sign that she is sick or thinking of some evil. But you . . .

Teresa. Ay, Mother! Where do you suppose that I came from?

Joanna. From Heaven, my daughter, as all of us have come.

Teresa. Do you really think that we have all come from Heaven?

Joanna. At least you have come from Heaven to me. You say that I am your mother more than the rest; I don't know—it may be. But I know that for years you have been all my happiness and joy.

Teresa. Mother!

Joanna. I was so glad to hear you laugh and see you run about the cloisters! It was absurd, but I always felt—not now, for you are grown-up now—but for years I always felt as if you must be I, myself, scampering and playing. For I was just your age now, a little more or less, when you came into the Convent. And it seemed to me as if I was a child again and had just begun to live. You were so little, so busy —yes, you were—but I was busy too, if you only knew, before I entered here, at home in our house in the village. I was always singing and dancing, although we were very poor. My mother went out every day to wash in the river or to do housework—she had so many children!—and I was always carrying one about in my arms. And when I entered here, as I could do, thanks to some good ladies, who collected the money for my dowry—God reward them for it— although I had a real vocation, I was sorrowful and homesick thinking of my little brothers and sisters! How I used to cry in the dark corners, and I never dared to say a word! Then the Mother told me that if my melancholy didn't leave me she would be obliged to send me home. And then you came and I forgot everything! That is why I say you came to me from Heaven. And I don't want you to think I am angry, or ashamed—or that it has ever given me a moment's pain to have loved you.

Teresa. Is that the reason that you scold me so?

Joanna. When have I ever scolded you?

Teresa. Oh, so many times! But no matter. I always tell Antonio, Sister Joanna of the Cross is my mother. She is my mother, my real mother! So now he always calls you mother whenever he speaks of you.

Joanna. My daughter, will you be happy with him?

Teresa. Of course! I am sure I will. He is so good, he is so happy! He says he doesn't know where it is all his happiness comes from, because his father, who is dead now, was more mournful than a willow, and his mother, poor lady, whenever anything happened to her that was good, burst right out crying. How do you suppose it was she ever managed to have such a boy? It must be that sad mothers have happy children. How does it seem to you?

Joanna. How do I know?

Teresa. It must be that way. The first boy I have is going to be—what is the solemnest thing in the world? No, the first is going to be an architect, like his father; but the second can be a missionary, and go to China if he wants to, and convert the heathen. Just think what it would be to have a son who was a saint! I shouldn't have to be so humble in Heaven, then, should I? I should have inflence. And here you are all the time, Sister Joanna of the Cross, praying for me and preparing miracles. So you see I have a good start already.

Joanna. How you do love to talk!

Teresa. Isn't it foolish, Mother? Don't I? Listen! When you were little didn't you ever want to be a boy? I did. I used to cry because I thought then that I could have been anything I wanted to be—this, that, I didn't care what it was—Captain-General, Archbishop, yes, Pope, even! Or something else. It used to make me mad to think that because I was a girl I couldn't even be an acolyte. But now, since—well, since I love Antonio, and he loves me, I don't care; it doesn't make any difference any more, because if I am poor and know nothing, he is wise and strong; and if I

am foolish and of no account, he is, oh, of so much worth!
And if I have to stay behind at home and hide myself in the
corner, he can go out into the world and mount, oh, so high
—wherever a man can go—and instead of making me en-
vious, it makes me so happy! Ah, Sister Joanna of the Cross,
when she truly loves a man, how humble it makes a girl!

Joanna. Do you really love him so?

Teresa. More than life itself! And that is all too little.
Maybe it's a sin, but I can tell you. Do you believe that
we will meet in Heaven the persons we have loved on earth?
Because if I don't meet him there and I can't go on loving
him always just the same as I do now, no, more than I do
now . . .

Joanna. (*Interrupting.*) Hush! Peace! You mustn't
say such things. It is a sin.

Teresa. Ay, Sister Joanna of the Cross! How sweet it
is to be in love!

Joanna. But he . . . he . . . Does he love you too,
so much?

Teresa. Yes, he loves me. How much, I don't know;
but it doesn't make any matter. What makes me happy is
that I love him. You needn't think that sometimes—very
seldom though—I haven't been afraid that perhaps some
day he might stop loving me. It used to make me sad. But
if I had ever thought that some day I could stop loving him
. . . No, it would be better to die first; for then, what would
be the good of life?

Joanna. Ah, my child! To continue in God's love!

Teresa. Do you know how I would like to spend my life?
All of it? Sitting on the ground at his feet, looking up into
his eyes, just listening to him talk. You don't know how
he can talk. He knows everything—everything that there
is to know in the world, and he tells you such things! The
things that you always have known yourself, in your heart,
and you couldn't find out how to say them. Even when he
doesn't say anything, if he should be speaking some language which you didn't understand, it is wonderful . . .

his voice . . . I don't know how to explain it, but it is his voice—a voice that seems as if it had been talking to you ever since the day you were born! You don't hear it only with your ears, but with your whole body. It's like the air which you see and breathe and taste, and which smells so sweetly in the garden beneath the tree of paradise. Ah, Mother! The first day that he said to me "Teresa"—you see what a simple thing it was, my name, Teresa—why, it seemed to me as if nobody ever had called me by my name before, as if I never had heard it, and when he went away, I ran up and down the street saying to myself "Teresa, Teresa, Teresa!" under my breath, without knowing what I was doing, as if I walked on air!

Joanna. You frighten me, my child.

Teresa. Do I? Why?

Joanna. Because you love him so. For earthly love . . . I mean . . . it seems to me it is like a flower, that we find by the side of the road—a little brightness that God grants us to help us pass through life, for we are weak and frail; a drop of honey spread upon our bread each day, which we should receive gladly, but with trembling, and keeping our hearts whole, daughter, for it will surely pass away.

Teresa. It cannot pass away!

Joanna. It may; and then what will be left to your soul, if you have set your all on this delight, and it has passed away?

Teresa. (*Humbly.*) You mustn't be angry with me, Mother. No! Look at me! It isn't wrong, I know. Loving him, I . . . he is so good, he is so good . . . and good, it cannot pass away!

Joanna. Is he a good Christian?

Teresa. He is good, Sister.

Joanna. But does he fear God?

Teresa. One day he said to me: "I love you because you know how to pray." Don't you see? And another time: "I feel a devotion toward you as toward some holy thing." He! Devotion! To me! And whenever I think of that, it seems to me as if I was just growing better, as if all at once I was capable of everything there was to do or suffer in the world—so as to have him always feel that way!

Joanna. I hear some one in the parlor. Draw the curtains.

* * *

Act II

Parlor of a Convent.

Characters: *Teresa, Doctor, Prioress, Mistress of Novices, Vicaress,* and *Sister Joanna of the Cross.*

(*Sister Joanna of the Cross and Teresa enter. It is plain that they both have been crying. Teresa, wearing a mantilla, and with her coat on, carries a shawl over her arm for use as a wrap on the voyage. She stops in the middle of the room and stands still, not daring to say good-bye.*)

Doctor. Well? Are we ready now?

Teresa. Yes . . . Now . . .

Doctor. Then say good-bye. It is late. We must be going, daughter.

Prioress. Yes, you must not delay.

Teresa. (*Throwing herself on her knees before the Prioress and kissing her scapular.*) Mother!

Prioress. Rise, my daughter, rise.

Teresa. Bless me, Mother! Bless me!

Prioress. May God bless you; so. Rise. (*As Teresa rises, the Nun embraces her.*)

Teresa. Mother! I don't know what to say to you—I don't know how to leave you . . . but you must forgive me all the wrong I have ever done in all these years. I have been foolish, wilful. I have made so much trouble for you all. You must forgive me. I would like to do something great, something splendid for you all. But—but may God reward you! May God reward you! God reward you! (*She bursts into tears.*)

Prioress. My daughter, come! You must not cry. You must not allow yourself to be afflicted so.

Teresa. I am not afflicted, Mother; but . . . it's . . . Mother, I can never forget you! You must pray for me, pray for me! And you must never forget me!

Prioress. Ah, no, my child! Never! We will pray God to help you, and to be with you, and you must pray to Him for guidance and for counsel always, whenever you are troubled or perplexed in anything. For the liberty which they enjoy in the world is like a sword in the hands of a child, and life is hard, and bitter oftentimes.

Novices. Be thankful that your heart is well steeled to resist all temptations that may come. Is it not, my daughter?

Teresa. It is, Mother.

Prioress. Will you promise always to be reverent and good?

Teresa. Yes! Yes, Mother!

Vicaress. Remember that your obligation is greater than that of others, because you have come forth from God's own house.

Teresa. Yes! Yes, Mother.

Prioress. Remember all the blessings He has showered upon you from the cradle; remember that your whole life has been as a miracle, that you have lived here as few have ever lived, that you have been brought up as few have ever been brought up, like the Holy Virgin herself, in the very temple of the Lord.

Novices. As He was to the Evangelist, so God has been to you a father and a mother, more than to any other living thing.

Prioress. Remember that you are the rose of His garden and the grain of incense upon His altar.

Teresa. Yes! Mother, yes! I will! . . . I will remember all . . . all . . . all . . .

Novices. And do not forget each day to make an examination of your soul.

Teresa. No, Mother.

Joanna. And write often.

Teresa. Yes, Mother.

Doctor. It is time to go, Teresa.

Teresa. (*Throwing herself suddenly into his arms.*) Oh, father! Promise me never to leave them! Never abandon them!

Doctor. Child of my heart! Ah, may they never abandon me!—for this is my house. For more than forty years I have been coming here day by day, hour by hour, and now there is nobody within these walls who is older than I. I have no children. I have had my loves—yes, a moment's flame— but it was so long ago! I have forgotten them. And these Sisters, who have been mothers to you, have been daughters to me; and now, when I come, they no longer even cover their faces before me. Why should they? It seems to me as if I had seen them born. And in this house (*Greatly moved.*) I should like to die, so that they might close my eyes, and say a prayer for me when life itself has closed!

Novices. Who is thinking of dying, Doctor?

Prioress. It is time to go.

Teresa. (*looking from one to the other.*) Aren't you going to embrace me? (*The Nuns, after hesitating and glancing a moment doubtfully at the Mother Prioress, embrace Teresa in turn, in perfect silence. Only Sister Joanna of the Cross, taking her into her arms, says:*)

Joanna. My child!

Prioress. May you find what you seek in the world, daughter, for so we hope and so we pray to God. But if it should not be so, remember, this is your Convent.

Teresa. Thanks . . . thanks. . . . (*Sobbing.*)

Doctor. Come, daughter, come. . . . (*The Doctor and Teresa go to the door, but Teresa turns when she reaches the threshold and embraces Sister Joanna of the Cross, passionately. Then she disappears. Sister Joanna of the Cross rests her head against the grille, her back to the others, and weeps silently. A pause. The bells of the coach are heard outside as it drives away.*)

Novices. They are going now. (*The chapel bell rings summoning the Nuns to choir.*)

Prioress. The summons to the choir.

Novices. Come, Sisters! Let us go there.

(*All make ready to go out sadly. The Vicaress, sensing the situation, to her mind demoralizing, feels it to be her duty to provide a remedy. She, too, is greatly moved, but making a supreme effort to control herself, says in a voice which she in vain endeavors to make appear calm, but which is choked in utterance by tears.*)

Vicaress. One moment. I have observed of late . . . that some . . . in the prayer . . . have not been marking sufficiently the pauses in the middle of the lines, while on the other hand, they drag out the last words interminably. Be careful of this, for your Reverences know that the beauty of the office lies in rightly marking the pauses, and in avoiding undue emphasis on the end of the phrase. Let us go there. (*The Nuns file out slowly. Sister Joanna of the Cross, unnoticed, remains alone. With a cry, she falls upon her knees beside an empty chair.*)

LADY WINDERMERE'S FAN
by
Oscar Wilde

ACT I

SCENE—Morning-room of Lord Windermere's house in Carlton house terrace.

Lady Windermere is at table R. arranging roses in a blue bowl. Enter Parker.

Parker. Is your ladyship at home this afternoon?

Lady W. Yes—who is calling?

Parker. The Duchess of Berwick and Lady Agatha Carlisle.

Exit Parker.

Enter the Duchess of B. and Lady A. C.

Duchess of B. (*Coming to Lady W. and shaking hands.*) Dear Margaret, I am so pleased to see you. You remember Agatha, don't you? How sweet you're looking! Where *do* you get your gowns? And now I must tell you how sorry I am for you, dear Margaret. (*Crosses to sofa and sits with Lady W.*) Agatha, darling!

Lady A. Yes, Mamma. (*Rises.*)

Duchess of B. Will you go and look over the photograph album that I see there?

Lady A. Yes, Mamma. (*Goes to table.*)

Duchess of B. Dear girl! She is so fond of photographs of Switzerland. Such a pure taste, I think. But I really am so sorry for you, Margaret.

Lady W. (*Smiling.*) Why, Duchess?

Duchess of B. Oh, on account of that horrid woman. She dresses so well, too, which makes it much worse, sets such a dreadful example. Augustus—you know my dis-

475

reputable brother—such a trial to us all—well, Augustus is completely infatuated about her. It is quite scandalous, for she is absolutely inadmissible, into society. Many a woman has a past, but I am told that she has at least a dozen, and that they all fit.

Lady W. Whom are you talking about, Duchess?

Duchess of B. About Mrs. Erlynne.

Lady W. Mrs. Erlynne? I never heard of her, Duchess. And what *has* she to do with me?

Duchess of B. My poor child! Agatha, darling!

Lady A. Yes, Mamma.

Duchess of B. Will you go out on the terrace and look at the sunset?

Lady A. Yes, Mamma. (*Exit through window L.*)

Duchess of B. Sweet girl! So devoted to sunsets! Shows such refinement of feeling, does it not? After all, there is nothing like nature, is there?

Lady W. But what is it, Duchess? Why do you talk to me about this person?

Duchess of B. Don't you really know. I assure you we're all so distressed about it. Only last night at dear Lady Fansen's every one was saying how extraordinary it was that, of all men in London, Windermere should behave in such a way.

Lady W. My husband—what has *he* to do with any woman of that kind?

Duchess of B. Ah, what indeed, dear? That is the point. He goes to see her continually, and stops for hours at a time, and while he is there she is not at home to any one. Not that many ladies call on her, dear, but she has a great many disreputable men friends—my own brother in particular, as I told you—and that is what makes it so dreadful about Windermere. We looked upon *him* as being such a model husband, but I am afraid there is no doubt about it. My dear nieces—you know the Saville girls, don't you?— such nice domestic creatures—plain, dreadfully plain, but so good—well, they're always at the window doing fancy

work, and making ugly things for the poor, which I think
so useful of them in these dreadful socialistic days, and
this terrible woman has taken a house in Curzon Street,
right opposite them—such a respectable street, too. I
don't know what we're coming to! And they tell me that
Windermere goes there four and five times a week—they
see him. They can't help it—and although they never talk
scandal, they—well, of course—they remark on it to every
one. And worst of it all is, that I have been told that this
woman has got a great deal of money out of somebody, for
it seems that she came to London six months ago without
anything at all to speak of, and now she has this charming
house in Mayfair, drives her pony in the Park every afternoon, and all—well all—since she has known poor dear
Windermere.

Lady W. Oh, I can't believe it!

Duchess of B. But it's quite true, my dear. The whole
of London knows it. That is why I felt it was better to
come and talk to you, and advise you to take Windermere
away at once to Homburg or to Aix where he'll have something to amuse him, and where you can watch him all day
long. I assure you, my dear, that on several occasions after
I was first married I had to pretend to be very ill, and was
obliged to drink the most unpleasant mineral waters, merely
to get Berwick out of town. He was so extremely sus-
ceptible. Though I am bound to say he never gave away
any large sums of money to anybody. He is far too high-
principled for that.

Lady W. (*interrupting*). Duchess, Duchess, it's impossible!
(*rising and crossing stage C.*) We are only married two years.
Our child is but six months old. (*Sits in chair R. of table.*)

Duchess of B. Ah, the dear, pretty baby! How is the
little darling? Is it a boy or a girl? I hope a girl—Ah, no,
I remember it's a boy! I'm so sorry. Boys are so wicked.
My boy is excessively immoral. You wouldn't believe at
what hours he comes home. And he's only left Oxford a
few months—I really don't know what they teach them there.

Lady W. Are *all* men bad?

Duchess of B. Oh, all of them, my dear, all of them, without any exception. And they never grow any better. Men become old, but they never become good.

Lady W. Windermere and I married for love.

Duchess of B. Yes, we begin like that. It was only Berwick's brutal and incessant threats of suicide that made me accept him at all, and before the year was out he was running after all kinds of petticoats, every color, every shape, every material. In fact, before the honeymoon was over, I caught him winking at my maid, a most pretty, respectable girl. I dismissed her at once without a character.—No, I remember I passed her on to my sister; poor dear Sir George is so short-sighted, I thought it wouldn't matter. But it did, though it was most unfortunate. (*Rises.*) And now, my dear child, I must go, as we are dining out. And mind you don't take this little aberration of Windermere's too much to heart. Just take him abroad, and he'll come back to you all right.

Lady W. Come back to me?

Duchess of B. Yes, dear, these wicked women get our husbands away from us, but they always come back, slightly damaged, of course. And don't make scenes, men hate them!

Lady W. It is very kind of you, Duchess, to come and tell me all this. But I can't believe that my husband is untrue to me.

Duchess of B. Pretty child! I was like that once. Now I know that all men are monsters. (*Lady W. rings bell.*) The only thing to do is to feed the wretches well. A good cook does wonders, and that I know you have. My dear Margaret, you are not going to cry?

Lady W. You needn't be afraid, Duchess, I never cry.

Duchess of B. That's quite right, dear. Crying is the refuge of plain women, but the ruin of pretty ones. Agatha, darling!

Lady A. (*Entering.*) Yes, Mamma.

Duchess of B. Come and bid good-bye to Lady Windermere, and thank her for your charming visit. And by the way, I must thank you for sending a card to Mr. Hopper— he's that rich young Australian people are taking such notice of just at present. His father made a great fortune by selling some kind of food in circular tins—most palatable, I believe,—I fancy it is the thing the servants always refuse to eat. But the son is quite interesting. I think he's attracted by dear Agatha's clever talk. Of course, we should be very sorry to lose her, but I think that a mother who doesn't part with a daughter every season has no real affection. We're coming to-night, dear. (*Parker opens doors.*) And remember my advice, take the poor fellow out of town at once, it is the only thing to do. Good-bye, once more; come, Agatha. (*Exeunt Duchess and Lady A.*)

* * *

From ACT III
SCENE—Lord Darlington's rooms.
(*Lady W. standing by the fireplace.*)

Enter Mrs. Erlynne.

Mrs. E. Lady Windermere! (*Lady W. starts and looks up. Then recoils in contempt.*) Thank Heaven I am in time. You must go back to your husband's house immediately.

Lady W. Must?

Mrs. E. (*Authoritatively.*) Yes, you must! There is not a second to be lost. Lord Darlington may return at any moment.

Lady W. Don't come near me!

Mrs. E. You must leave this place at once, my carriage is waiting at the corner of the street. You must come with me and drive straight home. (*Lady W. throws off her cloak and flings it on the sofa.*) What are you doing?

Lady W. Mrs. Erlynne—if you had not come here, I would have gone back. But now that I see you, I feel that nothing in the whole world would induce me to live under the same roof as Lord Windermere. You fill me with horror. There is something about you that stirs the wildest rage within me. And I know why you are here. My husband sent you to lure me back that I might serve as a blind to whatever relations exist between you and him.

Mrs. E. Oh! You don't think that—you can't.

Lady W. Go back to my husband, Mrs. Erlynne. He belongs to you and not to me. I suppose he is afraid of a scandal. Men are such cowards. They outrage every law of the world, and are afraid of the world's tongue. But he had better prepare himself. He shall have a scandal. He shall have the worst scandal there has been in London for years.

Mrs. E. Lady Windermere, you wrong me horribly— you wrong your husband horribly. He doesn't know you are here—he thinks you are safe in your own house. He thinks you are asleep in your own room. He never read the mad letter you wrote to him!

Lady W. Never read it!

Mrs. E. No—he knows nothing about it.

Lady W. How simple you think me! (*Going to her.*) You are lying to me!

Mrs. E. (*Restraining herself.*) I am not. I am telling you the truth.

Lady W. If my husband didn't read my letter, how is it that you are here! Who told you I had left the house you were shameless enough to enter? Who told you where I had gone to? My husband told you, and sent you to decoy me back.

Mrs. E. Your husband has never seen the letter. I— saw it, I opened it. I—read it.

Lady W. (*Turning to her.*) You opened a letter of mine to my husband? You wouldn't dare!

Mrs. E. Dare! Oh! to save you from the abyss into which you are falling, there is nothing in the world I would not dare, nothing in the whole world. Here is the letter. Your husband has never read it. He never shall read it.

(*Going to fireplace.*) It should never have been written. (*Tears it and throws it into the fire.*)

Lady W. (*With infinite contempt in her voice and look.*) How do I know that was my letter after all? You seem to think the commonest device can take me in!

Mrs. E. Oh! why do you disbelieve everything I tell you! What object do you think I have in coming here, except to save you from utter ruin, to save you from the consequences of a hideous mistake? That letter that is burning now *was* your letter. I swear it to you!

Lady W. (*Slowly.*) You took good care to burn it before I had examined it. I cannot trust you. You, whose whole life is a lie, how could you speak the truth about anything? (*Sits down.*)

Mrs. E. (*Hurriedly.*) Think as you like about me—say what you choose against me, but go back, go back to the husband you love.

Lady W. (*Sullenly.*) I do *not* love him!

Mrs. E. You do, and you know that he loves you.

Lady W. He does not understand what love is. He understands it as you do—but I see what you want. It would be a great advantage for you to get me back. Dear Heaven! what a life I would have then! Living at the mercy of a woman, a vile woman, a woman who comes between husband and wife!

Mrs. E. (*With a gesture of despair.*) Lady Windermere, Lady Windermere, don't say such terrible things. You don't know how terrible they are, how terrible and how unjust. Listen, you must listen! Only go back to your husband, and I promise you never to communicate with him again on any pretext—never see him—never to have anything to do with his life or yours. The money that he gave me, he gave me not through love, but through hatred, not in worship, but in contempt. The hold I have over him—

Lady W. (*Rising.*) Ah! you admit you have a hold!

Mrs. E. Yes, and I will tell you what it is. It is his love for you, Lady Windermere.

Lady W. You expect me to believe that?

Mrs. E. You must believe it! It is true. It is his love for you that has made him submit to—oh! call it what you like, tyranny, threats, anything you choose. But it is his love for you. His desire to spare you—shame, yes, shame and disgrace.

Lady W. What do you mean? You are insolent! What have I to do with you?

Mrs. E. (*Humbly.*) Nothing. I know it—but I tell you that your husband loves you. Lady Windermere, before Heaven your husband is guiltless of all offense towards you! And I—I tell you that had it ever occurred to me that such a monstrous suspicion would have entered your mind, I would have died rather than have crossed your life or his—oh! died, gladly died!

Lady W. You talk as if you had a heart. Women like you have no hearts. Heart is not in you. You are bought and sold.

Mrs. E. (*Starts, with a gesture of pain. Then restrains herself, and comes over to where Lady W. is sitting. As she speaks, she stretches out her hands towards her, but does not dare to touch her.*) Believe what you choose about me. I am not worth a moment's sorrow. But don't spoil your beautiful young life on my account! You don't know what may be in store for you, unless you leave this house at once. You don't know what it is to fall into the pit, to be despised, mocked, abandoned, sneered at—to be an outcast! to find the door shut against one, to have to creep in by hideous byways, afraid every moment lest the mask should be stripped from one's face, and all the while to hear the laughter, the horrible laughter of the world, a thing more tragic than all the tears the world has ever shed. You don't know what it is. One pays for one's sin, and then one pays again, and all one's life one pays. You must never know that.—As for me, if suffering be an expiation, then at this moment I have expiated all my faults, whatever they have been; for to-night you have made a heart in one who had it

not, made it and broken it.—But let that pass. I may have
wrecked my own life, but I will not let you wreck yours.
You—why, you are a mere girl, you would be lost. You
haven't got the kind of brains that enables a woman to get
back. You have neither the wit nor the courage. You
couldn't stand dishonor. No! Go back, Lady Windermere,
to the husband who loves you, whom you love. You have a
child, Lady Windermere. God gave you that child. He
will require from you that you make his life fine, that you
watch over him. Your husband loves you. He has never
swerved for a moment from the love he bears you. But
even if he had a thousand loves, you must stay with your
child.

(*Lady W. bursts into tears and buries her face in her hands.*)
(*Rushing to her.*) Lady Windermere!

Lady W. (*Holding out her hands to her, helplessly, as a
child might do.*) Take me home. Take me home.

Mrs. E. (*Is about to embrace her. Then restrains herself. There is a look of wonderful joy in her face.*) Come!
Where is your cloak? (*Getting it from sofa.*) Here. Put it
on. Come at once! (*They go to the door.*)

Lady W. Stop! Don't you hear voices?

Mrs. E. No, no! There is no one!

Lady W. Yes, there is! Listen! Oh! that is my husband's voice! He is coming in! Save me! Oh, it's some
plot! You have sent for him! (*Voices outside.*)

Mrs. E. Silence! I am here to save you if I can. But I
fear it is too late! There! (*Points to the curtain across the
window.*) The first chance you have, slip out, if you ever get
a chance!

Lady W. But you!

Mrs. E. Oh! never mind me. I'll face them.

JOHN FERGUSON
by
St. John G. Ervine

From Act I

Hannah Ferguson (*Bitterly.*) It's quare and hard to see what purpose there is in misfortune and trouble for people that never done nothing to deserve it! . . .

John Ferguson. Daughter, dear, you're a young slip of a girl, or you'd never talk that way. (*Sternly.*) Do you think God doesn't know how to look after His own world? (*The severity of his voice relaxes.*) Everything that happens is made to happen, and everything in the world, the commonest wee fly in the bushes before the door there, has a purpose and a meaning. There's things hid from you and me because we're not fit to know them, but the more we fill ourselves with the glory of God, the better we get to understand the world. It's people that's full of sin, Hannah, that can't see or understand. That's sin—not knowing or understanding! Ignorance is sin. Keeping your mind shut is sin. Not letting the sun and the air and the warmth of God into your heart—that's sin, Hannah!

JANE CLEGG

by

St. John G. Ervine

From Act I

Jane Clegg. I never see anything or go anywhere. I
have to cook and wash and nurse and mend and teach! . . .
And then I'm not certain of Henry. That's what's so hard.
I give him everything, and he isn't faithful.

Mrs. Clegg. 'E was always a man for women. There's
a lot like that. They don't mean no 'arm, but some'ow they
do it. I 'eard tell once of someone that said it was silly
of women to complain about things like that, and mebbe 'e
was right. They're not made like us, men aren't. I never
wanted but one man in my life, but my 'usband, bless 'im,
'e was never satisfied. 'E used to say it near broke 'is 'eart
to be a Christian! 'E 'ad a great respect for Turks an'
foreigners. 'Enry takes after 'im. (*She pauses for a moment.*) I dunno! Men's a funny lot wotever way you take
them, an' it's my belief a wise woman shuts 'er eyes to more'n
'alf wot goes on in the world. She'd be un'appy if she didn't,
an' it's no good bein' un'appy.

* * *

From Act III

Jane Clegg. You are an absolute rotter.

Henry Clegg. I don't know. I'm not a bad chap, really.
I'm just weak. I'd be all right if I had a lot of money and
a wife that wasn't better than I am. . . . Oh, I know, Jane!
You *are* better than I am. Any fool can see that! It doesn't
do a chap much good to be living with a woman who's his
superior, at least not the sort of chap I am. I ought to have
married a woman like myself, or a bit worse. That's what

485

Kitty is. She's worse than I am, and that sort of makes me love her. It's different with you. I always feel mean here. Yes, I am mean. I know that; but it makes me meaner than I really am to be living with you. (*He sits down at the table and begins to fill his pipe.*) Do you understand, Jane? Somehow, the mean things I do that don't amount to much, I can't tell 'em to you, or carry 'em off as if they weren't mean, and I do meaner things to cover them up. That's the way of it. I don't act like that with Kitty.

THE FOOL

by
Channing Pollock

From Act I

Goodkind. Dan, you're an awfully decent fellow, but I still think you made a mistake going into the church. If you ever want to talk it over with me, I'd be glad to help you—any time! You know that! Good-bye, Doctor! Good-bye, Dan, and a Merry Christmas! (*He exits L.*)

Dr. Wadham. Daniel, you're in trouble.

Daniel. (*Smiling.*) Doctor, I'm used to it.

Dr. Wadham. This time it's serious. I've warned you often. I don't see how you can have been so blind.

Daniel. I haven't been blind.

Dr. Wadham. Then you don't care for your position in this church.

Daniel. (*With feeling.*) There's only one thing I care for more.

Dr. Wadham. And that is?

Daniel. To be worthy of it.

Dr. Wadham. When you're as old as I am, Daniel, you'll understand that being honest doesn't necessarily mean being disagreeable.

Daniel. Doesn't it mean—telling the truth?

Dr. Wadham. Do you know the truth, Daniel?

Daniel. Yes; don't you? Doesn't every man—in his heart? And if we want to keep it in our hearts, and never think about it or look it in the face, shouldn't someone pry open the door and cry: "Behold"? . . . I didn't tell them anything they didn't know, Doctor. I don't *know* anything they don't know. I just reminded them—

487

Dr. Wadham. (*Exploding on the last word.*) That we were heathen!

Daniel. That we were Christians, and every man our brother, and that we were sitting, overdressed and overfed, in a Christian Church, while our brother froze and starved—outside—in a Christian World!

Dr. Wadham. That isn't fair! These good people have given—

Daniel. *Given*—what cost them nothing! Frumpery and trumpery and diamond stars! That's how all of us give—what we don't need; what we don't even want! . . . You're a good man, Doctor, and, honestly, what would you say tomorrow if your wife told you she'd sold her rings, and given the money to the poor?

Dr. Wadham. Why, I—

Daniel. You'd say she was crazy!

Dr. Wadham. But there's no necessity—

Daniel. Oh, yes, there is! There'll be people lying in the parks tonight. What would Mrs. Tice say if I invited them to sleep in her pew?

Dr. Wadham. That there's no reason why she should share dirt and disease!

Daniel. Exactly! We may *believe* in the brotherhood of man, but we *know* about germs! We're not sure what is truth, but there's one thing we *are* sure of, and *mean* to be sure of, and that's our own comfort! You know that, and I know it, and they know it—but we mustn't say it! All right; in God's name, what *are* we to say?

Dr. Wadham. (*Who has been nervously regarding this raving as confirming the worst fears of Mr. Goodkind.*) Precisely. And that brings us to tomorrow's sermon. I understand you intend to talk about the strike. (*Dan nods " Yes"*) And that's not a very pleasant subject for Christmas. Wouldn't it be more fitting to preach from the text, "Glory to God in the Highest"?

Daniel. "And on earth, Peace, good will toward men"?

Dr. Wadham. (*Delighted.*) Yes! You might say, "There are many kinds of peace—"

Daniel. But there aren't!

Dr. Wadham. There is physical peace—peace that came with the end of this cruel war!

Daniel. There *is* no peace! There is only fear—and hate—and vanity—and lust, and envy, and greed—of men and nations! There are only people preying on one another, and a hungry horde at the very doors of your church! . . . My text will be: "And Peter followed afar off."

Dr. Wadham. I don't understand.

Daniel. (*Into his tone, hitherto indignantly human, comes something mystic—something divine.*) We all follow—afar off.

Dr. Wadham. (*Alarmed; not at the words, but at that "something divine".*) Daniel . . . my dear fellow!

Daniel. Don't worry. I'm quite sane. Only—I've been wondering about that for a long time.

Dr. Wadham. Wondering?

Daniel. What would happen if anybody really tried to live like Christ.

Dr. Wadham. (*Shaking his head.*) It can't be done.

Daniel. Isn't it worth trying? Men risk their lives— every day—in experiments far less worth while. We've had centuries of "fear, and hate, and greed"—and where have they brought us? Why not try love?

Dr. Wadham. How can you make them try?

Daniel. By showing that it would work.

Dr. Wadham. It *won't* work, Daniel. It's a beautiful ideal, but it won't work. Times have changed, and things are different. Life isn't as simple as it was two thousand years ago. The trouble with you, Daniel, is that you're not practical.

Daniel. I wonder.

Dr. Wadham. And the great need of the church is practical men. We mustn't take the Scriptures too literally. We must try to interpret their spirit. And, above all, we must please our congregations, or we shan't have any. And then what becomes of our influence? Better fall back on my text for tomorrow, Daniel.

Daniel. I can't.

Dr. Wadham. At least, you must promise not to discuss the strike.

Daniel. I can't do that, Doctor.

Dr. Wadham. Or else let me take the pulpit.

Daniel. I won't do that! (*A pause.*)

Dr. Wadham. Very well! Preach your Christmas sermon, and afterward—

Daniel. Yes?

Dr. Wadham. I think you may find a greater field of usefulness elsewhere. (*A long pause. The men look at each other, and then Daniel turns away to conceal his emotion. He goes up for his hat, and returns.*) I'm sorry, Daniel. I know you've been very happy in your work here. I know how failure hurts. But you saw it coming, and you wouldn't turn aside.

Daniel. (*He looks up with flashing eyes.*) The man who turns away from his vision—lies! (*Shakes hands.*) It's all right, Doctor. (*He crosses L.*)

"AND SO THEY WERE MARRIED"
by
Jesse Lynch Williams

From Act I
Characters

John, the masterful type of successful business man.

Theodore, a cousin of John's, a care-worn rector, a noble soul, self-sacrificing and sanctified.

Lucy, John's wife, conspicuously a "sweet" woman.

The Judge, John and Lucy's Uncle Everett; a gentle satirist with a cynical tolerance of the ways of the world, which he understands, laughs at, and rather likes.

SCENE: The terrace. John, Lucy, Theodore and Uncle Everett are continuing an earnest discussion with the intimate manner of friendly members of the same family. John, Lucy and Theodore deeply concerned; Uncle Everett detached and amused.

Theodore. But, Uncle Everett, hasn't Aunt Julia always been a good wife to you?

Judge. Quite so, quite so, a good wife, Theodore, a good wife.

Lucy. And a devoted mother to your children, Uncle Everett?

Judge. Devoted, Lucy, devoted.

John. She has always obeyed you, Uncle Everett.

Judge. Yes, John—a true, old-fashioned woman.

Theodore. She has been a great help to me in the parish work, Uncle Everett.

Judge. An earnest worker in the vineyard, Theodore— in fact, I might say, a model female.

All. Then why, why do you want a divorce?

Judge. Because, damn it, I don't like her!

491

Lucy. But think of poor Aunt Julia!

Judge. But damn it, she doesn't like *me*.

Theodore. (*Wagging head sadly.*) Ah, yes, I suppose there has been fault on both sides.

Judge. Not at all! No fault on either side. . . . Both patterns of Christian fortitude to the end! We still are. Just listen to this telegram.

Lucy. (*Puzzled.*) From Aunt Julia?

Judge. Yes from Aunt Julia in Reno. Not used to travelling without me; knew I'd worry. Thoughtful of her, wasn't it? (*Puts on glasses.*) A night letter. Much cheaper; your Aunt Julia was always a frugal wife. Besides, she never could keep within ten words. (*Reads.*) "Arrived safely. Charming rooms with plenty of air and sunlight. Our case docketed for March 15th. Wish you were here to see the women in Divorcee Row—overdressed and underbred." Rather neat, eh? "Overdressed and underbred." "I should love to hear *your* comments on the various types." Now, isn't that sweet of her? Well, you know, I always *could* make her laugh—except when I made her cry. "Write soon. With love, Julia." Now (*Folds telegram*), isn't that a nice message? From a wife suing for divorce? You happily married people couldn't beat that. (*Pats telegram and pockets it tenderly.*)

John. (*Like a practical business man.*) But if there's no other woman, no other man—what's it all about?

Judge. She likes her beefsteak well done; I like mine underdone. She likes one window open—about so much (*Indicating four inches*); I like all the windows open wide! She likes to stay at home; I like to travel. She loves the opera and hates the theatre; I love the theatre and hate the opera.

Theodore. Stop! Aren't you willing to make a few little sacrifices for each other? Haven't you character enough for that?

Judge. We've been making sacrifices for twenty-five years, a quarter of a century! Why, I remember the first dinner we had together after we were pronounced man and

vife, with a full choral service and a great many expensive
lowers—quite a smart wedding, Lucy, for those simple days.
'Darling", I asked my blushing bride, "do you like tutti-
rutti ice-cream?" "I adore it, dearest", she murmured. I
nated it, but nobly sacrificed myself and gave her tutti-
frutti and gained character every evening of our honeymoon! Then when we got back and began our "new life"
together in our "little home", my darling gave *me* tutti-frutti
and indigestion *once a week* until I nearly died!

 Lucy. But why didn't you tell her?

 Judge. I did; I did. Got chronic dyspepsia and struck!
" *You* may adore this stuff, *darling,*" I said, "but I hate it."
"So do I, dearest", says she. "Then why in thunder have
you had it all these years, *sweetheart?*" "For your sake,
beloved!" And that tells the whole story of our married
life. We have nothing in common but a love of divorce and
a mutual abhorrence of tutti-frutti. "Two souls with but a
single thought, two hearts that beat as one!" It has been
the dream of our lives to get apart, and each has nobly re-
frained for the other's sake. And all in vain!

 John. Bah! All a cloak to hide his real motive. And
he knows it!

 Judge. (*After a painful pause.*) I may as well confess.
(*Looks around to see of overheard. Whispers*) For over twenty
years I—I have broken my marriage vow! (*Lucy drops her
eyes. Theodore aghast. John wags head.*) So has your Aunt
Julia!

 Theodore. No! Not that!

 Judge. Well, we solemnly promised to love each other
until death did us part. We have broken that sacred vow!
I don't love *her;* she doesn't love *me*—not in the least!

 John. Rot! A matured, middle-aged man, a distinguished member of the bar—break up his home for that?
Damned rot!

 Judge. Right again, John. That's not why I'm breaking
up my home. I prefer my club. What does the modern
home amount to? Merely a place to leave your wife.

Lucy. Of course, it doesn't matter about the poor little
wife left at home.

Judge. Wrong, Lucy, it does matter. That's why I
stayed at home and was bored to death with her prattle about
clothes and the opera, instead of dining at the club with my
intellectual equals, picking up business there, getting rich
like John, supplying her with *more* clothes and a whole *box*
at the opera, like yours, Lucy.

Lucy. (*Shoots a glance at her husband.*) Oh, that's the
way you men *always* talk. It never occurs to you that business, business, *business is just* as much of a bore to us!

Judge. Wrong again! It did occur to *me*—hence the
divorce! She couldn't stand seeing *me* bored; I couldn't
stand seeing *her* bored. Once we could deceive each other;
but now—too well acquainted; our happy home—a hollow
mockery!

Theodore. You ought to be ashamed! I love my home!

John. So do I. (*He glances sternly at Lucy.*)

Lucy. (*Nervously.*) So do I.

Judge. All right. Stick to it, if you love it. Only, don't
claim credit for doing what you enjoy. I stuck to my home
for a quarter of a century and disliked it the whole time.
At last I'm free to say so. Just think of it, Lucy, free to
utter those things about marriage we all know are true but
don't dare say! Free to be honest, John! No longer a hypocrite, no longer a liar! A soul set free, Theodore—two souls,
in fact. "Two souls with but a single thought. . . ."

Theodore. Stop! You have *children* to consider, not
merely your own selfish happiness!

Lucy. Yes, think of Tom and little Julia!

Judge. We did . . . for a quarter of a century—sacrificed everything to them, even our self-respect; but now—
what's the use? We are childless now. Tom and Julia have
both left us for "little homes" of their own to love.

Theodore. Ah, but don't you want them to have the old
home to come back to?

Judge. "No place like home" for children, eh? You're

right—can't have too much of it. Most children only have
one home. Ours will have *two*! When they get bored with
one they can try the other.

Theodore. But, seriously, Uncle Everett—"Whom God
hath joined together!"

Lucy. (*Clasping John's arm.*) Yes, Uncle Everett, mar-
riages are made in heaven.

Judge. I see; quite so; but your Aunt Julia and I were
joined together by a pink parasol made in Paris.

John. What rot! Stop your fooling and speak the truth,
man.

Judge. Just what I'm doing—that's why you think I'm
fooling. A very pretty parasol—but it wasn't made in
heaven. You see, God made poor, dear Julia pale, but on
that fatal day, twenty-five years ago, the pink parasol, not
God, made her rosy and irresistible. I did the rest—with the
aid of a clergyman, whom I tipped even more liberally than
the waiter who served us tutti-frutti. Blame *me* for it,
blame her, the tutti-frutti, the parson, but do not, my dear
Theodore, blame the Deity for our own mistakes. It's so
blasphemous. . . .

* * *

Act III

The butler now brings a telegram to the Judge.

Judge. From Julia! (*Tears it open eagerly, reads, and
then shouts.*) She's coming back to me, she's coming back!
Look at that, look at that! (*Jumps up and shows telegram to
John. Then taking it around to Lucy he sings to tune of
"Merrily we roll along"*):

> Aunt Julia is coming back
> Coming back—coming back
> Aunt Julia is coming back
> Coming back from Reno.

Helen. (*Laughing.*) From Reno? That sounds like
divorce, Uncle Everett.

Judge. Like divorce? Does *that* sound like divorce?

(*Takes telegram from Lucy and hands it to Helen.*) **Read it aloud.**

Helen. (*Reading.*) "Dear boy, I can't stand it, either. Come to me or I go to you."

Judge. (*Sings during the reading.*) Coming back from Reno. (*Breaks off—to Helen.*) So you thought we wanted a divorce, did you?"

Helen. I never dreamed of such a thing.

Judge. (*Looks at her a moment, then in a burst.*) Well, I did. The dream of my life—your Aunt Julia's too. We thought we believed in trial marriage, but we don't—we believe in trial *separation!*

Theodore. (*Uncomfortably.*) They thought they didn't love each other, but they do, you see.

Judge. We don't, we don't; but we can't get along without each other . . . got the habit of having each other around and can't break it. . . . This morning I telegraphed: "Are you doing this just for my sake?" She replied: "Tutti-frutti." (*Sings.*) Aunt Julia's coming back. Oh, I'm too happy to eat. (*Singing, while others eat and drink.*) . . .

MARY STUART
by
Schiller

ACT THIRD, SCENE IV

The Park at Fotheringay—*Mary and Elizabeth.*

Elizabeth. (*Coldly and haughtily.*) What would'st thou say to me? Thou did'st seek converse with me! Forgetting that I am an outraged Sovereign, I honor thee with my royal presence! 'Tis in obedience to a generous impulse that I now deservedly incur the reproach of having sacrificed my dignity.

Mary. How can I express myself, how shall I so choose my every word that it may penetrate, without irritating thy heart? Aid thou my lips, Oh, God of mercy, and banish from them everything that may offend my sister! I cannot relate to thee my woes, without appearing to accuse thee, and this is not my wish. Towards me thou hast been neither merciful or just. I am thine equal, and yet thou hast made a prisoner of me! A suppliant and a fugitive I turned to thee for aid—and thou, tramping on the rights of nations and of hospitality, hast immured me in a living tomb! Thou hast cruelly deprived me of my servants and my faithful friends— thou hast abandoned me to the most shameful need, and, finally, exposed me to the ignominy of a trial! But no more of the past—we are now face to face! Display the goodness of thy heart! Tell me the crimes of which I am accused. Ah! wherefore did'st thou not grant me this friendly audience when I so eagerly desired to see thee? It would have spared me years of misery; and this sad, painful interview would never have occurred in this abode of gloom and horror!

Elizabeth. Accuse not fate, but thine own wayward soul,

497

and the uncontrollable ambition of thy house! There was
no cause of quarrel between us, until thy most worthy ally
inspired thee with the mad and rash desire to claim for thyself my royal titles and my throne! Not satisfied with this,
he then urged thee to make war against me—to threaten
my crown and my life! Amidst the peace which reigned in
my dominions, he fraudulently excited my subjects to re-
volt. But heaven doth protect me, and the attempt was
abandoned in despair! The blow was aimed at my head,
but 'tis on *thine* that it will fall.

Mary. I am in the hand of God! but thou wilt not exceed thy power by committing so atrocious a deed!

Elizabeth. Who could prevent me! Thy kinsman has
showed monarchs how to make peace with their enemies!
Who would be surety for thee if, imprudently, I were to
liberate thee from thy fetters? How can I rely on thy
pledged faith? Nought but my power renders me secure.
No! there can be no friendship with a race of vipers!

Mary. Are these thy dark suspicions? to thine eyes, then,
I have ever seemed a stranger and an enemy. If thou had'st
but recognized me as heiress to thy throne, as is my lawful
right—love, friendship, would have made of me thy sister
and thy friend!

Elizabeth. What affection hast thou that is not feigned?
I declare thee heiress to my throne? Insidious treachery! In
order, forsooth, that thou mightest overturn the state, and,
wily Armida that thou art, entrap within thy snares the
youthful spirit of my kingdom, so that, e'en during mine
own lifetime, all eyes might turn towards thee—the new
constellation!

Mary. Reign on in peace! I renounce all right unto thy
sceptre! The wings of my ambition have long drooped, and
greatness has no longer charms for me! 'Tis thou who hast
it all! I am now but the shade of Mary Stuart! My pristine
ardor has been subdued by the ignominy of my chains! Thou
hast now put my spirit to its last test! Thou hast nipped
my existence in its bud! Now, hold! Pronounce those

magnanimous words for which thou camest hither—for I will not believe that thou art come to enjoy the base delight of insulting thy victim! Pronounce the words so longed for, and say—"Mary, thou art free! Till now thou hast only known my power; thou shalt now know my greatness!" Woe to thee, should'st thou not depart from me, propitious, beneficent, sublime, like to an invoked Deity. Oh, sister! not for all England, not for all the lands that the vast ocean embrace, would I present myself to thee with the inexorable aspect with which thou now regardest me!

Elizabeth. At length thou confessest thyself vanquished? At last thou hast emptied thy quiver of the artifices it contained? Hast thou no more *assassins?* Does there not remain to thee one single hero to undertake in thy defence the duties of knight errant? Gone, Mary—gone for ever are those days. Thou can'st no longer seduce a follower of mine; far other causes now inflame men's hearts! In vain thou'dst seek a fourth husband among my English subjects; they know too well that thou *murderest* thy husbands, as thou dost thy lovers!

Mary. (*Shuddering*). Oh, heavens! sister—grant *me*—resignation!

Elizabeth. (*Contemplating her with an air of haughty contempt. To Leicester.*) Earl, are these then the boasted features on which no mortal eye could gaze with safety? Is this the beauty to which no other woman's could be compared? In sooth, the reputation appears to have been easily won. To be thus celebrated as the reigning beauty of the universe, seems merely to apply that she has been *universal* in the distribution of her favors!

Mary. Ah! 'tis too much.

Elizabeth. (*With a smile of contempt.*) Aye, now thou showest thyself in thine own form. Till now thou hast worn a mask!

Mary. (*With dignified pride.*) They were mere human errors that overcame me in my youth; my grandeur dazzled me. I have nought to conceal or to deny my faults—my pride has ever disdained the base artifices of vile intriguers. The worst I ever did is known, and I may boast myself far better than my reputation. But woe to thee, thy malignant hypocrite, if ever thou lettest fall the virgin mantle beneath which thou concealest thine own shameless amours! Thou, the daughter of Anne Boleyn, hast not inherited virtue! The chaste virtues that brought thine adulterous mother to the block, are known to all! The throne of England is profaned by a bastard! The British nation is duped by a vile pretender! Did but *right* prevail, thou would'st now be grovelling at my feet,—for 'tis I who am *thy* Sovereign!

(*Elizabeth hastily retires.*)

Mary. (*Still violently excited.*) She departs, burning with rage and with the bitterness of death at heart! Anna! how happy I am! (*Throwing her arms around Anna's neck.*) I have degraded her in Leicester's presence! At last! at last! after long years of insult and contumely, I have at least enjoyed one hour of triumph and revenge!

(*Exeunt hastily.*)

MARY OF SCOTLAND
by
Maxwell Anderson

From Act Three

(*Elizabeth comes to the doorway. Mary looks at her questioningly.*)

Mary

I have seen but a poor likeness, and yet I believe
This is Elizabeth.

Elizabeth

I am Elizabeth.
May we be alone together?
(*At a sign from Mary the Maids go out the rear door. Elizabeth enters and the hall-door swings to behind her.*)

Mary

I had hoped to see you.
When last you wrote you were not sure.

Elizabeth

If I've come
So doubtfully and tardigrade, my dear,
And break thus in upon you, it's not for lack
Of thinking of you. Rather because I've thought
Too long, perhaps, and carefully. Then at last
It seemed if I saw you near, and we talked as sisters
Over these poor realms of ours, some light might break
That we'd never see apart.

Mary

Have I been so much
A problem?

Elizabeth

Have you not? When the winds blow down
The houses, and there's a running and arming of men,

501

And a great cry of praise and blame, and the center
Of all this storm's a queen, she beautiful—
As I see you are—

Mary

Nay—

Elizabeth

Aye, with the Stuart mouth
And the high forehead and French ways and thoughts—
Well, we must look to it.—Not since that Helen
We read of in dead Troy, has a woman's face
Stirred such a confluence of air and waters
To beat against the bastions. I'd thought you taller,
But truly, since that Helen, I think there's been
No queen so fair to look on.

Mary

You flatter me.

Elizabeth

It's more likely envy. You see this line
Drawn down between my brows? No wash or ointments
Nor wearing of straight plasters in the night
Will take that line away. Yet I'm not much older
Than you, and had looks, too, once.

Mary

I had wished myself
For a more regal beauty such as yours,
More fitting for a queen.

Elizabeth

Were there not two verses
In a play I remember:

> Brightness falls from the air;
> Queens have died young and fair—?

They must die young if they'd die fair, my cousin,
Brightness falls from them, but not from you yet; believe
me,
It's envy, not flattery.

Mary

Can it be—as I've hoped—

Can it be that you come to me as a friend—
Meaning me well?

Elizabeth

Would you have me an enemy?

Mary

I have plenty to choose among as enemies—
And sometimes, as your word reached out to me
Through embassies, entangled with men's tongues,
It has seemed you judged me harshly, even denying
My right to a place beside you. But now you are here,
And a woman like myself, fearing as I do,
With a little dark fears of a woman, the creeping of age
On a young face, I see truer—I think I see truer,
And that this may be someone to whom I can reach a hand
And feel a clasp, and trust it. A woman's hand,
Stronger than mine in this hour, willing to help.
If that were so—

Elizabeth

Aye.

Mary

Or, if that were so,
I have great power to love! Let them buzz forever
Between us, these men with messages and lies,
You'll find me still there, and smiling, and open-hearted,
Unchanging while the cusped hills wear down!

Elizabeth

(*Smiling.*)
Nay, pledge
Not too much, my dear, for in these uncertain times
It's slippery going for all of us. I, who seem now
So firm in my footing, well I know one mis-step
Could make me a most unchancy friend. If you'd keep
Your place on this rolling ball, let the mountains slide
And slip to the valleys. Put no hand to them
Or they'll pull you after.

Mary

But does this mean you can lend
No hand to me, or I'll pull you down?

Elizabeth

I say it
Recalling how I came to my throne as you did,
Some five or six years before, beset as you were
With angry factions—and came there young, loving truth,
As you did. This was many centuries since,
Or seems so to me, I'm so old by now
In shuffling tricks and the huckstering of souls
For lands and pensions. I learned to play it young,
Must learn it or die.—It's thus if you would rule;
Give up good faith, the word that goes with the heart,
The heart that clings where it loves. Give these up, and love
Where your interest lies, and should your interest change
Let your love follow it quickly. This is queen's porridge,
And however little stomach she has for it
A queen must eat it.

Mary

I, too, Elizabeth,
Have read my Machiavelli. His is a text-book
Much studied in the French court. Are you serious
To rede me this lesson?

Elizabeth

You have too loving a heart,
I fear, and too bright a face to be a queen.

Mary

That's not what's charged against me. When I've lost
So far it's been because my people believed
I was more crafty than I am. I've been
Traduced as a murderess and adulteress
And nothing I could have said, and nothing done
Would have warded the blow. What I seek now is only
My freedom, so that I may return and prove
In open court, and before my witnesses,
That I am guiltless. You are the queen of England,

And I am held prisoner in England. Why am I held,
And who is it holds me?

Elizabeth

It was to my interest, child,
To protect you, lest violence be offered to a princess
And set a precedent. Is there anyone in England
Who could hold you against my will?

Mary

Then I ask as a sovereign,
Speaking to you as an equal, that I be allowed
To go, and fight my own battles.

Elizabeth

It would be madness.

Mary

May I not judge of that?

Elizabeth

See, here is our love!

Mary

If you wish my love and good-will you shall have it freely
When I am free.

Elizabeth

You will never govern, Mary. If I let you go
There will be long broils again in Scotland, dangers,
And ripe ones, to my peace at home. To be fair
To my own people, this must not be.

Mary

Now speak once
What your will is, and what behind it! You wish me here,
You wish me in prison—have we come to that?

Elizabeth

It's safer.

Mary

Who do you wish to rule in Scotland,
If not my Stuart line?

Elizabeth

Have I said, my dear,
That I'd bar the Stuarts from Scotland, or bar your reign

If you were there, and reigned there? I say only
You went the left way about it, and since it's so
And has fallen out so, it were better for both our kingdoms
If you remained my guest.

Mary

For how long?

Elizabeth

Until
The world is quieter.

Mary

And who will rule in my place?

Elizabeth

Why, who rules now? Your brother.

Mary

He rules by stealth—

Elizabeth

But all this could be arranged,
Or so I'm told, if your son were to be crowned king,
And Moray made regent.

Mary

My son in Moray's hands—
Moray in power—

Elizabeth

Is there any other way?
(*A pause.*)

Mary

Elizabeth—I have been here a long while
Already—it seems so. If it's your policy
To keep me—shut me up—I can argue no more—
No—I beg now. There's one I love in the north,
You know that—and my life's there, my throne's there, my
 name
To be defended—and I must lie here darkened
From news and from the sun—lie here impaled
On a brain's agony—wondering even sometimes

If I were what they said me—a carrion-thing
In my desires—can you understand this?—I speak it
Too brokenly to be understood, but I beg you
As you are a woman and I am—and our brightness falls
Soon enough at best—let me go, let me have my life
Once more—and my dear health of mind again—
For I rot away here in my mind—in what
I think of myself—some death-tinge falls over one
In prisons—

Elizabeth

It will grow worse, not better. I've known
Strong men shut up alone for years—it's not
Their hair turns white only; they sicken within
And scourge themselves. If you would think like a queen
This is no place for you. The brain taints here
Till all desires are alike. Be advised and sign
The abdication.

Mary

Stay now a moment. I begin to glimpse
Behind this basilisk mask of yours. It was this
You've wanted from the first.

Elizabeth

This that I wanted?

Mary

It was you sent Lord Throgmorton long ago
When first I'd have married Bothwell. All this while
Some evil's touched my life at every turn.
To cripple what I'd do. And now—why now—
Looking on you—I see it incarnate before me—
It was your hand that touched me. Reaching out
In little ways—here a word, there an action—this
Was what you wanted. I thought perhaps a star—
Wildly I thought it—perhaps a star might ride
Astray—or a crone that burned an image down
In wax—filling the air with curses on me
And slander; the murder of Rizzio, Moray in that

And you behind Moray—the murder of Darnley, Throg-
    morton
Behind that too, you with them—and that winged scandal
You threw at us when we were married. Proof I have none
But I've felt it—would know it anywhere—in your eyes—
There—before me.

Elizabeth

What may become a queen
Is to rule her kingdom. Had you ruled yours I'd say
She has her ways, I mine. Live and let live
And a merry world for those who have it. But now
I must think this over—sadness has touched your brain,
I'm no witch to charm you, make no incantations;
You come here by your own road.

Mary

I see how I came.
Back, back, each step the wrong way, and each sign followed
As you'd have me go, till the skein picks up and we stand
Face to face here. It was you forced Bothwell from me—
You there, and always. Oh, I'm to blame in this, too!
I should have seen your hand!

Elizabeth

It has not been my use
To speak much or spend my time—

Mary

How could I have been
Mistaken in you for an instant?

Elizabeth

You were not mistaken.
I am all women I must be. One's a young girl,
Young and harrowed as you are—one who could weep
To see you here—and one's a bitterness
At what I have lost and can never have, and one's
The basilisk you saw. This last stands guard
And I obey it. Lady, you came to Scotland
A fixed and subtle enemy, more dangerous
To me than you've ever known. This could not be borne,

And I set myself to cull you out and down,
And down you are.

Mary

When was I your enemy?

Elizabeth

Your life was a threat to mine, your throne to my throne,
Your policy a threat.

Mary

How? Why?

Elizabeth

It was you
Or I. Do you know that? The one of us must win
And I must always win. Suppose one lad
With a knife in his hand, a Romish lad who planted
That knife between my shoulders—my kingdom was yours.
It was too easy. You might not have wished it.
But you'd take it if it came.

Mary

And you'd take my life
And love to avoid this threat?

Elizabeth

Nay, keep your life.
And your love, too. The lords have brought a parchment
For you to sign. Sign it and live.

Mary

If I sign it
Do I live where I please? Go free?

Elizabeth

Nay, I would you might,
But you'd go to Bothwell, and between you two
You might be too much for Moray. You'll live with me
In London. There are other loves, my dear.
You'll find amusement there in the court. I assure you
It's better than a cell.

Mary

And if I will not sign
This abdiction?

Elizabeth

You've tasted prison. Try
A diet of it.

Mary

And so I will.

Elizabeth

I can wait.

Mary

And I can wait. I can better wait than you.
Bothwell will fight free again. Kirkaldy
Will fight beside him, and others will spring up
From these dragon's teeth you've sown. Each week that
    passes
I'll be stronger, and Moray weaker.

Elizabeth

And do you fancy
They'll rescue you from an English prison? Why,
Let them try it.

Mary

Even that they may do. I wait for Bothwell—
And wait for him here.

Elizabeth

Where you will wait, bear in mind,
Is for me to say. Give up Bothwell, give up your throne
If you'd have a life worth living.

Mary

I will not.

Elizabeth

I can wait.

Mary

And will not because you play to lose. This trespass
Against God's right will be known. The nations will know
    it,
Mine and yours. They will see you as I see you
And pull you down.

Elizabeth

Child, child, I've studied this gambit

Before I play it. I will send each year
This paper to you. Not signing, you will step
From one cell to another, step lower always,
Till you reach the last, forgotten, forgotten of men,
Forgotten among causes, a wraith that cries
To fallen gods in another generation
That's lost your name. Wait then for Bothwell's rescue,
It will never come.

Mary

I may never see him?

Elizabeth

Never.
It would not be wise.

Mary

And suppose indeed you won
Within our life-time, still looking down from the heavens
And up from men around us, God's spies that watch
The fall of great and little, they will find you out—
I will wait for that, wait longer than a life,
Till men and the times unscroll you, study the tricks
You play, and laugh, as I shall laugh, being known
Your better, haunted by your demon, driven
To death or exile by you, unjustly. Why,
When all's done, it's my name I care for, my name and heart,
To keep them clean. Win now, take your triumph now,
For I'll win men's hearts in the end—though the sifting
    takes
This hundred years—or a thousand.

Elizabeth

Child, child, are you gulled
By what men write in histories, this or that,
And never true? I am careful of my name
As you are, for this day and longer. It's not what happens
That matters, no, not even what happens that's true,
But what men believe to have happened. They will believe
The worst of you, the best of me, and that
Will be true of you and me. I have seen to this.

What will be said about us in after-years
By men to come, I control that, being who I am.
It will be said of me that I governed well,
And wisely, but of you, cousin, that your life,
Shot through will ill-loves, battened on leachery, made you
An ensign of evil, that men tore down and trampled.
Shall I call for the lord's parchment?

Mary

This will be said—?
But who will say it? It's a lie—will be known as a lie!

Elizabeth

You lived with Bothwell before Darnley died,
You and Bothwell murdered Darnley.

Mary

And that's a lie!

Elizabeth

Your letters, my dear. Your letters to Bothwell prove it.
We have those letters.

Mary

Then they're forged and false!
For I never wrote them!

Elizabeth

It may be they were forged.
But will that matter, Mary, if they're believed?
All history is forged.

Mary

You would do this?

Elizabeth

It is already done.

Mary

And still I win.
A demon has no children, and you have none,
Will have none, can have none, perhaps. This crooked track
You've drawn me on, cover it, let it not be believed
That a woman was a fiend. Yes, cover it deep,
And heap my infamy over it, lest men peer
And catch sight of you as you were and are. In myself

I know you to be an eater of dust. Leave me here
And set me lower this year by year, as you promise,
Till the last is an oubliette, and my name inscribed
On the four winds. Still, STILL I win! I have been
A woman, and I have loved as a woman loves,
Lost as a woman loses. I have borne a son,
And he will rule Scotland—and England. You have noheir!
A devil has no children.

Elizabeth

By God, you shall suffer
For this, but slowly.

Mary

And that I can do. A woman
Can do that. Come, turn the key. I have a hell
For you in mind, where you will burn and feel it,
Live where you like, and softly.

Elizabeth

Once more I ask you,
And patiently. Give up your throne.

Mary

No, devil,
My pride is stronger than yours, and my heart beats blood
Such as yours has never known. And in this dungeon,
I win here, alone.

Elizabeth

(*Turning.*)
Goodnight, then.

Mary

Aye, goodnight.
(*Elizabeth goes to the door, which opens before her. She goes
    out slowly. As the door begins to close upon her Mary
    calls.*)
Beaton!

Elizabeth

(*Turning.*)
You will not see your maids again,
I think. It's said they bring you news from the north.

Mary

I thank you for all kindness.

(*Elizabeth goes out. Mary stands for a moment in thought, then walks to the wall and lays her hand against the stone, pushing outward. The stone is cold, and she shudders. Going to the window she sits again in her old place and looks out into the darkness.*)

Curtain

ELIZABETH, QUEEN OF ENGLAND
by
Paolo Giacometti

Act I

Note: Sir Francis Bacon solicits Elizabeth to witness the representation of Shakespeare's Henry VIII. She declines at first, but on hearing the flattering words respecting herself at the close of the play, orders its representation. She then attempts to dictate two letters at the same time.

Scene VI

A hall in the Queen's Palace (London).

Present: *Elizabeth, Sir George Jackson, Lord Burleigh, Davison, Sir Francis Bacon,* and courtiers.

Jackson. The courier from Brussels has brought a despatch for the Queen's most sacred Majesty.

Elizabeth. (*Joyously.*) It must be from our good Earl of Leicester.

Davison. Does your Majesty command that I—

Elizabeth. (*Reddening, and seizing the letter.*) Know, my new secretary, that I open all letters addressed to *me.* (*Opens it, and after reading a few lines, thumps the table, and exclaims.*) Death to the traitors!

Burleigh. What means this!

Elizabeth. 'Tis he!—'tis Leicester who writes! Listen: (*Reads.*) "We were received in Holland with the most undeniable demonstrations of enthusiasm. The inhabitants erected triumphal arches and gave splendid fetes in our honour." (*Aside.*) And for *him!* "Yesterday, a deputation consisting of the Counts Egmont, Horn, and Flessing, offered me, in the name of the United States, the crown of Belgium; and we now ask your Majesty whether we may

515

accept it." He has stolen our style from us. (*Tears the letter.*) King! Leicester *King!*

Davison. And have your Majesty's allies dared—

Elizabeth. My allies thought they were doing me an honour in honouring my vassal. He, the younger son of a fallen family, thinks now that he can share with me my bed and throne! (*Looking at the Earl.*) He, my subject—one of the many nobles whom I permit to kiss the hem of my robe—and yet I have not stricken down this angel of darkness! But strike him down I will!

Burleigh. 'Tis the second time to-day that your Majesty has been in a passion.

Elizabeth. Yes! and my doctor Lopez only allows me this privilege once in every twenty-four hours. 'Tis well. Retire! Let Davison remain.

Bacon. I had something to impart to your Majesty!

Burleigh. Some other time, nephew—

Elizabeth. No! We will listen to him, whilst Davison is inditing our answer to this King with a wooden crown!

Davison. How shall I couch the answer?

Elizabeth. Need I say!

Davison. (*Placing himself at the table.*) The duties of secretary are more difficult than I had imagined.

Elizabeth. Speak, Sir Francis.

Bacon. (*Kneeling.*) 'Tis a favour that I have to beg of your Majesty, in the name of England!

Elizabeth. We love England well, what would she?

Bacon. That Shakespeare's last masterpiece, "Henry VIII" should be performed!

Elizabeth. But who is this mad successor of Melpomene, who in his plays out-herods Herod, and now actually presumes to introduce our father and mother on the stage?

Bacon. Your Majesty has read the play?

Elizabeth. The first three acts only, and I found *them* quite sufficient!

Bacon. (*Producing a manuscript.*) Permit me then to read you the last scene.

Elizabeth. I have other things to think of now. Davison, does that letter require so long—

Davison. I crave pardon (*aside.*) The letter is no such easy matter.

Bacon. On my honour, I entreat your Majesty to hear the *end* of the play! (*Kneels once more.*)

Elizabeth. (*Angrily.*) Read on then!

Bacon. (*Still on his knees.*) The action of Henry the Eighth terminates with your Majesty's birth and baptism.

Elizabeth. We, too, then are dragged into this play!

Burleigh. 'Tis a marvellous piece of audacity.

Bacon. The Duchess of Norfolk presents to the king the new-born infant resplendent with gold and gems, whilst the reverend Cranmer pronounces the following words:— (*Reading.*)

"Let me speak, sir, for Heaven now bids me
"This royal infant, though in her cradle,
"Yet now promises upon this land
"A thousand, thousand blessings, which time
"Shall bring to ripeness. She shall be
"A pattern to all princes living with her,
"And all that shall succeed.
"* * * all princely graces
"That mould up such a mighty piece as this is,
"With all the virtues that attend the good,
"Still shall be doubled on her: truth shall bless her:
"Her foes shake like a field of beaten corn,
"And hang their heads with sorrow.

Elizabeth. (*Smiling complacently.*) Rise!

Bacon. I thank your majesty. (*Continuing with increasing animation.*)

"Wherever the bright sun of Heaven shall shine,
"Her honor and the greatness of her name
"Shall be, and make new nations.
"She shall be, to the happiness of England,
"An aged princess: many days shall see her.
"* * * But she must die—

"She must, the saints must have her; yet a virgin.

"A most unspotted lily shall she pass

"To the ground, and all the world shall mourn her!"

Elizabeth. Enough, enough! and has Popham read the last scene!

Bacon. Most surely.

(*Elizabeth takes the manuscript and writes something thereon—she then hands it to Bacon.*)

Bacon. (*Reading.*) "Within fifteen days we will witness the representation of 'Henry the Eighth' in our Court Theatre at Windsor.

(Signed) Elizabeth."

Elizabeth. (*To Davison.*) Is the letter finished?

Davison. Almost, your Majesty! (*Aside, wiping his brow.*)—How very warm I feel!

Bacon. Within fifteen days? That will be scarcely feasible, for William Shakespeare, in his capacity of poet, is now in prison for debt!

Elizabeth. This must be remedied immediately; place yourself there and write. (*Pointing to the table, Bacon obeys.*)

Davison. (*Rises and presents the paper on which he was writing to Elizabeth.*) If your Majesty will deign to glance— (*Elizabeth hastily looks over the paper, and shakes her head.*) All's well, 'twould seem!

Elizabeth. (*Tearing up the paper.*) Nothing could be worse! I will dictate it to you!

Davison. 'Twill be better.

Elizabeth. (*Dictating to Bacon.*) "To Chief Justice Popham"—(*turning to Davison*). Well—are you ready?

Davison. I was waiting until—

Elizabeth. Waiting—nonsense! Cesar was wont to dictate five letters at a time—surely I can dictate *two!* Write now—"Most arrogant Earl, crowns are not made for heads like yours"—(*Turning to Bacon.*) "Dear Popham—I have permitted the performance of 'Henry the Eighth,'" (*To Davison.*)—"far less that of Belgium which has already been refused by your Sovereign!" (*In the interim she speaks aside to Burleigh and Bacon.*) "But as Shakespeare is now in prison for debt"—(*to Davison*) "Resign forthwith the command of the troops in favour of Sir Walter Raleigh"—(*To Bacon.*) "for debt—you will therefore have the honour to pay those debts for him, in virtue of the order which Sir Francis Bacon will present to you." (*To Davison.*) "Otherwise we shall despatch a regiment of cavalry to arrest you." (*To Bacon.*) "I hope that another time you will put on your spectacles, in order to better distinguish white from black." (*To Davison.*) "And Chief Justice Popham, to whom at this moment we are inditing a most gracious epistle, will place on your head a crown of thorns. Yours, according to your deserts—Elizabeth. (*Signing, then to Bacon.*) "Your most clement sovereign—Elizabeth. (*Signing.*)

Bacon. (*After folding the letter, approaches the Queen, kneels, and says.*) In William Shakespeare's name—

Elizabeth. Rise—you can thank Popham. (*To Davison.*) Prepare the envelope.

Burleigh. (*Aside to Bacon.*) A famous courtier is Shakespeare—

Bacon. Say rather an expert doctor, for he has well known how to gild the pill!

Exit.

Elizabeth. Despatch the letter by means of a special courier—but be economical as regards expense—and afterwards betake yourself to the House of Commons.

Davison bows and exit.

*   *   *

From SCENE VII

Present: *Earl of Essex, Elizabeth,* and *Burleigh.*

Earl. (*Turning to Elizabeth, who appears absorbed in deep thought.*) Of what is your Majesty thinking?

Burleigh. What is the subject of this reverie?

Elizabeth. I was thinking that Mary Stuart, though steeped in misery, and a poor prisoner at Fotheringay, has yet a son, young, handsome, and valiant—whilst I, Queen of

England and Ireland, and perchance the terror of Europe—
like to a vine planted on the shore, and rendered barren by
the sea winds—do wither on the throne! And when I shall
have had Mary put to death, this warlike son will collect
his mother's blood in his helmet, and hasten hither to deluge
therewith my crowned head! But who, with loving hand,
will close my eyes? Who will e'en shed a tear o'er my marble
tomb? No one! No one!

Burleigh. Why, then, does not your Majesty comply
with the wish of the nation, so many times expressed?

Elizabeth. What? *marry?* The Lords and Commons
will not understand that to marry a foreign prince would be
to place the kingdom under tutelage, and that France, or
Spain, or Germany, might some day put forth claims to the
throne of England. 'Tis *thus* they thank me for my sacrifice.

Earl. Sacrifice!

Elizabeth. Yes! and a cruel one. When in the summer
I betake me to my royal parks, or the country seats of my
nobles, in order that I may listen to the petitions of the poor
peasantry,—and when I behold the joyous reapers, who,
though bare footed and ragged, are blessed with blooming
happy children,—I suffer bitterly. I feel that I could rush
between the mothers and children, and with insensate
cruelty—

*　　*　　*

Act IV

Note: Elizabeth is greatly agitated that the Earl of Essex
will not seek pardon by returning to her a ring that she had
given to him as a pledge for his safety.

Scene IV

Hudson enters.

Elizabeth. Has any message been sent me from the
Tower?

Hudson. None, your Majesty!

Elizabeth. To die thus, with his life depending on his

own option! Lady Anna will not go to the Tower. No!
Throughout all the years I have reigned, this is the first time
I have *wished* to be disobeyed—and they'll obey me! She
must be blind, senseless; could she not understand, that although my *lips* forbade her, my *heart* implored her to hurry
to the Tower. Ah! Essex, with his brow bent o'er his bonds,
deserves less compassion than I; even at the hour of his
death will he defy me!—defy me! Ay! he would have placed
the Stuarts on my throne—James, the son of that Mary
whose spectre eternally pursues me, and causes me to start
up from my bed! Still no message from the Tower! Be it
so then; he will not accept his *life* from me.—Let then his
death be ordained by my hand! (*Signs the sentence.*)

* * *

Scene V

Davison enters.

Davison. Your Majesty—the Lord Chancellor has re-
quested me to fetch the Earl's sentence!

Elizabeth. (*Giving him the document with a trembling hand.*)
'Tis here!

Davison. (*Watching her.*) What must I do with this?

Elizabeth. Affix thereunto the royal seal.

Davison. And afterwards—

Elizabeth. Why these questions?—

Davison. In order that—happen what may—I may not
have another ten thousand pounds to pay!

Elizabeth. Dar'st thou jest with a man's life in thy hands?
Go! (*Davison is about to withdraw. Elizabeth intently watches
his retreating figure, and when he has almost reached the door,
exclaims*), Ah!

Davison. Did your Majesty recall me?

Elizabeth. I! No, no—away! Steep the royal seal in
blood, and let the execution take place this very instant!
(*Exit Davison.*) Ah! 'tis *he* who has willed it thus—'tis *he*
who has willed it! (*Falls into a chair.*)

* * *

Scene VII

Lady Sarah enters.

Sarah. (*Throwing herself in the greatest agitation at Elizabeth's feet.*) Mercy! mercy!

Elizabeth. You!—are you come to implore mercy for your lover?

Sarah. O! cause the execution to be delayed—the Earl has confined to me the ring!

Elizabeth. Ah! where is it—where?

Sarah. They have taken it from me.

Elizabeth. 'Tis false!

Sarah. No! I call heaven to witness!

Elizabeth. Who can have robbed thee of it?

Sarah. The Duke, my husband! My husband was at the Tower, I know not why—when the earl entrusted the ring to me—he furiously drew, or rather dragged me to one of the Tower-gates, where a carriage awaited us—no sooner had we reached the Palace, than he brutally tore from me (unable as I was to offer a protracted resistance) the gem which I had received from Essex, and caused me to be confined in an apartment. The window thereof not being very high, I dropped from it to the ground, and although much shaken by the fall, I have had strength to drag myself here! (*Report of a cannon heard.*) Ah!

Elizabeth. Heavens! 'tis the signal.

Anna. Who knows? Perchance it may be—the Earl.

*   *   *

Scene IX

Lord Burleigh and Lord Bacon enter.

Burleigh. He is no more!

Elizabeth. Dead!

Sarah. (*Supporting herself by Anna.*) Ah!

Elizabeth. Dead! Robert is no more! The only man I ever really loved—and I have killed him! No one has said a single word to appease my wrath—they all hated him, and yet not one of them was worthy to kiss the dust raised by his charger's hoof on a day of battle! (*To Bacon.*) And you, vile, miserable wretch, you, that owe all the advantages you enjoy to his kindness and generosity. It was your duty to have opposed my sovereign will—yes my will, to have saved his life. You should have reminded me of Ireland subjugated by him, of the conquest of Cadiz, and its conflagration. You should have torn off his breastplate and counted his wounds one by one, and offered them as ransoms, each a trophy of his glorious deeds, and a demand upon my clemency. You should have disputed my authority—anything— rather than sacrifice a life so valuable to the welfare of England. But no; you chose rather to guide the hand that signed that fatal death-warrant—and—mine sealed it. . . . May the curse of Cain be yours! Begone! Out of my sight! Begone! Let all withdraw—I do command it. (*All retire.*) Here let me remain, surrounded by a lake of blood—alone, with my remorse and God! (*Falls on her knees in great agitation.*)

"VICTORIA REGINA"
by
Laurence Housman

WOMAN PROPOSES
15th October, 1839

SCENE: In a sitting-room at Windsor Castle Prince Albert of Saxe-Coburg Gotha and the young Queen are standing near the window.

Victoria. Won't you sit down, Albert? (*He takes a distant seat.*) Why don't you sit nearer? Talking then is so much easier. (*He comes towards her.*)

Albert. You are very kind, Cousin, ever since we came: to both of us, I mean.

Victoria. I am very fond of—Ernest.

Albert. Yes, so am I. (*He sits down.*)

Victoria. You've always been together, haven't you?

Albert. We've never been apart yet.

Victoria. How very nice that has been—for both. (*A pause.*) Would it be a great trial to you, if you had to live away from him?

Albert. Of course, the parting would be a trial. But one would get used to it—as to other things—if it had to be.

Victoria. My life has been so different from yours. I have never had anyone always with me like that—one of my own age. All my life I have been so much alone, except, of course, with Mamma. I don't know what it can be like—to have a brother.

Albert. One gets very fond of a brother.

Victoria. Yes; but one can get fonder of someone else—can one not?

Albert. It happens, sometimes. (*A pause.*)

Victoria. Albert! What are you doing?

Albert. I was listening to Ernest, practising. I can just hear him; it is Beethoven.

Victoria. Don't listen to Ernest! You must listen to me!

Albert. I beg your pardon, Cousin; I was listening. Please don't think I am inattentive.

Victoria. (*After a long pause.*) Albert . . . I have something to say to you.

Albert. Yes . . . what is it, Cousin?

Victoria. In my position, it is I who have to say it—unfortunately. Ordinarily it is not what a woman would wish to say herself. She would rather—*he* said it.

Albert. Is there anything you wish me to say—that I can say?

Victoria. (*Tremulously.*) To hear you say you *can* love me, is all I can hope—yet. If you could say that you already *do* love me, that would be—almost like Heaven.

Albert. I do . . . love you, Cousin.

Victoria. Enough to marry me?

Albert. More than enough to marry you. For people in our position often marry without any love at all.

Victoria. I couldn't do that—Albert.

Albert. Nor could I—Victoria.

Victoria. Then you will marry me?

Albert. If it is still your wish—when you know me—I will, very gratefully and humbly, accept this dear hand that you offer me.

Victoria. When I know you?

Albert. Yes; for I, too, have something to say. A few minutes ago, I did not know about myself what I know now. Even now I have no proof. Yet something tells me that it is true.

Victoria. Don't tell me—if it is anything I shouldn't wish to know, Albert.

Albert. But I must. My brother Ernest and I had the same mother; but not the same father.

Victoria. I don't understand.

Albert. I am sorry you should have to . . . My Mother and my Father (*Ernest's Father*) separated—after I was born. They did not love each other. . . . My Mother must have loved someone else.

Victoria. While she was married? (*His head makes silent assent.*) Before you were born—or after?

Albert. Before.

Victoria. Who?

Albert. I don't know. So neither do I know who I am. Perhaps I shall never know. Yet there must still be someone who could tell me—more than I have been able to tell you. . . . Shall I—? Do you wish me to go now? I had to tell you this.

Victoria. Yes . . . of course.

Albert. Then now—you wish me to go?

Victoria. No. . . . No . . . I wish you to stay. It makes no difference to *me*. . . . And besides, who knows?

Albert. Somebody must know. Ernest knows.

Victoria. Ernest?

Albert. It was he who told me. And his Father knows.

Victoria. But his Father sent you here—let you come.

Albert. Yes, but he hoped it would be Ernest.

Victoria. How very silly of him!

Albert. Why?

Victoria. How could it possibly be Ernest, after I had seen you? . . . Oh, Albert! Albert! What does it matter? It is not your Father that I shall marry: it is you!

(*And as she speaks they are in each other's arms. Her passionate abandonment awakens response, though of a more restrained nature.*)

Albert. My very dear Cousin! My sweet Wife that is to be.

Victoria. Aren't you going to kiss me?

Albert. If I may. (*The kiss is given.*)

Victoria. Again, please! . . . Again!

Albert. I pray God you do not ever have to repent of this.

Victoria. Repent? How could I repent! It is not in my nature, Albert. Besides, there isn't going to be time. We must be married quite soon. Everybody expects it.

Albert. Expects it? They don't know.

Victoria. Expects me to marry, I mean. I had to choose *somebody*. But I wasn't going to choose *any*body.

Albert. Not even Ernest?

Victoria. Oh, I liked Ernest very much, from the first. . . . I do still.

Albert. (*With a touch of humour.*) Is that why you sent him to practice? . . . He *knew*.

Victoria. That this was going to happen?

Albert. No; he did not know *that*.

Victoria. What, then?

Albert. That you were going to ask me.

Victoria. Well, then, what else could he suppose *would* happen?

Albert. He expected me to say no.

Victoria. (*Almost affronted.*) But you couldn't have said 'No' to a Queen—could you, Albert?

Albert. No, dear; one couldn't say 'no' to a Queen.

Victoria. But did you want to?

Albert. No, Dearest One. All it means is that Ernest will be disappointed.

Victoria. Oh, I see. Poor Ernest! . . . Well, we must both try to be very nice and kind to him. . . . And now it is quite time that we went for our ride.

Albert. Isn't Ernest to come, too?

Victoria. Why, yes, of course!

Albert. Then won't you send and say he may stop practicing? This hasn't taken an hour, you know.

(*Enter Ernest.*)

Victoria. Nor has he, either; for here he is. Are you ready to come riding, Ernest?

Ernest. Quite, if you are, Cousin.

Victoria. Oh, yes, we are quite ready *now*. Everything has been settled. Tell him, Albert.

Albert. Ernest. . . . You told me to remember . . . I *forgot.*

(Ernest has only to look at them, and the awful situation is explained. It will also have to be explained elsewhere. For when Victoria says that a thing is settled, it is settled—for good.)

THE BARRETTS OF WIMPOLE STREET

by
Rudolf Besier

From Act III

Robert Browning enters. He is a dark, handsome man in the middle thirties, faultlessly, perhaps even a trifle foppishly, dressed. Over his shoulder he wears a cape fastened with a chain at the throat. He carries his high hat, lemon-coloured gloves, and clouded cane. Browning's manner is sincere and ardent; his speech rapid, voluble, and emphasised by free gestures.

(*Henrietta goes out.*)

Browning. (*Pausing for a moment a few steps beyond the threshold.*) Miss Barrett?

Elizabeth. (*Stretching out her hand.*) How-do-you-do, Mr. Browning?

Browning. (*Quickly lays aside his hat, cane and gloves, and crossing to the sofa, takes her hand in both of his.*) Dear Miss Barrett—at last! (*Raises her hand to his lips.*) At last!

Elizabeth. (*Still all nerves, and rather overcome by the ardour and unconventionality of his manner.*) I—I've had to put off the pleasure of meeting you much longer than I wished. . . .

Browning. (*Still holding her hand.*) Would you ever have received me if I hadn't been so tiresomely insistent?

Elizabeth. As you know from my letters, I've not been at all well during the winter, and I—(*Realising that her hand is still in his, she gently withdraws it.*) But won't you take off your cape?

Browning. Thank you. (*Unfastens his cape and lays it aside.*)

Elizabeth. I—I hope you don't find the room very close, Mr. Browning?

Browning. No, no . . .

Elizabeth. My doctor obliges me to live in what I am afraid must be to you a—a hot-house temperature . . .

Browning. (*Who has thrown a quick glance round the room.*) Wonderful! You may think, Miss Barrett, that this is the first time I've been here. You're quite wrong, you know!

Elizabeth. But—

Browning. Quite wrong. I have seen this room more times than I can remember. It's as familiar to me as my own little study at home! Before I came in, I knew just how your books were arranged, just how that tendril of ivy slanted across the window panes—and those busts of Homer and Chaucer are quite old friends, and have looked down on me often before!

Elizabeth. (*Smilingly protesting.*) No, really—!

Browning. But I could never make out who the other fellows were on the top of the wardrobe, and—

Elizabeth. (*Laughing, and now quite at her ease.*) Oh, come, Mr. Browning! I know that dear Mr. Kenyon is never tired of talking about his friends; but I can't believe that he described my poor little room to you in detail!

Browning. (*Seating himself beside her.*) I dragged all the details I possibly could out of him—and my imagination supplied the rest. Directly after I had read your brave and lovely verses I was greedy for anything and everything I could get about you.

Elizabeth. (*Smilingly.*) You frighten me, Mr. Browning!

Browning. Why?

Elizabeth. Well, you know how Mr. Kenyon's enthusiasms run away with his tongue? He and I are the dearest of friends. What he has told you about poor me I quite blush to imagine!

Browning. You mean, Miss Barrett, about you—you *yourself?*

Elizabeth. I feel it would be hopeless for me to try to live up to his description.

Browning. He never told me anything about you—personally—which had the slightest interest for me.

Elizabeth. (*Puzzled.*) Oh!

Browning. Everything he could give me about your surroundings and the circumstances of your life I snatched at with avidity. But all he said about *you* was quite beside the point, because I knew it already—and better than Mr. Kenyon, old friend of yours though he is!

Elizabeth. But—Oh, Mr. Browning, do my poor writings give me so hopelessly away?

Browning. Hopelessly—utterly—entirely—to *me*! . . . I can't speak for the rest of the world.

Elizabeth. (*Smilingly.*) You frighten me again!

Browning. No?

Elizabeth. But you do! For I'm afraid it would be quite useless my ever trying to play-act with you!

Browning. Quite useless!

Elizabeth. I shall always have to be—just myself?

Browning. Always.

Elizabeth. Oh . . . (*quickly*). And you too, Mr. Browning?

Browning. Always—just myself! (*He stretches out his hand; she takes it with a smile. Then, with a sudden laugh.*) But really, you know, Miss Barrett, I sha'n't be able to take much credit for that! Being myself comes to me as easily as breathing. It's play-acting I can't manage—and the hot water I've got into in consequence. . . If life's to run smoothly we should all be mummers. Well, I can't mum!

Elizabeth. Yes, I can well believe that now I know you. But isn't it extraordinary? When you are *writing* you never do anything else but—play-act.

Browning. I know—

Elizabeth. You have never been yourself in any one of your poems. It's always somebody else speaking through you.

Browning. Yes. And shall I tell you why? I am a very modest man. (*Quickly, after a slight pause.*) I am really!

Elizabeth. (*With suppressed amusement.*) I didn't question it, Mr. Browning.

Browning. So modest, I fully realise that if I wrote about myself—my hopes and fears, hates and loves, and the rest of it—my poems would be intolerably dull.

Elizabeth. (*Laughing vivaciously.*) Well—since we are pledged to nothing but the truth, I won't contradict that—until I know you better!

Browning. (*With a laugh.*) Bravo!

Elizabeth. (*Ardently.*) Oh, but those poems, with their glad and great-hearted acceptance of life—you can't imagine what they mean to me! Here am I shut in by four walls, the view of Wimpole Street my only glimpse of the world. And they troop into the room and round my sofa, those wonderful people of yours out of every age and country, and all so tingling with life! life! life! No, you'll never begin to realise how much I owe you!

Browning. (*With emotion.*) You—you really mean that?

Elizabeth. Why, why Mr. Browning—

Browning. But of course you do, or you wouldn't say it! And you'll believe me when I tell you that what you have said makes up to me a thousand times over for all the cold-shouldering I've had from the public?

Elizabeth. (*Fiercely.*) Oh, it infuriates me! Why can we never know an eagle for an eagle until it has spread its wings and flown away from us for good? Sometimes—I detest the British public!

Browning. (*Lightly.*) Oh, no, no! Dear old British public! At least it gives us generously the jolly pastime of abusing it! And mind you, Miss Barrett, I've an uneasy feeling that my style is largely to blame for my unpopularity.

Elizabeth. (*A little too eagerly.*) Oh, surely not!

Browning. Didn't we agree never to play-act with each other?

Elizabeth. (*With a laugh.*) *Touché!* Well, perhaps, there *are* passages in your work a little invol—I mean a little too—too profound for the general reader.

Browning. Oh, no! it's not what I say, but how I say it.

Elizabeth. Oh, but—

Browning. And yet to me it's all simple and easy as the rule of three! And to you?

Elizabeth. Well . . . not *quite* always. Sometimes there *are* passages. . . . (*She picks up a book.*) I have marked one or two in your "Sordello" which rather puzzle me. Here, for instance. . . . (*She opens the book and hands it to him.*)

Browning. (*Taking the book.*) Oh, "Sordello!" Somebody once called it "a horror of great darkness!" I've done my best to forget it. However—(*He reads the passage to himself, smiling. The smile fades; he passes his hand over his brow and reads it again. She watches him covertly smiling. He mutters.*) Extraordinary. . . . But—but a passage torn from its context. . . . (*He rises and goes to the window, as though to get more light on the subject, and reads the passage a third time. Elizabeth has some difficulty in suppressing her amusement. He turns to her with an expression of humorous chagrin.*)

Elizabeth. Well? . . .

Browning. Well, Miss Barrett—when that passage was written only God and Robert Browning understood it. Now only God understands it. (*She laughs, and he joins in.*) What do you say—shall we lighten this great darkness by pitching it on the fire?

Elizabeth. (*Indignantly.*) No, indeed! We shall do nothing of the kind! Please give me back the book. (*He does so.*) Such passages are only spots on the sun. I love "Sordello."

Browning. (*Eagerly.*) You would! And shall I tell you why? Because it's a *colossal failure.*

Elizabeth. If by a failure you mean an attempt—yes! you're right! That's just why "Sordello" appeals to my very heart. I too am always making colossal attempts—and always failing.

Browning. Isn't one such failure worth a hundred small successes?

Elizabeth. Oh, a thousand and more!

Browning. (*Eagerly.*) You think so too? But, of course, I knew that! . . . Miss Barrett, you smiled when I told you that Kenyon had no need to describe you· because I knew you through and through already. And what you have just said about success and failure proves to me finally how right I was. All Kenyon did was to fill in the background. I—I had painted the portrait—with the true soul of you, ardent and lovely, looking out of it.

Elizabeth. Ardent and lovely! And you think you know me! (*With a bitter smile.*) Oh, Mr. Browning—too often impatient and rebellious. . . .

Browning. Well, what of it? I've no love for perfect patience under affliction. My portrait is the portrait of a woman, not a saint. Who has more right to be impatient and rebellious than you?

Elizabeth. Did Mr. Kenyon paint my background with a very gloomy brush?

Browning. Old Rembrandt would have envied him!

Elizabeth. (*Smilingly.*) Poor dear Mr. Kenyon! He is more Royalist than the Queen herself! I assure you my afflictions worry him a great deal more than they worry me. . . . I suppose he told you that I am a—a dying woman?

Browning. We are all of us—dying.

Elizabeth. And that our family life was one of unrelieved gloom?

Browning. Yes, he hinted at something of the sort.

Elizabeth. He really shouldn't say such things! Frankly now, Mr. Browning, do you find me such a very pitiable object?

Browning. I find you, as I expected to find you, full of courage and gaiety. . . . And yet, in spite of what you say, I'm not at all sure that Kenyon's colours were too sombre.

Elizabeth. But—

Browning. (*Eagerly interrupting.*) No, no, listen to me.

Those colours are not yet dry. They must be scraped off! The whole background must be repainted! . . . And if only you'll allow it—I must have a hand in that splendid work.

Elizabeth. But, Mr. Browning—

Browning. (*Carried away.*) No, listen! I'll dip my brush into the sunrise and the sunset and the rainbow! You say my verses have helped you—they're nothing. It's I—I who am going to help you now! We have come together at last—and I don't intend to let you go again.

Elizabeth. But—

Browning. No, listen. Give me your hands. (*Bends forward and takes them.*) I've more life than is good for one man—it seethes and races in me. Up to now I've spent a little of all that surplus energy in creating imaginary men and women. But there's still so much that I've no use for but to give! Mayn't I give it to you? Don't you feel new life tingling and prickling up your fingers and arms right into your heart and brain?

Elizabeth. (*Rather frightened and shaken.*) Oh, please . . . Mr. Browning, please let go my hands. . . . (*He opens his hands; but she still leaves hers lying on his palms for a moment. Then she withdraws them, and clasping her cheeks, looks at him with wide, disturbed eyes.*)

Browning. (*Softly.*) Well?

Elizabeth. (*A little shakily, with forced lightness.*) You —you are really rather an overwhelming person, and in sober truth, I'm—

Browning. No—don't tell me again that you are afraid of me! You're not. It's life you're afraid of—and that shouldn't be.

Elizabeth. Life?

Browning. Yes.

Elizabeth. Well, when life becomes a series of electric shocks!

Browning. (*Smiling.*) Was it as bad as all that?

Elizabeth. (*Smiling.*) Indeed, yes! Do you affect other people in the same way?

Browning. They've often told me so.

Elizabeth. (*Lightly.*) No wonder I hesitated about meeting you, much as I wanted to! Something of your disturbing vitality must have come to me from your letters and poems. . . . You'll laugh at me, Mr. Browning, but do you know we very nearly didn't meet to-day after all! When my maid told me you had arrived I was so panic-stricken that I all but sent down a message that I was too unwell to receive you. And it was a big effort to pull myself together, and behave like a sensible woman, when you came into the room!

Browning. I think I must have been quite as nervous as you at that moment.

Elizabeth. You, Mr. Browning!

Browning. Yes—and I'm anything but a nervous man as a rule. But that moment was the climax of my life—up to now. . . . Miss Barrett, do you remember the first letter I wrote to you?

Elizabeth. Yes, indeed! It was a wonderful letter.

Browning. You may have thought I dashed it off in a fit of whitehot enthusiasm over your poems. I didn't. I weighed every word of every sentence. And of one sentence in particular—this sentence: "I love your books with all my heart—and I love you too." You remember?

Elizabeth. (*Lightly.*) Yes—and I thought it charmingly impulsive of you!

Browning. (*Almost with irritation.*) But I tell you there was nothing impulsive about it. That sentence was as deeply felt and anxiously thought over as any sentence I've ever written.

Elizabeth. I hope I have many readers like you! It's wonderful to think I may have good friends all the world over whom I have never seen or heard of.

Browning. I am not speaking of friendship, but of love. (*Elizabeth is about to make a smiling rejoinder.*) No, it's quite useless your trying to put aside the word with a smile and a jest. I said love—and I mean love—

Elizabeth. But really, Mr. Browning, I must ask you—

Browning. (*Swiftly interrupting her.*) I'm neither mad nor morbidly impressionable—I'm as sane and level-headed as any man alive. Yet all these months, since first I read your poems, I've been haunted by you. And to-day you are the centre of my life.

Elizabeth. (*Very gravely.*) If I were to take you seriously, Mr. Browning, it would, of course, mean the quick finish of a friendship which promises to be very pleasant to both of us.

Browning. Why?

Elizabeth. You know very well that love—in the sense you, apparently, use the word—has no place, and can have no place, in my life.

Browning. Why?

Elizabeth. For many reasons—but let this suffice. As I told you before. I am a dying woman.

Browning. (*Passionately.*) I refuse to believe it! For if that were so, God would be callous, and I *know* that He's compassionate—and life would be dark and evil, and I *know* that it's good. You must never say such a thing again. I forbid you to.

Elizabeth. Forbid, Mr. Browning? . . .

Browning. Yes—forbid. Isn't it only fair that if you forbid me to speak of you as I feel, and I accept your orders, as I must, that I should be allowed a little forbidding as well?

Elizabeth. Yes, but—

Browning. (*Breaking in with sudden gaiety.*) Dear Miss Barrett, what a splendid beginning to our friendship! We have known each other a bare half hour, and yet we've talked intimately of art and life and death and love, and we've ordered each other about, and we've almost quarrelled! Could anything be happier and more promising? . . . With your permission, I'm going now. Mr. Kenyon impressed upon me to make my first visit as short as possible, as strangers tire you. Not that I'm a stranger!—still I can see that you are tired. . . . When may I call again?

Elizabeth. (*A little dazed.*) I don't quite know . . . I—

Browning. Will next Wednesday suit you?

Elizabeth. (*As before.*) Yes, I—I think so. But perhaps it would be better—

Browning. Next Wednesday then.

Elizabeth. But—

Browning. At half-past three again?

Elizabeth. Yes—but I—

Browning. (*Bowing over her hand.*) *Au revoir* then.

Elizabeth. Good-bye.

Browning. (*Gently masterful, retaining her hand.*) *Au revoir.*

Elizabeth. (*A little breathlessly, after a slight pause.*) *Au revoir.*

Browning. Thank you. (*He kisses her hand, turns and picks up his hat and cape, etc., and goes out.*)

The moment after the door has closed behind him Elizabeth sits up and clasps her face with both her hands. Then she slips off the sofa and unsteadily gets on her feet. With the help of the table and the chairs, she manages to cross the room to the window. Grasping the curtain to support herself, she stands looking down into the street after the departing Browning, her face as alive with excitement and joy as though she were a young girl. And the scene slowly closes.

5. PROBLEMS FOR ORAL INTERPRETATION

PROBLEMS FOR ORAL INTERPRETATION

1.   Swift as a spirit hastening to his task
    Of glory and of good, the sun sprang forth
    Rejoicing in his splendour, and the mask
    Of darkness fell from the awakened Earth—
              "The Triumph of Life"—Shelley.

2.   MUTABILITY

We are as clouds that veil the midnight moon;
  How restlessly they speed, and gleam, and quiver,
Streaking the darkness radiantly!—yet soon
  Night closes round, and they are lost for ever:

Or like forgotten lyres, whose dissonant strings
  Give various response to each varying blast,
To whose frail frame no second motion brings
  One mood or modulation like the last.

We rest—A dream has power to poison sleep;
  We rise—One wandering thought pollutes the day;
We feel, conceive or reason, laugh or weep,
  Embrace fond woe, or cast our cares away:

It is the same!—For, be it joy or sorrow,
  The path of its departure still is free:
Man's yesterday may ne'er be like his morrow;
  Naught may endure but Mutability.
                       Shelley.

3.   MUTABILITY

The flower that smiles today
    Tomorrow dies;
All that we wish to stay
    Tempts, and then flies.
What is this world's delight?
Lightning that mocks the night,
    Brief even as bright.

Virtue, how frail it is!
    Friendship how rare!
Love, how it sells poor bliss
    For proud despair!
But we, though soon they fall,
Survive their joy, and all
    Which ours we call.

Whilst skies are blue and bright,
    Whilst flowers are gay,
Whilst eyes that change ere night
    Make glad the day,
Whilst yet the calm hours creep,
Dream thou—and from thy sleep
    Then wake to weep.

                                        Shelley.

4. Mont Blanc yet gleams on high;—the power is there,
The still and solemn power of many sights
And many sounds, and much of life and death.
In the calm darkness of the moonless nights,
In the lone glare of day, the snows descend
Upon that Mountain; none beholds them there,
Nor when the flakes burn in the sinking sun,
Or the star-beams dart through them:—Winds contend
Silently there, and heap the snow, with breath
Rapid and strong, but silently! Its home

The voiceless lightning in these solitudes
Keeps innocently, and like vapour broods
Over the snow. The secret strength of things,
Which governs thought, and to the infinite dome
Of heaven is as a law, inhibits thee!
And what were thou, and earth, and stars, and sea,
If to the human mind's imaginings
Silence and solitude were vacancy?

"Mont Blanc"—Shelley.

5. All he had loved, and moulded into thought,
From shape, and hue, and odour, and sweet sound,
Lamented Adonais. Morning sought
Her eastern watch-tower, and her hair unbound,
Wet with the tears which should adorn the ground,
Dimmed the aerial eyes that kindle day:
Afar the melancholy thunder moaned,
Pale Ocean in unquiet slumber lay,
And the wild winds flew around, sobbing in their dismay.

* * *

6. The splendours of the firmament of time
May be eclipsed, but are extinguished not;
Like stars to their appointed height they climb,
And death is a low mist which cannot blot
The brightness it may veil. When lofty thought
Lifts a young heart above its mortal lair,
And love and life contend in it, for what
Shall be its earthly doom, the dead live there,
And move like winds of light on dark and stormy air.

* * *

7. The One remains, the many change and pass;
Heaven's light for ever shines, Earth's shadows fly;
Life, like a dome of many-colour'd glass,
Stains the white radiance of Eternity,
Until Death tramples it to fragments.—Die,
If thou would'st be with that which thou dost seek;

Follow where all is fled!—Rome's azure sky,
Flowers, ruins, statues, music, words, are weak,
The glory they transfuse with fitting truth to speak.
"Adonais"—Shelley.

8.　　　　The rainbow comes and goes,
　　　　　And lovely is the rose,
　　　　　The moon doth with delight
Look round her when the heavens are bare,
　　　　Waters on a starry night
　　　　Are beautiful and fair;
　　　　The sunshine is a glorious birth;
But yet I know, where'er I go.
That there hath passed away a glory from the earth.

* * *

9. Our birth is but a sleep and a forgetting;
The soul that rises with us, our life's star,
　　　　Hath had elsewhere its setting,
　　　　And cometh from afar;
　　　　Not in entire forgetfulness,
　　　　And not in utter nakedness,
But trailing clouds of glory do we come
　　　　From God, who is our home.
Heaven lies about us in our infancy;
Shades of the prison-house being too close
　　　　Upon the growing boy,
But he beholds the light, and whence it flows.
　　　　He sees it in his joy;
The youth, who daily farther from the east
　　　　Must travel, still is Nature's priest,
　　　　And by the vision splendid
　　　　Is on his way attended;
At length the man perceives it die away,
And fade into the light of common day.
　　　　"Ode: Intimations of Immortality"—
　　　　　　　　William Wordsworth.

10. O blithe new-comer! I have heard,
I hear thee and rejoice.
O Cuckoo! shall I call thee bird,
Or but a wandering voice?

   * * *

O blessed bird! the earth we pace
Again appears to be
An unsubstantial, faery place;
That is fit home for thee!
   "To the Cuckoo"—William Wordsworth.

11. The boast of heraldry, the pomp of power,
  And all that beauty, all that wealth e'er gave,
Awaits alike the inevitable hour.
  The paths of glory lead but to the grave.

   * * *

Full many a gem of purest ray serene,
  The dark unfathomed caves of ocean bear;
Full many a flower is born to blush unseen
  And waste its sweetness on the desert air.
    "Elegy"—Thomas Gray.

IF THIS GREAT WORLD OF JOY AND PAIN

12. If this great world of joy and pain
  Revolve in one sure track;
If freedom, set, will rise again,
  And virtue, flown, come back:
Woe to the purblind crew who fill
  The heart with each day's care;
Nor gain, from past or future, skill
  To bear, and to forbear!
    William Wordsworth.

13. All thoughts, all passions, all delights,
Whatever stirs this mortal frame,
All are but ministers of Love,
  And feed his sacred flame.
    "Love"—Wordsworth.

14.   O ye loud Waves! and O ye Forests high!
        And O ye Clouds that far above me soared!
     Thou rising Sun! thou blue rejoicing Sky!
        Yea, every thing that is and will be free!
        Bear witness for me, wheresoe'er ye be,
        With what deep worship I have still adored
        The spirit of divinest Liberty.
                              "France: An Ode"—Coleridge.

15.   Waken, lords and ladies gay,
           On the mountain dawns the day;
           All the jolly chase is here,
           With hawk, and horse, and hunting-spear!
           Hounds are in their couples yelling,
           Hawks are whistling, horns are knelling,
           Merrily, merrily, mingle they;
           "Waken, lords and ladies gay."
                              "Hunting Song"—Scott.

XCVI

16. Sky, mountains, river, winds, lake, lightnings! ye,
    With night, and clouds, and thunder, and a soul
    To make these felt and feeling, well may be
    Things that have made me watchful; the far roll
    Of your departing voices, is the knoll
    Of what in me is sleepless,—if I rest.
    But where of ye, O tempests, is the goal?
    Are ye like those within the human breast;
    Or do ye find at length, like eagles, some high nest?
                              "Childe Harold"—Lord Byron

XIII

17.   It might be months, or years, or days—
            I kept no count, I took no note,
        I had no hope my eyes to raise,
            And clear them of their dreary mote—
        At last men came to set me free;

I asked not why, and recked not where:
It was at length the same to me,
Fettered or fetterless to be,
    I learned to love despair.
And thus when they appeared at last,
And all my bonds aside were cast,
These heavy walls to me had grown
A hermitage—and all my own!
And half I felt as they were come
To tear me from a second home.

With spiders I had friendship made,
And watched them in their sullen trade,
Had seen the mice by moonlight play,
And why should I feel less than they?
We were all inmates of one place,
And I, the monarch of each race,
Had power to kill—yet, strange to tell!
In quiet we had learned to dwell.
My very chains and I grew friends,
So much a long communion tends
To make us what we are:—even I
Regained my freedom with a sigh.
            "The Prisoner of Chillon"—Lord Byron.

CXXVIII

18. Arches on arches!—as it were that Rome,
    Collecting the chief trophies of her line,
    Would build up all her triumphs in one dome,
    Her Coliseum stands; the moonbeams shine
    As 'twere its natural torches, for divine
    Should be the light which streams here, to illume
    This long-explored but still exhaustless mine
    Of contemplation; and the azure gloom
    Of an Italian night, where the deep skies assume

CXXIX

19. Hues which have words and speak to ye of heaven,
Floats o'er this vast and wondrous monument,
And shadows forth its glory. . . .

CXLIV

20. But when the rising moon begins to climb
Its topmost arch, and gently pauses there;
When the stars twinkle through the loops of time,
And the low night-breeze waves along the air
The garland forest, which the gray walls wear
Like laurels on the bald first Caesar's head;
When the light shines serene but doth not glare,
Then in this magic circle raise the dead:
Heroes have trod this spot—'tis on their dust ye tread.
"Childe Harold"—Lord Byron.

21.   Man, one harmonious soul of many a soul,
        Whose nature is its own divine control,
Where all things flow to all, as rivers to the sea;
        Familiar acts are beautiful through love;
        Labor, the pain, and grief, in life's green grove
Sport like tame beasts, none knew how gentle they could
        be!
"Prometheus Unbound"—Shelley.
From Act Fourth.

22.   No, the bugle sounds no more,
            And the twanging bow no more;
            Silent is the ivory shrill
            Past the heath and up the hill;
            There is no mid-forest laugh,
            Where lone Echo gives the half
            To some wight, amazed to hear
            Jesting, deep in forest drear.
"Robin Hood"—John Keats.

XIX

23.　I sometimes think that never blows so red
The rose as where some buried Caesar bled;
　　That every hyacinth the garden wears
Dropt in her lap from some once lovely head.

LXXI

24.　The Moving Finger writes; and, having writ,
Moves on; nor all your piety nor wit
　　Shall lure it back to cancel half a line;
Nor all your tears wash out a word of it.
　　　　　　　　　"Rubaiyat of Omar Khayyam"—
　　　　　　　　　　　　　Edward Fitzgerald.

25.　The world's course proves the terms
On which man wins content;
Reason the proof confirms—
We spurn it, and invent
A false course for the world, and for ourselves, false
　　powers.

Riches we wish to get,
Yet remain spendthrifts still;
We would have health, and yet
Still use our bodies ill;
Bafflers of our own prayers, from youth to life's last
　　scenes.

We would have inward peace,
Yet will not look within;
We would have misery cease,
Yet will not cease from sin;
We want all pleasant ends, but will use no harsh means;

Is it so small a thing
To have enjoyed the sun,
To have lived light in the spring,
To have loved, to have thought, to have done;
To have advanced true friends, and beat down baffling
　　foes—

That we must feign a bliss
Of doubtful future date,
And, while we dream on this,
Lose all our present state,
And relegate to worlds yet distant our repose?
                    "Empedocles on Etna"—Arnold.

THE THROSTLE

26. "Summer is coming, summer is coming.
    I know it, I know it, I know it.
Light again, leaf again, life again, love again."
    Yes, my wild little poet.

Sing the new year in under the blue.
    Last year you sang it as gladly.
"New, new, new, new!" Is it then *so* new
    That you should carol so madly?

"Love again, song again, nest again, young again."
    Never a prophet so crazy!
And hardly a daisy as yet, little friend.
    See, there is hardly a daisy.

"Here again, here, here, here, happy year!"
    Oh, warble unchidden, unbidden!
Summer is coming, is coming, my dear,
    And all the winters are hidden.
                    Alfred, Lord Tennyson.

27. Ye marshes, how candid and simple and nothing-
        withholding and free
    Ye publish yourselves to the sky and offer yourselves
        to the sea!
    Tolerant plains, that suffer the sea and the rains and the
        sun,

Ye spread and span like the catholic man who hath
    mightily won
God out of knowledge and good out of infinite pain
And sight out of blindness and purity out of a stain.

As the marsh-hen secretly builds on the watery sod,
Behold I will build me a nest on the greatness of God;
I will fly in the greatness of God as the marsh-hen flies
In the freedom that fills all the space 'twixt the marsh
    and the skies:
By so many roots as the marsh-grass sends in the sod
I will heartily lay me a-hold on the greatness of God:
Oh, like to the greatness of God is the greatness within
The range of the marshes, the liberal marshes of Glynn.
        "The Marshes of Glynn"—Sidney Lanier.

28. I have entered into the Desert,
    The place of desolation;
    Where is great silence.

           *   *   *

29. The mountains belt the Desert with amethyst
    And girdle her with opal;
    They lift their proud aspiring tops
    Into the vault of space,
    Above our tribulation and unanswered fret.

           *   *   *

30. I will refuse to be moulded in the common mould;
    To step regularly according to custom; or order;
    To measure myself among monotonous patterns;

           *   *   *

31. I know Life has not been hurled at us
    As a sharp and poisonous javelin.
    I know it is an alabaster-cup
    Offered by an unseen hand, holding sweet and bitter;
    Aloes and honey and the wine of dreams.

* * *

32. The clock of the Heavens is set for eternity.
    And the infinite Ages are but a point on a line
    From infinity to infinity, without beginning and with-
    out end.
    Man has never flown with wings,
    But slowly, as a snail, he has zigzagged along this in-
    finite.
    Groping, reaching, trying, feebly feeling, yet still crawl-
    ing upward.

* * *

33. Morning is a great architect, gilding the dome
    Of our habitation.

* * *

34. Cities, Omnipotent, Songful, Luxurious;
    Queens loaded with jewels, seated on thrones,
    Receiving much tribute.
    Monsters, powerful, restless, sinuous;
    Terrifying, vague, vast, mysterious;
    Mystic, relentless, beautiful; not yet beautiful;
    Lying on carrion, as a sleek and glossy lion,
    Roaring, muttering, sullenly growling,
    Devours his prey under the stars.

* * *

35. Blessed is leisure, gateway to the wonderful garden
    Where the mind puts forth leaves
    And the soul blossoms;

* * *

36. By Imagination, Man takes the hands
    Of the gods who look afar,
    Seeing the things which are not,
    And the things which are not
    Become more eternal than the things which are.
    Beauty is not wasted though it endure but an hour.

* * *

37. Joy is a beautiful young runner
Continually bringing to our lips,
A jar from the fountain.
But Sorrow is beloved of the eternities.
She descends to the hut of the fisherman,
Nestled in the rocks,
Just beyond the edge of foam,
And comes, also, to the palace
Built proudly on a hill.
Her eyes are sad as the Moon when it has fallen;
Her lips firm as the lips of a wrestler.
She is the great Sculptor, fashioning the soul.
She models us to beauty.

*   *   *

38. The black demon is riding.
Furiously he rides on the fore-front of the tempest
Which licks up the blossomry of the World
And blows it away as dust.
The wings of his coursers
Overwhelm the zenith and
The whistle of their pinions
Is the screaming of eagles.
Their manes toss out lightnings;
Flames shoot from their nostrils.
And their hoofs strike out a great stench.
They paw the air for hunger
And neigh terribly for drink.
Their hunger is for the flesh of young men.
The river they drink is blood.

I have seen War.

*   *   *

39. Whose is the quarrel?
Whose the profit?
Answer—whose the profit?
The greed for gain makes all war.

* * *

40. The soul of Man shattered contemptuously
By the greedy brute in Man;
Man's contemplative godhood smeared
With his own filth.

* * *

41. The Great Harmony builds on Freedom—
Justice—Equality—and Brotherhood

* * *

42. Love is All in All—the Cosmic Harmony.
By Love alone can the nations be preserved.

* * *

43. Man builds upon things of the body—falsities—
Injustice—Inequality—Wealth—Power—Conquest.
Rejecting Brotherhood, he invites Hate.

* * *

44. . . . But the strength beloved
By the Great Harmony, is the strength of the mind,
The strength of the Soul.
Thought is the god in Man. The chiefest attribute
Of gods is thought. . . .

> "The Poet in the Desert"—
> Charles Erskine Scott Wood.

45.   The very God! think, Abib; dost thou think?
So, the All-Great, were the All-Loving too—
So, through the thunder comes a human voice
Saying, "O heart I made, a heart beats here!
Face, my hands fashioned, see it in myself!
Thou hast no power nor mayst conceive of mine,
But love I gave thee, with myself to love,
And thou must love me who have died for thee!"
The madman saith He said so: it is strange.

> "An Epistle"—Robert Browning.

46. . . . Love, we are in God's hand.
How strange now, looks the life he makes us lead;
So free we seem, so fettered fast we are!

*   *   *

47. Ah, but a man's reach should exceed his grasp,
Or what's a heaven for?

"Andrea Del Sarto"—Browning.

SUCH A STARVED BANK OF MOSS
48.   (Prologue of The Two Poets of Croisic)

Such a starved bank of moss
   Till, that May-morn,
Blue ran the flash across:
   Violets were born!

Sky,—what a scowl of cloud
   Till, near and far,
Ray on ray split the shroud:
   Splendid, a star!

World,—how it walled about
   Life with disgrace,
Till God's own smile came out:
   That was thy face!

Robert Browning.

49. I shall never, in the years remaining,
Paint you pictures, no, nor carve you statues,
Make you music that should all-express me;
So it seems: I stand on my attainment.
This of verse alone, one life allows me;
Verse and nothing else have I to give you.
Other heights in other lives, God willing:
All the gifts from all the heights, you own, Love!

*   *   *

50. God be thanked, the meanest of his creatures
     Boasts two soul-sides, one to face the world with,
     One to show a woman when he loves her!

*   *   *

51. This I say of me, but think of you, Love!
     This to you—yourself my moon of poets!
     Ah, but that's the world's side, there's the wonder,
     Thus they see you, praise you, think they know you!
     There, in turn I stand with them and praise you—
     Out of my own self, I dare to phrase it.
     But the best is when I glide from out them,
     Cross a step or two of dubious twilight,
     Come out on the other side, the novel
     Silent silver lights and darks undreamed of,
     Where I hush and bless myself with silence.
                    "One Word More"—Browning.

52. All we have willed or hoped or dreamed of good shall
         exist;
       Not its semblance, but itself; no beauty, nor good,
       nor power
       Whose voice has gone forth, but each survives for the
       melodist
       When eternity affirms the conception of an hour.
     The high that proved too high, the heroic for earth too
       hard
         The passion that left the ground to lose itself in
         the sky,
     Are music sent up to God by the lover and the bard;
       Enough that he heard it once: we shall hear it by-and-
       by.
                    "Abt Vogler"—Browning.

53.   Grow old along with me!
         The best is yet to be,
     The last of life, for which the first was made:

Our times are in His hand
Who saith, "A whole I planned,
Youth shows but half; trust God: see all, nor be
afraid!"

"Rabbi Ben Ezra"—Browning.

54.   Poetry lifts the veil from the hidden beauty of the
world, and makes familiar objects be as if they were not
familiar.

* * *

55.   A great poem is a fountain forever overflowing with
the waters of wisdom and delight; and after one person
and one age has exhausted all of its divine effluence
which their peculiar relations enable them to share,
another and yet another succeeds, and new relations
are ever developed, and the source of an unforeseen and
an unconceived delight.

* * *

56.   The drama, so long as it continues to express poetry,
is a prismatic and many-sided mirror, which collects
the brightest rays of human nature and divides and
reproduces them from the simplicity of these elementary
forms, and touches them with majesty and beauty, and
multiplies all that it reflects, and endows it with the
power of propagating its like wherever it may fall.

* * *

57.   Dante was the first awakener of entranced Europe;
he created a language, in itself music and persuasion,
out of a chaos of inharmonious barbarisms. He was the
congregator of those great spirits who presided over the
resurrection of learning; the Lucifer of that starry
flock which in the thirteenth century shone forth from
republican Italy, as from a heaven, into the darkness of
the benighted world. His very words are instinct with
spirit; each is as a spark, a burning atom of inextinguish-

able thought; and many yet lie covered in the ashes of their birth, and pregnant with a lightning which has yet found no conductor.

"A Defence of Poetry"—Shelley.

58.   Humor draws its materials from situations and characteristics; Wit seizes on unexpected and complex relations.

* * *

59.   Wit is brief and sudden, and sharply defined as a crystal; it does not make pictures, it is not fantastic; but it detects an unsuspected analogy, or suggests a startling or confounding inference.

* * *

60.   Wit is an electric shock, which takes us by violence quite independently of our predominant mental disposition; but humour approaches us more deliberately and leaves us masters of ourselves.

* * *

61.   Heinrich Heine gives us some recollections in his wild poetic way, of the dear old town where he spent his childhood, and of his schoolboy troubles there: "But oh! the trouble I had at school with the endless dates. And with arithmetic it was still worse. What I understood best was subtraction, for that has a very practical rule: 'Four can't be taken from three, therefore I must borrow one.' But I advise every one in such a case to borrow a few extra pence, for no one can tell what may happen. . . . As for Latin, you have no idea, madam, what a complicated affair it is. The Romans would never have found time to conquer the world if they had first had to learn Latin. Luckily for them, they already knew in their cradles what nouns have their accusative in *im*. I, on the contrary, had to learn them by heart in the sweat of my brow; nevertheless, it is fortunate for me that I know them; . . . and the fact that I have them at my finger-ends if I should ever happen to want them sud-

denly, affords me much inward repose and consolation
in many troubled hours of life. . . . Of Greek I will not
say a word; I should get too much irritated. The
monks in the middle ages were not so far wrong when
they maintained that Greek was an invention of the
devil. God knows the suffering I endured over it. . . .
With Hebrew it went somewhat better, for I had always
a great liking for the Jews, though to this very hour they
crucify my good name; but I could never get on so far
in Hebrew as my watch, which had much familiar inter-
course with pawnbrokers, and in this way contracted
many Jewish habits—for example, it wouldn't go on
Saturdays."

"The Wit of Heinrich Heine"—George Eliot.

62.   In the tragedies of Sophocles there is a most distinct
recognition of the eternal justice of heaven and the un-
failing punishment of crime against the laws of God.

I believe you will find in all histories that that has
been at the head and foundation of them all, and that
no nation that did not contemplate this wonderful universe with an awe-stricken and reverential feeling that
there was a great unknown, omnipotent, and all-wise,
and all-virtuous Being, superintending all men in it, and
all interests in it—no nation ever came to very much,
nor did any man either, who forgot that.

*   *   *

63.   Silence is the eternal duty of a man.
"On the Choice of Books"—Carlyle.

64.   Speak not, I passionately entreat thee, till thy
thought hath silently matured itself. . . . Out of
Silence comes thy strength. "Speech is silvern, Silence
is golden; Speech is human, Silence is divine."

Carlyle.

65. "Impression must precede and determine all expression."
S. S. Curry.

66.   He practically distinguishes the kinds of religion that are in the world, and he makes out three reverences. The first and the simplest is that of reverence for what is above us. It is the soul of all the Pagan religions; there is nothing better in man than that. Then there is reverence for our equals, and to which he attributes an immense power in the culture of man. The third is reverence for what is beneath us—to learn to recognize in pain, sorrow, and contradiction, even in those things, odious as they are to flesh and blood—to learn that there lies in these a priceless blessing.
From "Choice of Books"—Carlyle.

67.   Thus the best sign of originality lies in taking up a subject and then developing it so fully as to make every one confess that he would hardly have found so much in it.

*   *   *

68.   And if we turn to that significant utterance, *Know thyself*, we must not explain it in an ascetic sense. . . . It simply means: pay some attention to yourself; so that you may know how you come to stand towards those like you and towards the world.

*   *   *

69.   It is said: Artist, study nature! But it is no trifle to develop noble out of the commonplace, or beauty out of uniformity.

*   *   *

70.   It is only by Art, and especially by Poetry, that the imagination is regulated. Nothing is more frightful than imagination without taste.

*   *   *

71.   Higher aims are in themselves more valuable, even if unfulfilled, than lower ones quite attained.

* * *

72.   In every kind of Art there is a degree of excellence which may be reached, so to speak, by the mere use of one's own natural talents, and at the same time it is impossible to go beyond that point, unless Art comes to one's aid.

* * *

73.   A man cannot live with every one, and therefore he cannot live for every one. To see this truth aright is to place a high value upon one's friends, and not to hate or persecute one's enemies.

"Literature and Art"—Goethe.

WINDOWS

74.   He who looks in through an open window never sees so many things as he who looks at a shut window. There is nothing more profound, more mysterious, more fertile, more gloomy, or more dazzling, than a window lighted by a candle. What we can see in the sunlight is always less interesting than what goes on behind the panes of a window. In that dark or luminous hollow, life lives, life dreams, life suffers.

Across the waves of roofs, I can see a woman of middle age, wrinkled, poor, who is always leaning over something, and who never goes out. Out of her face, out of her dress, out of her attitude, out of nothing almost, I have made up the woman's story, and sometimes I say it over to myself with tears.

If it had been a poor old man, I could have made up his just as easily.

And I go to bed, proud of having lived and suffered in others.

Perhaps you will say to me: "Are you sure that it is

the real story?" What does it matter, what does any
reality outside of myself matter, if it has helped me to
live, to feel that I am, and what I am?

Baudelaire.

75.   Toussaint was too dangerous to be left at large. So
they summoned him to attend a council; he went, and
the moment he entered the room the officers drew their
swords and told him he was a prisoner.

They put him on shipboard, and weighed anchor for
France. As the island faded from his sight he turned
to the captain and said: "You think you have rooted
up the tree of liberty, but I am only a branch; I have
planted the tree so deep that all France can never
root it up." He was sent to a dungeon twelve feet by
twenty, built wholly of stone, with a narrow window,
high up on one side, looking out on the snows of Switzerland. In this living tomb the child of the sunny tropic
was left to die.

Wendell Phillips.

76.   It is much easier to recognize error than to find
truth; for error lies on the surface and may be overcome;
but truth lies in the depths, and to search for it is not
given to every one.

Goethe.

77.   "I always read La Fontaine out loud whereas you
read the *Fables* as most people do; my voice tells me
when there is a danger of misinterpreting a line."
Legouve to Cousin, from "The Art of Thinking" by

Ernest Dimnet.

78.   Why take the artistic way to prove so much?
Because, it is the glory and good of Art,
That Art remains the one way possible
Of speaking truth, to mouths like mine, at least.

"The Ring and the Book"—Browning.

79.   Fitz-James was brave. Though to his heart
       The life-blood thrilled with sudden start,
       He manned himself with dauntless air,
       Returned the Chief his haughty stare.
       His back against a rock he bore,
       And firmly placed his foot before:
       "Come one, come all! this rock shall fly
       From its firm base as soon as I."
                     "The Lady of the Lake"—Scott.

80. *Green.* God save your majesty!—and well met, gentle-
       men:—
       I hope the king is not yet shipp'd for Ireland.
       Queen. Why hop'st thou so? 'tis better hope he is;
       For his designs crave haste, his haste good hope:
       Then wherefore dost thou hope he is not shipp'd?
       Green. That he, our hope, might have retir'd his power,
       And driven into despair an enemy's hope,
       Who strongly hath set footing in this land:
       The banish'd Bolingbroke repeals himself,
       And with uplifted arms is safe arriv'd
       At Ravenspurg.
       Queen. God in heaven forbid!

                     *   *   *

81. *Bushy.* Despair not, madam.
       Queen. Who shall hinder me?
       I will despair, and be at enmity
       With cozening hope,—he is a flatterer,
       A parasite, a keeper-back of death,
       Who gently would dissolve the bands of life,
       Which false hope lingers in extremity.
                     "King Richard II."—Shakespeare.

82. *King Richard.* What must the king do now? must he
       submit?
       The king shall do it: must he be depos'd?
       The king shall be contented: must he lose
       The name of king? o' God's name, let it go:

I'll give my jewels for a set of beads,
My gorgeous palace for a hermitage,
My gay apparel for an alms-man's gown,
My figur'd goblets for a dish of wood,
My sceptre for a palmer's walking staff,
My subjects for a pair of carved saints,
And my large kingdom for a little grave,
A little, little grave, an obscure grave;—
Or I'll be buried in the king's highway,
Some way of common trade, where subject's feet
May hourly trample on their sovereign's head;
For on my heart they tread now whilst I live;
And buried once, why not upon my head?—

Ibid.

83. *Boling.* I thought you had been willing to resign.
K. Rich. My crown I am; but still my griefs are mine;
You may my glories and my state depose,
But not my griefs; still am I king of those.
Boling. Your cares set up do not pluck my cares down.
My care is, care of loss, by old care done;
Your care is, gain of care, by new care won:
The cares I give, I have, though given away;
They tend the crown, yet still with me they stay.

Ibid.

84. *Queen.* And must we be divided? must we part?
K. Rich. Ay, hand from hand, my love, and heart from
        heart.
Queen. Banish us both, and send the king with me.
North. That were some love, but little policy.
Queen. Then whither he goes thither let me go.
K. Rich. So two, together weeping, make one
Weep thou for me in France, I for thee here;
Better far off than near, be ne'er the near.
Go, count thy way with sighs; I, mine with groans.
Queen. So longest way shall have the longest moans.

K. Rich. Twice for one step I'll groan, the way being
  short,
And piece the way out with a heavy heart.
Come, come, in wooing sorrow let's be brief,
Since, wedding it, there is such length in grief.
One kiss shall stop our mouths, and dumbly part;
Thus give I mine, and thus take I thy heart.
                    (*They kiss.*)
Queen. Give me mine own again; 'twere no good part
To take on me to keep and kill thy heart. (*They kiss.*)
So, now I have mine own again, be gone,
That I may strive to kill it with a groan.
                                        Ibid.

85. *Hor.* Hail to your lordship!
Ham. I am glad to see you well;
Horatio,—or I do forget myself.
Hor. The same, my lord, and your poor servant ever.

                *   *   *

Hor. My lord, I came to see your father's funeral.
Ham. I pray thee, do not mock me, fellow-student;
I think it was to see my mother's wedding.
Hor. Indeed, my lord, it follow'd hard upon.

                *   *   *

Ham. . . . .
Would I had met my dearest foe in heaven
Ere I had ever seen that day, Horatio!—
My father,—me thinks I see my father.
Hor. Where, my lord?
Ham. In my mind's eye, Horatio.
Hor. I saw him once; he was a goodly king.
Ham. He was a man, take him for all in all,
I shall not look upon his like again.
Hor. My lord, I think I saw him yesternight.
Ham. Saw who?
Hor. My lord, the king your father.
Ham. The king my father!

*   *   *

For God's love, let me hear.

Hor. Two nights together had these gentlemen,
Marcellus and Bernardo, in their watch,
In the dead vast and middle of the night,
Been thus encounter'd. A figure like your father,
Arm'd at all points exactly, cap-a-pe,
Appears before them, and with solemn march
Goes slow and stately by them.

*   *   *

Ham. But where was this?
Mar. My lord, upon the platform where we watch'd.
Ham. Did you not speak to it?
Hor. My lord, I did;
But answer made it none.

*   *   *

Ham. 'Tis very strange.
Hor. As I do live, my honour'd lord, 'tis true;
And we did think it writ down in our duty
To let you know of it.
Ham. Indeed, indeed, sirs, but this troubles me.
Hold you the watch tonight?
Mar. and Ber. We do, my lord.
Ham. Arm'd, say you?
Mar. and Ber. Arm'd, my lord.
Ham. From top to toe?
Mar. and Ber. My lord, from head to foot.
Ham. Then saw you not his face?
Hor. O yes, my lord; he wore his beaver up.
Ham. What, look'd he frowningly?
Hor. A countenance more in sorrow than in anger.

*   *   *

86. *Ham.* The air bites shrewdly; it is very cold.
Hor. It is a nipping and an eager air.
Ham. What hour now?
Hor. I think it lacks of twelve.
Mar. No, it is struck.

Hor. Indeed? I heard it not: then it draws near the season
Wherein the spirit held his wont to walk.

* * *

Look, my lord, it comes!
(*Enter Ghost.*)
Ham. Angels and ministers of grace defend us!—

* * *

Hor. It beckons you to go away with it.

* * *

Ham. It will not speak; then will I follow it.
Hor. Do not, my lord.
Ham. Why, what should be the fear? . . .
I'll follow it.

* * *

Mar. You shall not go, my lord.
Ham. Hold off your hands.
Hor. Be rul'd; you shall not go.
Ham. . . . . Unhand me, gentlemen;—
(*Breaking from them.*)
By heaven, I'll make a ghost of him that lets me.
I say, away!—Go on; I'll follow thee.
"Hamlet"—Shakespeare.

HAMLET'S INSTRUCTIONS TO THE PLAYER

87.　Speak the speech, I pray you, as I pronounced it to you,—trippingly on the tongue; but if you mouth it, as many of our players do, I had as lief the town-crier spoke my lines. Nor do not saw the air too much with your hand, thus; but use all gently: for in the very torrent, tempest, and, as I may say, whirlwind of your passion, you must acquire and beget a temperance that may give it smoothness. O, it offends me to the soul to hear a robustinous periwig-pated fellow tear a passion to tatters, to very rags, to split the ears of the groundlings, who, for the most part, are capable of nothing but inexplicable dumb show and noise. I would have such a fellow whipped for o'er-doing Termagant; it out-herods Herod. Pray you avoid it.

Be not too tame, neither, but let your own discretion be your tutor. Suit the action to the word, the word to the action; with this special observance, that you o'erstep not the modesty of nature: for anything so overdone is from the purpose of playing, whose end, both at the first and now, was, and is, to hold, as 'twere, the mirror up to nature; to show virtue her own feature; scorn her own image; and the very age and body of the time, his form and pressure. Now, this, overdone, or come tardy off, though it make the unskilful laugh, cannot but make the judicious grieve; the censure of which one must, in your allowance, o'erweigh a whole theatre of others. O, there be players, that I have seen play, and heard others praise, and that highly,—not to speak it profanely, that, neither having the accent of Christians, nor the gait of Christian, pagan, or man, have so strutted and bellowed, that I have thought some of Nature's journeyman had made men, and not made them well, they imitated humanity so abominably!

—Shakespeare.

88. *Iago.* My noble lord,—

Oth. What dost thou say, Iago?

Iago. Did Michael Cassio, when you woo'd my lady, Know of your love?

Oth. He did, from first to last: why dost thou ask?

Iago. But for a satisfaction of my thought; No further harm.

Oth. Why of thy thought, Iago?

Iago. I did not think he had been acquainted with her.

Oth. O, yes; and went between us very oft.

Iago. Indeed!

Oth. Indeed! ay, indeed:—discern'st thou aught in that? Is he not honest?

Iago. Honest, my lord!

Oth. Honest! ay, honest.

Iago. My lord, for aught I know.

Oth. What dost thou think?

Iago. Think, my lord!

Oth. Think, my lord!
By heaven, he echoes me,
As if there were some monster in his thought
Too hideous to be shown.—Thou dost mean something:
I heard thee say even now,—thou lik'dst not that,
When Cassio left my wife: what did'st not like?
And when I told thee he was of my counsel
In my whole course of wooing, thou criedst, *Indeed*!
And didst contract and purse thy brow together,
As if thou then hadst shut up in thy brain
Some horrible conceit: if thou dost love me,
Show me thy thought.

* * *

Iago. Good name in man and woman, dear my lord,
Is the immediate jewel of their souls:
Who steals my purse steals trash; 'tis something,
nothing;
'Twas mine, 'tis his, and has been slave to thousands;
But he that filches from me my good name
Robs me of that which not enriches him,
And makes me poor indeed.
"Othello"—Shakespeare.

89. *Macb.* How now! what news?

Lady M. He has almost supp'd: why have you left the
chamber

Macb. Hath he ask'd for me?

Lady M. Know you not he has?

Macb. We will proceed no further in this business:
He hath honour'd me of late; and I have bought
Golden opinions from all sorts of people,
Which would be worn now in their newest gloss,
Not cast aside so soon.

Lady M. Was the hope drunk
Wherein you dress'd yourself? hath it slept since?
And wakes it now, to look so green and pale
At what it did so freely? From this time
Such I account thy love. Art thou afeared
To be the same in thine own act and valour
As thou art in desire? Would'st thou have that
Which thou esteem'st the ornament of life,
And live a coward in thine own esteem;
Letting I *dare not* wait upon I *would*,
Like the poor cat i' the adage?
Macb. Pr'ythee, peace:
I dare do all that maye become a man;
Who dares do more is none.

90. *Macb.* I have done the deed.—Didst thou not hear a
       noise?
Lady M. *I* heard the owl scream and the crickets cry.
Did not you speak?
Macb. When?
Lady M. Now.
Macb. As I descended?
Lady M. Ay.
Macb. Hark!—
Who lies i' the second chamber?
Lady M. Donalbain.
Macb. This is a sorry sight. (*Looking on his hands.*)
Lady M. A foolish thought to say a sorry sight.
Macb. There's one did laugh in's sleep, and one cried
       Murder!
That they did wake each other: I stood and heard them:
But they did say their prayers, and address'd them
Again to sleep.

                                              Ibid.

Len. What's your grace's will?
Macb. Saw you the weird sisters?
Len. No, my lord.
Macb. Came they not by you?

Len. No, indeed, my lord.

Macb. Infected be the air whereon they ride;
And damn'd all those that trust them!—I did hear
The galloping of horse: who was't came by?

Len. 'Tis two or three, my lord, that bring you word,
Macduff is fled to England

Macb. Fled to England!

Len. Ay, my lord.

Ibid.

91.   *Doct.* I have two nights watched with you, but can perceive no truth in your report. When was it she last walked? . . . What, at any time, have you heard her say?

Gent. That, sir, which I will not report after her.

Doct. You may to me; and 'tis most meet you should.

Gent. Neither to you nor anyone; having no witness to confirm my speech. Lo you, here she comes!

(*Enter Lady Macbeth with a taper.*)

This is her very guise; and, upon my life, fast asleep. Observe her; stand close.

Doct. How came she by that light?

Gent. Why, it stood by her: she has light by her continually; 'tis her command.

Doct. You see, her eyes are open.

Gent. Ay, but their sense is shut.

Doct. What is it she does now? Look, how she rubs her hands.

Gent. It is an accustomed action with her, to seem thus washing her hands: I have known her continue in this a quarter of an hour.

Lady M. Yet here's a spot.

Doct. Hark! she speaks: I will set down what comes from her, to satisfy my remembrance the more strongly.

Lady M. Out, damned spot! out, I say!—One; two: why, then 'tis time to do't:—Hell is murky!—Fie, my

lord, fie! a soldier, and afeared? What need we fear who
knows it, when none can call our power to account?—
Yet who would have thought the old man to have had
so much blood in him?

Ibid.

92.   *Sooth.* Caesar!
    Caes. Ha! who calls?
    Casca. Bib every noise be still.—Peace yet again.
(*Music ceases.*)
    Caes. Who is it in the press that calls on me?
I hear a tongue, shriller than all the music,
Cry, *Caesar.* Speak; Caesar is turned to hear.
    Sooth. Beware the Ides of March.
    Caes. What man is that?
    Bru. A soothsayer bids you beware the Ides of
March.
    Caes. Set him before me; let me see his face.
    Cas. Fellow, come from the throng; look upon
Caesar.
    Caes. What say'st thou to me now? speak once
again.
    Sooth. Beware the Ides of March.
    Caes. He is a dreamer; let us leave him.—Pass.

       *   *   *   *   *

93.   *Casca.* You pull'd me by the cloak; would you
speak with me?
    Bur. Ay, Casca; tell us what has chanc'd today,
That Caesar looks so sad?
    Casca. Why, you were with him, were you not?
    Bur. I should not then ask Casca what had chanc'd.
    Casca. Why, there was a crown offered him: and
being offered him, he put it by with the back of his
hand, thus: and then the people fell a-shouting.
    Bur. What was the second noise for?
    Casca. Why, for that too.

Cas. They shouted thrice: what was the last cry for?

Casca. Why, for that too.

Bru. Was the crown offer'd him thrice?

Casca. Ay, marry, was't, and he put it by thrice, every time gentler than other; and at every putting by mine honest neighbours shouted.

Cas. Who offered him the crown?

Casca. Why, Antony.

"Julius Caesar"—Shakespeare.

94. *Dec.* Caesar, all hail! Good-morrow, worthy Caesar:
I come to fetch you to the senate-house.
Caes. And you are come in very happy time,
To bear my greetings to the senators,
And tell them that I will not come to-day:
Cannot, is false; and that I dare not, falser:
I will not come to-day,—tell them so, Decius.
Cal. Say he is sick.
Caes. Shall Caesar send a lie?
Have I in conquest stretch'd mine arm so far,
To be afeard to tell graybeards the truth?
Decius, go tell them Caesar will not come.
Dec. Most mighty Caesar, let me know some cause,
Lest I be laugh'd at when I tell them so.
Caes. The cause is in my will,—I will not come:
That is enough to satisfy the senate.
But for your private satisfaction,
Because I love you, I will let you know,—
Calpurnia here, my wife, stays me at home:
She dreamt to-night she saw my statue,
Which, like a fountain with a hundred spouts,
Did run pure blood; and many lusty Romans
Came smiling and did bathe their hands in it:
And these does she apply for warnings and portents,
And evils imminent; and on her knee
Hath begg'd that I will stay at home to-day.

Dec. This dream is all amiss interpreted;
It was a vision fair and fortunate:
Your statue spouting blood in many pipes,
In which so many smiling Romans bathe'd,
Signifies that from you great Rome shall suck
Reviving blood; and that great men shall press
For tinctures, stains, relics, and cognizance.
This by Calpurnia's dream is signified.
Caes. And this way have you well expounded it.
Dec. I have, when you have heard what I can say:
And know it now,—the senate have concluded
To give this day a crown to mighty Caesar.
If you shall send them word you will not come,
Their minds may change. Besides, it were a mock,
Apt to be render'd, for some one to say,
Break up the senate till another time,
When Caesar's wife shall meet with better dreams.
If Caesar hide himself, shall they not whisper,
Lo, Caesar is afraid?
Pardon me, Caesar; for my dear, dear love
To your proceeding bids me tell you this;
And reason to my love is liable.
Caes. How foolish do your fears seem now, Calpurnia!
I am ashamed I did yield to them.—
Give me my robe for I will go.

Ibid.

95. *Caes.* The Ides of March are come.
Sooth. Ay, Caesar; but not gone.
Art. Hail, Caesar! Read this schedule.
Dec. Trebonius doth desire you to o'er read,
At your best leisure, this his humble suit.
Art. O Caesar, read mine first; for mine's a suit
That touches Caesar nearer: read it, great Caesar.
Caes. What touches us ourself shall be last serv'd.
Art. Delay not, Caesar; read it instantly.
Caes. What, is the fellow mad?

Pub. Sirrah, give place.
Cas. What, urge you your petitions in the street?
Come to the Capitol.

Ibid.

96. *Bru.* Remember March, the Ides of March remember!
Did not great Julius bleed for justice' sake?
What villain touch'd his body, that did stab,
And not for justice? What, shall one of us,
That struck the foremost man of all this world
But for supporting robbers, shall we now
Contaminate our fingers with base bribes,
And sell the mighty space of our large honours
For so much trash as may be grasped thus?—
I had rather be a dog, and bay the moon,
Than such a Roman.
Cas. Brutus, bay not me,—
I'll not endure it: you forget yourself
To hedge me in; I am a soldier, I,
Older in practice, abler than yourself
To make conditions.
Bru. Go to; you are not, Cassius.
Cas. I am.
Bru. I say you are not.
Cas. Urge me no more, I shall forget myself;
Have mind upon your health, tempt me no further.
Bru. Away, slight man!
Cas. Is't possible?
Bru. Hear me, for I will speak.
Must I give way and room to your rash choler?
Shall I be frightened when a madman stares?
Cas. O ye gods, ye gods! must I endure all this?
Bru. All this! ay, more: fret till your proud heart break;
Go, show your slaves how choleric you are,
And make your bondmen tremble. Must I budge?
Must I observe you? Must I stand and crouch
Under your testy humour? . . .

* * *

Cas. I denied you not.

Bru. You did.

Cas. I did not: he was but a fool that brought
My answer back.—Brutus hath riv'd my heart:
A friend should bear his friend's infirmities,
But Brutus makes mine greater than they are.

Bru. I do not, till you practise them on me.

Cas. You love me not.

Bru. I do not like your faults.

Cas. A friendly eye could never see such faults.

Bru. A flatterer's would not, though they do appear
As huge as high Olympus.

Ibid.

(*Enter the Ghost of Caesar.*)

97. *Bru.* How ill this taper burns!—Ha! Who comes here?
I think it is the weakness of mine eyes
That shapes this monstrous apparition.
It comes upon me.—Art thou anything?
Art thou some god, some angel, or some devil,
That mak'st my blood cold and my hair to stare?
Speak to me what thou art.

Ghost. Thy evil spirit, Brutus.

Bru. Why com'st thou?

Ghost. To tell thee thou shalt see me at Philippi.

Bru. Well:
Then I shall see thee again?

Ghost. Ay, at Philippi.

Ibid.

98.   SONG OF THE CHORUS
From *The Frogs*, by Aristophanes
Translated by John Hookham Frere

Chorus. Now we go to dance and sing
In the consecrated shades;
Round the secret holy ring,
With the matrons and the maids.

Thither I must haste to bring
  The mysterious early light;
  Which must witness every rite
  Of the joyous happy night.
Let us hasten—let us fly—
Where the lovely meadows lie;
  Where the living waters flow;
  Where the roses bloom and blow
—Heirs of Immortality,
Segregated, safe and pure,
Easy, sorrowless, secure;
Since our earthly course is run,
We behold a brighter sun.
Holy lives—a holy vow—
Such rewards await them now.

6. BIOGRAPHICAL NOTES

VI. BIOGRAPHICAL NOTES

ADAMS, JAMES TRUSLOW. Born in Brooklyn 1878. Educated at Brooklyn Polytechnic, and did graduate work at Yale. Was in business in Wall Street until 1912, when he retired and devoted himself to study. Began writing local history. In 1922 his *The Founding of New England* was awarded the Pulitzer Prize for History. He has contributed to the Encyclopedia Britannica, and has written about one hundred lives for the *Dictionary of American Biography*.

ALDRICH, THOMAS BAILEY. Born, 1836 in New Hampshire, died 1907. His life was devoted to literature, as the literary critic of *The Evening Mirror*, editor of the *Atlantic Monthly*, and editor of *Every Saturday*.

ALLINGHAM, WILLIAM. Born in Ireland, 1824; died 1889. A friend of Dante Gabriel Rossetti. He is known today for his *Irish Songs and Poems*, and *Flower Pieces and Other Poems*.

ANDERSON, J. REDWOOD. Born, 1883, in Manchester, England. Has lived abroad and traveled extensively. Educated by private tutors, Brussels Conservatoire (violin), and Trinity College, Oxford. For past twenty years, has been Master at Hymers College, Hull. Author of *Flemish Tales, The Human Dawn, English Fantasies, The Tower to Heaven*.

ANDERSON, MAXWELL. Born, 1888. Was instructor in English Department, Stanford University, then with newspapers in North Dakota and California. Author of *What Price Glory, The Buccaneer, Elizabeth the Queen, Mary of Scotland*.

BAKER, KARLE WILSON. Born, 1878. Professor of English, Stephen F. Austin Teachers' College, Texas. Author of *Blue Smoke, Burning Bush, Old Coins*. "The Bride's Parable" was written under author's early pen-name, "Charlotte Wilson".

BAKER, RAY STANNARD. (David Grayson.) Born, 1870. Degrees from Michigan State College and Amherst. One time managing editor and later associate editor of *McClure's Magazine*. Served as Special Commissioner of the Department of State, in Europe, 1918. Author of *What Wilson Did at Paris* and *Woodrow Wilson—Life and Letters*. Under pseudonym of David Grayson, he has written *Adventures in Solitude* and many first-person essays and stories.

BENÉT, WILLIAM ROSE. Born in New York, 1886. Since his graduation from Yale in 1907, he has been editor in a publishing house, and has served on the staffs of four magazines, among them the *Century*, and the *Saturday Review of Literature*, which he with Christopher Morley and Henry Seidel Canby founded. *Man Possessed* was a collection of the best poems which had appeared in six volumes published between 1913 and 1920.

BESIER, RUDOLPH. Born in 1878 in England. Author of many plays—*The Barretts of Wimpole Street* is one of his best known. Katherine Cornell played the role of Elizabeth Barrett.

BISHOP, NORRIS. Born in Willard, N. Y., 1893. Assistant Professor of Romance Languages, Cornell University. Author of *The Odyssey of Cabeza de Vaca*, *A Gallery of Eccentrics*, *Paramount Poems*, *Pascal: the Life of Genius*, and *Love Rimes of Petrarch*.

BJORNSON, BJORNSTJERNE. (1832–1910.) Norwegian novelist, poet and dramatist. Was an advocate of Norwegian national rights against Sweden. Greatest distinctively Norwegian writer of his day. Awarded Nobel prize in literature in 1903.

CARRYL, GUY WETMORE. Born in New York City, 1873, died 1904. A graduate of Columbia University. He lived abroad and was the representative for various American publications. His books include: *Fables for the Frivolous*, *Mother Goose for Grown-Ups*, and *Grimm Tales Made Gay*.

CHASE, HARRY WOODBURN. Educator. Born, 1883. Now Chancellor of New York University. Member of National Advisory Committee on Education, and National Advisory Council on Radio in Education.

CLARK, BADGER. Born in Albia, Iowa, in 1883. He attended Dakota Wesleyan University. He has written *Sun and Saddle Leather*, *Grass Grown Trails*, and *Spike*, a novel.

COFFIN, ROBERT P. TRISTRAM. Brilliant poet, essayist, novelist, and biographer, author of a score of books. He was Phi Beta Kappa Poet at Harvard Commencement in 1932, Katherine Lee Bates Poet at Wellesley. At present he is Professor of English at Bowdoin College. His *Strange Holiness* was awarded the Pulitzer Prize for Poetry in 1936.

COLLINGE, PATRICIA. Actress. Born in Dublin, Ireland, 1894. Among her roles were: *Pollyanna*, *The Dark Angel*, *Hedda Gabler*, *What Every Woman Knows*.

COLLINS, FREDERICK LEWIS. Born, 1882. Degree, Harvard. Was editor of *McClure's Magazine*, 1913–1920. Author of *This King Business*, *Vacation Travel Charts and Travel Chats*, and *Glamorous Sinners*.

COLUM, PADRIAC. Born in Ireland, 1881. Entered the ranks of writers in his youth. One of the founders of *The Irish Review* in 1911. Some of his books are *Cross Roads in Ireland*, *Old Pastures*, and *Orpheus: Myths of the World*, which contains folk legends from all nations. In

1923 Mr. Colum went to Hawaii at the invitation of the Hawaiian Legislature to make a survey of native myths and folk-lore.

CONGREVE, WILLIAM. Born, 1670, died 1729. English dramatist.

CONNELL, RICHARD. Born, 1893. Degree from Harvard. Was reporter, *New York American*. Served in 27th Division, U. S. A., and with A. E. F. in France. Author of *The Sin of Monsieur Pettipon, The Mad Lover, Ironies*, and other books, stories, and motion pictures.

CULLEN, COUNTÉE. Born in New York City, 1903, the son of a minister. He has a B.A. degree from New York University, and a M.A. degree from Harvard. His books of poetry include *Color, Copper Sun*, and *Black Christ*, which deal for the most part with the Negro.

CUMMINGS, PARKE. Graduated from Harvard. Writes verse and other articles for periodicals and magazines.

DAVIS, MARY OCTAVIA. Graduated from Our Lady of the Lake College. Teaches in San Antonio Schools. Writes poetry, plays, pageants, articles, and illustrates them herself.

DE LA MARE, WALTER. Born in England, 1873. He worked in the London office of the Anglo-American Oil Company for 18 years, and wrote poetry at his desk. His first volume was *Songs of Childhood*. Later he received a pension which enabled him to step from the business world and devote himself to writing. Among his more than 25 published books are: *The Return, Peacock Pie, Flora*, and *Collected Poems*.

DE LEON, WALTER. His story, *The Boob*, was written, he says, as an experiment, the result of a dare. It first appeared in *Hearst's International* and later in Small, Maynard's *Best Love Stories of 1924*.

DRUMMOND, WILLIAM HENRY. Born in Ireland, died 1907. He was educated in Montreal schools, McGill University and Bishop University. He practiced medicine in Montreal. His literary works were *The Habitant, Johnnie Courteau*, and *The Voyageur: A Volume of Verse*.

DUGANNE, PHYLLIS. Born in Boston, 1899. Worked on New York newspapers. Married Eben Given, painter, and has a daughter. Author of a novel, *Prologue*, and many short stories.

DURANTY, WALTER. One of the best known United States foreign correspondents. During the war he was correspondent with the French armies, afterwards becoming the *New York Times* correspondent for Russia. Recent book, *I Write as I Please*.

EDGAR, DAY. Grew up near a village laid out by William Penn. Began writing at an early age. In sophomore year at Princeton, met Hugh MacNair Kahler, to whom he feels indebted for much literary help. Author of many short stories and a book, *In Princeton Town*, a collection of college stories.

EMERSON, ELIZABETH H. Born, 1885, in Illinois. Degrees from Earlham College and New Mexico Normal University. Taught in

Illinois high schools. Author of *The Cloth of Sendony* and other plays, articles, and poems.

ERSKINE, JOHN. Born, 1879. Poet, novelist, musician, teacher. Was professor at Columbia University. Author of *The Private Life of Helen of Troy, Galahad, Tristram and Isolde,* and other books.

ERVINE, ST. JOHN. Born in Ireland in 1883. Served in the World War and lost one leg. His plays have been enacted all over the world and translated into three languages. He was at one time the visiting dramatic critic for *The New York World.* Two of his novels are *Foolish Lovers* and *Changing Winds.*

FARR, FINIS. Born in Tennessee. Graduated from Princeton. Has done journalistic work. Versatile writer of radio dialogue: *Sherlock Holmes, Treasure Island, The Trial of Dolores Divine,* the famous Lucky Strike mystery thrillers, and others.

FIELD, SARA BARD. Wife of Charles E. S. Wood. Author of *The Pale Woman, Barabbas, Darkling Plain.*

FLETCHER, JOHN GOULD. Born in Arkansas, 1886. Educated at Harvard. He left this country as a young man and lived in England for 15 years, returning to the United States in 1933. Amy Lowell and Ezra Pound greatly encouraged him and helped him publish his first poems. His *Selected Poems* was awarded the Pulitzer Prize for Poetry in 1939.

FROST, FRANCES. Born, 1905. Degree from University of Vermont. Was newspaper reporter; later, instructor in Creative Poetry at the University of Vermont. Author of verse, *Hemlock Wall, These Acres, Pool in the Meadow,* and other poetry and fiction.

FROST, ROBERT. Born in California, 1875. After the death of his father, his mother moved to New England. He wrote poetry for twenty years without recognition. He studied at Dartmouth and later at Harvard, but did not complete either course. He has taught school, made shoes, edited a newspaper, and run a New Hampshire farm. Publication in 1893 of *A Boy's Will* in England first brought him recognition. Since then he has been granted the Pulitzer Prize for Poetry three times: 1924, 1931, 1937.

GALE, ZONA. Born, 1874, in Wisconsin. Died 1938. Degrees from University of Wisconsin. Has always written; printed and bound in ribbon, her first book of fiction and verse was illustrated by herself at seven. Her play, *Miss Lulu Bett,* won the Pulitzer Prize for 1921. Also author of novels, essays, short stories and poems. Among them: *Faint Perfume, Preface to Life, Borgia, Friendship Village Stories.*

GARLAND, HAMLIN. Born, 1860, in Wisconsin. Taught private classes in English and American Literature and lectured in and about Boston, 1885–1889. Author of *A Son of the Middle Border, A Daughter of the Middle Border* (Awarded the Pulitzer Prize for the best biography of 1921), *Trail Makers of the Middle Border*, *My Friendly Contemporaries*.

GIBBS, WOLCOTT. On the staff of *The New Yorker*.

GIRLING, KATHERINE PEABODY. Graduate of University of Illinois. Lecturer, and writer for periodicals and magazines. "Hannah" was Mrs. Girling's maid. The story of *Hannah* was published in *The Atlantic Monthly*, 1913, as a booklet by the Stokes Publishing Co., 1915, in *The Golden Book*, 1931, and reprinted by *The Atlantic Monthly*, 1932.

HANSEN, HARRY. Born, 1884. Was correspondent and later literary editor of Chicago and New York newspapers. Reviewer for *Harper's Magazine*. Lecturer on Reviewing at Columbia. Author of *Midwest Portraits, Carl Sandburg, the Man and His Poetry*, and *Your Life Lies Before You*. Edits the O. Henry Prize Stories every year.

HARVEY, ALEXANDER. Born, 1868, in Brussels, Belgium. Author of *Shelley's Elopement, Essays on Sophocles, Essays on Euripides, Essays on Jesus, Love Life of Hellenic Heroines*.

HILLYER, ROBERT. Born in New Jersey in 1895. After graduating from Harvard, he published his first book of poetry—*Sonnets and Other Lyrics*. During the World War he served as an ambulance driver in France. In 1920–21 he studied in Copenhagen as a fellow of the American-Scandinavian Foundation. *The Collected Verse of Robert Hillyer* was awarded the Pulitzer Prize for Poetry in 1934.

HOLMES, JOHN. Born in Massachusetts, 1904. Graduate of Tufts College 1929. Professor of English at Tufts College; Poetry critic of *Boston Evening Transcript* and author of the column "Poetry Now". His collection of poems, *Address to the Living*, was awarded the Golden Rose, annual award of the New England Poetry Club.

HOUSMAN, ALFRED EDWARD. Born in Shropshire, England, 1859. Elder brother of Laurence Housman. A poet and classical scholar. He was Professor of Latin at Cambridge; Honorary Fellow at St. John's College, Oxford; and Fellow of Trinity College, Cambridge. As a poet he is best known for *A Shropshire Lad*. He died in 1936.

HOUSMAN, LAURENCE. Born, 1865. English playwright and author, brother of A. E. Housman. Left school at 18 and went with his older sister to London to train as an art student. A rabid pacifist and internationalist. *Little Plays of St. Francis* is his largest series of plays; *Palace Plays* deal with the life and character of Queen Victoria. Also wrote many poems, novels, and short stories.

HUGHES, JAMES LANGSTON. Born in Missouri, 1902. He worked as a seaman on voyages to Europe and Africa, and has lived in Mexico, Paris and Italy. Vachel Lindsay "discovered" him while he was working in a Washington hotel. He was the first one to win the poetry prize

offered to Negro writers by *Opportunity Magazine*. He was also the
winner of the Witter Bynner undergraduate poetry prize contest in 1926.

HUGHES, RUPERT.   Author of *The Old Nest, What Will People Say,
Clipped Wings, The Old Home Town*. Has written and directed many
motion pictures.

ICKES, HAROLD L. Born, 1874, Pennsylvania. Degrees from
University of Chicago. Was engaged in newspaper work. Became a
lawyer and took active interest in politics. Has been Secretary of
Interior in the Roosevelt Cabinet (1933–1940).

JOHNSON, JAMES WELDON.   Born in Florida, 1871, died in 1938.
For several years was the principal of the Negro High School in Jackson-
ville. His first book *The Autobiography of An Ex-Colored Man* was
published anonymously in 1912, and in 1927 reappeared under his
name. *God's Trombones* is his best known book of poetry.

KEATS, JOHN.   Born 1795, died 1821. English poet who studied
medicine. At the age of 18 he produced one of the finest sonnets in
English *On First Looking Into Chapman's Homer*, which is known today
wherever English is spoken. His *Ode to a Grecian Urn* is also ranked
among the great short English poems.

KOMROFF, MANUAL.   Born, 1890, in New York. Author of *Coronet*.
Has a new historical novel in preparation on Napoleonic history.

LAIDLAW, LOUISE BURTON.   Graduated from Barnard College, was
a student at Oxford, and has a Doctor's degree from Columbia.

LEACOCK, STEPHEN.   Born in England in 1869. His parents moved
to Canada, where he was educated. He holds a Ph.D. degree from the
University of Chicago. In 1903 he joined the staff of McGill University
in Montreal where he has been ever since. He has published numerous
works, both humorous and serious.

LEAR, EDWARD.   Born in London 1812, died 1888. He was a writer
of nonsense verse and prose, landscape artist, and wanderer. He had a
passion for painting, and was sent by the Earl of Derby to Greece and
Italy where he painted landscapes. In 1845 he gave Queen Victoria
drawing lessons. However, he is best known today for his *Book of
Nonsense*, which has gone to the hearts of children.

LEES, HANNAH.   Born, 1904, in Philadelphia. Has written advertis-
ing. Calls herself a "haus frau" with a hobby (writing).

LE GALLIENNE, RICHARD.   Born in Liverpool, 1867. An English
poet, critic, editor, essayist, and journalist. For seven years he was in
the business world and later became secretary to Wilson Barrett, well-
known actor and dramatist. In 1887 he issued *My Ladies' Sonnets*,
which led to his introduction to John Lane, a London Publisher, and to
his becoming literary critic for the *London Star*. He is the father of
Eva Le Gallienne, the talented actress.

LE POER TRENCH, P. S. Claims that Parsons, in *Parsons Is Prepared*, represents himself.

LINDSAY, NICHOLAS VACHEL (1879–1931). Born in Springfield, Missouri. Attended Hiram College, studied at the Art Institute at Chicago and at the New York School of Art. For several years he traveled as a combination missionary and minstrel, distributing a pamphlet entitled, "Rhymes to Be Traded for Bread." His works include *The Congo and Other Poems*, *The Chinese Nightingale*, *A Handy Guide for Beggars*.

LIPPMAN, WALTER. Born, 1889. Was editor of *The New Republic* and *New York World*. Author of *A Preface to Politics*, *The Stakes of Diplomacy*, *The Political Scene*.

LOOMIS, CHARLES BATTELL (1861–1911). Born in Brooklyn, N. Y. Writer, humorist, and public reader of his own writings. His son describes him as having "a long, lugubrious face, a prime asset to a humorist." Once Mark Twain was asked if he knew him; he answered, "What? Know Loomis? I've always wished I had his face." Loomis wrote *Just Rhymes*, *Cheerful Americans*, *A Bath in an English Tub*, *Just Irish*.

LOWELL, AMY (1874–1925). Born in Brookline, Massachusetts. She is the best known of the "Imagist" poets. Her books include *Sword Blades and Poppy Seed*, *Men, Women and Ghosts*, *Can Grande's Castle*, and *What's O'Clock*, which was awarded the Pulitzer Prize for 1925.

MACLEISH, ARCHIBALD. Born in Illinois, 1892. He is a graduate of Yale University, and Harvard Law School. During the World War he served in France. After his return to this country, he practiced law in Boston, but later gave that up for literature. Two of his well-known collections of poems are *Happy Marriage* and *Streets in the Moon*. He was awarded the Pulitzer Prize for Poetry in 1933. Appointed Librarian, Library of Congress, 1939.

MAGARET, HELENE. Born, 1906, in Nebraska. Graduated from Barnard College. Writes lyrics for periodicals and magazines. Author of *The Trumpeting Crane*, a narrative poem.

MARKHAM, EDWIN. Born in 1852 in Oregon City. He was taken to California at the age of five, and lived on a cattle ranch. He became a teacher after graduating from the State Normal School at San Jose. Later he gave up teaching to spend his time writing. His "Man with the Hoe" has been called the most quoted poem of recent years. He has published five books of poems, the latest being *Eighty Songs at Eighty*.

MARLATT, EARL BOWMAN. A.B. and Litt.D. from DePauw University; B.S.T. and Ph.D. from Boston University. He has been a teacher, an officer in the U. S. Army, a journalist, and a clergyman. At present he is Dean, and Professor of Philosophy of Literature, Boston University School of Theology. In 1925 he was awarded the Golden Rose at the May Day Poetry Tournament in Boston, an award formerly won by Robert Frost, Robert Hillyer, Archibald MacLeish, and Robert P. Tristram Coffin. His collection of poetry is *Cathedral.*

MASTERS, EDGAR LEE. Born in Kansas, 1869. He went to school in Illinois. His formal education ended with one year in Knox College; afterwards he became a lawyer. His books are too numerous to list. Probably the best known is *Spoon River Anthology.*

MAUGHAM, W. SOMERSET. Born in 1874 in Paris. Educated to be a doctor, but made his fortune as a dramatist. In 1915 he published his *Of Human Bondage* which is today recognized as one of the modern classics.

McCARTHY, DENIS. 1817–1882. Irish poet who contributed to numerous periodicals. His collections of poems are *Ballads, Poems and Lyrics; The Bell-Founder;* and *Underglimpses.* He also wrote *The Early Life of Shelley,* and translated the works of Calderon, the Spanish dramatist.

McCREARY, FREDERICK R. Born, 1893. Author of *The Northeast Corner.*

MERRYMAN, MILDRED PLEW. Formerly of Chicago, now in Florida. In 1932 she made her first appearance in *Scribner's* with *Gossip* (1585 A.D.). She has contributed to the *Literary Digest, Commonweal,* and *Poetry.*

MITCHELL, GEORGE WILLIAM. Born 1873, in New York City. Author, illustrator, wood sculptor. Studied at the Conservatory of Music, Milan, Italy, and sang tenor in light and grand opera, 1897–1917. Author of *Kernel Cob, Sergeant Giggles, Old King Cole* and *The Ostrich* (on radio), and has collaborated on operattas.

MITCHELL, RUTH COMFORT. Born in San Francisco. She has contributed poetry to various periodicals. Her books of poems are *Night Court and Other Verse, The Wishing Carpet, Straight Gate.*

MITCHNER, ROBERT W. Born in Hutchinson, Kansas. Teacher of English and dramatics in Cannelton, Indiana. Says: "My existence— so far—has been calm, confortable, orderly, happy. A person who wants to write a regulation autobiography should arrange to be poor or an orphan; I am neither."

MONROE, HARRIET. Born in Chicago, 1860, died 1936. She wrote *Columbian Ode* in response to a request by the Committee on Ceremonies of the World's Columbian Exposition. The poem was partly read, partly sung before an audience of 120,000. In 1912 she published the first issue of her magazine *Poetry: A Magazine of Verse* which had an extraordinary success from the first, and introduced to the public many poets who later became famous.

MORRIS, I. V.   Born, 1903, in Chicago.   Educated at Harvard and at Heidelberg University, Germany.   Resides in France.   Author of *Covering Two Years*, a novel.

MORTON, DAVID.   Born, 1886.   Instructor at Amherst.   Author of *Ships in the Harbor and Other Poems, Harvest*.

O'NEILL, EUGENE.   Born in New York City, 1888.   His father was James O'Neill, a popular actor who was eminently successful throughout the country.   When O'Neill was in a hospital following a breakdown in his health, he decided to write plays.   Three times he has won the Pulitzer Prize for Drama: *Beyond the Horizon*, 1920; *Anna Christie*, 1922; *Strange Interlude*, 1928.   He is the foremost American dramatist today.   His plays are read and produced in six languages besides English.

OPPENHEIM, JAMES.   Born in Minnesota, 1882; died 1932.   He was educated in public schools and went to Columbia University, but left without degree.   He went in for social work and teaching.   In 1916 he became a psychoanalyst.   With two others he founded *Seven Arts Magazine*.   His novel *Idle Wives* is well known.

PERCY, WILLIAM ALEXANDER.   Born, 1885.   Lawyer.   Was with A. E. F. in France.

PHELPS, WILLIAM LYON.   Born in Connecticut 1865.   American critic, essayist and professor.   Educated at Yale and Harvard.   In 1901 he was appointed Lampson Professor of English Literature at Yale, a position in which he rose to national prominence.   He held it until his resignation in 1933.   His books, articles for magazines and newspapers, and lectures have covered a wide range of topics.   His Autobiography has just been published.

POLLOCK, CHANNING.   Born in Washington, D.C. 1880.   American playwright.   His play *The Sign on the Door* ran a year in New York and a year in London, and became perhaps the first American play to be presented in every country in the world that boasts a stage.   *The Fool* was the greatest success of its decade, toured this country and Europe after a sensational run in New York.   At the age of fifty-three, he started writing novels.

PORTER, KENNETH.   Born February 17, 1905, near Sterling, Kansas, of Scotch-Irish ancestry.   Received Ph.D. degree from Harvard University in 1936.   He is now instructor in history at Vassar College.   As historian, Porter is the author of *John Jacob Astor* and *The Jackson and the Lees*, Numbers 1 and 2 of the Harvard Studies in Business History.   As poet-pamphleteer, he is co-author of *Christ in the Breadline* and author of *Pilate Before Jesus*.   *The High Plains* is his first book of verse.

POWYS, THEODORE FRANCIS.   Born in Shirley, Derbyshire, England.   Author of *The House with the Echo, Mr. Weston's Good Wine*,

Soliloquies of a Hermit, *The Only Penitent*, *The Two Thieves*, and many other publications.

RICKETTS, ORVAL. Born, Missouri. Editor of New Mexico newspaper and Secretary of New Mexico Press Association. Writes verse as a hobby.

RILEY, JAMES WHITCOMB. Born in Indiana, 1849, died 1916. He created Little Orphan Annie and other famous American characters. Although he left school at the age of 16, his talents as verse writer, amateur musician and painter were already manifest. He joined the staff of the local newspaper, and at 18 he joined a troupe of traveling actors who sold medicine between the acts of the plays. In 1883 his first book was issued which contained *The Old Swimmin' Hole*, and brought him fame. During his long career as a writer he published the popular volumes *Old Fashioned Roses*, *Rhymes of Childhood*, and others.

ROBERTS, ELIZABETH MADOX. Born in 1885 at Perryville, Kentucky. Received Ph.B. from University of Chicago. Her works include *Under the Tree*, *The Time of Man*, *My Heart and My Flesh*, and *The Great Meadow*. *A Ballet Song of Mary*, won the John Reed Memorial Prize in Poetry in 1928.

ROBERTS, LESLIE. Born in Wales, and migrated to Canada in childhood. Educated at McGill University. Was engaged in newspaper work many years. Contributes to Canadian, English, and American magazines. Author of *These Be Your Gods*, *When the Gods Laughed*, *So This Is Ottawa*.

ROBINSON, EDWIN ARLINGTON. Born in Maine, 1869, died in 1935. He worked for some time as inspector on the New York subway, and as a clerk in the New York Custom House, writing poetry on the side, and struggling constantly against poverty. In 1916, he published *The Man Against the Sky*, which gained him his first wide reputation. The next year appeared *Merlin*, the first of three long poems on Arthurian themes of which the other two are *Lancelot* and *Tristram*. He was the recipient three times of the Pulitzer Prize for Poetry: 1922, 1925, 1927.

RUSSELL, IRWIN (1853–1879). Born at Port Gibson, Mississippi. He studied law and was admitted to the Bar. His poetry showed the possibilities of the use of Negro thought and speech and had great influence on other writers of the South.

SANDBURG, CARL. Born in Illinois, 1878. His education, except for a few years in public school and at Lombard College, has been acquired through the process of working as driver of a milk wagon, porter, scene-lifter, truck driver, dish-washer, harvest hand, soldier, salesman, and newspaperman. His first volume to attract attention *Chicago Poems*, was followed two years later by *Cornhuskers*. Since then he has published the first two volumes of a life of Lincoln, and a collection of native folk songs, called *The American Songbag*.

SARETT, LEW. Born in Chicago, 1888. As a boy of 12 he supported his mother and himself working as a bundle boy in a department store and peddling papers. At 18 he determined to get a college education. He worked his way through seven years of college, and in 1912 received a position to teach English at the University of Illinois. While there he began writing poetry. The title poem of *The Box of Gold* was awarded the Levison Prize in 1922 by *Poetry: A Magazine of Verse*. His third volume of poetry *Slow Smoke* was awarded the prize in 1925 offered by the Poetry Society of America.

SCHREINER, OLIVE. (1862–1920). Born in Basutoland, the daughter of a German missionary. Author of *The Story of an African Farm, Dreams, Woman and Labor*. Her husband, S. C. Cronwright wrote *The Life of Olive Schreiner*, published in 1923.

SIERRA, G. MARTINEZ. Born in Madrid, 1881. A Spanish playwright, novelist, poet and producer. *The Cradle Song* was an immediate success in 1911. Author of some forty plays. In 1931 he came to America to direct the Spanish Department of the Fox Studios, translating, adapting and directing films in his native language.

SILL, EDWARD ROWLAND. Born in Connecticut, 1841, died 1887. Poet and essayist.

SOUTHERN, CLARENCE E. Master's degree from Stanford University. Chairman of English Department of high school in Mesa, Arizona.

STEVENSON, ROBERT LOUIS. Born 1850, and died 1894. A Scottish novelist, poet and essayist. His formal education was greatly interrupted by illness. He studied for the Scottish Bar examinations and passed them, but made no attempt to practice. In 1875 he began to write for English magazines, and soon attracted the attention of the discerning. Came to America in 1887 to fulfill contracts and in hopes the climate would aid his frail health. In 1888 he sailed for the South Seas and spent his remaining days in Samoa. His works include *Treasure Island, Dr. Jekyll and Mr. Hyde*, and *Kidnapped*.

TEASDALE, SARA. Born in Missouri, 1884, died 1933. All her life she traveled extensively in Europe and the United States. Her *Love Poems* was given the Columbia University Poetry Society of America prize for the best book of poetry of 1917. Other collections of her poems are: *Flame and Shadow*, and *Dark of the Moon*.

THOMPSON, FRANCIS. Born in England 1859, died 1907. He was sent to college to prepare for the priesthood, but at 17 left to study medicine. He failed in his degree examination and sought his fortune in London. Unfortunately he fell prey to opium. His life was a succession of failures and extreme poverty. Finally he was rescued by the poet Alice Meynell and her husband, a publisher, who made it possible for him to write, and who published his poetry.

TILDEN, FREEMAN. Born, 1883. Was foreign correspondent for newspapers and magazines in Europe and South America. Author of *That Night and Other Stories, Second Wind, The Virtuous Husband*.

TOLLER, ERNST. Born 1893 in German Poland. Studied at the University of Greenoble, served at the Front for 13 months. In 1933, the Nazis burned his books and deprived him of citizenship. His years in prison were fruitful: he wrote his plays *Nation-Wreckers* and *Man of the Masses*.

TOWNE, CHARLES HANSON. Born, 1877. Was editor of *The Designer* and *The Smart Set*, managing editor of *McClure's Magazine*, and editor of *Harper's Bazaar*. He now conducts daily literary column, *New York American*. Author of *The Quiet Singer and Other Poems, Today and Tomorrow*.

TRULLINGER, RAY. Born in Oregon. Writes a daily rod and gun column for the *New York World-Telegram*. *The Duck Hunter's Honeymoon* was his first story. Hobbies, hunting and fishing. Professes to "love mongrel dogs and have a profound aversion for fresh kids, female business executives and bridge players".

UNTERMEYER, LOUIS. Born in New York City, 1885. At 16 he appeared as a semi-professional pianist; at 17 he entered his father's jewelry manufacturing business. In 1923 he retired, and after two years of study abroad he returned to America to devote himself entirely to literature. Since then he has become well known as a writer of poetry, parodies, and critical prose; as a translator, and an anthologist.

WALN, NORA. Born in Pennsylvania of Quaker parents. Attended Swarthmore College. Lived in China, 1920-1932. In China, married an Englishman in government service.

WARFIELD, FRANCES. Born, 1901, in Missouri. Graduated from Wellesley. Then society editor of paper in Massachusetts. Husband is John T. Hackett of *The Literary Digest*.

WELCH, DOUG. "Born Boston, Mass., June 21, 1906, educated Boston and Tacoma, Wash., schools and the University of Washington, class of '28. Worked as reporter for various newspapers. Is now with Seattle *Post-Intelligencer*." (From *Esquire*.)

WETSTEIN, ALEEN. Attended Ohio State University. Writes a daily column, *One Girl Chorus*, in the *Pittsburgh Press*.

WILDE, OSCAR. Born in Ireland, 1854, died 1900. Poet, dramatist, and wit. His works have been translated into most European languages. He lectured in the United States. His first dramatic success was *Lady Windermere's Fan*. His special form of wit lay in ingenious paradox, with particular fondness for the inverted proverb. In prose and verse alike, he was a craftsman.

WILLIAMS, JESSE LYNCH. 1871–1929. American author of short stories and plays. A graduate of Princeton University. His play *Why Marry?* was produced in 1917, and was awarded the Pulitzer Prize.

WOOD, CHARLES ERSKINE SCOTT. Born, 1852. Degrees from Columbia. Was in the United States Army many years, and later lawyer. Author of *The Poet in the Desert, Maia, Heavenly Discourses.*

YOUNG, OWEN D. Born, 1874, in New York State. Lawyer and corporation official.

INDEX TO AUTHORS

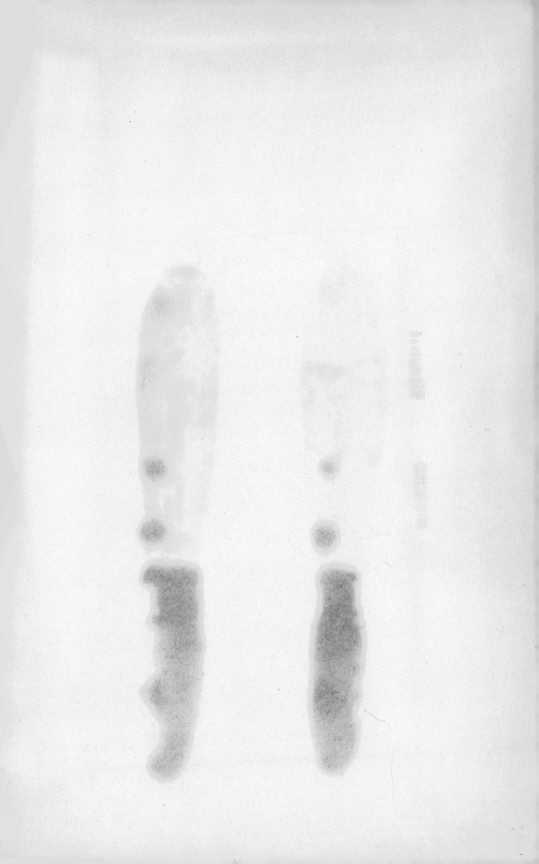